Section III:
Tool-Based Solutions for the Development
and Implementation of Learning Objects

Section IV:
Appendices

Foreword

One of the complexities about the field of learning objects is that it is highly organized yet highly diverse. As a veteran participant in and observer of the evolution of learning objects, it is clear to me that the promise afforded by these approaches is great and the applications many. It is also clear to me that how one might describe the promise of learning objects depends to a large extent on the applications to which you wish to put them.

Much of the early work in learning objects came from two related but almost competing directions: the proponents of e-learning, especially those who wished to meet the needs of corporations for rapid deployment of training; and those whose focus was on searching and finding learning objects based on carefully constructed metadata schema intended to make learning objects work seamlessly with learning management systems. For both groups, the objects themselves could take many forms, but were generally to be housed in a database called a repository. Each camp envisioned that learning objects would revolutionize course design and dramatically lower the costs of training and instruction. Rapid course assembly, "drag and drop" course design, just-in time learning, and a growing collection of shared materials (both within and outside intranets) were all part of the emerging vision.

Colleges and universities were quick to embrace the construction of metadata and repositories for learning objects, and as they did, repositories specializing in materials to support educational curricula began to emerge. The forerunner of all of them was the Educational Object Economy (EOE), a collection of java-based applets useful in primarily engineering and scientific applications housed in a framework based on the idea of exchange. The Multimedia Educational Resource for Learning and Online Teaching (MERLOT) soon followed, and extended that work to the social sciences and other disciplines.

Now with nearly a decade of development and experience behind us, it is fair to say that educational institutions have clearly embraced the idea of applying reusable learning objects to the development of content. As a result, learning objects have entered the mainstream of both e-learning and educational practice. Nonetheless, they have been applied in very different ways. There is a growing dichotomy between the needs and practices of e-learning and instruction as it relates to reusable learning materials.

Early proponents of learning objects often described them as a sort of "Lego" block, which could be snapped together with other blocks to create a curriculum. This metaphor persists in e-learning circles, but has fallen away in educational practice with the realization that a disciplinary context is often critical. As learning objects came to be applied more and more in educational contexts, the theoretical emphasis came to be placed more on reusability than adaptability, and the practical focus was to place learning objects within rather than across contexts and disciplines. At the same time, it became clear that educational learning objects were moving away from the "Lego" metaphor. While the objects being created for education were quite reusable, they were often very complex and detailed.

Today, educational learning objects are typically very rich and deep, and many carry the load of an entire curricular component. In contrast, learning objects for e-learning continue to hold to the vision of rapid course assembly, and so tend to stress adaptability more than do educational learning objects. If we were to create a new metaphor, it might be that e-learning objects are more like atoms than the complex molecules being assembled for instruction.

Much has been written about the e-learning side and training applications for learning objects, but little has appeared in print about how learning objects are being used within a curriculum. The essential value and contribution of this book, *Learning Objects for Instruction: Design and Evaluation*, is that it addresses that need very handily.

Editor Pamela T. Northrup has taken on the challenge of detailing the instructional applications of learning objects, and has assembled a group of authors who have considerable experience with the application of learning objects. To illustrate the broad applicability of these approaches, she has purposely taken a multidisciplinary approach in structuring the volume. She has organized the book into three broad areas that provide not only the theoretical underpinnings of the field, but also detailed case studies that emphasize the applications of learning objects across a number of disciplines, and a survey of emerging tools for creating learning objects.

In so doing, Northrup has filled an important gap in the literature, and readers will find much of value, no matter what their background in learning objects may be.

For those to whom this area is new, the comprehensive introduction to learning objects looks at not only the history of the field, but also several key aspects in depth. This introduction covers all the essential dimensions of learning object theory in a way practitioners will find very valuable and accessible. Many readers, especially those looking for a solid foundation in the field, will want to read the volume as a whole. Those who are more familiar with the theoretical underpinnings of learning objects will appreciate the eight detailed case studies that form the core of the volume. All readers will benefit from the descriptions of tools that close the volume.

The strength of *Learning Objects for Instruction: Design and Evaluation* lies in its focus on practice, and how learning objects are actually being applied in instructional contexts. The chapters detail these applications in ways that are easily generalizable, and highlight approaches that anyone interested in developing educational learning objects will appreciate. The chapters on the kinds of tools emerging to support the development of learning objects highlight how these tools have envisioned and tried to meet the needs of authors. Those who are developing or considering the development of new toolsets will benefit from the descriptions of how these tools were conceptualized, and the requirements they aimed to address.

Anyone interested in the educational applications of learning objects will want to place *Learning Objects for Instruction: Design and Evaluation* on a handy book-shelf, within easy reach, for it is one of those uniquely useful books you'll want to revisit often!

Laurence F. Johnson
Chief Executive Officer,
The New Media Consortium

Laurence F. Johnson is chief executive officer of the New Media Consortium (NMC), an international consortium of more than 200 world-class universities, colleges, museums, research centers, and technology companies dedicated to using new technologies to inspire, energize, stimulate, and support learning and creative expression. He is an acknowledged expert on the effective application of new media in many contexts, and has worked extensively to build common ground among museums and universities across North America and in more than a dozen other countries. He is the author of a number of important books, monographs, and articles exploring emerging trends and issues related to that work.

In his current post, Dr. Johnson routinely brings visionaries and thought leaders from across the globe together to define and explore new ways of thinking about and using technology, and to examine emerging trends and issues. The NMC's annual Horizon Report has become one of the leading tools used by senior executives in universities and museums to set priorities for technology planning. NMC summits and large-scale projects have helped set the agenda for topics such as visual literacy, learning objects, educational gaming, the future of scholarship, and the new Web. Recent examples are the NMC's high-profile experimental campus in the virtual world of Second Life and its leadership role in the MacArthur Foundation Series on Digital Media and Learning.

Having served as president and senior executive at institutions in both the higher education and not-for-profit realms, Dr. Johnson has more than 25 years of experience leading high-profile, high-stakes projects. His educational background includes an MBA in finance and a PhD in education that focused on research and evaluation. Among other recognitions, Dr. Johnson has been honored as a distinguished graduate by the University of Texas at Austin.

Preface

Learning objects have been a major topic of discussion for the past several years with most heated debates focusing on data standardization, interoperability, meta-data, SCORM, and the LOM. Most absent in this discussion are those responsible for designing instruction using learning objects. As a result, many of the objects and attributes that have been placed in massive learning object repositories are infrequently used by designers or instructors. This may be attributed to the lack of common features available in the collections or just the lack of understanding by designers and instructors on how these granular objects can be used in larger chunks of instruction. Or there may be bigger issues of context or lack of intellectual property policies. This text will focus on discussing learning objects from the view of learning and instruction with key sections highlighting design standardization using a theoretical approach, use of repositories for sharing, tools for classifying and capturing learning objects, a context for evaluating learning objects, and examples of learning objects in action.

Design Standardization

With all of the definition focused on standards, little time has been spent on stan-dardization or optimization of instructional elements that may be included. One framework representing standardization of learning objects is the model developed by Cisco (Barritt & Alderman, 2004). Cisco has defined instruction by lessons and topics with lessons representing reusable learning objects (RLOs) and content associated with that RLO defined as a reusable information object (RIO). Although Barritt and Alderman are very specific that this model is not intended to be a cookie cutter approach, it does provide for common attributes, common design elements, and specifications on granularity. In using this framework, designers are intended to develop solid objectives, tie RLOs and RIOs to those objectives, and content topics, practice and assessments for each RIO. Advantages to using this process include standardization of content that can be used and reused across designers, it can be clustered into complete lessons or units of instruction by capturing five to nine RIOs, and it can be more easily evaluated with tangible standard assessment techniques such as true/false, multiple choice, and matching. What isn't easily evident is how to extend this metaphor into instructional strategies that may not follow the RLO/RIO approach like problem-based learning, Webquests, and other more constructivist learning approaches. Likely, there will be many approaches to develop content for storage in repositories, but until more consistency, definition of granularity, and grappling with context are solved, there will still be missing puzzle pieces.

Repositories

With massive repositories available, it is anticipated that sharing and re-use would become commonplace and be an efficient way to organize instruction. Some well-known repositories such as MERLOT are expanding daily through its community members. Merlot is a peer reviewed repository intended to be used by higher education faculty and students to improve the quality of teaching and learning by increasing the number of easily available learning resources. Other notable repositories include The National Science Digital Library that houses thousands of learning objects for K-12 students and teachers and the Maricopa Learning Exchange for Community Colleges. The list of public repositories is expanding frequently. See the Academic ADL Co-Lab for ongoing updates. (http://www.academiccolab.org/).

With these and other repositories available for digital content sharing, users of repositories still appear to be most interested in interoperability and content management. Metadata management is still a major issue as inconsistent tagging may occur, thus making it difficult to classify specific objects consistently. Some research is underway to establish a workflow process for the human creation of metadata or automatic metadata creation and indexing. Either strategy would assist greatly with consistency. Whether developed by individuals or automated, there are many examples of taxonomies that have been generated to further describe the objects, to better assist the end user in searching and locating specific learning objects. For example, in *QuickScience*™ (Northrup, Rasmussen, & Dawson, 2004) metadata were further classified by Bloom's Taxonomy and by state and national standards to assist in keyword searching. Another example of taxonomy generation was a project called *Metasoft* generated by a consortium of school districts called Digital Districts Online. *Metasoft* enabled a similar taxonomy with classification around Bloom's Taxonomy. In addition, a taxonomy for professional development materials was also developed to further explain the objects. For final reviews, a team of cataloger's entered the final metadata into *Metasoft* before going live. Both examples provide a strategy for cataloging that will enable easier search and retrieval of learning objects (Peeples, Bunnow, & Holden, 2005).

Many organizations are struggling with how to create and share their learning objects in a manageable, stable environment. Additional issues remain in sharing and versioning of specific learning objects, which presents issues of intellectual property and copyright management.

Tools for Aiding in the Development and Implementation of Learning Objects

Tools that aid in the development of learning objects are beginning to become more commonplace through learning content management systems and stand-alone tools that can hook into repositories or even export to the end learning device such as the Web, a PDA, or other digital delivery device. Blackboard's Learning Object catalog (2004) can now assist faculty members in storing, retrieving and sharing its digital content at various user levels across courses, faculty, and institutions. Blackboard is in the process of expanding its workflow features for a more automated and scalable process. Desire2Learn and WebCT have similar tools that allow users to create and share content. In addition, both WebCT and Blackboard are delivering MERLOT learning objects through constant RSS feeds in several subject areas. Although these features dramatically include the potential for sharing and re-use, still missing is a structure for creating content and packaging as a learning object. Most faculty members developing instructional content do not have foundational knowledge in learning theory, instructional strategies, or techniques for building instruction. The advent of a tool, eLON™ created by the University of West Florida provides a structure for creating learning objects shaped around common instructional strategies tied to learning outcome. This tool assists non-designers and designers alike in structuring content for export into a range of LMS tools, repositories, and portals (Academic Technology Center, 2005).

In addition to the higher education view of learning objects, K-12 schools are beginning to engage in resource sharing through industry standard portals and digital dashboards to push information needed to the teachers or students desktop using predefined possible routines. For example, if a student diagnostic test score is low on specific standards, digital dashboards and portals can push targeted content, strategies, and even teacher professional development to the desktop in response to the need. Learning objects tagged to standard play a key role for use and re-use in this type of an environment.

Evaluating Learning Objects

Evaluating learning objects is a difficult task but must be taken into account if the expectation is for large-scale use. MERLOT's repository is a peer-reviewed system that requires all objects be reviewed before going live. This sometimes causes a massive bottleneck for new objects becoming available as communities continue to submit objects. However, peer-reviewed objects provide much merit to the academic community as a whole. A new repository being populated in Florida, The Orange Grove, requires several layers of evaluation and peer-review, starting with the home institution. Each Community College and University in Florida participating in the Orange Grove peer-reviews objects onsite, then forwards them to the Orange Grove for final analysis and public access. The system is intended to reduce bottleneck while ensuring ongoing quality.

On the other side of evaluation, it is important for those searching for and selecting objects to evaluate objects to meet instructional need. Evaluative questions may include (1) Does it align to stated goals and objectives? (2) Will it fit into the context of my lesson or course? (3) Is it of high quality? (4) Is it accurate and free of bias? (5) It is usable by my students, are plug-ins or additional software required to run? (6) Is the file size too large to download? (7) Do I download the object or point to it? (8) Do I have confidence that it will continue to be located in its designated link?

Conclusion

Overall, each area under investigation in the text provides a view of the issues still surrounding the successful use of learning objects for instruction. From the perspective of the designer, faculty member, or student who may be searching large repositories for matching content or those who are creating new content to align to the requirements of export to a repository. A myriad of issues exist, beginning with those involved in teaching and learning beginning to shape the direction that is being directed by the programmers and others in definition of metadata, interoperability, and standards. Both sides of the story should be considered for successful development, use, and re-use of learning objects for instruction.

Contribution and Scholarly Value

This text will tie together practical issues surrounding the instructional use of learning objects with real examples and case studies of how implementation of objects has occurred in a variety of settings. Designers, faculty, trainers, and teachers are beginning to partake of learning object repositories, but still fall short on how to develop instructional learning objects or the issues surrounding the objects into a repository in terms of tagging, designing in chunks, determining layers of granularity, and determining the need for contextualization.

There are many issues to consider, with this text providing a forum for experts in this newly emerging area to provide their scholarly view of each of the areas of emphasis. Simply defining learning objects from an instructional perspective still remains an issue. With only one leading definition from Wiley (2002), there is still more to discuss. The notion of designing instruction using learning objects located in repositories garners the question of metadata, tagging to a conventional standard, emphasizing the levels of granularity, and hoping that some common features exist among the unique pieces of the puzzle. Designing learning objects for re-use through repositories presents another unique set of challenges including serious change management and professional development for instructional designers and faculty. Many examples of learning objects in action across areas of K-12, higher education, community colleges, industry, and the military will be depicted through the chapters of this text.

Overall, this text will lay a foundation for areas currently being debated with designers of learning objects and provide some much needed guidance to the community of designers, faculty members, and developers.

Organization of the Book

The book is organized into fifteen chapters. A brief description of each of the chapters follows:

Introduction to Learning Objects

Chapter I provides a short history of learning objects in both the academic, governmental and corporate sectors. The origin of the term will be traced from 1992, as Wayne Hodgins coined it, to the present.

Chapter II presents an overview of the use of digital repositories in the field of education. The authors' purpose in writing this chapter is not only to provide their readers with general knowledge about educational repositories, but to give them some idea of the various issues and processes involved in launching a digital repository.

Chapter III provides a survey of 59 well-known repositories with learning resources and presents initial results from their analysis. The most important characteristics of these LORs are examined and useful conclusions made about the current status of development. A discussion of future trends in the LORs field is also included.

Chapter IV provides a theoretically grounded discussion of the creation of a reusable learning object that is effective from instructional and system perspective. A combination of frameworks, the Cisco model and the grounded instructional systems design model, have been integrated to develop a set of templates that can be used to help developers efficiently create RLOs and the reusable information objects that comprise them. The integration of psychological foundations into learning object creation is critical to a successful implementation of RLO architecture.

Chapter V describes the adaptation of the object-oriented software engineering design methodology for software objects to engineering reusable learning objects. The approach extends design principles for reusable learning objects with the design of learning object lessons being independent of, and complementary to, instructional design theory underlying the learning object design process, and metadata standards adopted by the IEEE for learning object packaging.

Developing Instruction Using Learning Objects

Chapter VI presents a background on learning objects including the use of American Sign Language learning objects in three higher education settings. Recommendations for the use of learning objects for multiple higher education disciplines and insights into future and emerging trends related to the use of learning objects in higher education will be provided.

Chapter VII discusses the lessons learned while designing a SCORM-conformant Web-based courseware product using an iterative instructional design process. In particular, it describes some of the design trade-offs between instruction that is highly modular vs. situational and instruction that is highly interactive vs. highly contextualized. Organizational issues, such as metatagging and asset naming procedures, and the challenge of designing realistic and motivating e-learning assessments are presented as well.

Chapter VIII proposes a category of tools called design objects that can be used by instructors to integrate existing content sources, including but not limited to learning objects, within teaching frameworks that engage learners with content in meaningful ways. Emphasis is on tools to support the K-12 instructor, although related issues are applicable across educational levels.

Chapter IX introduces the use of a learning objects content development tool, the eLearning Objects Navigator, (eLON™) as a strategy for creating, classifying and retrieving reusable learning objects and reusable information objects. Presented in this chapter is the underlying theoretical framework for the development of eLON™ as well as the specific design decisions made regarding the deployment of PDA mobile learning devices to military personnel.

Chapter X presents learning objects utilization in the corporate training world. The acceptance by corporate training can be attributed in part to the fact that learning objects provided those departments with a system and tools that they could present to their decision makers—a system that aligned with corporate goals. Some of the goals included the need to train a global workforce and the need to do it in an effective, competitive and efficient manner.

Chapter XI examines the issues and concerns of faculty regarding the development and use of learning objects as instructional resources. It describes the characteristics and benefits of learning objects, barriers to adoption, and strategies to increase learning object use.

Chapter XII presents a case study of a teacher education faculty member as she researches learning objects and integrates the concepts into her curriculum. The author provides examples of how to create an awareness of learning objects among her students and provides an experience where students are afforded opportunities to determine the value of using learning objects as an instructional tool.

Chapter XIII presents a collaborative development model that accomplishes the goal of bridging the academic environment and industry, specifically relating to the production of self-paced, Web-based learning objects, catalogued within workforce development curricula. The model provides a roadmap that maximizes the expertise of college faculty, industry managers, and multimedia production specialists to meet the needs of government sponsors, commercial corporations, non-profit postsecondary institutions, and individual learners.

Tool-Based Solutions for the Development and Implementation of Learning Objects

Chapter XIV discusses the reasoning behind the lack of the expected authoring of digital learning objects while presenting a tool, Pachyderm 2.0. The Pachyderm 2.0 software is discussed as a tool for faculty to utilize while creating engaging learning objects in an easy to use environment. The author hopes that discussing and enumerating the obstacles to learning object authoring and dissemination, combined with the proposal of using the Pachyderm software along with a model of working with organizational information technology (IT) staff, will assist all involved in circulating successful digital learning objects.

Chapter XV presents a support tool for teachers, QuickScience™, to assist teachers and students improve performance in science. QuickScience™ is designed using Cisco's approach with six unique classifications of reusable learning objects, including five types of instructional resources aligned to Bloom's Taxonomy, are used by teachers to help students improve their performance in science.

Chapter XVI explores the use of learning objects within the context of teacher education. The authors argue that learning objects can be useful in teacher education if we both create *and* code learning objects appropriately to the needs of the teacher education community. The chapter begins with framing the teaching and learning issues associated with the use of learning objects in higher education. Next, the chapter introduces a method for generating and marking up learning objects; examples are described where learning objects are created and coded to address the teaching and learning needs of teacher educators and teachers. The authors conclude with a discussion of the issues and prospects for the use of learning objects in teacher education.

References

Academic Technology Center. (2006). *What is eLON™?* Retrieved September 1, 2006, from http://uwf.edu/atc/projects/eLON.html

Barritt, C. & Alderman, F. L. (2004). *Creating a reusable learning objects strategy: Leveraging information and learning in a knowledge economy.* San Francisco: Pfeiffer.

Blackboard Media Center. (2004). *Blackboard launches enterprise wide learning objects repository.* Retrieved October 26, 2006, from http://www.blackboard.com/company/press/release.aspx?id=604710

Northrup, P. T., Rasmussen, K. L. & Dawson, D. B. (2004). *QuickScience research model.* University of West Florida. Retrieved October 26, 2006, from http://cops.uwf.edu/itc/itc-research/OverviewofResearch.pdf

Peeples, J., Bunnow, D., & Holden, C. (2005). *Learning objects across boundaries: A report from digital district's online K-20 learning objects community.* Paper presented at the 21st conference on Distance Teaching and Learning. Madison, WI. Retrieved October 15, 2006, from http://www.uwex.edu/disted/conference/Resource_library/proceedings/05_1992.pdf

Wiley, D. A. (2002). Connecting learning objects to instructional design theory: A definition, a metaphor, and a taxonomy. In D. A. Wiley (Ed.), *The instructional use of learning objects.* Retrieved May 02, 2002, from http:// reusability.org/read/chapters/wiley.doc

Acknowledgment

Special thanks go to all of the authors who shared their ongoing research and development efforts at individual institutions and organizations around the world. The collaboration with the authors was an inspiration that has sparked much creative thought for me and I can't wait to begin implementing some of the new, engaging ideas in my professional work.

Many of the authors included in this text also served as reviewers for chapters written by other authors. I was also able to include reviewers from around the world that were not chapter authors. Thanks to all who provided constructive and comprehensive reviews that substantially improved the quality of the text. Reviewers who provided the most comprehensive and constructive comments included Dr. Janette Hill from the University of Georgia and Dr. Karen Rasmussen from the University of West Florida.

Special thanks also to those who helped in the eleventh hour to resize images including Lam Chu and Karen Barth who electronically distributed chapters for final reviews and editing. I would be remiss not to mention the Academic Technology Center at the University of West Florida who provides me with innovation and creative thought to pursue emerging technologies for teaching and learning with vigor. Much of the inspiration for this text comes directly from projects we have worked on, conversations we have had, and things we have been thinking about for many years.

Thanks also to the publishing team at IGI Global. In particular, Kristin Roth, who continuously nudged via e-mail to keep the project on schedule and to make shifts in deadlines as hurricanes passed through our region.

Also, I would like to thank my family for their patience as mommy spent way too much time on the computer and way too little time playing. My kids, Haley (10) and Jack (8) kept asking if I had made my word count yet for the book, hoping that when I did, I would be finished. And, for my husband, Ron, I appreciate his unfailing support during the months I spent working on this book.

Finally, thanks to all of the authors for their excellent contributions to the book.

Pamela T. Northrup, PhD
University of West Florida
Pensacola, FL
October 2006

Section I

Introduction to Learning Objects

This section presents a foundation for the study of learning objects for teaching and learning. The foundation is undergirded with the evolution of learning objects, psychological theory, the construction of a repository, and the initial research on repositories and their usage.

Chapter I

An Abridged History of Learning Objects

Robert R. Saum, Daytona Beach Community College, USA

Abstract

What follows is a short history of learning objects in both the academic, governmental, and corporate sectors. This is by no means an exhaustive list of events. The origin of the term will be traced from 1992, as Wayne Hodgins coined it, to the present. Key standards will be listed as they occurred, such as the sharable content object reference model (SCORM). In addition, landmark collaborative applications and repositories will be mentioned along with their intended mission. Corporate and academic interpretations of the term are noted and its use within organizations.

Introduction

Querying the words learning and object in a search engine will yield tens of millions of results. Constraining the search to the phrase "learning object" yields a few hundred thousand to just over a million results depending on the search agent. Results are likely to grow exponentially into the millions in the coming years. Amazingly, only three years ago there were tens of thousands of records. Several reasons for this staggering phenomenon are supposed:

1.   The popularity of e-learning and the Internet along with the plethora of online communication technologies such as Web authoring tools, blogs, forums, and the like that allow almost anyone to create content and dub it as a learning object.

2.   Ambiguity in its meaning, as a variety of individuals and entities has offered numerous definitions depending on the context in which it is used.

3.   Reduced cost of production and rapid lesson development as the education arena shifts into technology-mediated instruction and away from traditional teaching-learning methods.

Additional explanations may be available; however, this chapter is concerned with the second reason and the understanding of the term learning object in its historical context. To divulge the forthcoming of the term *learning object*, a brief review of existing literature is necessary. To this end it is necessary to raise awareness of the various definitions and uses offered by a variety of scholarly works and trade publications.

Some selected applications of "learning object" in the literature are educational objects (Friesen, 2001), media object (Norton, 1996), knowledge object (Merrill, 1996), rapid learning object™, reusable learning object (Barritt, Lewis, & Wieseler, 1999), Oracle learning architecture (Ellwood, 1997), shareable courseware object (Dodds, 2000), shareable content object (Dodds, 2001), units of learning (Koper, 2001), e-learning objects (Collier & Robson, 2001), instructional object (Gibbons, Nelson, & Richards, 2000), intelligent object (Gibbons et al., 2000), and data object (Gibbons et al., 2000). Sometimes these terms are used interchangeably and at other times independently. The prolific usage of the coined term *learning object* is the most widely recognized of the variants. As such, its history is decidedly the focus of this investigation. What will follow is a brief historical listing of key events and publications related to this phrase and its inception into e-learning. This is by no means meant to be an exhaustive list.

The Timeline

1992

The term *learning object* is a fairly recent notion. Wayne Hodgins, a well-known e-learning expert and strategic futurist with Autodesk, Inc., is generally given credit for its penning. In 1992, Mr. Hodgins was watching one of his children playing with Lego [sic] building blocks while mulling over some problems regarding learning strategies. Wayne realized right there that the industry needed building blocks for learning plug and play interoperable pieces of learning. He termed those building blocks *learning objects* (Jacobsen, 2002). He defined learning objects as a collection of information objects assembled using metadata to match the personality and needs of the individual learner (Hodgins, 2000).

1994

A few years later Mr. Hodgins, now a former president of the Computer Education Management Association (CEdMA), established the learning architectures, APIs and learning objects working group (Polsani, 2003). This working group operates today as the learning architecture/learning objects (LALO) task force. Simultaneously a team was assembled by Oracle Corporation consisting of Chuck Barritt, Tom Kelly and several others to create a framework for converting computer-based training courses into a more flexible learning object authoring and delivery system.

While Oracle was still in the research and development phase, National Education Training Group, Inc. (NETg), a subsidiary of the Thomson Corporation, released a working e-learning application based on their interpretation of Hodgins' learning object model. NETg marketed their work under the trademarked term NETg learning object, or NLO (Barron, 2000). After researching this claim further, no active trademark could be located. There were, however, several applications filed. Regardless, NETg appears to have been the first business entity to market which was a remarkable feat considering that the Internet was in its neophyte stage.

1996

In January, the Alliance of Remote Instructional Authoring and Distribution Networks for Europe (ARIADNE) started with the financial support of the European Union Commission (ARIADNE, 2004). Their mission was to enable better quality learning through the development of learning objects, tools and methodologies that support a "share and reuse" approach for education and training (ARIADNE, 2003).

On September 22, EM-Assist, Inc., was granted a trademark for the term, rapid learning object™, with no further definition of the term released. The following month Mark Norton, an e-learning consultant who worked on the IMS abstract framework, posted an article about "media objects," which he defined as a user interface element with some physical appearance and associated interactive behavior. It has a default appearance, can be customized and may be coupled to a content element for display or manipulation (Norton, 1996).

November was a busy month as David Merrill suggested using the term *knowledge object* which consists of a set of predefined elements. Each of these elements is instantiated by way of a multimedia resource (text, audio, video, graphic) or a pointer to another knowledge object. Some of these elements include the name of the knowledge object, a portrayal of the knowledge object, the location of the knowledge object's portrayal, and other informational elements such as a description or demonstration (Merrill, 1996).

All of these developments did not go unnoticed. Later that month, the Learning Technology Standards Committee (LTSC) of the Institute of Electrical and Electronics Engineers (IEEE) formed to develop and promote instructional technology standards (LTSC, 2000). This was a critical component in achieving Mr. Hodgins' goal of achieving interoperability.

Oracle's learning object team's hard work came to fruition on December 5, 1996. The Oracle Corporation Education division launched the Oracle learning architecture (OLA), often mistakenly called the Oracle learning application. Seventy-five courses (Brown, 1996) were initially made available and by July of 1997 more than 93 courses were available online in more than 140 countries (Locklear, 1997). This was the first phase, an internet service (Ellwood, 1997), of a two-part rollout. The second phase, released in July of 1997, offered an Internet product and authoring environment where individual objects containing text, graphics, video and audio would be assembled by each student into a customized course (Brown, 1996).

The Gateway to Educational Materials[SM] (GEM) consortium formed and began developing a repository infrastructure. Their mission was to expand educators' capability to access Internet-based lesson plans, instructional units and other educational materials in all forms and formats (Laundry, 2006). This group established a national repository of educational materials. As such it was their goal to improve the organization and accessibility of the substantial collections of materials that were already available on various federal, state, university, nonprofit and commercial Internet sites (Laundry, 2006).

1997

This year produced numerous developments as Mr. Hodgins' original concept had captured national attention. The learning architecture/learning objects task force began operating under an open model welcoming all stakeholders (Conner, 1998).

In May of 1997, the national learning infrastructure initiative of EDUCOM, which later became EDUCAUSE, instituted the instructional management systems project and held its first metadata meeting (EDUCAUSE, 2004). Today this organization operates as the IMS Global Learning Consortium, Inc. This group has made a tremendous impact on education, in both the public and private sectors, across several continents (IMS, 2006). Shortly after EDUCOM's initiation of the IMS project, the United States Department of Defense birthed the advanced distributed learning initiative in an effort to identify better, more cost effective and efficient ways to educate and train Department of Defense service members (ADL, 2006). This initiative is a cooperative effort between the public and private sectors to develop and share common standards, reusable learning tools, and content (Department of Defense, 2000).

The Learning Technology Standards Committee (LTSC) of the Institute of Electrical and Electronics Engineers (IEEE) commenced working on the development and maintenance of the learning object metadata (LOM) standard (Duval, 1998).

Dr. James J. L'Allier, who is currently the chief learning officer at NETg, published a corporate brief in which he defined a learning object as the smallest independent structural experience that contains an objective, a learning activity and an assessment (L'Allier, 1997).

The California State University Center for Distributed Learning established the Multimedia Educational Resource for Learning and Online Teaching (MERLOT) system. This was modeled after the NSF funded project, "Authoring Tools and an Educational Object Economy (EOE)" (MERLOT, 2006).

The Gateway to Educational Materials[SM] (GEM) consortium officially launched its repository.

1998

In March, the Learning Technology Standards Committee published the draft standard for learning object metadata, which defined a learning object as any entity digital or nondigital that may be used for learning, education or training (Duval, 1998).

Both Tom Kelly and Chuck Barritt joined the Internet Learning Solutions Group (ILSG) at Cisco Systems, Inc. Mr. Kelly is the vice-president of this group and Mr. Barritt serves as Program Manager. They continued with the learning object research that they started while employed by Oracle Corporation. This work culminated in the release of a white paper in 1999 entitled "Reusable Information Object Strategy: Definition, Creation Overview, and Guidelines." In this document they added and coined two critical components supporting their strategy: a reusable information object (RIO) and a reusable learning object (RLO). A reusable information object is defined as a collection of content, practice and assessment items assembled around a single learning objective (Barritt et al., 1999).

A reusable learning object is created by combining an overview, summary, assessment, and five-to-nine RIOs. An RLO is based on a single objective, derived from a specific job task (Barritt et al., 1999). More specifically a RIO is a granular, reusable chunk of information that is media independent. Individual RIOs are then combined to form a larger structure called a reusable learning object (RLO) (Barritt et al., 1999).

Royal Roads University established the Centre for Economic Development and Applied Research (CEDAR) to develop new business enterprises, including applied research ventures, special training programs and partnerships with local industry (Heins, Mundell, & Muzio, 2001). To accommodate growing student demand for distance learning, the University installed a Microsoft exchange server to enable robust communication between faculty and students to deploy their learning objects. As part of this endeavor, the centre defined an e-learning object as a small piece of text, visual, audio, video, interactive component and so forth that is tagged, and stored in a database. They can also be other types of objects, for example, a FAQ or a glossary definition.

The IEEE Learning Technology Standards Committee stated that learning objects are defined here as "any entity, digital or nondigital, which can be used, reused or referenced during technology supported learning" (IEEE Standards, 1998).

1999

On January 12, President William Jefferson Clinton signed Executive Order 13111, titled "Using Technology to Improve Training Opportunities for Federal Government Employees," which established the president's task force on federal training technology. This task force was charged with providing leadership regarding the effective use of technology in training and education; make training opportunities an integral part of continuing employment in the federal government; and facilitate the ongoing coordination of federal activities concerning the use of technology in training (Clinton, 1999). Later that year, prompted by this charge, the first ADL Co-Lab was established in Alexandria, Virginia (ADL, 2006).

In March, Terry Anderson (1999), professor and Canadian research chair in Distance Education at the University of Alberta, submitted the proposal entitled "Campus

Alberta Repository for Educational Objects (CAREO)" to the Province of Alberta for a grant through their Learning Enhancement Envelope and Curriculum Redevelopment Fund. This work was influenced by the MERLOT project and its founders would become active participants. The purpose of CAREO was to establish an online repository of educational objects for postsecondary educators, and establish and support a professional development community that both creates, reviews and utilizes these objects through ongoing professional development activities (Buell, 2000).

In October, Rice University launched a repository project dubbed the "secret web initiative." This is a not only a learning repository but an authoring and collaboration application. This project would later become known as Connexions, which in 2000 would host 200 modules (Brent, 2006). This same year, Provost Robert A. Brown of Massachusetts Institute of Technology asked a committee comprised of students, faculty and staff to formulate a strategic e-learning plan (MIT, 2006a). The outcome of this project was the creation of the OpenCourseWare project. This is a repository of lessons and content authored by MIT faculty. The intent of the project was to provide free, searchable access to MIT's course materials for educators, students and self-learners around the world (MIT, 2006b).

Research continued on the theoretical and development fronts. David A. Wiley II, a research assistant and graduate student, and now a postdoctoral fellow in the Instructional Psychology and Technology Department at Utah State University, offered his definition of a learning object as anything digital, whether it has an educational purpose or not (1999). This same year CISCO unveiled their e-learning plans in a strategy paper branding their model as a reusable learning object. This defined a collection of RIOs, overview, summary and assessments that supports a specific learning objective (Barritt et al., 1999). Also, the Wisconsin Online Resource Center or Wisc-Online was created as a repository for the State of Wisconsin's technical colleges (Wisc-Online, 2000). This organization defined learning objects as Web-based, self-contained chunks of learning (Chitwood, 2000).

2000

January was an active month for the advancement of the e-learning industry and the learning object model. The Advanced Distributed Learning Initiative published the shareable courseware object reference model (SCORM), version 1.0 (ADL, 2006). These specifications defined a learning object as an interoperable, durable, computer-based course or component of a course packaged with sufficient information to be reusable and accessible (Dodds, 2000). At this same time four organizations collaborated on a grant solicitation to the National Science Foundations for a digital repository of learning objects. These four were the American Society for Engineering Education, the Institute of Electrical and Electronics Engineers, Inc., Iowa State

University and Virginia Polytechnic Institute and State University. Their solicitation was submitted to the National Science Technology, Engineering and Mathematics Education Digital Library (NSDL) program of the National Science Foundation (NSF solicitation 00-44) (Rahman, 2003). A final proposal was submitted to NSF entitled "A Digital Library Network for Engineering and Technology." The grant was awarded, NSF GRANT DUE-0085849, and in September the Digital Library Network for Engineering and Technology (DLNET) was launched (Rahman, 2003). The vision for the project was to create a platform complementing and supporting lifelong-learning and continuing education activities of practicing engineers and technologists (Rahman, 2003). Several works were developed in conjunction with this project including a paper defining a DLNET learning object. These works defined these items as structured, stand-alone resources that encapsulate high quality information in a manner that facilitates learning and pedagogy (Mahadevan, 2001). Stephen Downes, a senior research officer with National Research Council, suggested that learning objects are reusable and interoperable units of learning content (Downes, 2000).

In December, Clive Shepherd, an e-learning consultant, offered his interpretation that a learning object is a small, reusable digital component that can be selectively applied alone or in combination by computer software, learning facilitators or learners themselves, to meet individual needs for learning or performance support (Shepherd, 2000). David A. Wiley II authored materials that purposed a variant of the definition in his early work that identified these as any digital resource that can be reused to support learning (Wiley, 2000).

2001

The Advanced Distributed Learning (ADL) Initiative released an update to their shareable courseware object reference model. Under version 1.1, their learning object term became shareable content object and the model was now a shareable content object reference model. This work would again be updated in October with the release of the shareable content object reference model version 1.2.

A case-study was posted by Monson and South, of the Center for Instructional Design at Brigham Young University (BYU), about the principles, infrastructure and development of learning objects at their institution and their attempt of integrating this model into the institution's curriculum. In this work they use the term *media object*. Monson and South define such an object as digital media that is designed and/or used for instructional purposes. Such objects range from maps and charts to video demonstrations and interactive simulations (South & Monson, 2001).

In a paper submitted to the IMS Learning Design Group, Rob Koper, a professor of Educational Technology at the Educational Technology Expertise Centre (OTEC) of the Open University of The Netherlands, suggests using the term *Units of Study* in place of learning object. He goes on to define *unit of study* as the smallest unit providing learning events for learners, satisfying one or more interrelated learning objectives (Koper, 2001). It is contextually and semantically indivisible. Disassembly would yield the unit ineffective and no longer a component of the educational process, as it would merely be a series of disjointed assets or media elements. This paper also introduced educational modeling language (EML) which maintains a pedagogical focus that defines roles and activities for a unit of study. This paper and other collaborative works were to become the core of the IMS Learning Design standard.

The NETg catalogue eclipses 75,000 learning objects. These are used by leading companies such as Daimler-Chrysler, Honeywell, Proctor & Gamble and Dow Chemical (Business Wire, 2001).

Norm Friesen, an information architect with the CAREO project, contributes some materials supporting the project's definition of an educational object. It is said that a learning object is any digital resource with a demonstrated pedagogical value, which can be used, reused or referenced to support learning (Friesen, 2001).

2002

In November 2002, several more scholarly works were published. Among these was an article titled "(Learning) Objects of Desire: Promise and Practicality," in which Lori Mortimer, from the Open University of The Netherlands, stated that a learning object is a piece of content that is smaller than a course or lesson (Mortimer, 2002).

In February, the Centre for Learning and Teaching through Technology (LT3) at the University of Waterloo launched a collaboration project between Ontario's universities and colleges. This effort would not only build upon the MERLOT effort but also establish their own repository. This resulted in the creation of the Co-operative Learning Object Exchange (CLOE) (Goldsworthy, 2002).

2003

Polsani (2003), a professor at the University of Arizona, using Charles Sanders Pierce's theory of signs, defines a learning object as a form of organized knowledge content involving learning purpose and reusable value. Monique Doorten and colleagues, in a case study about the Open University of the Netherlands, proposed that learning objects are any reproducible and addressable digital or nondigital resources used to perform learning activities or support activities (Doorten, Giesbers, Janssen,

Daniels, & Koper, 2003).

2004

In January of 2004, the first edition of the shareable content object reference model version 2004 was released (ADL, 2006). In July the second edition is published. In October, a paper by Michael Engelhardt, a professor at the University of Applied Sciences, and colleagues stated that e-learning objects denote the smallest, atomic learning units covering a single, self-consistent subject (Engelhardt, Hildebrand, Lang, Schmidt, & Werlitz, 2004). Wesleyan University embarks on a mission to create their own repository. This endeavor is open for interinstitutional collaboration. The initiative becomes known as the LoLa Exchange: learning objects, learning activities (LoLa) as an exchange for facilitating the sharing of high-quality learning objects (LoLa, 2006).

Conclusion

In a relatively short time, a fair amount of work by both public and private sectors has contributed to the advancement of Mr. Hodgins' learning object concept. This is evident in the table that follows. This timeline marks each of the key events mentioned earlier in chronological order where possible.

Table 1. Condensed timeline of events

Year	List of Events
1992	Wayne Hodgins coins learning object
1994	LOLA task force established
	Oracle Research and Development begins
	NETg NLO published
1996	ARIADNE starts
	Rapid learning object™ trademarked
	Norton writes about "Media Objects"
	Merrill suggests using "Knowledge Objects"
	The IEEE Learning Technology Standards Committee forms
	Oracle Learning Architecture (OLA) released
	Gateway to Educational Materials℠ (GEM) organized
1997	IMS Global Learning Consortium, Inc. formed
	Advanced Distributed Learning (ADL) Initiative commissioned
	Dr. James J. L'Allier publishes work on NLOs
	MERLOT launches
	GEM repository opens
1998	Draft Standard for Learning Object Metadata is published
	CEDAR established
1999	Executive Order 13111 signed
	CAREO conceived and funded
	David A. Wiley II publishes his contributions
	Barritt and Lewis publish Cisco Systems, Inc. RLO strategy paper
	Rice creates Connexions
	MIT launches the OpenCourseWare project
	Wisc-Online established
2000	SCORM version 1.0 released
	DLNET launches
	Shepherd and Wiley publish additional findings
	Downes posts his thoughts
2001	SCORM version 1.1 and 1.2 released
	Monson and South published material on integrating learning objects into the curriculum
	"Units of Study" and Educational Modeling Language (EML) are suggested by Koper
	Norm Friesen suggests the term "Educational Object"
2002	Mortimer offers another definition
	CLOE commences
2003	Additional research is contributed by Polsani and Doorten
2004	SCORM version 2004 published
	Engelhardt suggests the term "E-learning Object"
	Wesleyan University launches LoLa

References

ADL. (2006). *History of ADL.* Retrieved February 21, 2007, from http://www.adlnet. gov/aboutadl/history.cfm

Anderson, T. (1999). *Campus Alberta Repository for Education Objects (CAREO)* (Learning Enhancement Envelope and Curriculum Redevelopment Fund Proposal). Edmonton, Alberta: University of Calgary.

ARIADNE. (2003, June 17). ARIADNE strategy status. Retrieved February 21, 2007, from http://www.ariadne-eu.org/common/docs/AriadneStrategyPaper.pdf

ARIADNE. (2004). *Alliance of Remote Instructional Authoring and Distribution Networks for Europe (ARIADNE).* Retrieved February 21, 2007, from http:// www.ariadne-eu.org/

Barritt, C., Lewis, D., & Wieseler, W. (1999). *Reusable information object strategy: Definition, creation, overview and guidelines.* Cisco Systems Version 3.0. Retrieved February 21, 2007, from http://www.cisco.com/warp/public/779/ ibs/solutions/learning/whitepapers/el_cisco_rio.pdf

Barron, T. (2000, March). Learning object pioneers. *Learning Circuits.* Retrieved February 21, 2007, from http://www.learningcircuits.org/2000/mar2000/barron.html

Brent, R. (2006, February 7). *Connexions history: Important past milestones.* Retrieved February 21, 2007, from http://cnx.org/aboutus/

Brown, J. (1996, November 4). Oracle lays out architecture for 'net-based training. *Network World.* Retrieved February 21, 2007, from http://www.findarticles. com/p/articles/mi_qa3649/is_199611/ai_n8755082/print

Buell, T. (2000, November). *Creating educational object repositories: The CAREO project.* Retrieved February 21, 2007, from http://www.ucalgary.ca/pubs/Newsletters/Currents/Vol7.7/careo.html

Business Wire. (2001, May 30). *NIIT-NETg relationship crosses a significant milestone.* Retrieved February 21, 2007, from http://www.highbeam.com/DocPrint. aspx?DocId=1G1:75118603

Chitwood, K. (2000). Learning objects defined. *Wisc-Online.* Retrieved February 21, 2007, from http://www.wisconline.org/about/woinfo/woinfo.html

Clinton, W.J. (1999). *Using technology to improve training opportunities for federal government employees* [Executive Order 13111]. Washington, DC: U.S. Office of Personnel Management.

Collier, G., & Robson, R. (2001). ELearning interoperability standards. In *Take it to the nth.* Sun Microsystems.

Conner, M. (1998, November 12). LALO. *What's that? Some history behind current learning standards initiatives and some updates!* Retrieved February 21, 2007, from http://www.learnativity.com/lalo.html

Department of Defense. (2000). *Department of Defense implementation plan for advanced distributed learning*, p. 117. Washington DC: Department of Defense.

Dodds, P. (Ed.). (2000). *ADL sharable courseware object reference model*. Concurrent Technologies Corporation (CTC). Retrieved February 21, 2007, from http://www.adlnet.gov/downloads/12.cfm

Dodds, P. (Ed.) (2001). *Advanced distributed learning sharable content object reference model*. Advanced Distributed Learning. Retrieved February 21, 2007, from http://www.adlnet.gov/scorm/history/12/index.cfm

Doorten, M., Giesbers, B., Janssen, J., Daniels, J., & Koper, R. (2003). *Transforming existing content into reusable learning objects*. Open University of the Netherlands.

Downes, S. (2000, October 14). *Exploring new directions in online learning*. Retrieved February 21, 2007, from http://www.downes.ca/files/Exploring.htm

EDUCAUSE. (2004). *National Learning Infrastructure Initiative*. Retrieved February 21, 2007, from http://www.educause.edu/content.asp?page_id=2601&bhcp=1

Ellwood, A. (1997). *Oracle learning architecture: Closing the training gap with Oracle's innovative Web-based solution*. Paper presented at the European Oracle User Group Conference, Brussels, Belgium.

Engelhardt, M., Hildebrand, A., Lang, A., Schmidt, T.C., & Werlitz, M. (2004). *A constructivist content exploration based on a hypermedia e-learning object system*. Retrieved February 21, 2007, from http://www.rz.fhtw-berlin.de/data/rz.Web/content/Materialien/Projekte/MIR/icl2004(2).pdf

Friesen, N. (2001). What are educational objects? *Interactive Learning Environments, 9*(3). Retrieved February 21, 2007, from http://www.ucalgary.ca/commons/careo/objectpaper.htm

Gibbons, A.S., Nelson, J., & Richards, R. (2000). The nature and origin of instructional objects. In D.A. Wiley (Ed.), *The instructional use of learning objects*. Association for Instructional Technology and the Association for

Educational Communications and Technology. Retrieved February 21, 2007, from http://reusability.org/read/chapters/gibbons.doc

Goldsworthy, P. (2002, February 14). *Ontario University collaborations for learning object development*. Retrieved February 21, 2007, from http://cloe.on.ca/news.html

Heins, T., Mundell, R., & Muzio, J. (2001). *Experiences with reusable elearning objects: From theory to practice.* Retrieved February 21, 2007, from http://www.udutu.com/pdfs/e-learning-objects.pdf

Hodgins, W. H. (2000, February). *Into the future: A vision paper. Commission on technology & adult learning.* Retrieved February 21, 2007, from http://www.learnativity.com/download/MP7.PDF

IEEE Standards. (1998). In E. Duval (Ed.), *Draft standard for learning object metadata* (p. 44). Piscataway, NJ: IEEE Standards Department. Retrieved February 21, 2007, from http://ltsc.ieee.org/doc/wg12/LOM_WD6_4.pdf

IMS Global Learning Consortium, I. (2006). *About IMS/GLC.* Retrieved February 21, 2007, from http://www.imsglobal.org/background.html

Jacobsen, P. (2002). Reusable learning objects: What does the future hold? *e-Learning Magazine,* p. 1. Retrieved February 21, 2007, from http://www.mcli.dist.maricopa.edu/ocotillo/retreat02/rlos.php

Koper, R. (2001). *Modeling units of study from a pedagogical perspective: The pedagogical meta-model behind EML.* DSpace at Open Universiteit Nederland. Retrieved February 21, 2007, from http://dspace.ou.nl/handle/1820/36

Koper, R., & Olivier, B. (2004). Representing the learning design of units of learning. *Educational Technology & Society, 7*(3). Retrieved February 21, 2007, from http://ifets.ieee.org/periodical/7_3/10.pdf

L'Allier, J.J. (1997). *Frame of reference: NETgs map to the products. Their structure and core beliefs.* NetG. Retrieved February 21, 2007, from http://www.netg.com/research/whitepapers/frameref.asp

Laundry, R. (2006, August 23). *About the GEM project.* Retrieved February 21, 2007, from http://64.119.44.148/about/gemingeneral/about-gem/

Locklear, C. (1997, July 30). Oracle offers interactive Web-based courseware for bBusinesses. *Newsbytes News Network.* Retrieved February 21, 2007, from http://www.findarticles.com/p/articles/mi_m0NEW/is_1997_July_30/ai_19682203/print

LoLa. (2006). *LoLa: learning objects learning activities.* Retrieved February 21, 2007, from http://www.lolaexchange.org/

LTSC. (2006, September 18). *Learning Technology Standards Committee.* Retrieved February 21, 2007, from http://ieeeltsc.org/

Mahadevan, S. (2001). *Brief introduction to learning objects in DLNET.* Retrieved February 21, 2007, from http://www.dlnet.vt.edu/Resources/reports/ARI_LO_Def.pdf

MERLOT. (2006). *How did MERLOT get started?* Retrieved February 21, 2007, from http://taste.merlot.org/howmerlotstarted.html

Merrill, M. D. (1996). Instructional transaction theory: An instructional design model based on knowledge objects. *Educational Technology, 36*(3). Retrieved February 21, 2007, from http://www.id2.usu.edu/Papers/IDTHRYK3.PDF

MIT. (2006a). *About OCW.* Retrieved February 21, 2007, from http://ocw.mit.edu/OcwWeb/Global/AboutOCW/about-ocw.htm

MIT. (2006b). *Our story.* Retrieved February 21, 2007, from http://ocw.mit.edu/OcwWeb/Global/AboutOCW/our-story.htm

Mortimer, L. (2002, April). (Learning) objects of desire: Promise and practicality. *Learning Circuits.* Retrieved February 21, 2007, from http://www.learningcircuits.org/2002/apr2002/mortimer.html

Norton, M.J. (1996, January 26). *Media objects.* Retrieved February 21, 2007, from http://www.nolaria.org/archi/MediaObjects.htm

Polsani, P.R. (2003). The use and abuse of reusable learning objects. *Journal of Digital Information, 3*(4).

Rahman, S. (2003). *DLNET: Digital Library Network for Engineering and Technology* (p. 162). Blacksburg: Alexandria Research Institute of Virginia Polytechnic Institute and State University.

Shepherd, C. (2000, December). *Objects of interest.* Fastrak Consulting Ltd. Retrieved February 21, 2007, from http://www.fastrak-consulting.co.uk/tactix/features/objects/objects.htm

South, J.B., & Monson, D.W. (2004). *A university-wide system for creating, capturing, and delivering learning objects* (p. 28). Provo: Brigham Young University.

Wiley, D.A.(2000). *Connecting learning objects to instructional design theory: A definition, a metaphor, and a taxonomy.* Utah State University. Retrieved February 21, 2007, from http://reusability.org/read/chapters/wiley.doc

Wisc-Online. (2000). *About Wisc-Online.* Retrieved February 21, 2007, from http://www.wisconline.org/about/woinfo/woinfo.html

Chapter II

Repositories

Cathleen S. Alfano, Florida Distance Learning Consortium, USA

Susan L. Henderson, Florida Distance Learning Consortium, USA

Abstract

This chapter presents an overview of the use of digital repositories in the field of education. The authors' purpose in writing this chapter is not only to provide their readers with general knowledge about educational repositories, but to give them some idea of the various issues and processes involved in launching a digital repository. The chapter first discusses key concepts and general functions of repositories, and offers the authors' thoughts on the most important functions of repository software management tools. A case study of repository implementation for the State of Florida is briefly described. The chapter closes with a look at some of the different ways repositories are being used nationally and globally, and with the authors' expectations on future developments in this area.

Introduction

This chapter focuses on the relatively recent emergence of digital repositories in the field of education. The authors discuss the definition and general function of repositories, and the authors' recommendations for important repository software functionality. To give readers a look at the processes and issues involved in repository implementation, we describe a case study of repository implementation for the State of Florida. The chapter closes with a look at how repositories are being used nationally and globally.

Definitions

Repositories are systems created to house and manage digital resources. They exist primarily to facilitate discovery of existing resources, and to enable their sharing and reuse. These structures are often quite large, encompassing statewide, regional, or national systems, so that multiple levels of appearance, accessibility, and control mechanisms become important issues.

You might wonder why repositories came to be, and what needs they serve. After all, the Internet is a fantastic and seemingly limitless research tool that is available to anyone with a Web browser. Why would you need yet another content resource? The problem is that there is so much information online already, and the number of digital educational resources continues to expand. And, as more educational content becomes electronically available, institutions and individuals are faced with the question of how to store this content, manage it, and make it available to those who should have access to it.

Currently, as you may have already experienced, it takes lots of time and energy to find an appropriate resource using common search engines. You may face challenges in learning about and locating different collections, interacting with different interfaces, and finally finding the relevant resources and determining if the resource is accurate and reliably available. As you will learn, a repository solves content management issues and can set standards for the quality of its resources while making it easier for content searchers to quickly find the exact resources they need. For example, a Google search for the "Declaration of Independence" returns 15.1 million hits in 0.6 seconds. How do you identify the resources that are relevant to your search?

Main Repository Functions and Key Terminology

What is happening inside these resource management systems? Just as a department store provides access to a variety of consumer goods, most repositories provide access to many types of digital resources, ranging from single files such as documents, photos, videos, slideshows, and audio files to more complex content groupings such as lessons, modules, or courses. An important aspect of repositories is that, like a warehouse, users do not need to know anything about what goes on behind the scenes. Users just want to show up at the warehouse, get exactly what they need, and get back to the task at hand.

Some repositories focus on specific types of resources while others are more diverse. Richards, McGreal, and Friesen (2002) offer the Australian AVIRE repository, which contains only architectural resources, as an example of a repository focused on the needs of a specific community. Besides various kinds of physical files, repositories may also store and catalog links (URLs) to resources located outside the repository. Another kind of repository is sometimes defined as a *referatory*. A referatory stores links to resources, rather than the physical files themselves. Multimedia Educational Resources for Learning and Online Teaching (MERLOT), a referatory that may be familiar to many U.S. educators, includes resources in a variety of content areas such as documents, games and puzzles, practice exercises and assignments, and also catalogs strategies for using a resource.

Repositories must store descriptive information about each resource—similar to the way a library's electronic catalog stores information about items in the library's collection. The descriptive information is associated with each repository resource and is known as *metadata*. Metadata usually includes the resource title, author, resource description, relevant keywords, copyright statements, and potentially many other elements. Sufficient metadata are the key to discovery of an item within the repository warehouse. Because a repository may only reference some resources that are actually physically located elsewhere, and because collections can quickly become extremely large, a key repository function is to perform targeted searches for resources. Ensuring that robust metadata is associated with each and every repository resource makes discoverability more likely, and makes it possible for users to locate resources that exactly match their specified needs.

By tagging objects according to an accepted international metadata standard, a repository ensures that items in the home repository can be discovered by searches conducted from other repositories. Even though Repository A may use a different tagging scheme (e.g., DublinCore) than Repository B (e.g., IEEE LOM v 1.0), if they both use a standard scheme, the repositories can communicate this descriptive information to each other through a crosswalk of the related fields. Efforts among repositories to communicate are discussed more fully in a later section of this chapter.

A type of resource that is frequently associated with repositories is a *learning object*. The definition of learning objects has been widely debated. The Learning Technology Standards Committee of the Institute of Electrical and Electronics Engineers (IEEE) formed in 1996 to create and promote technology standards. This group initially identified a learning object as any entity, whether digital or nondigital, that is "used, re-used, or referenced during technology supported learning" (Wiley, 2000, p. 4). Other definitions have been more specific. David Wiley has written extensively on the topic of learning objects, and his definition of a learning object provides the most value for our discussion: a small (relative to the size of an entire course) instructional component that can be reused a number of times in different learning contexts (Wiley, 2000). A challenge associated with the concept of reusability is the need to ensure that the learning object is self-contained—that it stands alone, and exists completely autonomously without need to reference other external learning objects or resources.

McLean (2001) suggests that the shareable content object reference model (SCORM) specification establishes a definition for a learning object through its standards for tagging, storing, and organizing content components Extrapolating from the specification, McLean offers a description of a learning object as a "granular" topic, ranging from 5 to 15 minutes in length, which can be reused while still maintaining its relationships with its associated objects. These relationships might include links to outcomes or objectives, assessment items, as well as to the object's metadata. The SCORM specifications also ensure technical compatibility standards that allow the learning object to be reused in multiple learning management systems.

You might be thinking that a repository is like a library, and you are correct in some respects. Repositories and libraries do have many similarities: They both exist to store resources and to offer access to resources. They both have systems for cataloging, searching, and retrieval. However, repositories are different in way that their users impact their contents. A library is a place where resources are stored but where the library patrons have little or no input on what is housed in the library. Repositories, on the other hand, may permit their users to take part in creating and contributing resources, commenting on resources, and determining whether resources are to be included in a collection. The users may not only be encouraged to share resources, but may have access to tools to assist in resource repurposing and to create completely new content. Users may then choose to share back with the community by contributing their new or revised resources to the repository. Repositories also invite peer input on resources. For example, MERLOT provides space for and access to peer reviews of resources, and members' comments on resources. Florida's K20 digital repository, The Orange Grove, mandates a quality peer-review process to ensure resource accuracy, instructional and editorial quality, and adherence to the repository technical and metadata standards.

The repository system works with existing learning management systems (LMSs) and authoring tools, but it focuses on the aspects of storage, access, tagging, and copyright issues, while an LMS generally focuses more on administration of the learning content, managing user and faculty interactions, and tracking and recording learner progress. An LMS often duplicates materials that are used across several courses, whereas in a repository, the content is stored only once and then accessed from multiple locations. The repository storage mechanism is much more efficient in terms of server space, and it also enables easy updating of content from one location.

Repositories are constantly evolving, and more are coming online every day. Some institutions have built their own systems, while others rely on commercial software. As Richards, McGreal, Hatala, and Friesen (2002) point out, it is unlikely that one repository could collect or manage all of the available digital resources in any given field. This situation has led to the next step in repository evolution, which is the ability of repositories to search metadata in other trusted repositories based on the international library standard Z39.50 and the emerging standards, SRU and SRW. This *federated search* allows the user to search resources distributed among state, regional, national, and international repositories and libraries. The Academic ADL Co-Lab (n.d.) delineates two current approaches to facilitating interaction among repositories. The CORDRA approach, discussed later in this chapter, collects resource metadata from member repositories into a central repository that serves as a "gateway" to the resources. A second approach is being developed as part of the Open Knowledge Initiative (OKI), which started at MIT in 2001. The OKI repository OSID tool is an interface used to enable integration among repository systems for the purpose of information exchange. The existence of standardized metadata systems enables these different repository systems to communicate. Some external repositories may already be integrated with the user's own repository and thus easily accessed. Other repositories may require separate authentication for the user to be granted permission to access their resources.

Important Repository Software Features

Ideally, a repository can integrate easily with multiple repositories and with multiple learning management systems (LMS), for example, Angel, Blackboard, Desire2Learn, Sakai, or Educator, to enable single sign-on for each learning management system (LMS) user. This is especially useful for higher education faculty members, many of whom are now accustomed to their institution's LMS. Integration may allow faculty to log into their LMS and then have a seamless entry into their repository, without additional log-ins required, to quickly access or share resources.

Some products also offer the opportunity to customize many aspects of the repository management system. For example, users may wish to customize the types of user information to be collected at an institutional, departmental, district, or state level and to control the interface look and feel. Some repository management software also allows control of metadata fields at multiple levels, control of searching at multiple levels, and setting up and managing workflows to control content creation or quality reviews of content. Other important issues to consider if you are software shopping are the ability to set copyright/access restrictions and to ensure access for persons with disabilities. There may be multiple options for notifying users when new resources are added to the repository or of items to be reviewed (e.g., reviews to ensure accuracy, standards conformance, quality ratings by peers).

Another useful software function is the types of personal spaces the software provides for users. Some repositories provide users with the ability to bookmark resources, or historical records on resources that have been downloaded. Notifications of new resources of personal interest can also be controlled by the user. Users may also wish to comment on resources and have those comments visible to other users through some type of peer rating mechanism.

Consider your needs to collect data on repository usage, as well as being able to quickly and easily produce statistical reports with information such as total number of items, information on items under review, weekly usage, user log-in times, and counts of external queries. Automated tracking and reporting on any nonfunctioning URLs within the repository is also valuable. Some repositories also track student performance data, through integration with their course management system.

Examine the kind of environment that the repository presents to your community of users. Is the interface simple, attractive, and easy to use for not-so-technically-savvy users? Does the repository provide any tools to assist users in creating resources? Is collaboration supported, and how flexible is that system? You and your users will be happiest if it is a simple process to contribute resources, link to resources, and download resources.

Finally, consider how easy it will be to move your repository resources, and the metadata associated with them. At some future point, you might need to migrate to a new software version, or to a new vendor.

Case Study: The Orange Grove K20 Digital Repository

This section provides you with a brief overview of how a statewide group in Florida, the Florida Distance Learning Consortium, implemented an educational repository. The Florida Distance Learning Consortium is a service organization, open to all of Florida's educational institutions, that supports technologies to enhance and deliver instruction. As consortium staff and members became aware of the repository effort, they first began to research repositories and their implementation. Over the course of the next year, they pooled information gathered at conferences, hired consultants, and organized policy planning workshops. They defined the repository project as a separate and high-priority consortium initiative and developed a set of key principles to guide the development of their repository:

1. Shareable content object reference model (SCORM) specifications for e-learning were creating the opportunity for a global marketplace of reusable content
2. Quality must be assured
3. Metadata must be standardized, required and yet customized
4. User trust must be developed and ensured
5. Content requires management
6. Content must be reusable in new and innovative teaching environments
7. Information about and training to use the system is critical for success

Repository vendors and their software were researched, and a choice of software was made and installed on a centralized consortium server. The group determined where to focus their collection and development efforts, and the scope of implementation. They selected several courses in higher education mathematics that had historically proved difficult for students, and for which instructors might be motivated to use additional resources for student mastery of concepts. This was done with an eye to obtaining documented results to solicit future funding. A core group of interested members from various Florida institutions emerged, and these institutions provided the test beds for pilot implementation efforts.

The consortium management team also worked hard to build networks and partnerships for the repository effort at the state, national, and international level, both in education, and in military and business sectors. At every opportunity, they utilized and built upon the talents and strengths of their partners to discuss intellectual property, workflow processes, quality review, and other policy issues related to implementing the key principles. The project director worked with state and regional organizations to develop standards and tools to guide users in adhering to the defined standards. Multiple funding possibilities were researched and grant proposal submitted.

Currently, this group has completed a limited repository implementation. The repository holds approximately 500 resources and has about 500 users from across the United States, but primarily Florida educators. Several online lessons have been developed asynchronously by teams composed of volunteer faculty members, developers, and project staff designers. A template has been developed and made freely available that assist Web developers in producing online lessons that meet interoperability standards.

Challenges that confront the project are adequate funding for statewide implementation and the need to raise faculty awareness about the repository and how digital resources can contribute to improved student performance. Relying on volunteers to conduct quality reviews of resources has also proved difficult, and metadata creation is time-consuming. While the project continues to pursue sufficient funding to take the repository statewide, it has recently been awarded a Fund for the Improvement of Postsecondary Education (FIPSE) grant to document and test a blueprint for repository implementation.

Current and Future Directions

International Efforts

While we do not promise to provide an exhaustive list, this section discusses several initiatives that are planned or underway that we think will affect the future of repositories. Although there are many efforts underway for repository development and federation among U.S. institutions, many international learning object repositories are well established.

Canada's Internet development organization, CANARIE, has invested heavily in online learning projects, including the design and development of learning object repositories. In a February 2005 discussion paper, MacLeod (2005) recommended that a cross-Canadian "infrastructure of interconnected learning object repositories be created" (p. 3) and that stakeholders develop the strategies for design, development, and implementation. This group has recognized that such a coordinated effort will not only benefit Canada's educational interests, but can provide international economic opportunities. MacLeod also reported that Australia, Sweden, and Holland are also moving rapidly in repository research and development and is hopeful that a universal repository model will result.

The European Union's ARIADNE project has a distributed repository of learning objects and associated metadata supported in multiple languages, the European Knowledge Pool System. This repository stores educational objects that are viewed as useful in training or teaching (Forte et al., 1999). In Australia, Education Network Australia (EdNA Online) has a tool that enables searches across multiple educational repositories and libraries. The MERLOT Federated Search allows users to choose from among the available digital libraries to search, and is scalable to allow incorporation of additional libraries.

Other global initiatives reported by Colin Steele (2006) include the University of California's eScholarship Repository and the Securing a Hybrid Environment for Research Preservation and Access (SHERPA) Initiative, which is investigating issues regarding the development of openly accessible institutional digital repositories in universities.

Another initiative, Japan's National Institute of Multimedia Education, is supporting higher educational institutions through information technology research and development and maintaining a global perspective. Their repository project, NIME-glad, has already federated with the EU's ARIADNE and has been preparing to federate with MERLOT in the U.S. In a January 2006 interview, NIME's president, Shimizu Yasutaka, discussed the Global Learning Objects Brokered Exchange (GLOBE) partnership formed in 2004 (Oblinger, 2006). This partnership brings several major repository players together to discuss potential joint development efforts: ARIADNE in the EU; education.au limited in Australia; eduSource in Canada; MERLOT in the United States; and NIME in Japan. LORNET replaced eduSourceCanada as the Canadian representative in the spring of 2006. The efficient sharing of educational resources is increasingly being seen a solution that makes the most sense for education and may help move us toward an international repository model.

The Content Object Repositories Digital Rights Administration (CORDRA) project is working to provide a central storehouse of metadata for resources and repositories that will enable the searching of multiple repositories at one time. The project goal is to specify the technologies and interoperability standards that can be used to create the needed infrastructure. Activities for the CORDRA initiative are being coordinated by the Advanced Distributed Learning Initiative (ADL), the Corporation for National Research Initiatives (CNRI), and the Learning Systems Architecture Lab (LSAL).

Repositories as Archive and Distribution Mechanisms

Educational repositories are generally used to store and manage educational materials for eventual use by teachers and their students. However, some institutions are using them to create a collaboration space and distribution vehicles for faculty research efforts and to document institutional efforts.

Some benefits of using repositories to store and manage research material were presented in a Scholarly Publishing and Academic Resources Coalition (SPARC) paper in 2002. This paper (Crow, 2002) suggested that repositories can help to stimulate a new type of dispersed scholarly publishing structure, as compared to the current culture of publishing in academic journals. Maintaining access to these journals is expensive for academic libraries. Repositories can also be used to document and to provide access to an institution's intellectual capital, and to assist in producing metrics for an institution's productivity and academic status.

The Massachusetts Institute of Technology (MIT) Libraries and Hewlett-Packard Labs have collaborated to develop an open source system called DSpace™ that stores and manages an institution's digital research and educational material (Massachusetts Institute of Technology, 2006). This project seeks to preserve and index academic output and to make it available for global sharing. The DSpace software and membership are free. Another interesting initiative that seeks to link research output through a more global network is The University of Melbourne ePrints Repository (University of Melbourne, n.d.). This repository is part of the Group of Eight (GO8) initiative that represents eight of Australia's leading universities involved in a collaborative effort to archive scholarly publications and to make them more visible and accessible.

Repositories As Collaboration Tools

Repositories also provide an opportunity for online collaboration in the creation and review of resources. Many repository software packages include tools for content creation and permit the definition and support of collaborative groups. When multifaceted teams of content developers work together, the software can facilitate the creation process for content creation. Tools are also evolving to permit easy content creation by users without Web development experience. These tools may allow authors to create many types of multimedia resources, to repurpose existing content by disassembling and modifying it and perhaps to reassemble it in new ways. Some software also permits easy conversion of proprietary documents and nonstandard image formats to HTML and JPEG formats and conversion of .zip files to IMS/SCORM content packages. A function valued by managers is the ability to monitor and manage items throughout the creation process and during any subsequent review processes via automated systems of participant alerts and reminders.

Conclusion

Undertaking repository construction is a significant effort, but one in which an increasing number of educational institutions and consortia are engaged. This chapter has introduced you to a range of potential repository functions and uses, to help you become aware of the options available to you. We have suggested issues that must be addressed and processes that we have found useful in repository implementation, but the repository landscape is changing rapidly. We anticipate that integration among learning management systems and repositories will continue to evolve in creative ways, providing greater support for collaboration and communication among digital contributors. As more repositories come online, and proliferation of digital content continues, federation among repositories will become increasingly important. Some aspects of metadata generation will hopefully be automated or facilitated in the near future.

While we are still working to ensure our own successful repository implementation, we are convinced that change management strategies are essential, coupled with a system that meets the needs of its users. Then, as in so many technology decisions, we make choices and take action using today's information while keeping one eye on the horizon.

References

Academic ADL Co-Lab. (n.d.). *Finding and sharing learning objects: Standards based interoperability and federated repositories.* Retrieved March 19, 2007 from: http://www.academiccolab.org/resources/Finding_Sharing.pdf

Crow, R. (2002). *The case for institutional repositories: A SPARC position paper.* The Scholarly Publishing & Academic Resources Coalition. Retrieved February 21, 2007, from http://www.arl.org/sparc/IR/IR_Final_Release_102.pdf

Forte, E., Haenni, F., Warkentyne, K., Duval, E., Cardinaels, K., Vervaet, E., et al. (1999, March). Semantic and pedagogic interoperability mechanisms in the ARIADNE educational repository. *ACM SIGMOD, 28*(1), 20-25. Retrieved February 21, 2007, from http://portal.acm.org/citation.cfm?id=309844.3098 70&dl=GUIDE&dl=ACM&idx=J689&part=periodical&WantType=periodic al&title=ACM%20SIGMOD%20Record#abstract

MacLeod, D. (2005, February). *Learning object repositories: Deployment and diffusion* (CANARIE Discussion Paper). Retrieved February 21, 2007, from http://www.canarie.ca/funding/elearning/2005_LOR_final_report.pdf

Massachusetts Institute of Technology. (2006). *Introducing DSpace.* Retrieved February 21, 2007, from http://dspace.org/index.html

McLean, N. (2001). Interoperability convergence of online learning and information environments. *The New Review of Information Networking, 7.* Retrieved February 21, 2007, from http://www.colis.mq.edu.au/news_archives/convergence.pdf

Oblinger, D. (2006, July-August). Sharing educational resources worldwide: An interview with Shimizu Yasutaka. *EDUCAUSE Review.* Retrieved February 21, 2007, from http://www.educause.edu/ir/library/pdf/erm0642.pdf

Richards, G., McGreal, R., & Friesen, N. (2002, June). Learning object repository technologies for telelearning: The evolution of POOL and CanCore. *In SITE.* Retrieved February 21, 2007, from http://proceedings.informingscience.org/ IS2002Proceedings/papers/Richa242Learn.pdf#search=%22Learning%20ob ject%20repository%20technologies%20for%20telelearning%3A%20The%2 0evolution%20of%20POOL%20and%20CanCore.%22

Richards, G., McGreal, R., Hatala, M., & Friesen, N. (2002). The evolution of learning object repository technologies: Portals for on-line objects for learning. *Journal of Distance Education, 17*(3). Retrieved February 21, 2007, from http://cade.athabascau.ca/vol17.3/richards.pdf#search=%22washburn%2019 99%20repositories%22

Steele, C. (2006, April 18). E-prints: The future of scholarly communication? *Incite*. Retrieved February 21, 2007, from http://alia.org.au/publishing/incite/2002/10/ eprints.html

University of Melbourne. (n.d.). *ePrints Repository*. Retrieved February 21, 2007, from http://eprints.unimelb.edu.au/

Wiley, D. A. (2000). Connecting learning objects to instructional design theory: A definition, a metaphor, and a taxonomy. In D. A. Wiley (Ed.), *The instructional use of learning objects: Online version*. Retrieved February 21, 2007, from http://reusability.org/read/chapters/wiley.doc

Appendix: Related Web Sites

- **Advanced Distributed Learning:** http://adlnet.org/
- **ARIADNE:** http://www.ariadne-eu.org/
- **CANARIE:** http://www.canarie.ca/about/index.html
- **Content Object Repositories Digital Rights Administration (CORDRA):** http://cordra.net/
- **Corporation for National Research Initiatives:** http://www.cnri.reston. va.us/
- **DSpace:** http://www.dspace.org/
- **Education Network Australia (EdNA) Online:** http://www.edna.edu.au/ edna/page1.html
- **eduSourceCanada:** http://www.edusource.ca/
- **Group of Eight (Go8):** http://www.go8.edu.au/
- **LORNET:** http://www.lornet.org/
- **Learning Systems Architecture Lab (LSAL):** http://lsal.org/
- **Multimedia Educational Resources for Learning and Online Teaching (MERLOT):** http://www.merlot.org/
- **National Institute of Multimedia Education (NIME):** http://www.nime. ac.jp/index-e.html
- **Securing a Hybrid Environment for Research Preservation and Access (SHERPA) Initiative:** http://www.sherpa.ac.uk

- **University of California's eScholarship Repository:** http://repositories.cdlib.org/
- **University of Melbourne ePrints Repository:** http://eprints.unimelb.edu.au/

Metadata Schemas

- **CanCore Guidelines for the Implementation of Learning Object Metadata (IEEE 1484.12.1-2002). Norm Friesen, Sue Fisher and Anthony Roberts. CanCore. Version 2.0** http://www.cancore.ca/en/guidelines.html
- **Dublin Core Metadata Initiative.** http://dublincore.org/
- **Draft Standard for Learning Object Metadata (IEEE.1484.12.1-2002). Learning Technology Standards Committee of IEEE. Institute of Electrical and Electronics Engineers, 2002.** http://ltsc.ieee.org/wg12/files/LOM_1484_12_1_v1_Final_Draft.pdf
- **GEM Documentation. 2006.** http://www.thegateway.org/about/documentation

Chapter III

An Overview of Learning Object Repositories

Argiris Tzikopoulos, Agricultural University of Athens, Greece

Nikos Manouselis, Agricultural University of Athens, Greece

Riina Vuorikari, European Schoolnet, Belgium

Abstract

Learning objects are systematically organised and classified in online databases, which are termed learning object repositories (LORs). Currently, a rich variety of LORs is operating online, offering access to wide collections of learning objects. These LORs cover various educational levels and topics, and are developed by using a variety of different technologies. They store learning objects and/or their associated metadata descriptions, as well as offer a range of services that may vary from advanced search and retrieval of learning objects to intellectual property rights (IPR) management. Until now, there has not been a comprehensive study of existing LORs that will give an outline of their overall characteristics. For this purpose, this chapter presents the initial results from a survey of 59 well-known repositories with learning resources. The most important characteristics of surveyed LORs are examined and useful conclusions about their current status of development are made. A discussion of future trends in the LORs field is also carried out.

Introduction

The evolution of information and communication technologies (ICTs) creates numerous opportunities for providing new standards of quality in educational services. The Internet is increasingly becoming one of the dominant mediums for learning, training and working, and learning resources are continuously made available online in a digital format to enable and facilitate productive online learning. Learning resources may include online courses, best practices, simulations, online experiments, presentations, reports, textbooks, as well as other types of digital resources that can be used for teaching and learning purposes. They may cover numerous topics such as computing, business, art, engineering, technology and agriculture. They are offered by various types of organisations, in different languages, at different cost rates, and aim at different learning settings. In general, the potential of digital resources that can be used to facilitate learning and training, and which are available online, is rapidly increasing (Friesen, 2001).

Recent advances in the e-learning field have witnessed the emergence of the *learning object* concept. A learning object is considered to be any type of digital resource that can be reused to support learning (Downes, 2003; Wiley, 2002). Learning objects and/or their associated metadata are typically organised, classified and stored in online databases, termed *learning object repositories* (LORs). In this way, their offering to learners, teachers and tutors is facilitated through a rich variety of different LORs that is currently operating online.

The LOR landscape would benefit from the examination of the characteristics of existing LORs in order to formulate a general picture about their nature and status of development. The contributions in this direction can be considered rather sporadic so far, focused on very particular topics or restricted in coverage (Balanskat & Vuorikari, 2000; Haughey & Muirhead, 2004; Neven & Duval, 2002; Pisik, 1997; Retalis, 2004; Riddy & Fill, 2004). More specifically, most of these contributions have a different focus and just include a brief LOR review in their literature review (e.g., Haughey & Muirhead, 2004; Retalis, 2004). Others include some that focus on some particular segment of LORs such as ones using a particular metadata standard (e.g., Neven & Duval, 2002), some that study the users and usage (e.g., Najjar, Ternier, & Duval, 2003), or some that have restricted geographical coverage (e.g., Balanskat & Vuorikari, 2000). Thus, we believe that current studies do not address largely enough interesting questions about today's LORs such as: what are the educational subject areas covered by LORs? In which languages are these resources available, and at what cost? Do LORs use metadata for classifying the learning objects, and, if yes, do they follow some widely accepted specifications and standards? What quality control, evaluation and assurance mechanisms do LORs use for their learning objects? How has intellectual property management been tackled?

This chapter aims to provide an introduction to the status of existing LORs, by reviewing a representative number of major LORs that are currently operating online and attempting to study some of their important characteristics. For this purpose, a survey of 59 well-known repositories with learning resources has been conducted. A selection of important LOR characteristics was reviewed and conclusions have been made about the current status of LORs' development. This chapter is structured as following: the next section provides the background of this study by defining learning objects and learning object repositories. The "LOR's Review" section provides an overview of the methodology followed to carry out the review of the LOR sample and presents the results of their analysis. In the "Discussion and Future Trends" section, the findings of the analysis are discussed and reflected on possible outcomes of LORs' development, in relation to the future trends arising in the LOR arena. Finally, the last section provides the conclusions of the chapter and outlines directions for future research.

Background

Learning Objects

Long before the advent and wide adoption of the World Wide Web (WWW), researchers such as Ted Nelson (1965) and Roy Stringer (1992) referred to environments where the design of information and courses could be based on the notion of reusable objects. During the past 10 years, relevant research in the e-learning area focused on describing the notion of reusable objects when referring to digital learning resources, introducing thus the concept of learning objects (Downes, 2003). One of the most popular definitions of a learning object is given by the IEEE Learning Technology Standards Committee in the IEEE Learning Object Metadata standard, stating that "a learning object is defined as any entity, digital or non-digital, that may be used for learning, education or training" (IEEE LOM, 2002). Wiley (2002) restricted this definition by characterising a learning object as "any digital resource that can be reused to support learning" (p. 6).

An interesting criticism on the above definitions has been provided by Polsani (2003), leading to a more constrained definition: "a learning object is an independent and self-standing unit of learning content that is predisposed to reuse in multiple instructional contexts" (p. 4). Metros and Bonnet (2002) note that learning objects should not be confused with information objects that have no learning aim. It has been argued by McCormick (2003) that learning objects should include (either within or in a related documentation) some learning objectives and outcomes, assessments and other instructional components, as well as the information object itself.

For the purposes of this chapter, we will use the following definition of learning objects, adopted by the New Media Consortium (NMC) as part of its Learning Object Initiative (Smith, 2004), which adds value to the above mentioned definitions by emphasising the meaningful structure and an educational objective dimensions:

A learning object is any grouping of materials that is structured in a meaningful way and is tied to an educational objective. The 'materials' in a learning object can be documents, pictures, simulations, movies, sounds, and so on. Structuring these in a meaningful way implies that the materials are related and are arranged in a logical order. But without a clear and measurable educational objective, the collection remains just a collection. (Smith, 2004)

This definition is not intended to be restrictive, so it refers to any digital asset which can be used to enable teaching or learning. It does not require a learning object to be of some particular size. It may refer to many different types of object, from simple images or video clips to collections of objects arranged in one or more sequences (Duncan, 2002). These learning objects can be delivered or accessed over the Internet or across a local or private network.

Learning Object Repositories

The digital resources that are developed to support teaching and learning activities must be easily located and retrieved, as well as be suitably selected to meet the needs of those to whom they are delivered. For this purpose metadata is used. The term 'metadata' is defined as data about data, and in the case of learning objects, it describes the nature and location of the resource (IEEE LOM, 2002; Miller, 1996). Related research has identified that systems that facilitate the storage, location and retrieval of learning resources are essential to the further integration of information technologies and learning (Holden, 2003). Such systems, termed *repositories*, are used to store any type of digital material. However, repositories for learning objects are considerably more complex, both in terms of what needs to be stored and how it may be delivered. The purpose of a repository with learning resources is not simply safe storage and delivery of the resources, but rather the facilitation of their reuse and sharing (Duncan, 2002). According to Holden (2003), a digital repository is a *learning* one if it is created in order to provide access to digital educational materials and if the nature of its content or metadata reflects an interest in potential educational uses of the materials.

According to Downes (2003), digital learning repositories can be distinguished in course portals, course packs and learning object repositories. A course portal is actually a Web site, offered either by a consortium of educational institutions or a private company working with educational partners, which lists courses from a number of institutions. The purpose of a course portal is to enable a learner to browse through or search course listings to simplify the learner's selection of an online course.

Course packs, the second type of learning repositories that Downes identifies, are packages of learning materials collected to support a course. Offered primarily by educational publishers, course packs are collections of learning materials offered to instructors for use in traditional, blended or online courses. The course pack may be predefined or custom built by the instructor. The instructor is expected to supplement the course pack with additional content, educational activities, testing and other classroom activities. Some course packs are stand-alone. Other course packs are available for use only in a learning management system (LMS).

Finally, the third type of learning repositories refers to those built for storing learning objects, the learning object repositories. There are two major categories of LORs. The first category includes those that contain both the learning objects as well as learning object descriptions in the form of metadata. The repository may be used to both locate and deliver the learning object. The second category includes LORs containing only the metadata descriptions. In this case, the learning objects themselves are located at a remote location and the repository is used only as a tool to facilitate searching, locating and accessing the learning objects from their original location. Thus, the LORs of this second category are sometimes called learning object "referatories" (Metros & Bennet, 2002).

The benefits of creating and using LORs of high-quality learning objects have been recognised by several educational institutions worldwide. These institutions have developed and published LORs, which offer a wide variety of learning resources. Examples include ARIADNE (www.ariadne-eu.org), MERLOT (http://www.merlot.org), CAREO (http://careo.netera.ca/), Online Learning Network (http://www.onlinelearning.net/), Digital Think (http://www.digitalthink.com/), EDNA (http://www.edna.edu.au) and SMETE (http://www.smete.org/).

LOR's Review

Methodology

The review of existing LORs took place in three phases. First, a set of LOR characteristics was identified as important to examine. These characteristics have been located from related studies (Haughey & Muirhead, 2004; Pisik, 1997; Retalis, 2004; Riddy & Fill, 2004) and evaluated by their importance within current research and development trends in the field. Our aim was to provide a general framework for the description and coding of the LOR characteristics. As a consequence, three main categories of characteristics have been identified and examined:

- **General and content characteristics:** This category refers to characteristics that generally characterise a LOR, such as the year when it started its operation, its geographical coverage, the language of its interface and so forth. They also refer to characteristics related to the content of the LORs, such as the language of the learning objects, the intended audience, discipline area and so forth.

- **Technical characteristics:** This category refers to the services that the LOR offers to its users, such as the possibility to browse and search the learning objects, to view the description of the learning objects, to contribute learning objects, to create and manage a personal account and so on. Furthermore, these characteristics refer to the usage of some metadata specification or standard for the description of the learning objects.

- **Quality characteristics:** This category refers to characteristics related to the existence of quality mechanisms in the LOR (e.g., a quality control policy, a resources' evaluation/reviewing policy, a copyright protection policy, etc.), as well as the existence of security-related services (e.g., user authentication, secure payment mechanisms, etc.).

The second phase concerned assembling an examination sample of LORs. Since the objective of this study has been to review existing and well-known LORs that are publicly available online, information from several resources has been gathered in order to identify some of the most popular LORs worldwide. The list, dating to 2003, of 40 LORs provided by the Advanced Distributed Learning (ADL) Co-lab (http://projects.aadlcolab.org/repository-directory/repository_listing.asp) has served as our initial basis. This list was updated and enriched with LORs that have been located throughout research in related publications and Internet sources. An overall set of 59 LORs has been assembled (see Appendix). Each LOR on the identified set has been visited and thoroughly analysed, according to the general framework of LOR characteristics.

The third phase of this study concerned encoding and importing the data into a statistical package for further investigation. A statistical software package was used for descriptive statistical analysis of the LORs' characteristics, as well as for the examination of combinations of characteristics. In the presentation of the results to follow, we discuss the most interesting findings of this analysis.

Results

First, we classified the number of learning objects that LORs offer into three major categories: those offering more than 50,000 learning objects (large LORs), those having from 10,000 to 50,000 learning objects (medium LORs), and those offering less than 10,000 learning objects (small LORs). Based on this classification, we could say that 5% of the examined LORs are large (3 LORs), 19% medium (11 LORs), and 76% small (45 LORs).

Furthermore, Figure 1 illustrates the graphical distribution of LORs according to the date of their establishment. It can be noted that the majority of LORs have been deployed during 2001-2002. This is the period that followed the *dot.com* explosion of 1999, during which numerous Internet-based applications and services started appearing in various business sectors (Benbya & Belbaly, 2002).

Figure 2 shows the distribution of the LORs according to the country they are located in, allowing the examination of their geographic origin. It illustrates that the majority of LORs surveyed are developed in U.S. (63%), followed by LORs that are developed in European countries (17%) and Canada (14%). Other countries that were part of this survey and have deployed LORs include Australia (5%) and Mauritius (2%).

Figure 1. Distribution of LORs according to their launch year

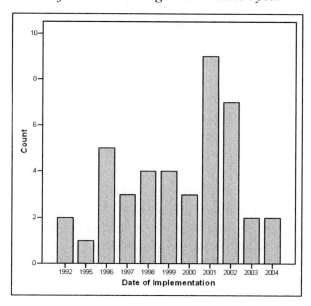

Figure 2. Distribution of LORs according to geographical region or country in which they are located

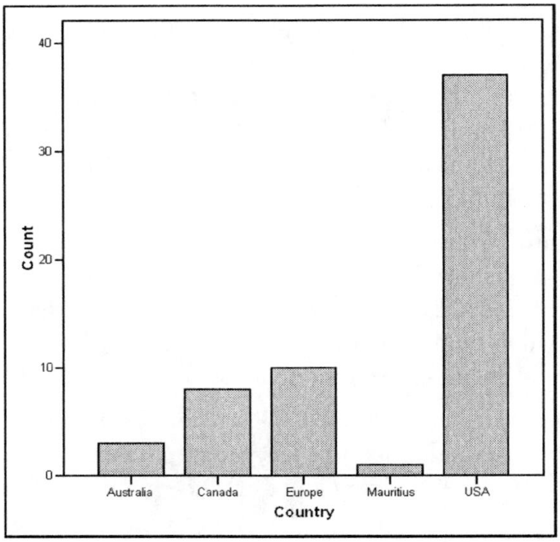

The language of each LOR's user interface is presented in Figure 3, in association to the country in which the LOR is based. This diagram demonstrates that all LORs in Australia, Mauritius and the U.S. offer user interfaces in English. On the other hand, Canadian and European LORs provide multilingual user interfaces, for example, in French, Spanish, German, Italian, Dutch and other.

In a similar manner, Figure 4 presents the language in which the offered learning objects are. It is noted that all LORs offer learning objects in English, independently from the country that they belong to. LORs that offer learning objects in other languages can be mostly located in Europe (14 LORs) and Canada (4 LORs).

Figure 5 illustrates the coverage of LORs is terms of content subjects. It can be observed that the majority of LORs (60%) covers comprehensive topics (that is, applying to more than one subject), 14% mathematical subjects, and 10% other science topics. Very little coverage of history, chemistry, biology, physics and social sciences exists (2% of the total number of LORs for each topic).

In the review of target audiences, a number of 26 repositories aim at more than one target audience, that is, comprehensive (44%), 22 at college-level (37%), 17 at graduate-level (29%), and 11 at continuous-and lifelong-learning audiences (19%). Eight LORs (14%) offer resources for primary school audiences and four LORs (7%) focus on middle school age, thus about one-fifth of LORs offer resources to school level audiences.

Figure 3. Analysis of distribution of LORs per country, according to the language of their interface

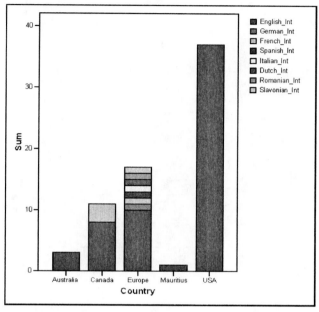

Figure 4. Analysis of the distribution of LORs per country, according to and the language of their objects

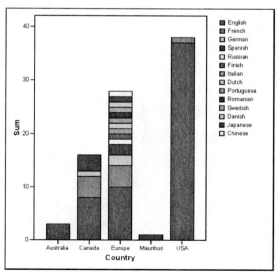

Figure 5. Distribution of LORs according to the subjects they cover

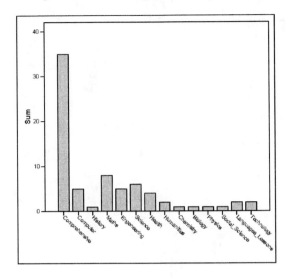

Figure 6. Distribution of LORs according to according to the technical services they offer

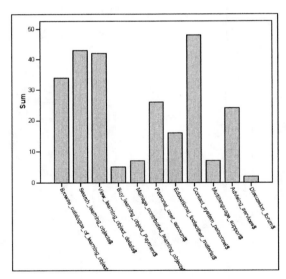

Examining the technical characteristics of the sample of LORs, Figure 6 presents the distribution of LORs according to the services they offer. In the majority of LORs, the users have the possibility to view learning object descriptions/details (71%), to search for learning objects (73%) and to browse a catalogue of learning objects (58%). A small number of LORs allows for the purchase of learning objects (8%) and manage a personal portfolio of learning objects (12%). Additionally, services such as the creation of a personal user account (44%), online advisory about the use of the LOR or the learning objects (41%), use of educational tools (27%) and participation in discussion forums (3%) are offered. Finally, there exist services such as contacting LOR system personnel (via e-mail, phone or online live chat) (81%) and accessing multilingual support (8%).

In addition, we have examined the application of some metadata specification or standard for the description of the learning objects. With regard to the distribution of LORs according to the metadata specification of standard, most of the examined LORs use the IEEE LOM (29%) and the Dublin Core (22%) standards (Dublin Core, 2004; IEEE LOM, 2002). Additionally 25% (15) use IEEE LOM compatible metadata such as IMS Metadata (2001) or CanCore (2002). Finally, there is also a small number (8) of LORs in the examined sample that does not use any particular metadata specification or standard for the description and classification of its learning objects.

Finally, the third category of examined characteristics concerned the quality and security aspects of the sample of LORs. Table 1 provides an overview of the examined dimensions. In particular, 56 LORs have some specific policy about resource submission (95%), from which 27 concerns submissions by the LOR staff (48%) and 29 submissions by the LOR's users (52%). Furthermore, there are 34 LORs that adopt some copyright protection policy (76%). Twenty-seven LORs follow some quality control policy (64%), whereas 23 have some resource evaluation/rating or review policy (43%). Finally, 13 LORs deploy digital rights management for the learning objects (25%).

Table 1. Quality characteristics of the examined LORs

	Total	Staff	Users
Policy Regarding Resource Submission	56	27	29
	Total	Yes	No
Quality Control Policy	42	27	15
Resource Ratings or Review Policy	53	23	30
Copyright Protection Policy	45	34	11
Digital Rights Management	52	13	39

Discussion and Future Trends

LORs Coverage

The majority of LORs surveyed have been deployed around the year 2000. A slight decline in the number of new LORs can be witnessed after 2002. This observation does not however necessary reflect the situation in the global sphere of LORs. The interest and awareness of e-learning, as well as the use of digital resources for learning and teaching purposes, is increasing around the world. It is therefore likely that there exists more and more interest in setting up LORs by educational institutions, international and national authorities, as well as by commercial educational content providers who seem to be moving towards the domain of digital publishing. Identifying such new efforts is rather challenging, as there is no up-to-date international or national indexes of major LORs available. Also, the information about these new LORs is not necessarily made readily available, since it does not appear in research publications, nor does it always exist in easily accessible languages. In conjunction to the somewhat contradictory decline in number of LORs established in recent years, it can be noted that, for example, in Europe extensive work continues to be conducted. Many universities and educational institutions currently have initiated educational repositories. Moreover, national and local educational authorities in the majority of European countries maintain a LOR of public and/or commercial digital learning material for the use in compulsory education, a number of which is increasing, especially in central and eastern European countries as they are re-designing their e-learning policies (Balanskat, 2005). Also, European schoolbook publishers, including GiuntiLab, Hachette, SanomaWSOY and Young Digital Poland, are acquiring their share of the market, thus a number of LORs containing only commercial learning material and assets have been established (McCormick, Scrimshaw, Li, & Clifford, 2004).

The omnipresence of English learning objects in all repositories is, on the one hand, due to the large Anglo-Saxon representation in the study, and on the other hand, indicates interest in having English material along the side of other national languages, as seen especially in the case of the European countries. Localisation of learning resources, both linguistic and to fit to local curriculum and educational culture, is a continuing challenge for countries or institutions who are interested in cross-border codevelopment of learning resources or in localisation of existing products. The dominance of U.S.-based and Anglo-Saxon educational repositories in this survey probably gives them more visibility at the cost of other national and local efforts, provided in languages other than English. In 2000 for instance, 68 educational repositories using more languages than English have been identified during a survey in 18 European countries (Balanskat & Vuorikari, 2000). Consequently, the scope of this chapter could be considered somewhat geographically and linguistically biased, lacking global coverage of existing LORs. Extending the coverage of this study will require more international coordination and an extensive linguistic effort. Albeit this limitation, this chapter still gives a comprehensive overview of representative LORs in the field. Its aim has been to serve as an initial roadmap to LORs, rather than thoroughly analysing all existing LORs, in all languages, from all countries. The examination of LORs with particular lingual and geographical characteristics may be the focus of future studies.

According to our survey, most of the repositories (60%) cover comprehensive subject matters, whereas there is a long trail of LORs focusing on more specific disciplines such as mathematics, physical sciences, engineering and computers, humanities and social sciences, as well as language learning. When it comes to the distribution of learning resources by intended audiences, it can be noted that there are two poles: digital learning resources for college age (37%) and graduate (29%) make one major pole (particularly focusing on higher education), and slightly less than half (44%) cover comprehensive age ranges. About one fifth of LORs offer learning resources for school audiences. Moreover, it would be important to mention that although professional, on-the-job training (termed vocational education and training) is increasingly supported by digital training resources, less than 20% of examined LORs offer resources targeted to this area. This aspect would benefit from further studies. For instance, a plethora of major companies, like CISCO and Microsoft, carry extensive private repositories of learning objects for their internal training purposes. Furthermore, specialised initiatives focus on the development of digital repositories for the vocational education and training sector (e.g., the European e-ACCESS repository at http://eaccess.iti.gr/).

Interoperability

When it comes to the use of metadata in the repositories reviewed, it has been observed that about half use some standardised form of metadata, namely 54% IEEE LOM compatible metadata (IEEE LOM itself, the IMS Metadata, or the CanCore specifications) and 22% Dublin Core. With the adoption of IEEE LOM as an international standard, this percentage is expected to continuously rise.

Apart from efforts on search interoperability, development work has been conducted to connect repositories together in a federation such as the CELEBRATE network (http://celebrate.eun.org) (Massart & Le, 2004). This was developed into the EUN Federation of Internet Resources for Education by European Schoolnet (http://fire. eun.org). There is also CORDRA—the content object repository discovery and registration/resolution architecture (http://cordra.lsal.cmu.edu/cordra/) that is coordinated by ADL. IMS Global Learning Consortium released Digital Repositories Specification in 2003. Moreover, memorandums of understandings on the international level have been established to allow access to quality educational content, for instance, the Global Learning Object Brokered Exchange (http://www.educationau. edu.au/media/040927globe.html), with its global founding members such as the ARIADNE Foundation in Europe, Education Network Australia (EdNA Online) in Australia, eduSource in Canada, Multimedia Educational Resources for Learning and Online Teaching (MERLOT) in the U.S. and National Institute of Multimedia Education (NIME) in Japan.

As LORs are extending to the global level to allow the exchange of metadata and learning objects as well as federating the searches, more information, research and development are still needed to assure semantic interoperability (Simon et al., 2005; OKI, 2007). Semantic interoperability is related to, for example, vocabularies used to describing learning objects, their intended audiences, topics, and so forth that characteristically serve localised needs. Harmonisation of these vocabularies on the local and global level and mapping between different concepts and vocabularies still remain challenges for the field. For example, ISO SC36, which develops International Standards in information technology in the areas of learning, education, and training has a working groups on vocabularies. IMS has created the Vocabulary Definition Exchange (VDEX) specification that defines a grammar for the exchange of value lists of various classes, that is, vocabularies (http://www.imsproject.org/vdex/), and the CEN/ISSS Workshop on Learning Technologies has published a CEN Workshop Agreement (CEN/ISSS, 2005) on harmonisation of vocabularies for e-learning.

Services

After a decade of extended development in the field of LORs it appears that the consensus about metadata standards that allow interoperability on the local and global level are well established and used. It could be speculated (based on the recent research papers and literature) that the next trend would be around the services that LORs could offer to enhance their functionalities and add more quality for the content. Recent papers, such as the LOM Research Agenda and the Learning Object Manifesto, have outlined research areas for development in the field of learning objects focusing on topics such as novel access paradigms, information visualisation and social recommendation, authoring by aggregating, as well as automated metadata generation (Cardinaels, Meire, & Duval, 2005; Duval, 2005; Duval & Hodgins, 2003).

From our survey, the most common combination of search services offered by LORs is the search and browse functionalities with previewing of learning objects' details in the format of metadata. What remained outside of the scope of this study, but worth mentioning, is that a number of current repositories offer search functions to multiple repositories through 'federated' searches (Van Assche & Massart, 2004). For example ARIADNE, EdNA Online and MERLOT cross-search each other's repositories for learning objects, a service that multiplies the availability of learning objects. Services that support the use of learning objects by end users exist; about 40% of the studied LORs offer online advisory about the use of the LOR or the learning objects; about a quarter of LORs offer some kind of educational tools and about 10% tools to manage a personal portfolio of learning objects. Such services cover a need that is also identified in a survey of teachers in about 350 schools concerning the use of a LOR to support their teaching activities (McCormick et al., 2004). In this survey, participants indicated that more pedagogical support on the actual use of LO, for instance, in the form of a lesson plan, would be appreciated. This area could benefit of further studies, for instance, in conjunction to the other new services that could be envisioned to support the creation of pedagogically oriented user communities where sharing of best practices and promotion of the reuse could take place (Chatzinotas & Sampson, 2005).

Future digital content providers and infrastructure providers who operate through LORs may expand to offer more services to their users. For example, communication tools offered for users are currently very basic, and services, such as payments for learning objects, are only reported to be offered by less than 10% of repositories. This implies that especially older repositories are still only focusing on the basic services rather than offering more elaborate services and support. However, as noted in the results, a positive correlation was seen between the new LORs and services offered. Furthermore, as learning objects are widely used in the context of learning management systems (e.g., Blackboard, WebCT, Moodle), services and APIs to connect a repository directly to such systems would be needed (Broisin, 2005; Hatala, Richards, Scott, & Merriman, 2004). Additional research on services in this direction would benefit the field.

Furthermore, personalised services such as learning object recommendation based on collaborative filtering and social networks deployed in the context of LORs will probably become more and more common, as they are currently researched at an academic level (Ma, 2005; Rafaeli, Dan-Gur, & Barak, 2005; Recker, Walker, & Lawless, 2003), as well as already widely used in commercial applications of other domains (e.g., the book recommendation service of Amazon.com). As users becomes more and more familiar with e-commerce services that allows user's evaluations and individual remarks alongside recommendations based on user modeling and previous behaviour, users can be expected to anticipate similar services by LORs (Vuorikari, Manouselis, & Duval, in press). These types of services are based on extensive data mining and tweaked algorithms, which LORs are also starting to capitalise on (Lemire, Boley, McGarth, & Ball, 2005). Furthermore, tracking on the diverse use of learning objects is being explored in using Attention.XML (Najjar, Meire, & Duval, 2005) which can also contribute to better recommendation mechanisms for learning objects.

Other Topics

The area of intellectual property within the surveyed LORs was addressed in 76% of the repositories that have such information publicly available (since about 15% of LORs did not make it available) by using a copyright policy. Additionally, digital rights management (DRM) is evident in 25% of LORs that have publicly available information. Finally, from the five LORs that allow commercial transactions concerning learning objects, 80% deploy DRM. As repositories are by definition about reuse and sharing, it should be considered essential to have proper policies in place that clearly indicate for the end users their rights and responsibilities in use, reuse, sharing and aggregating the learning resources found in a LOR.

One way to address the issue is by concentrating more on DRM frameworks (Ianella, 2002; Simon & Colin, 2004; Turnbull, 2005) that allow the expression, negotiation and management of digital rights of learning objects. It would be important that such systems be designed to handle both the needs of commercial and 'open' content creators (such as content using the licensing regime of Creative Commons, http://www.creativecommons.org), as well as to reassure users about their own rights. If users of LORs are not sure about their right to reuse, manipulate, aggregate and sequence learning objects, the development and sharing of learning objects will probably remain rather limited.

It could be speculated that learning object quality and evaluation services would become more of the focus of the LOR development. When the number of resources grows in LORs, the end users become more focused on the quality and evaluations from peers and experts to support their decision making process while choosing the right learning object. Evaluations can also be extended to include ratings, votes or comments and annotations from users on how to use a learning object in a lesson or in a different pedagogical setting (Nesbit et al., 2002; 2004). This type of quality management with shared evaluation responsibility by LOR owners and end users seems more likely to be able to capitalise on the community building among users that promotes use, reuse and sharing. It has been identified from our study that the majority of repositories follow a policy for the submission of resources into the collections, in most cases appearing to be guidelines for users to submit resources. It was not possible to find quality control policies for about 15% of the surveyed repositories, but for those that made this information available, two thirds claimed to follow a policy to assure the quality of resources and services. Furthermore, when looking at available review policies and resources ratings, it was possible to identify that 43% of LORs made some available to support users with the selection of resources. Making quality control policies explicitly available for the users of a LOR could be a practice encouraged among LOR owners and providers. However, the fact that many large and well established repositories seem to trust their internal quality policy or intrinsic quality of their own services is not always positively accepted by end users who have no means to verify, for example, what kind of approval procedures are there for learning objects to be accepted in the repository. Also, resources review or rating policies, both done by internal experts or end users, could become a part of the good practice to enhance the services around LORs.

Conclusion

This chapter presents the initial results from a survey of 59 well-known repositories with learning resources. It aims to progress, to some extent, existing knowledge about the current status of learning object repositories. For this purpose, the most important characteristics of examined LORs have been analysed, leading to useful conclusions about the general picture of currently operating LORs. In addition, it has also been possible to identify and discuss future trends in the LOR area, focusing on LOR topics that will require further attention from the people operating, deploying and researching LORs.

In the future, we plan to further elaborate on the analysis of the characteristics studied in this chapter, in order to identify possible combined trends and common evolutions. In addition, we may extend the sample of LORs examined to include a larger number of repositories. For example, large repositories from several Asian countries exist (e.g., ISO/IEC, 2004), which should be included in a future analysis of LORs (considering though the linguistic barriers). Additionally, we plan to focus on the analysis of LORs for particular user communities, geographical areas, or subject areas. For example, we are particularly interested in examining the area of LORs that cover agricultural topics or aim to support agricultural actors (e.g., farmers, processors or traders) for the Mediterranean countries (Tzikopoulos, Manouselis, Costopoulou, Yalouris, & Sideridis, 2005). Finally, we aim to focus on analysing more the quality characteristics of the examined LORs, in order to explore additional quality models and/or tools that can be proposed to support the quality control and evaluation of learning objects in large LORs.

References

Academic ADL Co-Lab. (n.d.). *Content repositories as eLearning tools community building with repository services.* Retrieved February 20, 2007, from http://www.academiccolab.org/resources/Repositories_Tools.pdf

Balanskat, A. (2005). *Country reports.* Retrieved February 20, 2007, from http://insight.eun.org/ww/en/pub/insight/misc/country_report.cfm

Balanskat, A., & Vuorikari, R. (2000). Survey on school educational repositories (D 2.1). *European Treasury Browser*, European Schoolnet.

Benbya, H., & Belbaly, N. (2002, December). The "new" new economy lessons learned from the burst of dot-com's bubble: Dispelling the myths of the new economy. *Journal of E-Business*, *2*(2).

Broisin, J. (2005). Sharing & re-using learning objects: Learning management systems and learning object repositories. In *Proceedings of World Conference on Educational Multimedia, Hypermedia and Telecommunications 2005*, Norfolk, VA (pp. 4558-4565).

CanCore. (2002). *Canadian core learning resource metadata application profile.* Retrieved February 20, 2007, from http://www.cancore.ca/indexen.html

Cardinaels, K., Meire, M., & Duval, E. (2005, May 10-14). *Automating metadata generation: The simple indexing interface.* Paper presented at the International World Wide Web Conference, WWW 2005, Chiba, Japan.

CEN/ISSS. (2005). *Harmonisation of vocabularies for elearning.* CEN/ISSS Learning Technologies Workshop, CWA 15453.

Chatzinotas, S., & Sampson, D. (2005, February). Exploiting the learning object paradigm for supporting Web-based learning communities. In *Proceedings of the 4th IASTED International Conference on Web-based Education (WBE 2005)*, Grindelwald, Switzerland (pp. 165-170).

Downes, S. (2003, January 7). Design and reusability of learning objects in an academic context: A new economy of education? *USDLA Journal.*

Dublin Core Metadata Element Set, Version 1.1 (2004). *Reference description.* Retrieved February 20, 2007, from http://dublincore.org/documents/2004/12/20/dces/

Duncan, C. (2002, September). Digital repositories: The 'back-office of e-learning or all e-learning?' In *Proceedings of ALT-C 2002*, Sunderland.

Duval, E. (2005, May 19-20). *A learning object manifesto towards share and re-use on a global scale.* Paper presented at the elearning Conference, Brussels, Belgium.

Duval, E., & Hodgins, W. (2003). A LOM research agenda. In *Proceedings of the 12th International World Wide Web Conference*, Budapest, Hungary (pp. 1-9).

Friesen, N. (2001). What are educational objects? *Interactive Learning Environments*, *9*(3) 219-230.

Hatala, M., Richards, G., Scott, T., & Merriman, J. (2004, June 21-26). Closing the interoperability gap: Connecting open service interfaces with digital repository interoperability. In *Proceedings of the International Conference (Ed-Media)*, Lugano, Switzerland (pp. 78-83).

Haughey, M., & Muirhead, B. (2004). Evaluating learning objects for schools. *e-Journal of Instructional Science and Technology, 8*(1). University of Southern Queensland, Australia.

Holden, C. (2003, November 11). *From local challenges to a global community: Learning repositories and the global learning repositories summit* (Version 1.0). Academic ADL Co-Lab.

Ianella, R. (2002, June 20). *Digital rights management (DRM) in education: The need for open standards.* Paper presented at the Digital Rights Expression Language Study Workshop. Kirkland WA.

IEEE LOM. (2002, July 15). *Draft standard for learning object metadata.* IEEE Learning Technology Standards Committee.

IMS. (2001). IMS learning resource meta-data specification. Retrieved February 20, 2007, from http://www.imsglobal.org/metadata

IMS Global Consortium. (2003). *IMS digital repositories v1.0: Final specification.* Retrieved February 20, 2007, from http://www.imsglobal.org/digitalrepositories/

ISO/IEC. (2004). *Report: LOM implementation in Japan. ISO/IEC JTC1 SC36 Information technology for learning, education, and training.* Retrieved February 20, 2007, from http://jtc1sc36.org/doc/36N0720.pdf

ISO/IEC JTC1 SC36. (n.d.). *Working group 1: Vocabulary, international standardisation organisation (ISO).* Retrieved February 20, 2007, from http://vocabulary.jtc1sc36.org/

Lemire, D., Boley, H., McGarth, S., & Ball, M. (2005). Collaborative filtering and inference rules for context-aware learning object recommendation. *International Journal of Interactive Technology and Smart Education, 2*(3). Retrieved February 20, 2007, from http://www.daniel-lemire.com/fr/abstracts/ITSE2005.html

Ma, W. (2005). *Learning object recommender systems.* Paper presented at the IASTED International Conference, Education and Technology, Simon Fraser University.

Massart, D., & Le, D.T. (2004). Federated search of learning object repositories: The CELEBRATE approach. In M. Bui (Ed.), *Actes de la Deuxieme Conference Internationale Associant Chercheurs Vietnameniens et Francophones en Informatique*, (pp. 143-146). Hanoï, Vietnam. Studia Informatica Universalis.

McCormick, R. (2003). *Keeping the pedagogy out of learning objects.* Paper presented at the Symposium Designing Virtual Learning Material, EARLI 10th Biennial Conference, Improving Learning: Fostering the Will to Learn.

McCormick, R., Scrimshaw, P., Li, N., & Clifford, C. (2004). *CELEBRATE evaluation report.* Retrieved February 20, 2007, from http://www.eun.org/eun.

org2/eun/Include_to_content/celebrate/file/Deliverable7_2EvaluationReport-02Dec04.pdf

Metros, S.E., & Bennet, K. (2002, November 1). Learning objects in higher education (Research Bulletin). *EDUCAUSE Center for Applied Research, 19.*

Miller, P. (1996). Metadata for the masses. *Ariadne, 5.*

Najjar, J., Meire, M., & Duval, E. (2005, June 27-July 2). Attention metadata management: Tracking the use of learning objects through attention XML. In *Proceedings of the ED-MEDIA 2005 World Conference on Educational Multimedia, Hypermedia and Telecommunications,* Montréal, Canada.

Najjar, J., Ternier, S., & Duval, E. (2003). The actual use of metadata in ARIADNE: An empirical analysis. In *Proceedings of the 3rd Annual Ariadne Conference* (pp. 1-6).

Nelson, T. (1965). A file structure for the complex, the changing and the indeterminate. In *Proceedings of the ACM National Conference.*

Nesbit, J., Belfer, K., & Vargo, J. (2002, Fall). A convergent participation model for evaluation of learning objects. *Canadian Journal of Learning and Technology, 28*(3).

Nesbit, J. C., & Li, J. (2004, July 21-25). *Web-based tools for learning object evaluation.* Paper presented at the International Conference on Education and Information Systems: Technologies and Application, Orlando, FL.

Neven, F., & Duval, E. (2002). Reusable learning objects: A survey of LOM-based repositories. In *Proceedings of the 10th ACM International Conference on Multimedia* (pp. 291-294).

OKI the Repository Open Services Interface Definitions (OSID). (n.d.). Retrieved February 20, 2007, from http://www.okiproject.org/specs/osid_12.html

Pisik, G.B. (1997, July-August). Is this course instructionally sound? A guide to evaluating online training courses. *Educational Technology*, pp. 50-59.

Polsani, P. (2003). Use and abuse of reusable learning objects. *Journal of Digital Information, 3*(4). Retrieved February 20, 2007, from http://jodi.ecs.soton.ac.uk/Articles/v03/i04/Polsani/

Rafaeli, S., Dan-Gur, Y., & Barak, M. (2005, April-June). Social recommender systems: Recommendations in support of e-learning. *Journal of Distance Education Technologies, 3*(2), 29-45.

Recker, M., Walker, A., & Lawless, K. (2003). What do you recommend? Implementation and analyses of collaborative filtering of Web resources for education. *Instructional Science, 31*(4/5), 229-316.

Retalis, S. (2004). Usable and interoperable e-learning resources and repositories. S. Mishra & R.C. Sharma (Eds.), *Interactive multimedia in education and training.* London: IGI Global.

Riddy, P., & Fill, K. (2004). *Evaluating e-learning resources.* Paper presented at the Networked Learning Conference, Lancaster, UK.

Simon, J., & Colin, J.N. (2004, July 5-7). A digital licensing model for the exchange of learning objects in a federated environment. In *Proceedings of the IEEE Workshop on Electronic Commerce,* San Diego, CA.

Simon, B., David, M., Van Assche, F., Ternier, S., Duval, E., Brantner, S., Olmedilla, D., & Miklós, Z. (2005, May 10-14). *A simple query interface for interoperable learning repositories.* Paper presented at the International World Wide Web Conference (WWW 2005), Chiba, Japan.

Smith, R.S. (2004). *Guidelines for authors of learning objects* (White paper). Retrieved February 20, 2007, from New Media Consortium, http://www.nmc.org/guidelines

Stringer, R. (1992). Theseus: A project at Liverpool Polytechnic to develop a hypermedia library for open and flexible learning. *Attention Metadata Management, 18*(3), 267-273. International Federation of Library Assistants.

Turnbull, G. (2005). *eCOLOURS: Analysis of copyright and licensing issues* (CO-developing and localizing learning resources for schools: A feasibility project EDC 40291.2005).

Tzikopoulos, A., Manouselis, N., Costopoulou, C., Yalouris, C., & Sideridis, A. (2005, October 12-14). Investigating digital learning repositories' coverage of agriculture-related topics. In *Proceedings of the International Congress on Information Technologies in Agriculture, Food and Environment (ITAFE05),* Adana, Turkey.

Van Assche, F., & Massart, D. (2004, August). Federation and brokerage of learning objects and their metadata. In *Proceedings. of the 4ᵗʰ IEEE International Conference on Advanced Learning Technologies (ICALT 2004),* Joensuu, Finland.

Vuorikari, R., Manouselis, N., & Duval E. (in press). Using metadata for storing, sharing, and reusing evaluations in social recommendation: The case of learning resources. In D. H. Go & S. Foo (Eds.), *Social information retrieval systems: Emerging technologies and applications for searching the Web effectively.* Hershey, PA: IGI Global.

Wiley, D. (Ed.) (2002). *The instructional use of learning objects.* Bloomington. IN: AECT. Retrieved February 20, 2007, from http://reusability.org/read/

Appendix: Related Web Sites

- **AESharenet:** http://www.aesharenet.com.au—*AEShareNet Web site facilitates the trading of licences for learning materials. It also provides detailed general information on copyright and licensing.*

- **Alexandria:** http://alexandria.netera.ca—*Various, Web pages, videos, etc.*

- **Apple Learning Interchange (ALI):** http://newali.apple.com/ali_sites/ali/— *The ALI collection is made up of exhibits which ALI defines as "a collection of media assets organized as a series of pages that tells a story of educational practice."*

- **European Knowledge Pool System (ARIADNE):** http://www.ariadne-eu.org/— *The collection contains a variety of materials, primarily text documents, followed in order of frequency by hypertext, slide sets, video clips, and interactive educational objects. Interactive objects include documents like multiple-choice questionnaires, quizzes, auto-evaluations, and simulations.*

- **BIOME:** http://biome.ac.uk/—*BIOME is a free catalogue of hand-selected and evaluated Internet resources for students, lecturers, researchers, and practitioners in health and life sciences.*

- **Blue Web'n:** http://www.kn.sbc.com/wired/blueWebn/—*Materials, and Web sites leading to further collections of materials, of interest to educators both because of their educational function either online or printed, or because of content relating to various academic subjects.*

- **Canada's SchoolNet:** http://www.schoolnet.ca/home/e/—*Web sites of interest to educators for various reasons, ranging from professional and private home pages, through pages for projects and programs. Collection also includes materials to be used in an educational context, and descriptions of materials that require membership or payment to use.*

- **CAPDM Sample Interactive LOS:** http://www.capdm.com/demos/software/—*Experiments.*

- **CAREO:** http://careo.ucalgary.ca/—*Various, Web pages, videos, browser-based interactive educational games, etc.*

- **CITIDEL:** http://www.citidel.org—*Most of the resources within the Computing and Information Technology Interactive Technology Interactive Digital Education Library (CITIDEL) collection are articles and technical reports but the collection does contain some materials created for the educational setting.*

- **Co-operative Learning Object Exchange (CLOE):** http://lt3.uwaterloo.ca/CLOE/—*All materials are interactive and browser based, combining various media into the learning experience. Assets or non-interactive materials may be "components of the learnware objects in the database."*

- **Computer Science Teaching Center (CSTC):** http://www.cstc.org—*.pdf and .ppt documents, produced in the course of computer science classes or educational programs.*

- **Connexions:** http://cnx.rice.edu—*The project's collection is made up of modules, each an XML document meeting specific criteria allowing their use and reuse in various contexts. Each item is written in cnxML, a format that contains both the metadata for a material and the content itself.*

- **Digital Library for Earth System Education:** http://www.dlese.org— *Resources and collections of resources to be used in the course of earth science education, or containing content of use or interest to earth science professionals and researchers. The collection includes resources such as lesson plans, maps, images, data sets, visualizations, assessment activities, curricula, online courses, and other materials.*

- **Digital Scriptorium:** http://www.scriptorium.columbia.edu/—*The Digital Scriptorium is an image database of medieval and renaissance manuscripts, intended to unite scattered resources from many institutions into an international tool for teaching and scholarly research.*

- **DSpace (MIT):** https://dspace.mit.edu/index.jsp—*A digital repository created to capture, distribute, and preserve the intellectual output of MIT.*

- **EducaNext (UNIVERSAL):** http://www.educanext.org/ubp—*Contains various pages, videos, and papers for educational use. Also includes many online resources for self-directed learning.*

- **Education Network Australia (EdNA):** http://www.edna.edu.au/go/browse/— *Materials of interest and use to educators due their potential classroom use, or content of interest to learners or educators interested in educational subjects or pedagogy.*

- **Educational Object Economy (EOE):** http://www.eoe.org/eoe.htm—*A repository with Java base objects in various themes.*

- **ESCOT:** http://www.escot.org/—*Educational Software Components of Tomorrow (ESCOT) is a research tested investigating replicable practices that produce predictably digital learning resources (Basically Java Applets).*

- **Eisenhower National Clearinghouse for Mathematics and Science Education:** http://www.enc.org/resources/collect—*Extremely large collection of curriculum resources, materials either of use in the classroom themselves or resources that could supplement and direct teaching.*

- **e-Learning Research and Assessment Network (eLera):** http://www.elera. net/eLera/Home—*eLera provides tools and information for learning object evaluation and research, maintains a database of learning object reviews, and supports communication and collaboration among researchers, evaluators, and users of online learning resources.*

- **Enhanced and Evaluated Virtual Library:** http://www.eevl.ac.uk/—*Digital resources of use or interest to teachers and learners within engineering, mathematics, and computer science.*

- **Exploratories:** http://www.cs.brown.edu/exploratories/home.html—*Materials are applets for use in science education.*

- **Fathom Knowledge Network Inc:** http://www.fathom.com—*"Courses" or seminars requiring two hours to complete. Courses are also associated with online text resources ("features"), book recommendations, and Web pages ("related links"), all of which are locatable individually.*

- **Filamentality:** http://www.kn.pacbell.com/wired/fil/—*Filamentality is a fill-in-the-blank tool that guides the user through picking a topic, searching the Web, gathering good Internet links, and turning them into learning activities.*

- **Gateway to Educational Materials (GEM):** http://www.geminfo.org—*Browser based, interactive learning materials as well as lesson plans or class materials that are either for teacher use or must be printed out to be used by students.*

- **Geotechnical, Rock and Water Resources Library:** http://www.grow.arizona.edu/—*Digital Library was created with support from the National Science Foundation by the University of Arizona's Department of Civil Engineering, Center for Campus Computing, University Library, and a host of other contributors across campus in the fall of 2001.*

- **Global Education Online Depository and Exchange:** http://www.uw-igs.org/search/—*A repository of University of Wisconsin-Milwaukee with various themes.*

- **Harvey Project:** http://harveyproject.org—*Interactive digital instructional materials.*

- **Health Education Assets Library (HEAL):** http://www.healcentral.org/healapp/browse—*Current collection contains a number of images and Medline tutorials.*

- **Humbul Humanities Hub:** http://www.humbul.ac.uk/—*Humbul refers to a variety of materials through its repository. Collecting materials to be used primarily by educators and students Humbul has put together a collection that includes educational materials and links to academic institutions, as well as academic research projects, and such various resources as the Web pages of companies producing educational software.*

- **Iconex:** http://www.iconex.hull.ac.uk/interactivity.htm—*An academic repository with various themes.*

- **Interactive Dialogue with Educators from Across the State (IDEAS):** http://ideas.wisconsin.edu—*IDEAS provides Wisconsin educators access to high-quality, highly usable, teacher-reviewed Web-based resources for curricula, content, lesson plans, professional development, and other selected resources.*

- **iLumina:** http://www.iLumina-dlib.org—*Assets for use in construction of teaching materials are for use during teaching. These range from individual images to interactive resources and tests.*

- **Interactive University (IU) Project:** http://interactiveu.berkeley.edu:8000/DLMindex/—*DLMs are collections of digital artifacts, readings, exercises, and activities that address specific topic- and standard-based instructional needs in K-12 classrooms.*

- **JORUM:** http://www.jorum.ac.uk—*Under development.*

- **Knowledge Agora:** http://www.knowledgeagora.com/—*Thousands of learning objects are contained within subcategories of the upper level subject categories.*

- **Learn-Alberta:** http://www.learnalberta.ca/—*Interactive, browser-based educational materials that directly relate to the Alberta programs of study.*

- **Le@rning Federation** (*http://www.thelearningfederation.edu.au/*): The Le@rning Federation (TLF) works with the educational multimedia industry and vendors of learning applications to support the creation of a marketplace for online curriculum content.

- **LearningLanguages.net:** http://learninglanguages.net—*Materials of various interactivity level of use to educators and learners of French, Spanish, and Japanese, as well as materials relating to the cultures and nations associated with those languages.*

- **Learningobject.net (Acadia University LOR):** http://courseware.acadiau.ca/lor/index.jsp—*A database of digital objects created to educate both students and faculty on a broad range of skills, functions, and concepts.*

- **Learning Matrix:** http://thelearningmatrix.enc.org—*The Learning Matrix provides resources that are useful to faculty teaching introductory science and mathematics courses, either through their use in the classroom setting or by providing resources with which those teachers can develop their pedagogical skills.*

- **Learning Object Repository, University of Mauritius:** http://vcampus.uom.ac.mu/lor/index.php?menu=1—*Text based and interactive materials for use by students and educators.*

- **Learning Objects for the Arc of Washington:** http://education.wsu.edu/ widgets/—*The project calls its materials "Wazzu Widgets," which it defines as interactive computer programs in Shockwave that teach a specific concept and can be used in a variety of educational settings.*

- **Learning Objects Virtual College (Miami Dade):** http://www.vcollege. org/portal/vcollege/Sections/learningObjects/learningObjects.aspx—*Virtual College are constantly pushing the technological edge of the envelope in order to serve this ever-growing and diverse student population with 16 new, sharable, Web-based learning objects with a pilot team of Medical Center Campus faculty.*

- **Learning-Objects.net:** http://www.learning-objects.net/modules. php?name=Web_Links—*Some browser-based interactive learning materials, some text-driven lessons.*

- **Learning Objects, Learning Activities (LoLa) Exchange:** http://www. lolaexchange.org/—*Various materials of mixed interactivity.*

- **Maricopa Learning Exchange:** http://www.mcli.dist.maricopa.edu/mlx—*The collection is made up of "packages," which are defines as "anything from Maricopa created for and applied to student learning."*

- **Math Forum:** http://mathforum.org—*The Math Forum contains a variety of materials. Some of these are provided by the project staff themselves, such as Problems of the Week, the Internet Math Hunt, and various projects. External pages include online activities, content of interest to mathematics educators, and Web pages containing links to other resources.*

- **Merlot-CATS: Community of Academic Technology Staff:** http://cats. merlot.org/Home.po—*Reference, technical, and some educational materials of use to those implementing or administrating academic technology systems and networks.*

- **MIT OpenCourseWares:** http://ocw.mit.edu/index.html—*Coursewares: Documents produced in preparation for a real-world instructional environment. Some materials include online materials but this is intended to be a source for various materials from practical teaching as it is currently practiced and thus presumes a traditional teacher as LMS framework.*

- **MERLOT:** http://www.merlot.org—*Multimedia Educational Resource for Learning and On-Line Teaching (MERLOT) provides access to a wide range of material of various interactivity levels for use either in the classroom or for direct access by learners. Other materials contain content of interest to educators and learners.*

- **MSDNAA:** http://msdn.microsoft.com/academic/—*Microsoft's MSDNAA provides faculty and students with the latest developer tools, servers, and platforms from Microsoft at a very low cost.*

- **NEEDS:** http://www.needs.org—*National Engineering Education Delivery System (NEEDS) describes types of materials found in repository, specifying their intended pedagogical use, their interactivity, and their format.*

- **National Learning Network: Materials:** http://www.nln.ac.uk/Materials/default.asp—*Interactive browser-based materials for online learning.*

- **National Science, Mathematics, Engineering, and Technology Education Digital Library (NSDL):** http://www.nsdl.nsf.gov/indexl.html—*A digital library of exemplary resource collections and services, organized in support of science education at all levels.*

- **OpenVES:** http://www.openves.org/documents.html—*Material and documents of interest to PK-12 e-learning.*

- **PBS TeacherSource:** http://www.pbs.org/teachersource/—*Interactive materials associated with PBS programs that can be integrated into a teaching environment through provided activity plans.*

Chapter IV

Psychological Principles for Reusable Learning Object-Based Learning System Design

David B. Dawson, University of West Florida, USA

Abstract

The creation of a reusable learning object that is effective from instructional and system perspectives must be guided by a framework that is founded on theory and research. A combination of frameworks, the Cisco model and the grounded instructional systems design have been integrated to develop a set of templates that can be used to help developers efficiently create RLOs and the reusable information objects that comprise them. The integration of psychology foundation into learning object creation is critical to a successful implementation of RLO architecture.

Standards and Theory

Many approaches to the development of tools using learning objects reflect the focus of the United States federal government's advanced distributed learning (ADL) initiative, which is directed toward the technological specifications and metadata standards that enable the reusability and transportability of learning objects across applications (Singh, 2000). Less attention is generally directed toward the integration of sound instructional design principles, particularly grounded instructional design theory, in the development of design tools for object-based learning systems (Wiley, 2002). Even less attention is paid to the underlying theories that should frame the development of the learning object and the resulting instruction.

To respond to these issues, a set of theoretical constructs can be merged to create a heuristic that can be used throughout the design and development process. Hannafin, Hannafin, Land, and Oliver (1997) have suggested an underlying theoretical concept of five dimensions using a grounded learning systems design model to structure design, development, and implementation of learning environments. Dimensions of psychological, pedagogical, technological, cultural, and pragmatic serve as a framework for examining integrated learning object-based instructional systems development. Such systems possess characteristics, features, and processes that embody the theoretical foundations and reflect the contexts within which those processes are developed. The framework may be used to organize, as well as characterize, the links between practical expressions and the underlying theoretical concepts of systems.

The focus of this chapter will be the description the fundamental properties of a reusable learning object-based learning system and specifically examine psychological concepts and supporting tools that promote successful implementation. An examination of these concepts and their implications provides insight to individuals who design, develop, refine, and adapt tools that focus on learning object architecture.

Why the Sense of Urgency?

Web-based delivery is a common distributed learning technology often embraced by institutions and organizations with a certain degree of urgency. Demand for the production of Web-based instructional programs is great, but resource inadequacies for their production threaten their timeliness (Hawkins, 1999). Production problems for a distributed learning program are compounded by the unique demands of Web-based instruction, particularly if developers choose to follow traditional theory-based instructional design models. Using a system as the one suggested by Hannafin et al. (1997) permits a framework that addresses alignment early in the design process so that general design decisions can be made within preset constraints. The intent of this process is to ensure that developers have done everything possible to maximize the effectiveness of the instruction (Hannafin et al., 1997).

The demand and desire for resources, whether professional development workshops, courses, or programs, in combination with the demand to roll out those events quickly, places the instructional design team in a precarious position. The challenge is to quickly provide effective Web-based learning opportunities, aligned with standards or institutional objectives, with a minimum investment in professional development related to their production and delivery. Learning object technology is a solution that offers promise in meeting these design challenges. The simplicity and efficiency of the instructional development process provides an attractive response to quickly provide content that can be scaled to large projects. The integration of sound principles of design along with the dimensions presented by Hannafin et al. (1997) ensures that a quality product is produced, especially when the processes of learning are considered and templates are used to guide the development process.

What is a Reusable Learning Object?

In the route to design high quality, standards-based instruction, using grounded instructional design and reusable learning object technology, an examination of issues related to learning objects is appropriate. This view forms a context through which developers can approach the actual development of an instructional product. The first step in this process is an examination of learning objects.

The Basics of Learning Objects

Wiley (2002) proposes a view of learning objects based on the Institute of Electrical and Electronics Engineers, Inc. (IEEE, 2001) Learning Technology Standards Committee's definition: "any digital resource that can be reused to support learning" (p. 7). Wiley's definition describes reusable digital resources and rejects nondigital, nonreusable objects. The definition focuses on the purposeful, supportive role the object plays in learning, not simply its usability in learning activity, according to Wiley.

Wiley (2002) expresses concern over the general disinterest of the instructional design implications of learning objects among those involved with the development and facilitation of learning object technology. For example, he notes that the Learning Objects Metadata Working Group standard fails to include any instructional design information in its specifications for metadata and that other standards bodies (as well as vendors) offer as a fundamental, valuable attribute, the instructional theory-neutral character of their products. Wiley also suggests that the Legos analogy commonly used to describe learning objects has been harmful because it implies that learning object can be combined with any other object in any sequence, by anyone, to create instruction. Wiley proposes that if there is no interest in an instructionally-grounded approach to learning object sequencing from a system level, there is little hope that the user will have any other motivation than to do likewise.

An issue related to linking learning objects and instructional design is that of *granularity*, which Wiley (2002) characterizes as the most difficult problem facing designers of learning objects. As learning objects grow in size, their reusability becomes increasingly problematic, especially when the documentation and categorization expense of objects (that may be as small as individual images or paragraphs of text) quickly become prohibitive, even when taking potential reuse into account. The scope of an object, or how much or how little to include in it, is a decision that Wiley insists must be made with instructionally grounded, principled deliberation.

Added to the issues of sequencing and granularity are issues of categorization. Wiley (2002) suggests that users of instructional learning objects cannot easily benefit from the application of any instructional design theory without adopting a taxonomy that addresses the distinguishing characteristics of different learning object types. This taxonomy can take several forms, but one solution is to align the learning object to psychological constructs which, in turn, align to learning objects.

Based on these issues, Wiley (2002) proposes that three components constitute a successful learning object implementation: an instructional design theory, a learning object taxonomy, and prescriptive linking material to connect theory to taxonomy. Each one of these elements is discussed in the following sections.

Instructional Design Theory

Instructional design theories frame the process of designing learning objects that are efficient in terms of use and reuse. When planning the design and development of learning objects, two perspectives, the Cisco reusable learning object model (Barritt & Lewis, 2001) and the grounded instructional design systems approach (Hannafin et al., 1997) can be integrated to guide development initiatives.

The Cisco Reusable Learning Object Model

While Wiley (2002) approaches the concept of reusable learning objects from the perspective of describing features reflecting instructional design theory, Barritt and Lewis (2001) address the concept of reusable learning objects from the perspective of production and systems management efficiency. Barritt and Lewis suggest that the demands placed on modern training organizations require a move away from the development of static, custom-designed, single-purpose courses to "reusable, granular objects that can be written independently of a delivery medium and accessed dynamically through a database" (p. 4). They proposed as a solution the system developed by their Internet Learning Solutions Group at Cisco Systems, the reusable learning object (RLO) strategy. RLOs are comprised of reusable information objects.

- **Reusable information objects:** The structure of the model described by Barritt and Lewis (2001) begins with the fundamental unit: a Reusable Information Object (RIO). From the instructional perspective, each RIO focuses on a single objective and is assigned a cognitive level value in the object's metadata that identifies how learners will remember or use the RIO content. The cognitive level scale developed by Clark (1989) and employed in Barritt and Lewis' model is a hybrid of Bloom and Krathwohl's (1994) taxonomy and Merrill's (1983) component display theory. Where Merrill divides cognitive level into two categories—that which must be remembered or that which must be used—Bloom and Krathwohl use six levels: (a) knowledge, (b) comprehension, (c) application, (d) analysis, (e) synthesis, and (f) evaluation. Barritt and Lewis require that all RIOs be tagged either remember or use. Assigning the remember tag for cognitive level automatically corresponds the object to Bloom and Krathwohl's knowledge level, but if the use tag is assigned, a sublevel designation from one of the top five levels (excluding knowledge) from Bloom and Krathwohl is required.

- **Assembly of RLOs:** Composed of RIOs, the RLO as defined by Barritt and Lewis (2001) is "a single learning objective derived from a specific job task" (p. 7). A RLO is composed of an overview, between five and nine RIOs, and a summary. The overview provides the learner with an advance organizer that includes an introduction, an explanation of the importance of the information contained in the RLO, the objectives of the RLO, a list of any prerequisites that may be required before using the RLO, and an outline of the RLO. It may also include a job-based scenario as a model for how the information in the RLO may be applied in the "real world."

- **The RLO summary:** This brings the RLO to a close, provides a review of the material covered in the RIOs, and serves as a transition between the RIOs and the assessment section. The assessment section is comprised of assessment items from each RIO. Depending on the instructional needs of the student, the summary may also provide information about the next steps the learner must follow and point to additional resources the learner might explore (Barritt & Lewis, 2001).

- **Advantages of reusable learning object use:** In discussing the benefits of the RLO model for instructional designers, Barritt and Lewis (2001) outline several advantages of using their system in the design and development of the RLO. The Cisco model facilitates the use of templates that ensure consistency throughout a system both for development and delivery. The use of templates improves the efficiency of instructional development and helps to ensure instructional effectiveness by helping developers structure the learning objects that are aligned to learning theories and associated instructional strategies. Including metadata (the information that describes the object) allows the learning object to be easily located and subsequently reused. These attributes of metadata and templates enable object users to reuse objects in any combination and permit resources of varying granularity to be stored and reused. In this environment, the format and output of the instructional materials are independent of content, enabling authors to focus on instructional requirements without concern for format, stylistic requirements, or limitations. The objects, consequently, can be implemented through any number of delivery methods and for multiple purposes.

Barritt and Lewis (2001) further identify advantages of the RLO model for delivering instruction to learners. Templates and stylesheets ensure that the learner is presented a consistent interface that facilitates predictable tool performance across instructional units. Objects serve, not only as instructional units, but also as support for learner performance in the context of the learning environment. The learning style of the learner can be accommodated through customization of the interface. Unique instructional or performance requirements of the individual can be addressed through individualized learning paths, where the learner may access a range of object types, from smallest and most specific to largest and most generalized. Overall, flexibility in delivery is facilitated through using the RLO model.

The Cisco model provides a technical protocol and baseline for the creation of the RLO and the RIOs that compose each complete object. This technical perspective is only one of the constructs needed to make the instruction successful. The Cisco Model, in conjunction with the grounded instructional systems design approach, can be used to create a learning environment that meets instructional goals and learner needs.

Grounded Instructional Systems Design

Hannafin et al. (1997) suggest that interest in constructivist learning theories presents opportunities for the evolution of instructional design theory to resolve disconnection between theoretical prescriptions for instructional design and actual design practices, particularly in the context of technology-enhanced learning environments.

Hannafin et al. respond to the mismatch between theory and practice in instructional design by proposing an approach called grounded learning systems design, which they define as "the systematic implementation of processes and procedures that are rooted in established theory and research in human learning" (p. 102). A grounded learning systems design does not provide designers with explicit, algorithmic steps that are to be rigidly applied; rather, the design processes and procedures are guided by heuristics that incorporate a number of approaches and perspectives reflecting the proposition that learning is not a unitary concept.

A Five-Dimensional Framework

While many instructional design practices produce good results and many designers employ successful approaches to instructional design that they have developed through experience, Hannafin et al. (1997) suggest that many designers can neither explain exactly why such practices are successful nor accurately predict their effectiveness in other similar applications. They contrast this with grounded learning systems design, which consistently links foundations and assumptions to specific instructional methods in a defensible theoretical framework rooted in related research.

The essence of Hannafin and Land's (1997) position is that "Learning environments are rooted in five foundations: Psychological, pedagogical, technological, cultural, and pragmatic" (p. 172). This framework provides a recognized, familiar class of concepts through which designers can characterize the features of a learning system. Structuring the environment based on these dimensions ensures that all aspects of the learning environments are taken into consideration during design and development processes (Northrup & Rasmussen, 2001).

Beliefs about how knowledge is acquired and used are fundamental to learning environment designs (Hannafin & Land, 1997). Such beliefs form the psychological dimension in their characterization of learning environments and they suggest that changes in thought about the character and form of learning environments trace a path in concert with the evolution and focus of psychological theory.

From the pedagogical perspective, Hannafin and Land (1997) suggest learning systems must "reflect, and be consistent with, the underlying psychological model upon which they are based" (p. 174). Hannafin and Land propose that student-centered learning environments must, therefore, place great weight concepts that learners are constructors of their own knowledge, context is critical to understanding, and experience is essential to learning.

A learning system's technology component drives the types of possible learner-system transactions, but design decisions regulate the range and character of their implementation (Hannafin & Land, 1997). Hannafin and Land suggest that technology (a) facilitates the understanding of abstract concepts through concrete experiences,

(b) facilitates selection and experimentation through the manipulation of objects, and (c) provides for the personalization of instruction with advice or appropriately timed and guided access to information.

Prevailing beliefs, cultural values, and individual societal roles lie at the heart of Hannafin and Land's (1997) cultural dimension for technology-enhanced, student-centered learning environments. They suggest that the desire to increase, decrease, or shift educational focus follows the progression of changes in its attitudes, beliefs, and social mores of the culture. This linkage exists at every level of organization in learning systems and reflects the philosophical shifts regarding the nature of teaching, learning, and technology experienced by the stakeholders in those systems.

The pragmatic dimension of grounded instructional design and technology-enhanced, student-centered learning environments reflects what Hannafin and Land (1997) identify as unique situational constraints that bridge the gap between theory and reality. While pragmatic concerns are often associated with technical constraints, Hannafin and Land note that learning requirements may force a blend of contrasting pedagogical approaches for instructional expediency.

The framework of the Cisco model and grounded instructional design provide designers with principles that can be used to jump start work on reusable information objects that can effectively combined to create RLOs. Once the framework of the instructional design process is established, the next consideration for the RIO and RLO is the categorization of the object using a taxonomy. This taxonomy can be based on the psychological dimension described by Hannafin and Land (1997).

Learning Object Taxonomy

The psychological dimension of grounded learning systems design addresses fundamental concepts regarding knowledge and the nature of knowing. These concepts, when framed in the context of learning object-based tool development, fall into four areas: (a) the acquisition of information, (b) knowledge representation, (c) knowledge organization in individuals, and (d) the role of social context in the acquisition and usability of knowledge. The psychological dimension of a grounded learning object-based instructional design tool builds on the recognition that although there may be a common process for acquiring information from the senses and storing that information, the methods for representing that information, organizing it, and acting upon it varies widely among individuals. The variance depends on individual cognitive processing preferences, the schema in an activated state at a given time, the robustness of the organizational state of their cognitive structure, and both the depth and range of their experiences. Once these frames are identified, the learning outcome can be classified. A full description of these concepts can be found in

Table 1. Setting up a psychological framework for developing RIOs

Learning Outcome	Foundational Learning Theory Area
Knowledge	Information Acquisition
	Knowledge Representation – exemplars
Comprehension	Knowledge Representation – generic tasks
	Information Acquisition – assimilation of new information into natural language structures
Application	Knowledge Representation – schema, types
	Information Acquisition – active learning
	Knowledge and Social Context – State of knowing that
Analysis	Knowledge and Social Context – State of knowing how
Synthesis	Knowledge Representation – Mental Models
	Knowledge and Social Context – Cyclic and Dynamic Movement of Thought
Evaluation	Knowledge and Social Context – Distributed Intelligence

Note: See Appendix A for full descriptions of foundational learning theories

Appendix A. In Table 1, the association of the learning outcome with a theory area is presented. The learning outcomes and theories are hierarchical in nature in that lower-level outcomes are used to support higher-level outcomes.

The frames provide direction and suggestions for instructional strategies within the learning theory that can, in turn, be used as a framework to develop RIOs and, ultimately, a RLO. In other words, knowledge representation, organization, and social context, as well as information acquisition, provide a foundation for developers of learning objects as they align to a learning outcome, such as the taxonomy proposed by Bloom and Krathwohl (1994). During the development process, templates from a support system that guides developers as they pursue RLO creation.

Connecting Theory and Taxonomy: Templates

To meet Wiley's (2002) suggestion about the theoretical framework for learning objects and their relative success, psychological constructs support the developer

Table 2. Learning object templates

Learning Outcome	Template	Description
Knowledge	Readings	Content narrative related to the objective. Alternative assessments can be included to help learners demonstrate that they have acquired the knowledge.
Comprehension	Tutorials	Self-contained lessons that include an orientation, and 3-9 reusable learning objects, followed by a summary. Each RIO contains items for practice and assessment.
Application		
Analysis	Application	Structured experiences that assist students in analyzing problems and sharing solutions to those problems. Template areas for tips on discussing results and conclusions are included.
Synthesis	Simulation	Open-ended learning environment that promotes active and exploratory learning where student collaborate with peers and experts and teachers facilitate the learning process.
Evaluation	Case Study	Complex situations presented in a way that require students to interpret and propose multiple solutions.

through the design and development process. In other words, application of psychological constructs when using templates permits the designer to apply the constructs in a heuristic fashion, permitting development of a high-quality environment while attending to the theories of learning.

To facilitate development of learning objects, templates provide a structure that can streamline development and reduce costs (Northrup, Rasmussen, & Dawson, 2004). Templates can be considered to be systems that direct content development. One way to organize the choice of templates is by aligning the template to a learning outcome, such as found in Bloom's taxonomy using instructional strategies suggested by an area of learning theory. Aligning learning outcomes to templates that have, as their foundation, learning needs as represented by theories of information processing, knowledge representation, types of knowledge, and mental models. One template system for developing a resource set of learning objects is presented in Table 2.

Each of the templates provides an instructional strategy, aligned to a learning outcome that can be used to develop the learning object. Developers select the most appropriate template that helps to create a learning environment that is, hopefully, active and engaging. Each template is populated with the associated required elements that serve as the guide. Table 3 outlines the elements of each template.

Table 3. Template components and description

Template	Components and Description
Reading	• The **Context** element of establishes a framework of issues addressed characterizing significance to the learner in terms of a learning outcome. Historical, cultural, political, or scientific events that play a role in those issues may be referenced to help define the impact of the new information. • The **Body** element contains the actual readings story, article, reading, Web site, or multimedia clip containing the information that is the subject. • The **Summary** element provides the learner the opportunity to express mastery of specific knowledge extracted from the story and relate its significance to issues identified in the Context element of the template. The summary may also include an assessment for retention and transfer.
Tutorials	• A Tutorial **Overview** establishes the subject matter of the tutorial, and identifies the expected learning outcomes that the completion of the tutorial should produce. It may serve as an advance organizer to prepare the learner for the concepts to be introduced and to establish a context or frame of reference for the lesson. • The **Lesson** element presents the content that supports achievement of the learning outcomes. Between three and nine narrowly defined, but interrelated concepts comprise a lesson. The knowledge represented as a concept may include a single fact, principle, process, or procedure. Opportunities for the learner to demonstrate mastery of each concept through practice activities are built into the lesson. • The **Summary** restates the essence of the concepts addressed within the context of the tutorial. It connects the concepts to the learning outcomes.
Application	• An Application **Introduction** establishes the subject matter of the Application, and identifies the learning outcomes that the completion of the application should produce. It may serve as an advance organizer to prepare the learner for the activities to be performed and to establish a context or frame of reference for those activities. • The **Materials** element identifies and describes objects, equipment, tools, software, or documents that are required to complete the application. Sources for these materials may be provided and may include hyperlinks to digital materials. • The **Procedures** element provides the learner with an organized sequence of tasks to be performed. Procedures are structured and unambiguous, and although the learner is not specifically told what results to expect, the procedures are designed to consistently yield predictable results that are also aligned with the strategy's learning outcomes. • The **Discussion** element provides focused information regarding key components of the learning outcome within the context of the procedures the learners are to follow. The connections between main underlying principles and knowledge to be exercised through execution of the procedures are outlined to direct attention and focus effort in applying that knowledge. • The **Results** element provides a structured format for learners to report the outcomes of the procedures they have followed. Guided questions may provide opportunities for learners to connect underlying principles to the effects from specific elements of the procedures and to characterize those connections in depth. Outcomes that are different from those anticipated are opportunities for the learner to identify factors that may account for the variance and explain their roles. • The **Summary** element restates the broad principles addressed and relates their roles in the procedures to the expected results of those procedures. Common factors that produce results often unexpected by the learner are addressed and explained in terms of the principle they prove.

continued on following page

Table 3. continued

Template	Components and Description
Simulation	• The *Overview* element provides the learner with a detailed description of the purpose of the simulation and identifies the learning outcomes expected from its completion. • The *Strategies* element provides the learner a framework for approaching the problems presented in the simulation that are directly aligned with the targeted learning outcomes. Special instructions, including orientation hints, prioritized objectives and contingency plans are examples of the types of material presented to the learner. • The *Experience* element presents the learner with a model of real world situations and conditions focused on a set of problems the Learner must resolve to achieve the desired learning outcomes. Experiences may range from virtual environments such as interactive Flash animations, through branching vignette video clips, to face-to-face small group role-playing exercises. Experiences are often open-ended and the paths learners may choose to reach the outcomes may widely vary. • The *Summary* element draws the learner's attention back to the underlying principles that are the focus of the target learning outcomes. The Summary relates significant events in the experience in the context of those principles and illustrates how those principles and the events in the experience can be synthesized to solve encountered problems.
Web Research	• An *Introduction* establishes the subject matter of the Web Research, and expresses the expected learning outcomes its completion should produce. It may serve as an advance organizer to prepare the learner for the issues to be introduced and to establish a context or frame of reference for the information. • A *Task* element itemizes and describes the specific activities the learner is to perform. The tasks provide a broad framework for the activity to be completed. The final project should be described. • The *Process* element presents the sequence of steps required to complete the strategy's tasks. Instructions for accomplishing the tasks are detailed, specific, and sufficiently comprehensive to insure all learners are able to complete the tasks. By design, Web Research is a collaborative strategy and the process element includes instructions for setting roles and establishing cooperative groups. Additionally, worksheets, external Web sites, or additional instructions are usually incorporated. Guidance is often provided in the form of checklists or questions to help learners evaluate the quality and significance of the information they discover. • The *Evaluation* element includes a rubric, checklist, or description of the assessment to be used to grade the project. Learners and instructors refer to the evaluation tool. • The *Conclusion* summarizes the events of the Web Research project, drawing relevant ideas together and discussing the evaluation process the learner followed to determine task completion. Common problems are discussed and solution strategies that are aligned with the desired learning outcomes are provided (Dodge, 1999).
Case Study	• In the Introduction, the learning outcomes, performance objectives, and issues are identified to set the stage for the situation or scenario. • The Presentation is comprised of a scenario description, relevant documents, and preliminary analysis questions that are created by the designer. • For Processing the Case, learners identify the problem, key players, and develop a recommended solution. • In the *Conclusion*, learners present their solutions, reflect on the case study, prepare an action plan, and debrief/report out their findings.

Future Research

As the process for developing RLOs becomes more and more mature, the case for reuse must be made. At the current time, researchers seem to be focusing on the use of the RLO, with a hope that it will be able to be reused in the future, at some point. The reuse process must be fully examined if the promise of RLO architecture is to be realized.

Combined with the idea of reuse, future research into Hannafin et al.'s (1997) other four dimensions of the grounded instructional design system and how those dimensions can be integrated into the template system must be conducted. Whether embedded support into a template system or external professional development for RLO creators, overt inclusion of the other dimensions will facilitate creation of exciting, active learning environments.

Conclusion

Fundamental psychological theories must be applied to the systematic development of reusable learning objects for them to be effectively used. The importance of these theories to the structural character of reusable learning objects and learning systems, upon which they are based, is significant to their development and implementation.

Perhaps the most important revelation to come from this examination is the recognition that instructional strategies can be aligned to learning outcomes and learning theory through the use of templates. Developers of the tools for creating reusable learning objects and the learning systems that instructors may use for delivering them can find much of value in these concepts. They may take advantage of the efficiencies gained through adoption of these principles to reduce the duration of development cycles. More importantly, this approach could soften the curve of development mastery so that it may become less the exclusive domain of highly specialized professionals and more the domain of engaged practitioners.

References

Barritt, C., & Lewis, D. (2001). *Reusable learning object strategy: Designing information and learning objects through concept, fact, procedure, process and principle templates* (Version 4.0). Retrieved February 20, 2007, from http://www. cisco.com/warp/public/10/wwtraining/elearning/implement/rlo_strategy.pdf

Bloom, B., & Krathwohl, D. (1994). *Taxonomy of educational objectives: Cognitive domain*. Boston: Addison-Wesley.

Clark, R. (1989). *Developing technical training: A structured approach for the development of classroom and computer-based instructional materials*. New York: Performance Technology Press.

Dodge, B. (1997). *Some thoughts about Webquests.* Retrieved February 20, 2007, from http://webquest.sdsu.edu/about_webquests.html

Hannafin, M., Hannafin, K., Land, S., & Oliver, K. (1997). Grounded practice and the design of constructivist learning environments. *Education Technology Research and Development, 45*, 101-110.

Hannafin, M., & Land, S. (1997). The foundations and assumptions of technology-enhanced student-centered learning environments. *Instructional Science, 25*, 167-202.

Hawkins, B. L. (1999). Distributed learning and institutional restructuring. *Educom Review, 34*(4), 12-15.

Institute of Electrical and Electronics Engineers, Inc. (2001). *Scope and purpose.* Retrieved February 20, 2007, from http://ltsc.ieee.org/wg12/s_p.html

Merrill, D. (1983). Component display theory. In C. Reigeluth (Ed.), *Instructional design theories and models* (p. 279). Hillsdale, NJ: Lawrence Earlbaum.

Northrup, P. T., & Rasmussen, K. L. (2001). A Web-based graduate program: Theoretical frameworks in practice. C. D. Maddux & D.L. Johnson (Ed.), *The Web in higher education: Assessing the impact and fulfilling the potential* (pp. 33-46). NY: The Haworth Press.

Northrup, P. T., Rasmussen, K. L., & Dawson, B. (2004). Designing and reusing learning objects to streamline Web-based instructional development. In. A. M. Armstrong (Ed.), *Instructional design in the real world: A view from the trenches* (pp. 184-200). Hershey, PA: IGI Global.

Singh, H. (2000). Achieving interoperability in e-learning. *Learning Circuits, 1*(3). Retrieved February 20, 2007, from http://www.learningcircuits.org/mar2000/singh.html

Wiley, D. A. (2002). Connecting learning objects to instructional design theory: A definition, a metaphor, and a taxonomy. In D. A. Wiley (Ed.), *The instructional use of learning objects* (Section 1.1). Retrieved February 20, 2007, from http://reusability.org/read/chapters/wiley.doc

Chapter V

Engineering Reusable Learning Objects

Ed Morris, RMIT University, Australia

Abstract

We adapt the object-oriented software engineering design methodology for software objects to engineering reusable learning objects. Our approach extends design principles for reusable learning objects. The resulting learning object class is a template from which individualised learning objects can be dynamically created for, or by, students. The properties of these classes refine learning object definitions and design guidelines. We adapt software object levels of cohesion to learning object classes. We demonstrate reusability increases when learning object lessons are built from learning objects, like maintainable software systems are built from software objects. We identify facilities for learning management systems to support object-oriented learning object lessons that are less predetermined in sequencing activities for each student. Our overall approach to the design of learning object lessons is independent of, and complementary to, instructional design theory underlying the learning object design process, and metadata standards adopted by the IEEE for learning object packaging.

Perspective

We approach the shared aim to design reusable e-learning objects by adapting software engineering methodology, where it enhances the reusability of software objects. Our work (Morris, 2005) contributes software engineering techniques to the design and evaluation of learning objects with enhanced reusability.

We also provide a different perspective on the continuing pedagogical debate over granularity and context for optimal e-learning object reusability (Littlejohn, 2003) as we focus on the user interface and internal structure of a learning object to enhance its reusability.

Objectives

The objectives of this chapter are:

1. To explain how object-oriented software engineering design methodology can be applied to the design of a learning object to enhance its reusability. See the "Designing Learning Objects as Software Objects" subsection and the "Example Learning Object Classes" section.

2. To show how object-oriented software engineering extends and refines Boyle's (2002) design principles for authoring dynamic reusable learning objects by enabling individual learning objects to be dynamically created for or by students from a template learning object, which we call a learning object class. See the "Designing Learning Objects as Software Objects" subsection and the "Example Learning Object Classes" section.

3. To contribute toward a learning object lesson design methodology that will facilitate the design and implementation of larger scale lessons, courses, and educational programs. See the "Developing Learning Object Lessons as Software Systems" subsection and the "Object-Oriented Design Principles for Learning Objects" section.

4. To explain how the properties of a learning object class refine existing learning object definitions and design guidelines. See the "Criteria That Define Object-Oriented Learning Objects" subsection.

5. To show how reusability is further enhanced by standardising the interface of a learning object class to provide its learning activities as services that can be invoked by other learning objects. See the "Developing Learning Object Lessons as Software Systems" subsection and the "Example Learning Object Classes" section.

6.   To explain how software object levels of cohesion can be applied to the design of a learning object class, such that the higher the level of cohesion, the more it is reusable. See the "Object-Oriented Design Principles for Learning Objects" section.

7.   To identify facilities required in a learning management system to support learning object lessons that are less predetermined in their sequencing of activities for each student. See the "Support for Object-Oriented Learning Objects" section.

8.   To explain how our object-oriented software engineering approach to the design of learning object lessons is independent of, and complementary to, (a) instructional design theory underlying the learning object design process, and (b) metadata standards adopted by the IEEE for learning object packaging. See the "Support for Object-Oriented Learning Objects" section.

Introduction

Early research and development of online learning materials did not focus on their reusability. For example, our previous research focussed on the cost effectiveness (Zuluaga, Morris, & Fernandez, 2002) and educational effectiveness (Morris & Zuluaga, 2003) of our online learning approach. This involved both online course development and online course delivery phases. We also addressed the deployment, management, and scalability of our online courses over a network of learning management system servers (Zuluaga & Morris, 2003).

Most of our early online courses (1999-2002) were developed for 100% online delivery, utilising mostly textual learning materials, plus (on average) four short multimedia supplements such as Java applets, Flash animations, voice overs, and video clips. During online delivery of such a course we relied more on students interacting with staff via e-mail or chat than on building interactivity into the online course material during its development. We assumed these early generation online course materials would soon be replaced as multimedia and learning management systems matured and standardised. So we were not so much concerned with upgrading the original online materials over the years, repurposing them for new educational programs, or repackaging them for different media in the future. Nor were we particularly concerned with standardising the packaging of online course materials so that they could be reassembled with online materials from other institutions.

However, during this early period of research and development (R&D) it became increasingly clear that e-learning materials need to satisfy all the 'bilities': *interoperability* among different systems connected by the Internet, *accessibility* anytime from another location, *reusability* by other developers to save time and money, *discoverability* in repositories using metadata, *extensibility* of existing courses due to their modular construction, *affordability* due to reduced development costs, and *manageability* by allowing easy changes and updates to small chunks (Computer Education Management Association, 2001).

The concept of a unit of e-learning material or 'learning object' is central to these objectives. A range of definitions of *learning object* or 'instructional object' exist (Wiley, 2001). One that captures a common theme defines learning objects as "small but pedagogically complete segments of instructional content that can be assembled as needed to create larger units of instruction, such as lessons, modules and courses. Learning objects should be stand-alone, and be built upon a single learning objective, or a single concept" (Hamel & Ryan-Jones, 2002).

Boyle (2002) proposed learning object design principles synthesised from pedagogy and software engineering for authoring dynamic reusable learning objects. From pedagogy, a learning object should have a single learning objective. From software engineering, a learning object should do one thing and only one thing (strong cohesion). And a learning object should have minimal bindings to other learning objects (weak coupling).

Contents

In the second section of this chapter, we expand the above synthesis by applying object-oriented software engineering design methodology to the design of learning objects. We introduce the 'abstraction' of a learning object to enable a designer to produce a 'learning object class'. A *learning object class* is a template from which similar but individualised learning objects can be dynamically created during a lesson. (Object-oriented software engineering refers to similar 'objects' being 'instantiated' (created) from a 'class', which encapsulates their shared attributes and activities.) We introduce 'inheritance' so that a designer can evolve a 'child' learning object class from its 'parent' learning object class, extending and modifying its attributes and activities as desired. The instructional designer can use inheritance to reuse learning object classes or repurpose a lesson by extending and coupling inherently cohesive learning object classes. The instructional designer can use instantiation during a lesson to enable student interaction to determine the actual sequence of possible events in a lesson.

In the third section we illustrate the application of object-oriented software engineering design methodology to the design of two learning object classes. Broadly speaking, one is for the programming discipline, and the other is for psychology. The first is based on the Java programming language while-loop learning object of Boyle et al. (2003). The second is based on a conflict resolution learning object that explains Maddux's five styles of conflict resolution (Rathsack, 2001). These two learning object classes from different disciplines demonstrate the general applicability of our approach.

In the fourth section, we adapt to learning objects a scale for grading the cohesion of software objects. We show how to classify a learning object's level of cohesion and explain how each of the lower levels further reduces learning object reusability. This informs the design of learning objects, as we illustrate with the examples from the third section.

Finally, in the fifth section, we identify facilities required in a learning management system to support object-oriented learning object lessons. We point out that our object-oriented software engineering approach to the design of learning object lessons is independent of, and complementary to, the instructional design theory underlying the learning object design process, and the metadata standards adopted by the IEEE (LTSC, 2003) for learning object packaging.

Application of Object-Oriented Software Engineering to Learning Objects

Software engineering is concerned with the design and implementation of large scale, complex information processing systems that are robust, maintainable, modularly reusable, scalable, and extensible (Pfleeger, 2001). These properties overlap the 'bilities' required of learning objects. This observation underlies the application of software engineering design principles to the design of learning objects. Boyle introduced this approach with reference to coupling and cohesion principles for the design of learning objects (Boyle, 2002). We extend this approach by applying *object-oriented* software engineering design methodology to the design of learning objects. Object-oriented software engineering has evolved into a dominant 'branch' in the software engineering design methodology 'tree'.

In the "Designing Learning Objects as Software Objects" subsection we show how learning objects can be designed with essentially the same techniques used to design software objects. In the "Developing Learning Object Lessons as Software Systems" subsection we explain how flexible learning object lessons can be built from reusable learning objects in the same way that maintainable software systems are built from software objects with well-designed interfaces. Our application of object-oriented software engineering to the design of object-oriented learning object lessons leads us in the "Criteria That Define Object-Oriented Learning Objects" subsection to synthesise criteria that define a truly object-oriented learning object.

Designing Learning Objects As Software Objects

Object orientation is an approach to software development that organises both the problem and the solution as a collection of discrete 'objects' (Pfleeger, 2001). Each software object can be based on a physical or abstract object in the problem space. In the software system solution, the software objects collaborate to answer a user's requests.

- **Problem:** Model an employee-employer relationship. This could be a fundamental requirement of a software application to manage staff. Solution: We consider an employee software object below; the reader can similarly consider an employer software object later.

In the object-oriented approach to software design the nouns in the problem statement generally identify the software objects and their attributes. The 'has-a' relationship governs a software object and each of its attributes.

Let us say that an employee software object (at least) has a *name*, a social security (tax) *number*, and regular *pay*.

Other attributes of a software object can be discovered by asking "if I am an employee, what should I know?" For instance the problem could indicate that an employment *history* is required.

In general the verbs in the problem statement identify the activities (behaviours, actions, responsibilities, operations) required of a software object.

An employee software object at the very least *works* and gets paid; the latter possibly comprising two activities: *receivePay* and *showPay*.

Other activities of a software object can be discovered by asking "if I am an employee, what should I be able to do?" For instance the problem could indicate that *reportWork* is also required.

The state of a software object at any time is given by the values of its attributes, as determined by the software object's activities. For instance showPay should show a higher pay value after receivePay provides a pay rise.

By analogy with a software object, we consider a learning object to have attributes and activities to deliver a single learning objective. Just as the users of a software system (solution) cause interactions between software objects to solve a problem, the students of a 'lesson' can cause interactions between learning objects to achieve the lesson's learning outcomes.

Adapting the above example of the object-oriented approach to software design, consider the overall learning outcome: understand the employee-employer relationship. A learning objective could be to know the responsibilities of employees in an employment hierarchy. We develop an employee learning object below in the same way that we developed an employee software object above.

Importantly, the attributes and activities of a learning object can be identified in the same manner as they were identified for a software object.

For the employee learning object we identify the exact same attributes and activities in the same manner as they were identified for the employee software object above.

By comparison with a software object, the activities of a learning object provide a form of explanation, rather than a computation.

For instance the receivePay activity in the employee learning object could explain that pay is in return for work.

In the object-oriented approach to software design a software object is an instance of a software object class. The process of abstraction enables software objects with shared attributes and activities to be defined as a single software object class. A *software object class* acts as a template from which individualised software objects are instantiated (created), as determined by the user's interactions with the software system.

As a user interacts with a software system that simulates the employee–employer relationship, let us say that employees, *bob, ted, carol*, and *alice* are instantiated. Each of these software objects has a distinct *name*, social security (tax) *number*, and *pay*. If bob's showPay activity is invoked, the pay value need not be that same as the other employees. If we define an extra *work* attribute and appropriate activities in the employee software object class, all these employee software objects could collaborate to perform their collective work.

Analogously, learning objects can be created as customised instances of a learning object class. A learning object class is not only a container of learning materials for a single learning objective (attributes), but also a container of operations defined on the materials (activities) that a student interacts with to attain the intended learning outcomes.

During a lesson, a student could create employees, *bob, ted, carol*, and *alice*. Each learning object has at least the distinct attributes identified above. These learning objects could collaborate to explain their *work*.

In general, a student initiates a lesson by interacting with a learning management interface that instantiates a learning object to service the student's initial request. During the learning object lesson, other learning objects are likely to be instantiated from one or more learning object classes. The student interacts with these collaborating learning objects to attain their desired learning experience.

In the object-oriented approach to software design, abstraction promotes generality, and instantiation provides flexibility and individuality. We assert that the design of learning objects can similarly benefit from essentially the same approach.

Figure 1. Class Employee and four instance objects

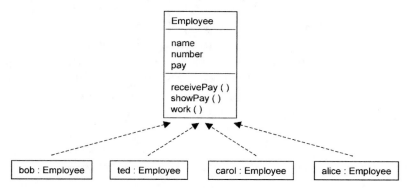

The unified modeling language (UML) is a standard for diagrammatically depicting relationships between classes (software object classes), via class diagrams, and between software objects, via object diagrams (Priestley, 1996). Figure 1 shows the Employee software object class in UML and four (4) instance Employee software objects. The attributes and activities of the Employee class are also shown.

Figure 1 could equally show the Employee learning object class in UML and its four (4) instance Employee learning objects.

Access to the attributes and activities encapsulated by a software object is determined by its software object class. In general, attributes of one software object cannot be directly manipulated by another software object. Instead, the software object encapsulating the attribute in question performs the relevant activity in response to a request from another software object. For instance, an employee software object's pay cannot be directly accessed by other software objects; they can only request an employee software object to showPay or receivePay. Not all activities of a software object need be accessible to other software objects. The public activities supplied by a software object class define an interface that protects the private attributes and activities of its software objects. In effect, software objects request each others' 'services' via the public interface activities supplied by their software object classes. This allows the internals of a software object class to be modified by a programmer without affecting collaborating software objects, provided its interface remains unchanged; for example receivePay could incorporate a bonus without upsetting any software object that requests showPay.

Encapsulation can be equally applied to learning object classes. We assert that encapsulation enhances manageability by facilitating updates without requiring changes to collaborating learning object classes. Other 'bilities' such as reusability and affordability also benefit.

A software object class can be extended into a more specialised software object class without changing the original (parent) class. The 'child' software object class inherits the parent's attributes and activities while encapsulating extra attributes and activities. The 'is-a' relationship governs a child as a specialised extension of its parent. The child can selectively modify its inherited characteristics too (called polymorphism). For example an Employee software object class could define employment *history* in terms of career achievements. A junior employee could reimplement its history in terms of final school courses and grades. Inheritance enhances reusability and adaptability of software object classes.

An *Employee* software object class can be extended to an *AirlineEmployee* software object class on the one hand, and a *HospitalEmployee* software object class on the other hand. An *AirlineEmployee* could add to its inheritance a knowledge of the *travelIndustry* and *airlinePolicies*. A *HospitalEmployee* could add to its inheritance a knowledge of *healthCareIssues* and *hospitalPolicies*. A *Nurse* software object class could further extend the *HospitalEmployee* with knowledge of *patientCare* and the activities to *takeBloodPressure* and *giveInjection*.

Figure 2 depicts the above inheritance hierarchy in a UML class diagram.

Figure 2. Class Employee and its 'child' classes

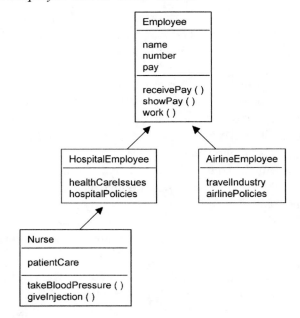

Figure 2 could equally depict an Employee learning object class inheritance hierarchy in a UML class diagram. We assert that inheritance can enhance reusability and extensibility of learning object classes.

Developing Learning Object Lessons as Software Systems

Software systems can be large and complex. Their design can comprise hundreds of software object classes and thousands of interactions of many kinds. Their implementation can amount to millions of lines of code. The software development life cycle (comprising requirements elicitation, analysis, specification, design, implementation, testing, and maintenance) can involve numerous teams of professionals of various kinds over many human years.

On the other hand, most learning objects are designed and implemented by one or two individuals, or a small team, over weeks or months, rather than years (Boyle et al., 2003; MIT OCW, 2005). No more than a handful of learning objects comprise a typical lesson. So there is at least an order of magnitude difference in the current scale of software systems design and learning object lesson design. However, software systems were originally far smaller. As the underlying hardware improved exponentially, it was still the advent of software engineering design methodologies that facilitated production of larger scale reliable software (Pfleeger, 2001). Hopefully, this chapter is a contribution toward a learning object lesson design methodology that will facilitate the design and implementation of larger scale lessons, courses, and educational programs.

An *interface* in object-oriented software engineering terms is the boundary around an object that defines which of its attributes and activities are accessible to other objects. An object's attributes remain private by default, but a public 'accessor' activity can be defined in an object to return an attribute to any other object that requests it. An object may also define a public 'mutator' activity to enable an attribute to be altered at the request of other objects. Each interaction between two objects is in the form of a request and an answer. Data can be transferred in both directions—in and out. Such interactions in software systems are generally driven by the user(s). In general, objects are dynamically created to provide services in response to user requests.

This software object interaction model is also entirely applicable to a learning object lesson. An instructional designer can define the interface of a learning object class to provide certain learning activities as services. During a lesson, learning objects instantiated from several learning object classes can interact to provide a (student) user responsive learning experience.

The Java language also provides a special interface type that can be used to group a number of classes by insisting each class implements all activities specified by the interface. The grouped classes can be considered to have the same 'look and feel'. We think the Java interface type suggests a mechanism for combining learning object classes into learning object lessons. If a learning object class, L, implements interface I along with other learning object classes, all these learning object classes share a single look and feel. So a (student) user should experience an interactively integrated lesson. If the learning object class, L, also implements another interface, say J, then L can integrate with other learning object classes that implement interface J. This facilitates reuse of learning object class L in a new learning object lesson. Multiple interface types can act as 'wrappers' or 'skins' to provide different contexts for the one learning object class (and its learning objects) in different learning object lessons. This should aid the 'bilities', in particular, reusability and extensibility.

Criteria That Define Object-Oriented Learning Objects

Our above application of object-oriented software engineering design methodology to the design of learning object classes and learning object lessons leads us to synthesise the criteria that define a truly object-oriented learning object class. Our criteria (as follows) refine the learning object definition work of Wiley (2001) and others, and extend learning object design guidelines (Hamel & Ryan-Jones, 2002).

*   Each learning object class has attributes and activities that meet a single well-defined learning objective and implement measurable learning outcomes in accordance with an instructional theory.
*   Each learning object class and its attributes are identified by the nouns in its learning objective and learning outcomes. The verbs identify its activities.
*   Each learning object class encapsulates learning activities that are stand-alone and achievable in a single sitting.
*   Each learning object class's attributes and activities contribute packaging metadata (LTSC, 2003), to enhance the 'bilities' (see the "Determining Learning Object Cohesion" subsection).
*   Each learning object class in general extends (specialises) its parent learning object class's attributes and activities. Inheritance enhances the 'bilities'.
*   Each learning object class in general implements a Java-like interface type (see the "Developing Learning Object Lessons as Software Systems" subsection), which can also be implemented by other learning object classes. A single interface for multiple learning object classes provides the 'look and feel' for a learning object lesson. Implementing multiple interfaces enables a learning object class to integrate into a different learning object lesson with other learning object classes. Learning object class interfaces enhance the 'bilities'.

Each learning object lesson involves student interaction to create learning objects on demand and to drive interactions between these learning objects to achieve the lesson's learning outcomes. The overall learning activity is necessarily interactive and in general involves (self-)assessment against the learning objectives.

Example Learning Object Classes

In this section we demonstrate our adaptation (see previous) of object-oriented software engineering design methodology to the design of learning object classes. The first example is based on the learning object developed by Boyle et al. (2003) for students to learn how while loops work in the Java programming language. The second example is based on a conflict resolution learning object that explains Maddux's five styles of conflict resolution (Rathsack, 2001).

We assert that our two learning object classes for different disciplines (programming and psychology) demonstrate the general applicability of our object-oriented software engineering approach to the design of learning object classes. Although we write each learning object class in Java, the design is our focus, and is language independent. In the "Cohesion of Example Learning Objects" subsection, we demonstrate the advantages of our design over the originals, as measured by the design principles of coupling and cohesion (elaborated in the "Learning Object Levels of Cohesion" subsection).

While Loop

The Java programming language while-loop learning object of Boyle et al. (2003) starts by showing the student how a program hammers a nail into wood: while (nail is not flush) hit the nail. Next, the Java code to move a car over a given distance is displayed, explained, and the student can animate the loop. The student can also step through the code, statement by statement. A second example shows a submarine submerging to a given depth. The code is displayed, explained, animated, and the student can step through. Then the student is asked to build the code from a given set of Java statements to move a horse a specified distance. Finally, the student is asked to spot errors in the code to move a lorry a given distance.

Our object-oriented software engineering design for a while-loop learning object class is shown (see Figure 3) as an incomplete class in Java. Class While has one attribute—the loop in question, represented as a string of characters. When an object of class While is instantiated, the loop can be initialised to an input string, or the default generic loop. Class While defines the following activities as operations on this loop—display, explain, animate, step_thru, build, and debug.

Figure 3. Class While

```
class While {

  String loop;

  While (String input) {
    // constructor given a loop
    loop = input
  }
  While ( ) {
    // default constructor with generic loop
    loop = "pre-action;" + "while (condition)" + "loop action;" + "post-action";
  }

  display ( );
  explain ( );
  animate ( );
  step_thru ( );
  build ( );
  debug ( );
}
```

The student interacts with a Java program that instantiates requisite While objects. For example, if the student follows the sequence intended in Boyle's learning object, the hammer object would be instantiated first. Its code would be displayed, explained, and animated. Next, the submarine object would be instantiated, its code displayed, explained, animated, and stepped through if desired. Next, the horse object would be instantiated, and the student would build its code. Finally, the lorry object would be instantiated, and the student would debug its code.

Note that another student, perhaps more advanced, could interact with class While to instantiate While objects (learning objects) in another sequence, bypassing some learning objects as desired.

Conflict Resolution

Rathsack's conflict resolution learning object explains Maddux's five styles for managing conflict. The learning object begins by stating that people can disagree, that this can be an opportunity for growth and learning, or it can be detrimental as conflict arises. The ability to manage conflict is important to succeed in one's career and life. The learning object then introduces Maddux's matrix depicting five styles for managing conflict: avoiding, accommodating, winning/losing, collaborating, and compromising. Each style is explained. Then the learning object explains that the matrix y-dimension shows increasing assertiveness and the x-dimension shows increasing cooperation, starting from zero at bottom left. This explains the location of each style in the matrix: winning/losing at top left, collaborating at top

Figure 4. Class Conflict

```
class Conflict {

    String style;

    Conflict (String input) {
        // constructor given a style
        style = input
    }

    display ( );
    explain ( );
    animate ( );
    identify ( );
}
```

right, accommodating at bottom right, avoiding at bottom left, and compromise in the centre. The learning object then presents five conflict scenarios and asks the student to identify the style in use. Finally, the learning object explains that Maddux believes no one style is always best for all situations.

Our object-oriented software engineering design for a conflict resolution learning object class is shown (see Figure 4) as an incomplete class in Java. class Conflict has one attribute—the conflict style in question, represented as a string of characters. When an object of class Conflict is instantiated, the style is initialised to an input string. Class Conflict defines the following operations on this style—display, explain, animate, and identify.

The student interacts with a Java program that instantiates requisite Conflict objects. For example, if the student follows the sequence intended in Rathsack's learning object, the 'avoiding' object would be instantiated first. This style would be displayed on the matrix (in relation to the other four styles), explained, and animated on the matrix (in terms of the x and y dimensions). Next, the 'accommodating' object would be instantiated. Similarly, this style would be displayed on the matrix (in relation to the other four styles), explained, and animated on the matrix (in terms of the x and y dimensions). Next, the remaining three Conflict style objects would be instantiated. Finally, the Java program that instantiates Conflict objects would ask the student to identify the style in use in a conflict scenario. The Conflict objects could cooperate to randomise this test.

Note that another student, perhaps more advanced, could interact with class Conflict to instantiate Conflict objects (learning objects) in another sequence, bypassing some learning objects if desired.

Object-Oriented Design Principles
for Learning Objects

In a software system, *coupling* measures how cleanly objects are partitioned. And *cohesion* measures how closely activities in an object are related. Coupling and cohesion are interdependent measures—the less cohesive an object, the more likely it is coupled with other objects. The more coupled an object is with other objects, the harder it is to alter or upgrade the object in isolation, which lowers maintainability. A strongly coupled object is less reusable without significant maintenance (Pfleeger, 2001).

In our terminology, the 'objects' referred to above are software object classes, not individually instantiated software objects. Following Boyle (2002), we assert the above applies as much to learning object classes in a learning object lesson as to software object classes in a software system. Weak coupling between learning object classes in a learning object lesson promotes the 'bilities' in that the maintainability of software object classes is essentially the manageability of learning object classes. The more cohesive each learning object class is, the less coupling is required when learning object classes are reused in a new learning object lesson.

Stevens and Myers devised a table (Yourdon & Constantine, 1978) to classify the level of cohesion of a software module—in our terminology, a software object class. (Although their work predated object-oriented software engineering design methodology, it is readily accommodated.) In the "Learning Object Levels of Cohesion" subsection we adapt their seven-level scale to learning object classes. In the "Determining Learning Object Cohesion" subsection, we show how to classify the level of cohesion of a learning object class. We explain how each of the lower levels further reduces learning object class reusability. We assert that awareness of cohesion levels can improve the design of learning object classes, as we illustrate in the "Cohesion of Example Learning Objects" subsection with the examples from the "Example Learning Object Classes" section.

Learning Object Levels of Cohesion

In Table 1 we adapt a seven-level scale of cohesion for software object classes (Yourdon & Constantine, 1978) to learning object classes. We describe a learning object class at each level and provide an example. The strongest level of cohesion is called *functional*, and the weakest cohesion is called *coincidental*. Each level in Table 1 is less cohesive that the level above it.

Table 1. Learning object class cohesion levels

Cohesion level	Description	Example
Functional (strongest)	Each activity in a learning object class contributes to a single learning objective related task or learning outcome.	Learn to calculate net employee salary. This could be one of many tasks an accountant learns. It comprises: getting the gross salary, subtracting legal deductions, computing taxes. Every step contributes to the single purpose outcome of this learning object class.
Sequential	The outcome (output) of each activity in a learning object class is the input to the next activity in the learning object class.	Learn to paint a picture. This learning object class could comprise: sketching, painting outlines, coloring shapes, adding texture, signing, and dating. Each activity uses the result of the previous activity on the canvas. The picture may be complete, but learning to paint could still be a life-long objective, so the learning object class is not functionally complete.
Communicational	The activities in a learning object class share the same attributes, or inputs and outputs.	Learn to summarise, say, a chapter of a book. This learning object class could comprise: reading the chapter, highlighting headings in the chapter, listi;ng key words in the chapter, writing sentences that connect key words in the chapter. Each activity uses the chapter, but not necessarily the result of the previous activity.
Procedural	Control flows from one activity to the next in the learning object class, i.e., the activities are related solely by their order of execution, which is arbitrary. Data passing in and out of the learning object class are unrelated.	Learn to dissect, say, a fish or mouse. This learning object class could comprise: cleaning the bench, arranging implements, preparing the specimen, starting experimental notes, using scalpel, recording observations. Each activity leads to the next, but it does not necessarily use the result of any previous activity.
Temporal	The activities in a learning object class are related in time only, i.e., the activities are executed at about the same time.	Learn to study. This learning object class could comprise: turning off the radio and TV, collecting pen, paper, and textbook, working at one's desk, ignoring phone calls and other distractions, making notes, etc. All these activities occur during study time, but they need not occur in this exact order.
Coincidental (weakest)	The activities in a learning object class are unrelated by any of the above.	Learn to tidy up a room. This learning object class could comprise: disposing of litter, hanging clothes, finishing a snack, making the bed, vacuuming, etc. Not all these activities need be done (together). The activities are not logically related, nor connected by flow of execution or data.

The reusability issue for each level below functional cohesion is explained in Table 2. Note that the issue at a given level is often in addition to reusability issues at higher levels.

Table 2. Learning object class cohesion levels and reusability

Cohesion level	Reusability issue
Sequential	Not as reusable as a functional learning object class because the sequencing of its activities cannot be easily altered.
Communicational	Either the input or output coupling is generally broader than for the above levels of cohesion. Reuse often needs a subset of this coupling, hence redundant coupling; or a cut down version of the learning object class is created, which still duplicates functionality. A communicational learning object class can often be split into functional learning object classes.
Procedural	Intermediate or partial results are often passed into or out of a procedural learning object class, reducing reusability. It is tempting to combine distinct activities for 'efficiency' or 'convenience' further reducing reusability.
Temporal	Activities in a temporal learning object class tend to be related to activities in other learning object classes, increasing coupling. Activities in a temporal learning object class are often combined because they can occur together. But this compromises reusability in another situation where the activities can occur at different times.
Logical	Broad input coupling is required for a logical learning object class to select which activity to perform. The activities are typically combined because they share common parts. Reusability suffers.
Coincidental	A combination of inputs often determines the selected activity. As a result it can be hard to understand a coincidental learning object class unless its internal detail is examined. This reduces reusability.

Determining Learning Object Cohesion

The description or name of a learning object class may suffice to determine its level of cohesion, as shown in Table 3.

We note that the presence of any of the above key words could be a valuable indicator for metadata tagging purposes, but further research is required to evaluate reliability.

Table 3. Determining learning object class cohesion by its name or description

Cohesion Level	Name or Description
Functional	Simple verb-object phrase.
Sequential	Commas often required.
Communicational	The word 'and' is often present.
Procedural	The word 'or' is often present, or words synonymous with repetition, e.g., 'while', 'until'.
Temporal	Time related words apparent, e.g., 'start', 'end', 'before', 'after'.
Logical	An 'umbrella' word is present, e.g., 'all', 'every', 'total'.
Coincidental	Description or name is meaningless, e.g., 'miscellaneous', 'X', 'Z-process'.

Figure 5. Cohesion decision tree

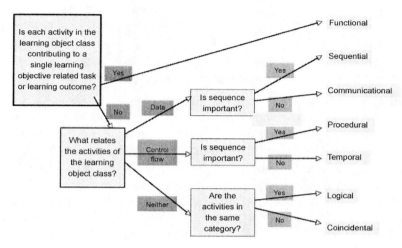

In Figure 5, we adapt a decision tree (Page-Jones, 1998) that enables the level of cohesion of a learning object class to be more accurately determined by asking and answering a few questions, starting at top left.

If all the activities in a learning object class share more than one level of cohesion, the learning object class has the highest (strongest) of the shared levels of cohesion—according to the 'chains in parallel' rule. If the activities in a learning object class exhibit various levels of cohesion, the learning object class has the lowest (weakest) level of cohesion—according to the 'chains in series' rule.

Cohesion of Example Learning Objects

In this section we use Figure 5 to establish the cohesion of the learning object examples in the "Example Learning Object Classes" section. Similar analysis of other learning objects could establish their levels of cohesion, and hence their reusability.

When we address the first question (top left of Figure 5) for Boyle et al.'s Java while-loop learning object, the answer at first appears to be 'yes'—the While learning object appears functionally cohesive in that each activity contributes to understanding how while loops work, which is the learning object's learning objective. But on closer examination, the activities performed by the While learning object do not contribute to one and only one learning objective related task. The learning object performs two pairs of similar analysis activities in sequence (hammer and submarine, horse and lorry), followed by one synthesis activity. Data are not passed between the activities, so the sequence is program controlled (i.e., chosen by the instructional designer). So the learning object exhibits procedural cohesion at best. If we similarly address our object-oriented software engineering design for a while loop learning object class, shown in Figure 3, a learning object can be instantiated for each of hammer, submarine, horse, and lorry. The sequence is determined by the student (via input data), so at least the learning object class exhibits communicational cohesion, which is better than procedural cohesion.

The situation is similar for Rathsack's conflict resolution learning object and our Conflict learning object class shown in Figure 4. When we address the first question (top left of Figure 5) for Rathsack's learning object, the answer at first appears to be 'yes'—the learning object appears functionally cohesive in that each activity contributes to understanding Maddux's five styles for managing conflict, which is the learning object's learning objective. But after closer examination, the activities performed by the Conflict learning object do not contribute to one and only one learning objective related task. The learning object performs five similar activities in sequence, one for each style. Data are not passed between the activities, so the sequence is program controlled (i.e., chosen by the instructional designer). So the learning object exhibits procedural cohesion at best. If we similarly address our object-oriented software engineering design for a Conflict learning object class, shown in Figure 4, a learning object can be instantiated for each of the five styles. The sequence is determined by the student (via input data), so at least the learning object class exhibits communicational cohesion, which is better than procedural cohesion.

Since each object-oriented software engineering designed learning object class exhibits stronger cohesion than the original learning object, our learning object class is likely to require weaker coupling with other learning object classes in a new learning object lesson, thereby enhancing its reusability.

Support for Object-Oriented Learning Objects

We henceforward refer to our above described object-oriented software engineering approach to designing learning objects and learning object lessons as 'object-oriented learning'. We claim benefits of object-oriented learning include the following, in addition to enhancing the 'bilities'. Dynamic instantiation of a learning object from its learning object class in response to a student's input/choice enables a learning object lesson to not only be more highly interactive but also far less predetermined in its sequence of activities for each student. Also the instructional designer need not build lessons as a predetermined sequence of learning object classes, as the student can be given more choices.

Below we investigate supports available for our object-oriented learning approach. We outline how object-oriented learning can be accommodated in a learning object development project from initial application of an instructional design theory to final implementation in a learning management system (e.g., Blackboard, WebCT, Moodle).

Object-Oriented Learning and Instructional Design Theory

It is reasonable that the design of learning objects and learning object lessons should be informed by an instructional design theory (Wiley, 2001). After these pedagogical choices are made, an instructional designer can apply our object-oriented learning approach, where the focus is on structuring the functionality provided by learning object classes. We assert that object-oriented learning is independent of, and complementary to, instructional design theory. Further research and development is needed to confirm this.

In fact we are presently using object-oriented learning to design a substantial learning object lesson, which is composed of several learning object classes. We intend to use UML during the design process in order to report on its usefulness as a tool for communicating the design of a learning object lesson. But the focus of our study will be on evaluating the effectiveness of our object-oriented learning approach on learning object class 'bilities'. We also expect to demonstrate most of the objectives of this chapter.

Object-Oriented Learning and Learning Management Systems

- Learning management systems like Blackboard, WebCT, and Moodle currently facilitate the development of e-learning courses, their collection in a repository, and their delivery to online students at anytime over any distance. Learning management systems are also starting to support standardised metadata tagging of learning objects to better facilitate the combination of learning objects into lessons, courses, and educational programs. Our object-oriented learning approach contributes to learning object metadata tagging as explained in the "Determining Learning Object Cohesion" subsection. We contend that our approach is automatically accommodated within the pedagogically neutral standards adopted by the IEEE (LTSC, 2003) for learning object packaging.

- Learning management systems will also need to provide the 'programming language' that enables instructional designers using object-oriented learning and students to realise the full potential of the dynamics inherent in the design of learning object classes. Our use of Java in the "Example Learning Object

Classes" section was not only to illustrate the application of object-oriented software engineering to the design of learning objects. Java can also be the programming language used in a learning management system to implement student-centered combination of learning object classes and the dynamic instantiation of their learning objects. However, the power of a general programming language environment such as Java is not necessary for this purpose. Indeed, further research is desirable to produce a complete yet simple programming tool for instructional designers to use across learning management systems. One avenue to explore is the programmability introduced into the computer aided instruction systems of the past (Gibbons & Richards, 2001). Fortunately, today's graphic user interfaces, more powerful computers, and faster connectivity will make the experience far more friendly for both today's instructional designers and students.

Conclusion

We have applied object-oriented software engineering design methodology to the design of learning objects. Our object-oriented learning approach extends and refines Boyle's (2002) design principles for authoring dynamic reusable learning objects as follows. The attributes and activities of a prospective learning object are first 'abstracted' into a learning object class. This facilitates dynamic instantiation of an individualised learning object for, or by, a student during a lesson; as we illustrated in the "Example Learning Object Classes" section with two example learning object classes for different disciplines. We introduced the unified modeling language to illustrate the learning object class design process (Figures 1 and 2). We showed how inheritance and polymorphism further enhance learning object class reusability in new lessons.

We explained how our object-oriented learning approach can benefit the design of lessons comprising several learning object classes. We identified a Java-like interface type as a useful mechanism to assist reuse and repurposing of learning object classes into new learning object lessons. This application of object-oriented software engineering design methodology led us to synthesise the criteria that define a truly object-oriented learning object class. Our criteria refine the learning object definition work of Wiley (2001) and others, and extend learning object design guidelines (Hamel & Ryan-Jones, 2002).

We adapted to learning object classes a scale for grading the cohesion of software modules (Yourdon & Constantine, 1978). We showed in the "Object-Oriented Design Principles for Learning Objects" section how to classify the level of cohesion of a learning object class, and described how each of the lower levels further reduces reusability. To illustrate we outlined two object-oriented software engineering designed learning object classes that exhibit stronger cohesion than the original learning objects. These learning object classes are likely to require weaker coupling with other learning object classes in a new learning object lesson, thereby enhancing reusability. Our adaption of cohesion levels to learning objects further extends and refines Boyle's design principles for authoring dynamic reusable learning objects (Boyle, 2002).

We explained in the "Support for Object-Oriented learning objects" section how our object-oriented learning approach is independent of, and complementary to, (a) the instructional design theory underlying the learning object design process, and (b) the metadata standards adopted by the IEEE (LTSC, 2003) for learning object packaging. Pedagogical decisions can be made by the instructional designer before applying our approach to structuring the functionality of learning object classes. Our object-oriented learning approach is pedagogy neutral in this respect. Our approach also contributes to learning object metadata tagging by identifying attributes and activities for each learning object class.

We assert that our object-oriented learning approach expands and informs the options available to instructional designers for structuring and interfacing learning object. We believe our approach assists the systematic development of more complex, authentic lessons, composed of student-centered, dynamically created learning objects. We expect further contributions toward an object-oriented learning methodology will facilitate the design and implementation of larger scale lessons, courses and educational programs, composed of learning objects that increasingly exhibit the 'bilities'.

References

Boyle, T. (2002). Design principles for authoring dynamic, reusable learning objects. In A. Williamson, C. Gunn, A. Young & T. Clear (Eds), *Winds of change in the sea of learning: Proceedings of the 19th Annual Conference of the Australasian Society for Computers in Learning in Tertiary Education* (pp. 57-64). Auckland, New Zealand: UNITEC Institute of Technology. Retrieved February 19, 2007, from http://www.ascilite.org.au/conferences/auckland02/proceedings/papers/028.pdf

Boyle, T., Chalk, P., Fisher, K, Jones, R., Bradley, C., Haynes, R., et al. (2003). *Example learning objects.* Retrieved February 19, 2007, from http://www.londonmet.ac.uk/ltri/learningobjects/examples.htm

Computer Education Management Association (2001). *Learning architecture learning objects overview*. Retrieved February 19, 2007, from http://learnativity. com/lalo.html

Gibbons, A., & Richards, R. (2001). The nature and origin of instructional objects. In D. Wiley (Ed.), *The instructional use of learning objects.* Retrieved February 19, 2007, from http://www.reusability.org/read/

Hamel, C. J., & Ryan-Jones, D (2002, November). Designing instruction with learning objects. *International Journal of Educational Technology, 3*(1). Retrieved February 19, 2007, from http://www.ed.uiuc.edu/ijet/v3n1/hamel/index.html

Littlejohn, A. (Ed.). (2003) *Reusing online resources: A sustainable approach to e-learning.* London: Kogan Page.

LTSC—IEEE Learning Technology Standards Committee. (2003). *Standard for learning object metadata* (LOM P1484.12). Retrieved February 19, 2007, from http://ltsc.ieee.org/wg12/index.html

Morris, E. (2005). Object oriented learning objects. *Australasian Journal of Educational Technology, 21*(1), 40-59. Retrieved February 19, 2007, from http://www. ascilite.org.au/ajet/ajet21/morris.html

Morris, E. J. S., & Zuluaga, C. P. (2003). Educational effectiveness of 100% online I.T. courses. In G. Crisp & D. Thiele (Eds.), *Interact : Integrate : Impact: Proceedings of the 20th Annual Conference of the Australasian Society for Computers in Learning in Tertiary Education* (pp. 353-363). Adelaide, Australia: Adelaide University. Retrieved February 19, 2007, from http://www. adelaide.edu.au/ascilite2003/program/conf_prog_index.htm

MIT OCW. (2005). *MIT OpenCourseWare process*. Retrieved February 19, 2007, from http://ocw.mit.edu/OcwWeb/Global/AboutOCW/publication.htm

Page-Jones, M. (1998). *The practical guide to structured systems design* (2nd ed.). Retrieved February 19, 2007, from Wayland Systems Inc., http://www.waysys. com/ws_content_bl_pgssd_ch06.html

Pfleeger, S. L. (2001). *Software engineering theory and practice* (2nd ed.). Upper Saddle River, NJ: Prentice Hall.

Priestley, M. (1996). *Practical object-oriented design with UML*. Maidenhead, Berkshire, UK: McGraw-Hill International.

Rathsack, R. (2001). *Conflict resolution styles*. Retrieved February 19, 2007, from http://www.wisc-online.com/objects/index.asp?objID=PHR300

Wiley, D. (2001). Connecting learning objects to instructional design theory: A definition, a metaphor, and a taxonomy. In D. Wiley (Ed.), *The instructional use of learning objects.* Retrieved February 19, 2007, from http://www.reusability.org/read/

Yourdon, E., & Constantine, L. (1978). *Structured design: Fundamentals of a discipline of computer program and systems design* (Yourdon Press Computing Series). Englewood Cliffs, NJ: Prentice Hall.

Zuluaga, C. P., & Morris, E. J. S. (2003). A learning management model for mixed mode delivery using multiple channels (Internet, Intranet, CD-ROM, Satellite TV). In G. Crisp & D. Thiele (Eds.), *Interact : Integrate : Impact: Proceedings of the 20th Annual Conference of the Australasian Society for Computers in Learning in Tertiary Education* (pp. 562-568). Adelaide, Australia: Adelaide University. Retrieved February 19, 2007, from http://www.adelaide.edu.au/ascilite2003/program/conf_prog_index.htm

Zuluaga, C. P., Morris, E. J. S., & Fernandez, G. (2002). Cost-effective development and delivery of 100% online I.T. courses. In A. Williamson, C. Gunn, A. Young & T. Clear (Eds.), *Winds of change in the sea of learning: Proceedings of the 19th Annual Conference of the Australasian Society for Computers in Learning in Tertiary Education* (pp. 759-766). Auckland, New Zealand: UNITEC Institute of Technology. Retrieved February 19, 2007, from http://www.ascilite.org.au/conferences/auckland02/proceedings/papers/109.pdf

Section II

Developing Instruction
Using Learning Objects

This section provides practical significance to the study of learning objects by discussing examples of implementation, struggles associated with creating learning objects, and new models that have emerged as a result of implementations in higher education, the military, K-12 environments, and in industry.

Chapter VI

American Sign Language Learning Objects for Instruction:
A Higher Education Perspective

Rosemary M. Lehman, University of Wisconsin-Extension, USA

Simone C. O. Conceição, University of Wisconsin-Milwaukee, USA

Abstract

Little consideration has been given to involving the deaf community in higher education teaching and learning as it relates to the use of instructional technology. The University of Wisconsin-Milwaukee was mindful of this need and collaborated with Instructional Communications Systems, University of Wisconsin-Extension to work with instructors in the use of technology and develop American Sign Language (ASL) learning objects as components of ASL courses. The purpose of this chapter is to present a background on learning objects; the use of ASL learning objects in three higher education settings; recommendations for the use of learning objects for multiple higher education disciplines; and insights into future and emerging trends related to the use of learning objects in higher education.

Introduction

Today, 54 million Americans—20% of the population—have some form of disability that affects their capabilities of hearing, seeing, or walking (Freedom Initiative, 2001). Nearly 20 million people nationally, and 500 million people worldwide are deaf and hard of hearing (National Deaf Education Network & Clearinghouse, 1989). Historically, society has tended to isolate and segregate people with disabilities. Despite some improvements, such forms of discrimination against these individuals continue to be a serious and pervasive problem that persists in many areas.

In July of 1990, the Americans with Disabilities Act (ADA) was signed into law by President George H. Bush. This act describes a clear and comprehensive national mandate to provide consistent and enforceable standards to address any type of discrimination against individuals with disabilities. The Telecommunications Act, Section 508 of the Rehabilitation Act Amendments of 1998, and the Workforce Reinvestment Act are more recent mandates that address technology accessibility and instructional design, requiring systems to be designed with accessibility built-in, where possible, for instructors and learners (Freedom Initiative, 2001). These mandates have served to bring technology accessibility and program design to the attention of higher education.

Little consideration, however, has been given to involving the deaf community in higher education teaching and learning as it relates to the use of instructional technology. In order to meet the changing needs of learners and instructors, the University of Wisconsin-Milwaukee (UWM) has been mindful of this need. This university collaborated with Instructional Communications Systems, University of Wisconsin-Extension to train instructors in the use of technology, assisted in the development of 351 basic-level video-based American Sign Language (ASL) learning objects, and applied and promoted their use in undergraduate education. The first use of the ASL learning objects was in a distance education course offered in the summer of 2001. Subsequently, these learning objects have also been used as instructional aids in traditional face-to-face classes and in independent learning.

The purpose of this chapter is to present: (1) a background on learning objects (definitions and characteristics of learning objects, and ways in which they have been used in general); (2) the use of ASL learning objects in three higher education settings; (3) recommendations for the use of learning objects for multiple higher education disciplines; and (4) insights into future and emerging trends related to the use of learning objects in higher education.

Background on Learning Objects

According to Wiley (2000), learning objects are units of information that are reusable in multiple contexts. For the purpose of this chapter, learning objects are digital entities: (1) deliverable or retrievable over the Internet through a learning management system (LMS) or a repository of knowledge, enabling individuals to access and use them simultaneously or for global sharing; (2) accessible through a CD-ROM for individual use via a computer at the person's own pace; and (3) viewable on a handheld device for individual mobile use (Conceição & Lehman, 2002).

One may find a variety of definitions to describe the different types of learning objects. Wiley (2000) created a taxonomy that differentiates different types of learning objects. What separates each type is "the manner in which the object to be classified exhibits certain characteristics" (p. 22). These characteristics are the same across environments, no matter where the learning objects reside, and they include number of elements combined, types of objects contained, reusable component, common function, extra-object dependence, type of log-in contained in object, potential for intercontextual reuse, and potential for intracontextual reuse. Other authors describe learning objects as dependent on six key characteristics: accessibility, interoperability, adaptability, reusability, durability, and granularity (Learning Object Authoring Zone Networks, 2004).

In order to standardize the use of learning objects, the U.S. Department of Defense created the shareable content object reference model (SCORM) initiative. SCORM sets interrelated e-learning technical standards, specifications, and guidelines using an XML-based framework to define and access information about learning objects so they can be easily shared among different learning management systems (Advanced Distributed Learning, 2006). A term that is commonly used today is shareable content objects (SCOs), but this term is often confused with learning objects. The difference is that not all learning objects are shareable because they do not have metadata, nor do they use an XML-based framework. Our chapter describes learning objects in three formats. The learning objects used in the Web format have metadata and are SCORM conformant, so they can be shared in different environments. Our learning objects are used with LMS and learning object repositories.

Repositories for Learning Objects

Learning objects require some type of receptacle for the purpose of holding and sharing with others. The term used for these receptacles is learning object repositories. These repositories have well researched user interfaces and architectures that make them easy to use and permit various levels of interactivity (Instructional Resource

Center, 2003). Since the field of repositories is relatively new, repository types and characteristics are only now beginning to be defined.

Repositories are of two general types. They may be either preconstructed or customized. They enable instructors to organize the learning objects, enhance learning opportunities, improve efficiencies, and strengthen both the reuse of the learning objects and collaboration with others. Important factors to be taken into consideration when selecting a preconstructed repository or creating a new one are flexibility, accessibility, and usability for the end user.

Using a repository necessitates the metatagging of each learning object with information that will facilitate its retrieval. The selection or creation of a repository also takes into consideration the context sensitivity of the repository for coding and retrieval, editing, and combining and repurposing. There are several metatagging protocols. The protocol that proved to be effective for the ASL project was SCORM.

The Use of ASL Learning Objects in Higher Education Settings

Learning objects have been used in different settings for different purposes. They have been used for training, instruction, instructional aids, orientation materials, and independent learning. UWM and ICS created 351 basic-level video-based ASL learning objects: (1) for a continuing education course taught at a distance, (2) in a traditional face-to-face setting for undergraduate students, and (3) for independent learning. This section will provide an overview of the implementation and evaluation of the use of the ASL learning objects in these three higher education settings.

Continuing Education Course at a Distance

The use of the learning objects in the distance education course was part of a pilot project in the summer of 2001 (Conceição & Lehman, 2003a). In this course, the learning objects were short video clips with text, showing the ASL instructor demonstrating words and phrases integral to the course. The course design included a workbook with a videotape, weekly synchronous videoconferencing sessions coupled with asynchronous online work, resource and course content access, and online discussions. Course participants met once a week for three hours during seven weeks via videoconferencing, in conjunction with instructional activities on the Web using the LMS Blackboard®. In Blackboard®, learners participated in online discussions and accessed the video-based learning objects for review and rehearsal of the signs prior to and following class sessions.

Participants in the distance education course gave high ratings to the use of the ASL learning objects. They thought the learning objects were a valuable resource for review and practice of the signs, but found them cumbersome to use because they could not go directly to a particular sign. Signs were grouped by categories per unit; thus when students clicked on a category they had to view the whole category and not individual signs (Conceição & Lehman, 2003a). As a result of this feedback, it was changed for future use.

Traditional Face-to-Face Classes

In 2003, participants in traditional semester-long undergraduate face-to-face classes also used the 351 video-based learning objects. In these classes, however, the learning objects were placed on CD-ROM and purchased by students as part of their course materials. Course participants met three to four times a week for 50 to 75 minutes. The design of the courses was based on lectures, in-class examples and drill, and a workbook with a videotape. In these traditional face-to-face classes, the learning objects were used by learners at their own pace and time as instructional aids. For these courses, the learning objects were used for review and practice of the signs and phrases before the beginning of a unit or prior to a quiz or exam (Conceição & Lehman, 2003b).

In the traditional face-to-face classes, evaluation results indicated that learners' inexperience with using the technology emerged during the course, and it became apparent that some of the students were not able to problem solve these technology issues. For example, in some instances students did not check the computer requirements prior to downloading the CD-ROM. When the CD-ROM did not download or their computer crashed, they became frustrated and decided not to use the learning objects. In other instances, students were not familiar with downloading the required software, and rather than asking for assistance made the decision not to use the CD-ROM (Conceição & Lehman, 2003b).

Also, there are various ways of expressing words and phrases in sign language, just as there are in any language. The instructors in the ASL courses occasionally used their preferred methods of signing some of the words and phrases. In some instances these were different from the signs on the CD-ROM, which created confusion for the students who were reviewing the signs on the CD-ROM (Conceição & Lehman, 2003b). These instances are being remedied for future courses.

Independent Learning

Requests for the ASL video-based learning objects from the general public led to a revised noncopyright version for sale on CD-ROM. This version was later placed in a customized learning object repository, and in a handheld device for independent use. The learning objects for the knowledge repository were metatagged for SCORM compliance and recategorized for easy access by the general public. The opening page of the repository provides an example of a learning object to introduce the users to the format of the individual signs. It then directs users to the appropriate signs. The repository is password protected for the purpose of tracking the number and affiliation of the users.

The use of the learning objects in the handheld devices is still in the experimental stage. The purpose of using the learning objects in this device is for ease of mobility. For example, handheld devices that have video capability are easy to carry and can be used anywhere, anytime. A variety of delivery formats can enhance the use of learning objects by providing greater access in various learning contexts. In addition, these delivery formats can offer flexibility and mobility for learners. For these reasons, the use of the ASL learning objects in multiple formats was explored and implemented, and is now in the process of being evaluated.

The ASL learning objects indicate that their use can be flexible and accessible because users can access them from different environments in remote locations such as LMS or knowledge repositories. The ASL learning objects are interoperable due to their ability to be transferred from one environment to another, while preserving the integrity of the object. They are reusable and can be incorporated into multiple applications. The ASL learning objects can also stand alone (i.e., they are independent of the platform or software learning application) and are self-sufficient (i.e., require no outside resources such as Web links). ASL signs are less likely to change, thus there is no need to redesign or recode the learning objects. This means that the ASL learning objects have an extended degree of durability (Learning Object Authoring Zone Networks, 2004).

Application of Learning Objects for Multiple Higher Education Institutions

Feedback from course participants and suggestions by other users of learning objects indicated that learning objects can be valuable instructional aids and educational enhancements in contexts other than ASL (Conceição & Lehman, 2003a, b). Below are several examples of ways in which learning objects are being used and can be used in multiple subject areas in higher education.

In the discipline of math, learning objects can provide a three-dimensional example of a math formula. For example, an animation of an explanation of the Pythagorean Theorem can enable students at a distance to view the mathematical calculation and visual representation of the Pythagorean formula. This example of a mathematical learning object can be posted to the web, easily placed on a CD-ROM, transferred to a repository of knowledge, and imported into a handheld computer.

Medical procedures are now simulated with computer graphics and videotaped for use by students and professionals in the medical field. These procedures can become part of a lesson plan in an online course where students can read about them, view and interact with them, and review them repeatedly before actually practicing the procedures in real life. Professionals in the medical field can use learning objects to review procedures that are not routinely available. These learning objects can be flexibly used in CD-ROM, learning object repositories, and handheld computer delivery formats.

Using role-play for real experiences for psychology courses, instructors can video-tape a simulated session between a patient and a psychologist. This video can then be edited and developed in more depth with complementary text. The video and text can be made available on the Web, on CD-ROM, in a learning object reposi-tory, and on a handheld computer. Students can then read the text, view the video, analyze, and discuss with their peers.

With the use of audio and video for foreign languages, a series of language learn-ing objects can be developed to include information on the culture and language of various countries. Using these learning objects, employees who will be work-ing with peers from other countries or who will be traveling overseas can become familiar with both the language and environment of other cultures. These learning objects can be developed for the Web, CD-ROM, learning object repository, and handheld computers.

Future Trends

When we first developed the ASL video-based learning objects, we used Web-based and CD-ROM technology. For the CD-ROM technology, users had to download a plug-in to view the learning objects. This proved to be confusing and inefficient because users with low technology skills found this to be a barrier and became frustrated with the installation process, and often chose not to use the CD-ROM format.

As a result we are now placing learning objects on a DVD video format (text-based and video-based). With this format, users do not have to download a video player or plug-in to view the learning objects. Once the user places the DVD into the disk drive and activates the DVD program, the learning objects are easily accessible and played, and appear as a high quality full screen video.

An important aspect of using the learning objects is the organization, design, and search capabilities of the learning object in a specific format. The organization of the content should be designed to provide the user with a variety of layouts to select from. For example, in a case like the ASL project, the learning objects were arranged in units and in categories that paralleled the course sequence. This arrangement was based on the instructional design of the course. In other cases, learning objects may be organized around modules, themes, scenarios, critical incidents, or case studies. The use of search features within all formats can help the user locate a specific topic, phrase, word, video, or graphic precisely when needed.

Today the iPod is the most recent technology format that allows users even greater flexibility and mobility. This new technology is less expensive than a computer or high-end handhelds and is already in high demand and use by the younger generation. The iPod technology adds a new feature: interactive teaching and learning. For a language class or lab, instructors can record lectures and assignments on the iPod and place them in a folder on a specified server. The students can in turn record their verbal assignments and upload them to the folder on the server. The instructor can then access the folder, download the file, listen to the assignment, and upload verbal feedback on the assignment to the student's folder for retrieval. This can all be done in a short period of time. At Duke University, faculty are integrating iPods and digital editing tools into many of their courses. One example involves a Spanish course in which faculty use iPods for audio flashcards to challenge students' vocabulary, discourse markers, and connectors. Students then use their iPods for practice and review, as well as for class journaling. In another instance, music faculty require students to record and review their voice lessons, and record vocal and language pronunciation exercises (Duke Center for Instructional Technology, 2006). iPod examples in higher education and all areas of learning continue to grow at a remarkable rate.

Conclusion

A number of mandates during the past decade have served to raise awareness of the importance of technology accessibility and program design. This awareness was the motivation for the development of the ASL pilot project that included video-based ASL learning objects in the higher education setting. The learning objects helped to meet the learning needs of students in the context of deaf culture. The success of the use of the learning objects in the ASL pilot project stimulated their continued use in ongoing courses; their development for advanced ASL levels; their adaptation for a variety of delivery formats; and the consideration of their application for multiple higher education disciplines. As new technologies continue to emerge, there will be new formats to consider; thus, we should continually look for new opportunities for their effective application and use in higher education settings.

References

Advanced Distributed Learning Co-Lab. (n.d.). Retrieved February 18, 2007, from http://adlnet.org

Conceição, S., & Lehman, R. (2002). Creating learning objects to enhance the educational experiences of American Sign Language learners: An instructional development report. *Canadian Journal of Learning and Technology, 28*(3). University of British Columbia, Canada.

Conceição, S., & Lehman, R. (2003a, February 26-March 2). Evaluation of the effectiveness of the design of a distance education course in American Sign Language offered to continuing education students. In *Academy of Human Resources Development Proceedings,* Minneapolis, MN.

Conceição, S., & Lehman, R. (2003b, October 8-10). *An evaluation of the use of learning objects as an instructional aid in teaching adults.* Paper presented at the Midwest Research-to-Practice Conference in Adult, Continuing, and Community Education, Ohio State University, Columbus, OH.

Duke Center for Instructional Technology. (2006). Retrieved February 18, 2007, from http://cit.duke.edu/about/ipod_faculty_projects_spring06.do#french63

Freedom initiative: Fulfilling America's promise to Americans with disabilities. (2001, February). Retrieved February 18, 2007, from http://www.whitehouse. gov/news/freedominitiative/freedominitiative.html

Instructional Resource Center (2003). *Teaching with technology: Introduction to learning object repositories.* Retrieved February 18, 2007, from http://www. irc.gmu.edu/resources/findingaid/twt_guides/repos.htm

Learning Object Authoring Zone Networks. (2004). Retrieved February 18, 2007, from http://www.loaz.com/learning-objects/learning-object-characteristics. html

National Deaf Education Network and Clearinghouse (NCIC). (1989). Gallaudet University.

Wiley, D. A. (2000). Connecting learning objects to instructional design theory: A definition, a metaphor, and a taxonomy. In D. A. Wiley (Ed.), *The instructional use of learning objects.* Retrieved February 18, 2007, from http://reusability. org/read/chapters/wiley.doc

Chapter VII

Transforming Instructional Design Ideas into SCORM-Conformant Learning Products

Vanessa P. Dennen, Florida State University, USA

Kira S. King, Instructional Systems Design Consultant, USA

Abstract

This chapter discusses the lessons learned while designing a SCORM-conformant Web-based courseware product using an iterative instructional design process. In particular, it describes some of the design trade-offs between instruction that is highly modular vs. situational and instruction that is highly interactive vs. highly contextualized. Organizational issues, such as metatagging and asset naming procedures, and the challenge of designing realistic and motivating e-learning assessments are presented as well.

Introduction

Sharable content object reference model (SCORM)-conformant learning systems have quickly moved from being an idea to a reality—a required reality for e-learning content developed for use by many organizations, including federal agencies of the United States. The concept behind SCORM is to provide a standardized format for e-learning content so that it may be used with any conformant learning management system and reused in other SCORM-conformant system. This concept makes SCORM attractive to many organizations or agencies that develop Web-based training for large audiences and multiple uses. While following the SCORM guidelines may at first sound simple and almost procedural, however, in practice it may require rethinking instructional design plans and compromising some pedagogical ideas in the interest of making the technology work. Additionally, the implementation of SCORM standards is a relatively recent phenomenon, meaning there is much theory but little practical experience to guide the instructional design process.

This chapter describes the lessons learned while designing Web-based courseware as part of a partnership between the Department of Veterans Affairs, the Department of Defense, and Image Technical Services, Inc. The goal of the courseware, entitled *Emergency Response to Weapons of Mass Destruction* (WMD) Course, while in development, is to prepare health care clinicians and leaders at Veterans Affairs medical facilities to respond to a potential terrorist attack. It is based on a six-section handbook created by the Department of Veterans Affairs that will serve as a paper version of the course for learners who prefer this mode of instruction, and in case of a power failure during an actual terrorist attack. This chapter discusses our design process and some of the challenges and decisions we faced during the development of engaging courseware that meets the SCORM 1.2 standard and the objectives for the WMD course.

Client and Learner Needs

As experienced instructional designers, we knew that addressing the client's needs would be critical to the success of the courseware. At the same time, we wanted to meet the learners' needs by supporting a variety of learning styles as well as providing contextual information to support effective learning. The client entered the project with a clearly defined idea and mission, although there was room for creativity within the execution. In other words, the instructional goal, learners, content, and technology were predetermined, but how we merged these four areas to create an effective learning product was up to us. This section presents some of the predetermined project parameters.

SCORM Conformant

First and foremost, the client wanted the courseware to be SCORM-conformant. This means that it would need to follow the SCORM specifications and pass the SCORM Conformance Test Suite, which is a self-test of compliance. Conformance is different from Advanced Distributed Learning (ADL) certification, which means a product has been independently tested by an ADL Certification Testing Center (Advanced Distributed Learning, 2005). Per ADL, theoretically both conformant and certified products meet the same technical standards and should function the same; the only difference is the label. However, our programmer indicated that in practice this may not be the case and that the only way to be certain an learning management system (LMS) meets the standard is to look for a certified product.

Designing to meet SCORM specifications was important not only because of the federal government's endorsement and adoption of SCORM conformance for all e-learning, but also because the client wanted us to help set the standard for e-learning development. Developing SCORM-conformant e-learning was new to the client, and while both instructional designers had worked with SCORM previously, we had never done so on a project of this scale or complexity. Fortunately, our programmer did have prior experience and was able to provide guidance as needed.

Predetermined Content

The content for the project was already well defined, having already been developed as part of a larger information-dissemination initiative undertaken by the Veterans Administration. The client required us to use the existing handbook as primary content and supplement it as we deemed necessary. Thus, the primary content-related task was not to develop, but rather to determine how to best structure, chunk, and present the WMD course.

Multiple Learner Audiences

There were multiple learner audiences for the courseware, each requiring a different customization. At the onset of the project, there were three audiences, each of whom had different learning needs. The first learner group, clinicians, required training that would prepare them to triage, diagnose, and treat various conditions related to terrorist attacks. The second group, emergency planning coordinators, required instruction on how to prepare for a terrorist emergency as well as what to do in the event that one occurred. The final group, medical facility leaders, required instruction that would prepare them for following required guidelines and providing leadership should a terrorist attack occur. Over the course of the project, the number of learner audiences was collapsed to two (leaders and clinicians) because it was determined that emergency planning coordinators and medical facility leaders would have similar instructional needs. We chose to develop the clinician version first, since it was the largest in scope and had the most technical content; much of the clinician version could then be reused in the leader version.

Performance Support Tool

Although the primary intent of the WMD was instructional—to create a collection of brief e-learning lessons—the client also had an informational request—to develop a performance support tool reusing same content. In other words, should a terrorist attack occur, both clinicians and leaders should be able to access all of the content included in the courseware without going through the lessons. If there was a power failure, however, they would utilize the paper-based handbook.

Continuing Education Units

Assessments had to be designed to comply with continuing medical education (CME) requirements. A CME unit had to be available for completion of brief, 15-minute lessons or larger course-level instruction. This requirement meant tracking learner performance on assessments was very important, and in some cases the assessments themselves had to be approved by accrediting bodies such as the American Psychological Association.

Chunking

The courseware specifications required the instruction to be chunked into brief, 15-minute segments to accommodate busy learner schedules as well as their focused learning needs. For example, a clinician may not have an afternoon to devote to a course on biological terrorism weapons, but he could likely spend 15 minutes learning about Anthrax.

Reusability

Not only were we relying on sharable courseware objects (SCOs) within the project—reusing content for both the leader and clinician versions of the WMD course—but we also sought to make the SCOs and assets developed within this course available to others who might reuse them for other purposes. This goal is one that is relevant to many government agencies as well as institutions and organizations that provide emergency response and medical services.

Design Process

The design process for the WMD course has been iterative in nature. The project began with a meeting between the client, designers, and developers. From the onset, we divided the content into modules (see Figure 1). Doing so was easy, since we simply adopted each of the six handbook sections as a module area. Topically, each area was distinct and there was little obvious crossover. Three of the module topics appear at surface level to be parallel in nature; biological, chemical, and radiological all are types of warfare agents that might be used in terrorist attack. A fourth area, blast, represents a possible method of attack. The remaining two modules, psychological effects and leadership, contain content that spans any type of attack.

Biological Warfare Agents was the first module developed. It was divided it into nine lessons, each representing a different type of agent. We chose this module to develop first, since it had a well defined content structure and was of moderate complexity and length. A module introduction and scenario-based assessment also were developed, for a total of 11 sub-units within the module; these last two parts are for use in the instructional part of the WMD course, but will not be part of the performance-support tool when it is developed. They are inserted into the course as context wrappers (see Figure 2), or nonreusable objects that help customize the content for a given audience (Ruyle, 2001). This structure was followed for all modules.

Figure 1. Course structure

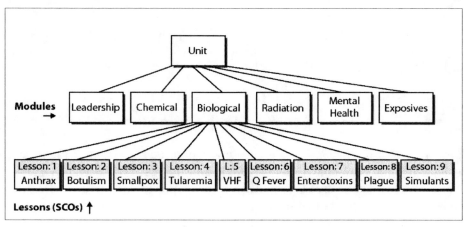

Figure 2. Module and unit structure with wrappers

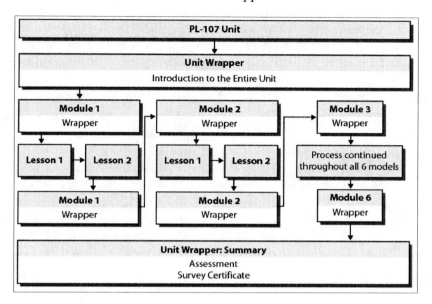

We began work by creating a design document that provided expectations about how to storyboard the lessons, preliminary asset labeling conventions, and media specification guidelines. The storyboarding process began using a MicroSoft Word-based template system, with a Web-based storyboarding tool being adopted during the process. The Web-based tool helped us see what the finished product would look like, complete with navigation and features such as pop-ups.

Client meetings and reviews took place periodically throughout the design process, and changes were made to the design document and storyboards as we encountered various challenges related to both content and technology along the way.

Engaging the Learner

Two of the concerns for the instructional component of the WMD course were retention and application. Given the unpredictable nature of terrorist attacks, there is no way to tell exactly when or if a learner might have the opportunity to apply the course content. Further complicating the design, we did not know if a learner would choose to complete one lesson or a full module and needed to design for either case.

In the end product, individual lessons are focused and brief. Within a module, however, they are tied together by a scenario that was intended to make the learning task rich and engaging. In our original design, the scenario was to be presented to all learners, whether they were engaged in a single lesson or an entire module. Whereas each lesson ends with a mastery-based assessment, the scenario was designed to provide an application-level assessment, varying by how many lessons were completed.

The concept behind the scenario-based design was to place the learner in a potential terrorist attack situation. Using a fictitious city called DisasterPrep City, each scenario positions the learner as someone who supports the leaders and/or clinicians in the DisasterPrep VA Medical Center as they respond to a terrorist attack. In the original design, each module would have one global scenario that would apply to each lesson and to the module context wrappers. The same characters would appear in each module, but the situation itself would change. Either a clinician or leader would describe the current urgent situation and appeal to the learner for assistance. Once the learners had successfully completed an assessment task, such as diagnosing and treating patient cases, they would see a DisasterPrep City Map and a multimedia animation narrating the sequence of events in the scenario. For example, if learners correctly identified anthrax, they would see a map of the city and an explanation that a flatbed truck had dispersed aerosol anthrax, including location and time, and so forth. After completing each lesson, the learner would see a different part of the city and would thereby view another part of the scenario mystery. This would encourage the learner to continue with the lessons until the entire module was complete.

As we tried to implement this design, however, we encountered a push and pull between interactive design, narrative design, and SCORM 1.2 conformance. In fact, Bizzocchi and Woodbury (2003) also suggests that interactivity and narrative storytelling can detract from each other. A unique power of simulations and scenarios is the narrative aspect. The goal is to immerse someone in the context and engage them emotionally in this other world. Sequences of events and continuity of characters play a major role in this storytelling. However, such sequencing and continuity is not in keeping with the concept of reusable learning objects, and the ability to develop it is not of foremost importance to SCORM-comformant LMS vendors.

For this course, to fully immerse the learner in the story, our first choice was to weave the narrative throughout the lessons and assessments of each module. In this approach, the context wrappers would introduce the scenario, then the learner would complete the lessons (SCOs) and scenario-based assessment. Additionally, as per Bizzocchi and Woodbury's (2003) recommendation, on-screen interactive elements such as navigation would be customized to support the story. We envisioned creating customized menus that resembled patient charts for each lesson; however, it was not manageable. First, to provide learners the choice of either completing a single lesson or an entire module, the lessons had to stand alone. This meant that any introductory material would have to be repeated continually for each lesson, and that the context wrapper at the module level (with the scenario introduction and solution) had to be kept separate from each lesson SCO. In other words, a learner completing the anthrax, botulism, and plague lessons would have to repeat the same introductory material three times because of tracking and navigational constraints. A further complication was added in that the LMS could not support customizable menus, requiring that we use standard menus instead. Thus, the development team had to choose between instruction that was highly modular and interactive and instruction that was highly situational and contextual (see Figure 3).

As we explored the issue, it became apparent that these items have indirect relationships. That is, situational instruction with rich narrative story and context is difficult to achieve when learners have a lot of choice regarding navigation and level. For example, one option was to increase the narrative context and weave the story throughout the lessons and modules. To do this, the material would have to be bundled at the module level. This would be a lower level of granularity than originally called for and would limit learner control by only allowing learners to take the course one module at a time (see Figure 4). Additionally, the LMS's in-

Figure 3. Instructional choices

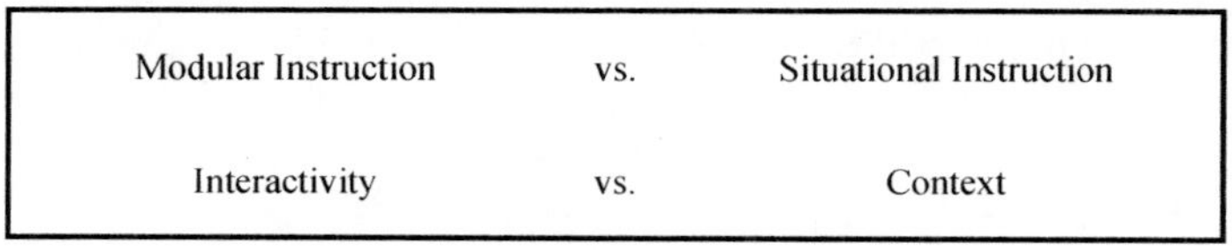

Modular Instruction	vs.	Situational Instruction
Interactivity	vs.	Context

Figure 4. High situation and context

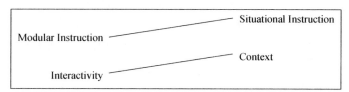

Figure 5. High granularity and interactivity

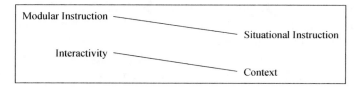

ability to support customizable menus meant we could not use menus as vehicles to carry the story.

Conversely, highly modular instruction that is SCORM 1.2 conformant and has high levels of granularity seems to function best with lower levels of situational context. For example, a second option was to increase interactivity and learner control by stripping narrative context from the lessons and placing it only at the module level. This would allow the learner to take the course one lesson at a time, which would help retention and performance support for actual emergency situations. It would also limit the power of the story itself, however, and would limit the ability of the scenario to provide a realistic context that emotionally engages the learners and requires them to apply content in authentic situations (see Figure 5).

For this course, the development team determined that modularity took higher priority over situational instruction. Modularity is particularly important in this experience because the content also has to serve as a performance support tool enabling clinicians and staff to access information in small chunks very quickly in case of an actual emergency. The final appears to be a suitable compromise that blends the two approaches of modular and situational instruction. At the lesson level, the instruction is entirely context-free with no scenario. This allows for high granularity and easy access to support quick review, enabling it to be used in case of an actual emergency. On the module level, however, a scenario is integrated into the final assessment. Learners are informed of the scenario-based test during the introduction to the module via the context wrapper. Then they will continue to work through each lesson, earning CME credits along the way. Once all of the lessons are completed, the learner then goes on to the scenario involving DisasterPrep City and the DisasterPrep VA Medical Center. To pass this final test, the learner must apply the material (e.g., diagnose and treat several patients, some of whom have been victims of a WMD terrorist attack). Once the learners pass the test, they view a multimedia presentation using a map of the city to detail key elements of the terrorist attack.

Design Challenges and Decisions

Designing the WMD course was not without challenges. Some challenges were typical of many instructional design projects. For example, we had to juggle our multiple goals of creating a product that would be interesting and motivating for the learners that would present the material in an effective manner; that would assess the learners' abilities to use what they had learned in as authentic a manner as possible; and that would be useful to both clinicians and leaders for their on-the-job learning and performance needs. Other challenges included following SCORM 1.2 design specifications and making them work within an LMS environment. Although much has been written that theorizes about the long-term benefits of reusable learning objects in general and SCORM-based design in particular, there is little practical guidance for applying SCORM (Barker, 2004). We began the project with faith that whatever we designed would work with the standard and the technology. In the end, we found it was necessary to make some creative and pedagogical compromises in the interest of functionality. Fortunately, these compromises do not sacrifice the integrity of the instruction; rather, they limit some of the flexibility and interaction we would have liked to build into the course.

Defining the SCO

The scale of the sharable content object, or reusable learning object (RLO), required definition before the course could be packaged within the learning management system. SCOs are the smallest chunks of information in the courseware that are tagged. As recommended by Beyer (2005), it was a joint decision made by the instructional designers, the programmer, and the client. Determining at what level the content made up an SCO provided a challenge for the team. Factors impacting the decision were efficiency, flexibility, the client's needs, and technical constraints.

Each SCO must be individually packaged within a learner management system. The LMS tracks and assesses learner progress at the SCO level; within SCO tracking is not possible within the LMS. As our design and development team deliberated how best to define SCO, the client's LMS vendor suggested that most often they wrap entire courses as SCOs. They were not well versed in dealing with multiple SCOs that together constituted a course and would allow learners to take flexible paths customized to meet their own learning needs.

Realizing the functionality that the technology was prepared to support, we had to determine carefully how to make our design work within these parameters. The decision required consideration of possible learner paths through the course, considering how it would work in terms of redundancy, tracking, and assessment. For example, we wanted a learner to be able to choose to take the Anthrax Lesson, which would include introductory information for a new learner and then select the Botulism Lesson without having to repeat any introductory information. However, a first-time learner in the course taking the Botulism Lesson should encounter the introductory information. Supposing a learner entered planning only to take the Smallpox Lesson, the learner should be able to change his/her mind and decide to complete the entire Biological Warfare Agents module without covering the smallpox content again.

We could have defined the SCO at any number of levels. Had we gone for a high level of granularity, which means that each chunk of content or topic—typically a one to five screen segment of the instruction is considered an SCO. Initially, this was how some members of the project team had envisioned a SCO and certainly it is in keeping with much of the rhetoric on learning objects as small, stand-alone pieces of content. At the opposite end of the spectrum was the option of wrapping the entire WMD course as a SCO. Neither of these solutions was really feasible. In the end, we defined each lesson, essentially a 15-minute chunk of content followed by a 5-question assessment, as an SCO because dividing it into smaller units would have created extra packaging work and technical challenges. Defining it any larger would have impeded our ability to track the learner's progress.

Remaining Context Free

One of the main concepts behind RLOs is that they must be context-neutral or context-free so they may be used in other courses or settings. Certain types of contextual information were easy to remove from the course content, but other parts were relevant and necessary to our individual learners. Clinician content focused on particular conditions, and their treatment was fairly context-neutral. Wrappers that provided information about instructional objectives and CEU written specifically for the DVA were sufficient to anchor such content for these learners.

However, some of the leader and procedural oriented content was particular to the Department of Veterans Affairs. Thus, we were faced with two opposing options: creating context-neutral instruction or creating instruction that truly met our learners' needs. In the end, our decision was influenced in part by how we chose to define SCOs, with each lesson as a SCO unto itself. It simply was not feasible to design SCOs that would be entirely devoid of contextual information, nor was it likely that someone else would want to reuse a SCO of that scope. As suggested by Greene (n.d.), at some point the quest to be context-free compromises one's ability to create a product that meets the current target learners' needs. We surmised, then, that part of the reusability of this project would be that one could use the metatags to locate the desired content and then simply copy the content, but not the SCO, over into their own project.

That said, we did follow as many of the context-related guidelines as possible, including not referencing the location of the SCO itself or of other SCOs in the overall instruction (e.g., "This is Module 1") (Beyer, 2005). Keeping the SCOs context-neutral in this sense was important because of the sequencing and modularity of the course. Although there is a big-picture sequence for completing the course as a whole, learners can complete all or part of the course in whatever order they wish, so any such references needed to be avoided.

Metatagging

It was necessary to determine who else might want to use this content and in what setting in order to identify the appropriate types of metatags to assign to SCOs.

Spigarelli (2004) suggests that metadata identification take into consideration secondary audiences for the content. The client was concerned with others being able to find content on particular topics readily and to trace the SCOs back to the client. Thus, the three most important bits of metadata from the client's perspective were keywords, learning objectives, and SCO owner. Also included was information about the last instructional designer to work on the SCO, which was intended to help our team know who to go to with questions.

The level of detail to be used for recording metadata on this project is still uncertain at this time. While conceptually it sounds nice to have thorough tag data recorded throughout the course, the process of generating this information can be time-consuming. Indeed, it may be more trouble than it is worth (Barker, 2004). Just the Biological Warfare Agents module alone will result in nine SCOs, each focused on different agents, and two context wrappers, one providing a module introduction and one for a module scenario assessment. An additional SCO that is the entirety of the module and the wrappers contained as one linear object will become a tenth. These SCOs are not the only parts for which metadata needs to be determined and entered; each asset or media file must include its own metadata. Most instructional screens in the course include graphics, making the number of files to be tagged for one module considerable.

The metadata will not affect the intended learner's experience of the course at all. It could enable future course design teams to search for and reuse some of the course content and assets, but that is dependent on there being a searchable, shared SCO repository. At this time, such a repository does not exist and to invest a great deal of time on creating tags that may or may not be used seems like a task that might not be the wisest use of time and money from a cost-benefit standpoint.

Asset Naming

It was necessary to develop a descriptive naming convention for media files, or assets, to assist with file management during the development process. The asset naming possibilities were endless. After a discussion, the client put forth a request that we followed. Assets located in and specific to lessons were named by their location in the course, with a three-letter code for each level of the instruction, ending in a number. For example, a photo that first appears in the Anthrax Lesson would be named WmdBioAnt001.jpg, indicating its location in the WMD course, Biological Warfare Agent Module, and Anthrax Lesson. The use of numbers at the end rather than greater descriptive titles is counter to some naming advice that advocates filenames that describe the file's contents (Beyer, 2005). However, such recommendations seem somewhat oversimplified, not taking into consideration the large number of asset files, many with content not readily summarized in one or two words, generated within a course of this scope. Assets that spanned lessons or modules, such as scenario graphics and standard instructional cues like topic introduction graphics, were named descriptively because it did not make sense to tie their names to a specific course location. This naming convention made it easy for the designers to keep track of and place the assets in the correct screens.

Creating Realistic Assessments

The team was challenged with creating assessments that would work for various levels of instruction (lesson, module, or unit level) and that could be reusable for other instructional systems. For example, imagine that a learner creates a customized course of three learning objects, each covering a different biological agent. A simple approach would be to place mastery-based assessments within each of the three learning objects. This approach does allow for reuse of each learning object. However, it generates a limited depiction of the learner's comprehension and does not provide the learner with an opportunity to synthesize learning across the three instructional units. The tests simply measure if the learner has mastered each condition in isolation.

What is required in the real world is for the clinician to be able to distinguish between the different conditions and prescribe the proper treatment for each. When a patient presents at a hospital with an unknown infection, the clinician must consider several possibilities, not just whether the patient has or has not been affected by a particular agent. Many symptoms are common to multiple conditions, and these conditions may be caused by an intentional terrorist act or not. To address the real world situation is a higher level of learning, and it requires a higher level of assessment. To fulfill this need, we used a guided discovery approach (Clark, 1999) to develop end of course assessments. These assessments engage learners in realistic scenarios, as described earlier in this chapter, requiring them to apply the learning covered in all learning objects by distinguishing conditions and prescribing appropriate treatment.

The only way to ensure reusability was to situate the scenarios at the end of a larger learning object, such as at the modular level consisting of several lessons. Therefore, the best approach has been to include the scenario in context wrappers (Ruyle, 2001) outside of the learning objects. The learning objects and context wrappers are then bundled for the different levels of instruction and type of learner. The result is mastery-based assessment within small learning objects (lessons) and a scenario-based assessment at the end of larger learning objects (modules).

Lessons Learned

Using a short, iterative design process was important to this project. Given that the end product was to be modular in nature, we capitalized on this modularity and developed it in phases. Had we designed all of the modules before checking how it would work within the constraints of the LMS and SCORM 1.2 requirements, there would have been considerable revision time required on this project. We were able to adjust our design document along the way, as necessitated by our experiences developing the first module. Some of the issues that affected us were related to how the LMS has interpreted SCORM 1.2; in other words, the LMS is more restrictive than the standard itself, and while it meets the standard, it is designed with a very static, linear form of instruction in mind and does not allow for the realization of all design possibilities that would potentially be SCORM-conformant. Although it is frustrating to have technology dictate design options, sometimes it is necessary to work within or around such restrictions. Each subsequent module has required less design time as we perfect the process.

Also critical to our design success was maintaining regular communication among various members of the project team. For example, the programmer was involved from the beginning, even though the bulk of her work was not done until the end. However, her guidance about what would or would not be technically feasible and her ability to communicate with the LMS vendor and check out our design options was essential to the instructional design process. Furthermore, knowing in advance what our functionality requirements would be helped her plan. Thus, having her involved from the beginning has made the transition from design to development as smooth as it could be.

Conclusion

Developing SCORM-conformant courseware is not quite as simple or template-driven of a process as it may appear. Had we been designing a simple page-turner type product, the process likely would have been much simpler. However, the value of providing interaction and authentic or situated instruction in a training area with such critical implications for peoples' health and welfare was well worth both the effort and the challenge.

Careful consideration must be given to the needs and expectations of the learners for whom the courseware is being designed as well as to remaining context-neutral and to tagging content so it can readily be found and used by others. Additionally, juggling desired features such as flexible navigation, modularity, and authentic macro-level assessment within a learning object environment may require some creative thinking and design compromises.

References

Advanced Distributed Learning (ADL). (2005). *Sharable content object reference model* (SCORM®) (2004 Conformance Requirements Version 1.3).

Barker, B. S. (2004). Adopting SCORM 1.2 standards in a courseware production environment. *International Journal on E-Learning, 3*(3), 21-24.

Beyer, M. (2005). *Storyboarding for reusable content.* Retrieved February 18, 2007, from http://www.adlnet.org/scorm/articles/9.cfm

Bizzocchi, J., & Woodbury, R. F. (2003, December). A case study in the design of interactive narrative: The subversion of the interface. *Simulation and Gaming, 34*(4), 550-568.

Clark, R. C. (1999). *Developing technical training: A structured approach for the development of classroom and computer-based instructional materials* (2nd ed.). Washington, DC: International Society for Performance Improvement.

Greene, T. (n.d) Objects of my desire: Reusable learning objects design ruminations. Retrieved March 24, 2007 from http://askintl.contentbox.com/index.cfm/1,a852,4710,1548,0,html.

Ruyle, K. E. (2001). Meet me in RIO: Implementing reusable information object. In *Proceedings of the 48th Annual Conference of the Society for Technical Communicators.* Retrieved February 18, 2007, from http://www.stc.org/confproceed/2001/PDFs/STC48-000087.PDF

Spigarelli, B. (2004). *Introduction to the SCORM for instructional designers.* Retrieved February 18, 2007, from http://www.adlnet.org/scorm/articles/3.cfm

Chapter VIII

Teaching Frameworks for Context-Rich Instruction:
Design Objects

Kevin Oliver, North Carolina State University, USA

Abstract

This chapter proposes a category of tools called design objects that can be used by instructors to integrate existing content sources, including but not limited to learning objects, within teaching frameworks that engage learners with content in meaningful ways. Emphasis is on tools to support the K-12 instructor, although related issues are applicable across educational levels. Examples of teaching-oriented design objects are provided along with related development systems, however it is argued the former represent more viable options for teachers given limitations in the learning object economy, conceptualizations of teachers regarding objects, complexity in packaging objects, and classroom control issues. The possibility of design objects and development systems working in tandem is discussed, with development systems prescribing effective educational strategies for novice teachers and design objects supporting more personalized content development. Various sources for new design objects are suggested to encourage further development and research.

Introduction

One of the primary assumptions and touted benefits of learning objects is that they will be reused by others and thereby reduce replication effort and cost. This assumption may be faulty, however, based on instructor difficulties in removing context from others' learning materials that may be inappropriate for their own classes (Parrish, 2004). In fact, the reusability of a learning object is thought to be inversely related to the amount of its internal context, leading many to decontextualize learning objects to boost the likelihood they will be reused (Wiley et al., 2004). Given that many learning objects are very small, covering only one objective or content chunk (Bradley & Boyle, 2004; Duval, Hodgins, Rehak, & Robson, 2004), context is often stripped that might provide cues to the big picture of how discrete content meshes with a broader topic. Obvious problems ensue from over decontextualizing, given recent attention in learning theory on the benefits of contextualizing content in anchored or situated formats (Cognition and Technology Group at Vanderbilt, 1993; Garrison, 1995). A challenge is left with teachers, then, to piece back together a number of disparate resources into a meaningful collection for their learners, and to design activities and provide tools that provide for learner interaction with these materials.

Partially addressing this dilemma of too-much/too-little context in learning objects are "design objects." Design objects are empty instructional design shells that facilitate the generation of an instructional sequence known to be effective in supporting a specific thinking process or type of learning (e.g., reasoning, inquiry, case analysis). Design objects provide a structure for content and activities to be specified by each instructor, which may or may not include existing learning objects, and they also provide the functionality necessary for students to carry out assigned activities. Thus, the "design" in design objects refers to not only the teacher's instructional design, but also to the students' original knowledge designs created by manipulating the structured material according to the manner specified by the teaching framework. In most design objects, the manner in which students manipulate rich resource sets is consistent with constructivist approaches to teaching. For the teacher, a design object supports multiple incarnations of a teaching strategy such as concept mapping or a teaching/learning model such as problem-based learning (PBL), instead of forcing the instructor to adopt or adapt activities created by others. The design shell and its underlying strategy or model are replicable and reusable, while the contextualized content specific to a course remains locally defined.

Open-ended and empty design objects empower instructors to infuse relevant context from their own courses and possibly from existing learning objects when appropriate. Design objects may inherently support higher-order learning from Bloom's taxonomy (i.e., analysis, synthesis, evaluation), given their close connection to authentic or context-bound situations that often require higher levels of thinking and problem solving (Wiley et al., 2004). A stand-alone learning object, in contrast, may be so decontextualized that it can only serve to transfer basic knowledge (i.e., lower-order learning), with notable exceptions when a learning object is classified as supporting a task or exercise (Koppi, Bogle, & Lavitt, 2004). Design objects serve a different purpose than most learning objects, guiding instructors to use effective strategies and models in their courses with the content that is most relevant to their teaching goals.

The objectives of this chapter are to help the reader:

1. Define characteristics of design objects and classify appropriate tools into different categories of design objects

2. Differentiate design objects focused on teaching and learning from instructional content systems, and understand the conditions under which each may be appropriate

3. Describe a range of potential foundations for future design objects

Background

Baruque and Melo (2004) distinguish learning theories or how learning occurs from instructional theories or the best strategies to promote learning. They describe behavioral, cognitive, and constructivist learning theories, suggesting an "eclectic" mix of each is appropriate for the design of learning object content. This chapter approaches the subject from the standpoint of instructional theories with a discussion of design objects or tools that promote the design of instructional sequences around teaching frameworks (e.g., cooperative learning). A design object is more inclusive than a learning object, in that some allow for the import or use learning objects as part of their overall scope, and most provide some student functionality to engage embedded content. Following a shift noted by Dodds and Fletcher (2004), this chapter emphasizes how instructors and students can utilize existing content in meaningful ways, rather than how designers and developers can best package content objects in strategy frameworks.

Some of the assumed benefits of traditional learning objects include: flexible content designed for use across varying contexts, updatable and customizable content with the ability to search for and filter out relevant segments, and interoperable content across systems (Longmire, 2000). While such features are desirable, a design object of the sort advocated here accomplishes these benefits for a specific instructor, while imposing only an instructional approach (e.g., inquiry). To the extent a teaching model like inquiry is desirable for teaching a portion of content, the related design object can be employed to generate an instructional sequence that accomplishes flexibility, customization, and interoperability for the instructor developing it.

What comprises a design object and what does not? A design object is a tool or tool suite employed by any instructor that supports an educational strategy or teaching model, and can be customized to fit the instructor's own concepts, problems, issues, cases, and so forth. Common characteristics of design objects are outlined below:

- Design objects are not learning objects themselves, but rather, the tools to structure and implement a lesson based on a teaching framework. Some consider the original "learning designs" created by design objects to be a type of comprehensive learning object that can be tagged and reused (see, for example, Kang, Lim, & Kim, 2004; Lukasiak et al., 2004). Design objects that emphasize content packaging into reusable learning designs, however, may not include added features to support user interaction with the material (i.e., developer-oriented only). This trend may result from the assumption that a teacher would import a packaged learning design into whatever learning management system (LMS) was at their disposal, using the student tools embedded in that course shell. The assumption that learning management systems contain appropriate student tools for constructivist activity, however, may be faulty (Oliver, 2001).

- Design objects include features that explicitly support instructional strategies (e.g., KWL charting, sequencing, guided writing, mind mapping, role playing, evaluating) or teaching models (e.g., anchored instruction, case-based instruction). The more explicit this relationship the better, since novice instructors may not readily make the connection between a set of features and the strategy or model being encouraged.

- Design objects come in the form of an empty shell that allows individual instructors to customize a lesson or project to fit their different subject-specific or grade-level needs. While a design object guides the instructor to set up an activity with specific steps as recommended by the instructional strategy or model being supported, it allows for customization of such elements as guiding questions and imported resources.

- Contemporary design objects are predominantly Web-based, allowing instructors to import and leverage increasingly rich online content resources as part of planned lessons. Some design objects allow for and may emphasize the import of tagged learning objects, although the most flexible design objects will allow for the import of any content whether its been tagged and archived in an object catalog or not (e.g., Web pages and articles referenced on the fly). Some design objects allow content to be imported by students as well, supporting information processing activities such as collecting, sorting, organizing, and synthesizing.

- In line with open learning environments (Hannafin, Land, & Oliver, 1999), design objects include student tools and scaffolds that allow information collected by the teacher or the students themselves to be processed in generative ways (e.g., collect, sort, rank, annotate, cite, share, analyze, compare, relate, evaluate) toward the goal of constructing new meaning (Bannan-Ritland, Dabbagh, & Murphy, 2002).

- To enhance their usability by instructors, quality design objects provide for several classroom management features: the ability to set up multiple lessons or projects within a strategy or model framework; the ability to set up individual and small group folders for students to store their work; the ability to assign a selected lesson or project to student folders; the ability to comment on or grade student work; the ability to collapse, compare, or look across multiple student folders, which also supports a whole-class discussion or peer critique of student work; and the ability to save or print student work.

At least two categories of design objects may be envisioned based on available examples: micro-level design objects that enable the structuring/manipulation of content within a relatively concise strategy framework (e.g., diagramming cause and effect); and macro-level design objects that enable the structuring/manipulation of content within a more complex teaching model framework (e.g., problem-solving, inquiry, case analysis).

In its most basic or micro-level form, a design object enables an instructor to import resources and create activities around an effective teaching strategy framework. For example, Cmap is a micro-level design object that supports the concept mapping strategy with its underlying skills of collecting, sorting, describing, and relating information. Instructors create student project folders into which they can drop various content elements (e.g., audio/video files, text-based articles, images, Web links). Students create concept maps and can attach resource files and annotations to the various "nodes" in their maps to exemplify and elaborate their concepts. Attached resources can be pulled from the instructor-provided set, or can be collected by the students through their own research. Cmap allows instructors to compile "knowledge soups" or aggregations of relationship/proposition statements across student maps, to aid in discussing the most prevalent relationships found by a group or class. Additional collaboration tools are built-into Cmap to support student work, including the ability for individuals in different locations to synchronously or asynchronously co-edit a map, and the ability to attach discussion boards and chat rooms to map elements.

The Fablusi role play design engine is another micro-level design object, helping an instructor create a simulated role play, outline key events, define stakeholders and roles, embed appropriate resources for the roles, and establish virtual meeting spaces for communication during events (Ip, Linser, & Naidu, 2001). As noted by the developers, "the use of the simulation generator has transformed the previously tedious, technically complicated process of creating a simulation into a rapid cyclic development environment for academics to design and experiment [with] different learning episodes and transform learning into a goal-directed activity."

The Intel® (2006) Teach to the Future Workshop on Teaching Thinking with Technology provides extensive training on micro-level design objects tied to specific thinking strategies. The *Visual Ranking* tool allows an instructor to create a list of items for students to practice sequencing and ordering skills (see Figure 1). Students can leave comments for each item in their list to explain their reasoning behind a certain order. The instructor can compare student lists to see correlations and prompt discussion. The *Seeing Reason* tool enables the instructor to generate an orienting question for student research (e.g., Is light rail a logical transit option for a medium-sized city?), then create group work spaces for students to generate related factors identified through research (pollution, ridership) and map the relationship between factors (as ridership increases, pollution decreases) (see Figure 2). This tool promotes the strategy of mapping cause and effect relationships.

In a more detailed or macro-level form, a design object enables an instructor to adopt an entire teaching model, specifying the embedded resources and activities. The Web-based Inquiry Science Environment (WISE) is one example, promoting

Figure 1. Intel® (2006) Visual Ranking tool (Courtesy of Intel Corporation)

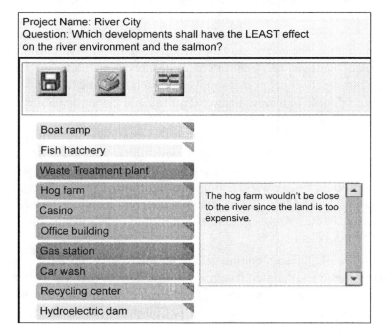

Figure 2. Intel® (2006) Seeing Reason tool (Courtesy of Intel Corporation)

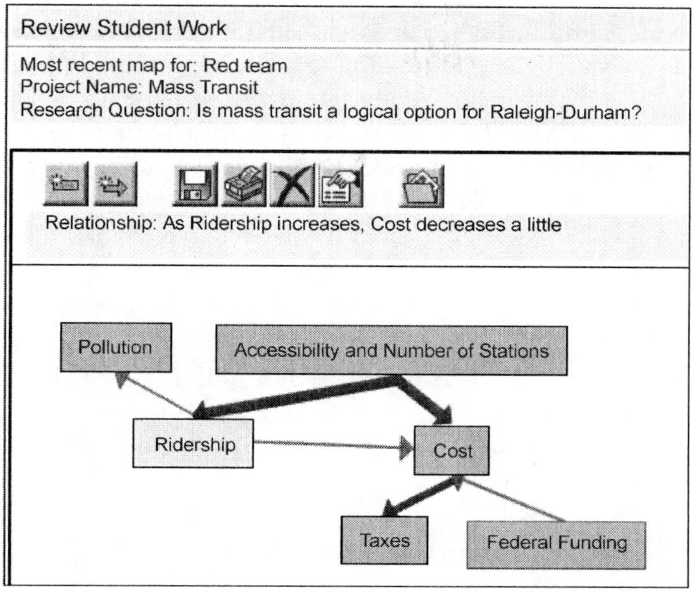

the inquiry teaching model (Williams, Linn, Ammon, & Gearhart, 2004). Teachers establish project spaces and connect external Web evidence for students to critique. Students have access to various tools that scaffold their inquiry, including note-taking, discussion, and visualization tools. A curriculum library is offered, although teachers can create their own projects through an authoring environment.

The Intel® (2006) *Showing Evidence* tool also supports the inquiry teaching model with instructors preselecting evidence for student inquiry around an orienting question. Students make a claim and then move information from the evidence bin into their claims workspace. Students must indicate whether the information supports or refutes their claim and to what degree. Students can work exclusively with teacher-selected evidence or add their own information to the evidence bin. Finally, students rank their work, indicating whether their claim has been adequately proven by the evidence analyzed. This design object supports several thinking skills underlying inquiry, including grouping, sorting, analyzing, and evaluating information.

The IThink case analysis tool may also be classified as macro-level design object, supporting the case-based teaching model (Center for Internet Imaging and Database Systems, 2005). Through IThink, instructors are empowered to collect and structure exhibits in the form of spreadsheets, media, text, and various other digital assets. The collection of exhibits represents the case, with built-in tools for student analysis and response.

Northrup, Rasmussen, and Pilcher (2001) describe a Web-based electronic performance support system (EPSS) that supports teacher development of lessons tied to the Florida Sunshine State Standards. The EPSS includes a lesson architect for instructional planning around teaching model frameworks (e.g., project- and problem-based learning), with the ability for instructors to tie developed lessons to specific state standards. Model units and a unit digest provide educators with sample instructional plans as well as the resources embedded in them (e.g., presentations, graphics, worksheets) for implementation in the classroom. This EPSS is closely related to macro-level design objects, supporting lesson development around strategic frameworks, external resources, and state standards, minus the added functionality for teachers to set up virtual project spaces and engage students with the content through embedded tools.

It has been recommended that one of the best uses of learning objects is to serve as background material for students involved in active learning such as collaborative, problem-based, or case-based learning (Parrish, 2004). Design objects support such models by enabling instructors to set up student work spaces with embedded tools that encourage student thinking and processing of information (e.g., construct a concept map to highlight the main relationships presented in learning objects X and Y). In such environments, traditional learning objects may work with rather than counter to design objects, with the former providing content and the latter providing the structure and means to engage it.

Researchers have developed theoretical models for macro-level design objects that allow instructors to integrate learning objects in teaching model frameworks. Wiley et al. (2004) describe their O_2 approach for employing learning object content, which involves designing a project or problem first (i.e., project-based learning), then selecting learning objects and other digital content that will support student work on project tasks. Further, ongoing research into "learning designs" remains a part of the smart learning design framework (SLDF), with a goal to allow teachers to compile units of study around a case-based learning design and integrate learning objects as resources (Lukasiak et al., 2004). While the creation of tools to integrate learning objects within teaching model frameworks is a positive step, the most flexible design objects will allow instructors to integrate any relevant content within a framework, not just learning objects that have been tagged and cataloged. This factor is particularly important for K-12 educators who may lack access to substantial learning object repositories directed at their subject areas.

Several development systems are available for layering existing learning objects onto teaching templates and creating lessons. These systems might be considered a type of design object by some defining characteristics, but with important distinctions from the teaching-oriented systems presented thus far (see Table 1).

On this last point, the goal of "packaging" for reuse represents a constraint for development systems, since it requires designers to aggregate tagged learning objects exclusively as the sole resource type. Those using most teaching-oriented systems

Table 1. Defining characteristics of development and teaching-oriented systems

Development Systems	Teaching-Oriented Systems
can include prescriptive features that recommend a teaching strategy/model or learning sequence based on instructor inputs about their content and/or learners	tend to support a skill set or one learning strategy specifically that the instructor intentionally selects for implementation
can prescribe or call on certain learning objects for student users as part of programmed adaptive intelligence that determines what the student needs to view next (Dodds & Fletcher, 2004)	rely on nonprogrammed intelligence from the instructor or student to sequence and sort resources—activities which may benefit student thinking/promote higher-order thinking
compile content and activity objects into tagged learning objects that may need to be imported into another system for intentional use (e.g., a Web browser or learning management system)	organize content directly in their intended place of implementation (e.g., in a Web space) and provide embedded tools to support student activities and processing of the material (e.g., sorting, mapping, discussing)
emphasize content packaging into courses or products that can be disseminated or reused by others	emphasize content use in lessons by individual instructors with the added inclusion of classroom management features (e.g., student project folders)

could certainly import learning objects as resources, but they are not held to objects tagged in catalogs exclusively.

Learning Designer is a development system for creating e-learning courses (Kang et al., 2004). The system first assists designers with creating and tagging content objects. Designers then input their desired objectives and describe the structure of their content. Based on inputs, learning models and underlying activities are prescribed by the system. Learning models include jigsaw cooperative learning, simulation, goal-based scenarios, among others, while underlying activities include discussion, brainstorming, evaluation, and so forth. Those creating content can choose from one of the prescribed models, or select their own. Depending on the model chosen, appropriate activity templates are displayed onto which existing content objects are imported or new content objects are built. The activity objects and content objects are combined into a learning object that represents an e-learning module or course. Learning Designer supports novice learning object developers by prompting for necessary metadata entry and content aggregation.

The REDEEM authoring environment is a development system for teachers to develop computer-based tutorials (Ainsworth & Fleming, 2005). Teachers are given tools to structure the sequence of domain material from courseware catalogs, as well as interactivity tools to embed questions with feedback or prompts that encourage students to reflect by taking notes. Teachers can modify the tutorial strategy to one of discovery with more student control over material viewed and questions answered, versus the guided approach with specified content and questions. Different student categories can be created with individualized approaches assigned to students in different categories.

One of the first development systems for creating packaged lessons with learning objects was the IDXelerator (Merrill & Thompson, 1999). "Knowledge objects" in the form of entities, properties, activities, and processes, are defined by an author and reused by a student in any of three instructional strategy types: presentation, practice, and learner guidance. The learner can select their preferred strategy and the system controls the subsequent presentation/sequence of the content. As noted by Bannan-Ritland et al. (2002), this system works well for its intended purposes of cognitive information processing, but is constrained by a limited number of preconfigured strategies.

In making decisions about which type of system to create or employ (i.e., development vs. teaching-oriented), designers and teachers should be aware of key issues tied to each.

Issues, Controversies, Problems

A key issue associated with design objects is whether instructors, particularly novices, will know which design object to employ in response to a set of learner-, context-, or content-dependent conditions. If you have no prior experience with case-based teaching, would you know when to employ a case-based teaching design object to teach a certain goal? It may be that prescriptive development systems are more supportive of novice or first-year teachers, because they provide structured guidance in aligning effective instructional strategies with goals and carefully delineated content. Development systems, however, often emphasize content/lesson packaging for reuse, while other teaching-oriented design objects seem to emphasize teacher preparation of lessons for individual use. Several problems exist for development systems that help to illustrate the more flexible capabilities of teaching-oriented design objects.

First, there is a resource problem for development systems related to the lack of a learning object economy at the K-12 level in particular. A learning object economy may be defined as the individuals and groups involved in creating learning object content and the systems to access them. For development systems to work well, they must package content efficiently and perhaps prescriptively, thus many systems work with tagged learning objects exclusively that can be searched for and pulled into a teaching framework. Given that many learning object catalogs are geared toward university-level instruction (Joint Information Systems Committee, 2006; Koppi et al., 2004; Kusiak et al., 2004; National Learning Network, 2006), systems that rigidly encourage the integration of learning objects as the sole resource type may not be feasible for K-12 teachers. Even in higher education, Koppi et al. (2004) found the lack of a reward structure for developing learning objects and innovative teaching materials was a key barrier for faculty contributors to a learning object catalog. To encourage a learning object economy, Liber (2005, p. 370) suggests a need exists to fund, support, and reward "communities of teachers committed to particular pedagogical approaches," and that the demand for objects will emerge more from sustaining these groups than from funding more content development. Models may also need to be considered by which teachers are given release time for development collaborations or for payments whenever their shared materials are reused (Liber, 2005). At this time, however, design objects for using content in pedagogical frameworks may require greater flexibility, allowing the import of any content, not just cataloged learning objects that may not exist depending on one's subject or grade level.

A second issue with development systems is largely conceptual and relates to the first issue. A need exists for more learning objects directed at K-12 subject areas, but this is difficult to improve since teachers tend to focus on lessons and courses as their basic unit of development, not on objects (Liber, 2005). Teachers do not necessarily understand the concept of learning objects, they do not necessarily think of their own materials as objects, and even if they do, they may not believe their own materials are worthy of contributing to a sharable database (Koppi et al., 2004). These conceptions may ultimately impact the availability of learning objects needed to support development systems, since teachers are not developing them. These conceptions may also impact the willingness of teachers to employ development systems which emphasize object "packaging," if such lesson development models fail to match with their own prior experiences and beliefs. It makes sense that teachers may be more comfortable employing teaching-oriented systems that use familiar concepts and capabilities (e.g., project folders, grading/marking).

Third, technical concerns are also tied to development systems, since some seem more appropriate for content developers familiar with learning object standards than for teachers. As noted by Liber (2005, p. 369), "if teachers are to become learning object authors, they need tools that make this as easy as possible, supporting the creation of the media assets, the assembly, sequencing, and packaging of these, and the description of the objects (metadata tagging). "Packaging learning designs with metadata descriptors, presumably for reuse by others, likely increases the overall complexity and time involved in the task. Menu-driven editors have been created to make packaging easier for novices (Kang et al., 2004; Lukasiak et al., 2004), but the number of standards to mark-up can still be overwhelming. Designers of the Learning Resources Catalog (LRC), a collection of learning objects from across the Universitas 21 Consortium, cut back the required number of metadata tags required of their content contributors from 90 in the IMS learning object metadata (LOM) set to five (Koppi et al., 2004). Others have mentioned the possibility of a "wizard" to assist developers with describing just the metadata elements relevant to their application, further hinting at the need to scaffold this detailed process (Lukasiak et al., 2004). The time available to teachers for planning is so severely limited that systems must significantly reduce their complexity if they have any hope of being employed by teachers and not just content developers.

A fourth issue with some development systems is tied to the overall control of the learning environment—how much teachers are willing to give up, and how giving up control may influence what can be learned. This issue is more of a concern for development systems that emphasize direct teaching strategies than for newer development systems that attempt to create learning designs around more democratic strategies like cooperative and situated learning (e.g., Kang et al., 2004). Dodds and Fletcher (2004), for example, describe "engineered" instruction in which adaptive intelligent tutoring systems compare target learning objectives to student knowledge states, adjusting the information presentation and locating relevant learning objects to help a student master the material. It is uncertain whether instructors are willing to release this much control to a system. Ainsworth and Fleming (2005) found that instructors using the REDEEM authoring system primarily created computer-based tutorials with a controlled presentation that aligned with their teaching beliefs, rather than instruction that REDEEM would adapt on the basis of student performance. Even if instructors were willing to let systems choose and structure a set of learning objects based on student characteristics or performance, Wiley et al. (2004) suggest it will take more than the concatenation of decontextualized resources to ensure meaningful learning. Someone, presumably the teacher, must also be responsible for reintroducing context. Further, some controlled systems emphasize self-paced or individualized instruction for foundational knowledge, using such strategies as present, practice, and guide (Merrill & Thompson, 1999). To teach complex skills and processes, however, students might need to retain control of information for processing in higher-order ways (e.g., analyze, synthesize, evaluate).

Some have hypothesized that the divide between teachers and the practice of instructional design is partially based on the alignment of instructional design with instructional technology and the subsequent change in focus from technology as a tool to support teachers' lessons to technology as a management system to which teachers could not relate (Earle, 1998; Heinich, 1995). If instructional technology systems are viewed as a culprit in driving teachers from instructional design practice, it should also be true that technology tools easily applied by teachers in the classroom could serve to bring the two together again. Indeed, the recent attention on using technology as a tool for student thinking is widely touted and increasingly accepted as part of classroom technology integration practice (Jonassen, Peck, & Wilson, 1999). Conceptually then, design objects that are readily applied to classroom teaching, may be viewed as more usable than rigid systems focused on content packaging and reuse.

Solutions and Recommendations

Many of the problems associated with using learning object content as part of development systems represent vicious cycles: you may solve technical problems but still be left with inadequate resources to employ new systems, you may solve resource problems but be left with complex systems to which teachers cannot relate, you may find teacher conceptions of content aggregation and use do not match the object model and thereby preclude the use of any related resource or technical system, or you may find teachers prefer to relinquish control for aggregating content to their students as part of thinking activities rather than to systems for rigid concatenation. Any solutions for development systems would need to be comprehensive and target several problems simultaneously. This is indeed change on a large scale. An opportunity may exist, however, to combine the best aspects of development and teaching-oriented systems to help mitigate problems tied to each.

As noted, it is an assumption that teachers will know when to employ a certain design object to teach a certain goal. Experienced teachers would likely have little trouble employing many of the teaching-oriented tools introduced in this chapter in response to a learning need. Novice teachers, however, may be assisted by development-type systems in that they offer strategy/model prescriptions for teaching certain content and/or learners. It may be that prescriptive systems and teaching-oriented design objects work well together, at least for those novice teachers willing to invest time in prescriptive systems. Systems might be employed in the first stage of a planning process to help select an appropriate teaching strategy or learning model based on the content/learner conditions input into the system by the teacher (e.g., Kang et al., 2004). After receiving a few prescribed strategies or models, related teaching-oriented design objects would then be offered by the system for implementation. At this stage, the focus of the prescriptive system changes from learning design packaging for reuse to lesson development for teaching, given the resource, conceptual, technical, and control issues outlined for the former. To help improve this comprehensive system further, teaching-oriented design objects might add the functionality to search for and import tagged learning object content from designated repositories—a feature most lack currently. The Cmap design object allows teachers and students to search for resources attached to others' concept maps across the diverse Cmap network. Such connections to rich resource databases should be planned as part of new design object development, as learning object content continues to increase.

Design objects represent teacher-friendly tools to address technical concerns with development systems, they specifically support classroom projects and lessons with which teachers are familiar to address conceptual concerns, and they allow for the easy integration of varying content resources to address both technical and resource concerns. Further, design objects may inherently support more constructivist modes of teaching by keeping control in the hands of teachers and learners, rather than relinquishing decisions about content aggregation and use to a system. This is not to say a good "learning design" system could not be created to support a subject like environmental science, with teachers importing a rich set of subject-specific learning objects in a framework of appropriate strategies, and packaging their lesson for reuse among a supported community. It is to say, however, these systems are currently few in number as a result of the constraints discussed, and design objects represent a realistic alternative for teachers, particularly in K-12 learning environments.

Future Trends

In this section, foundations for future design objects are discussed with suggestions for research. To develop new design objects, one can consider student skills and processes that are desirable to support which may be framed by state standards or curriculum. Similarly, one could base the design of new design objects on teaching strategies and models or learning theories that provide frameworks for effective student processing of information.

Ultimately, the viability of design objects rests in their ability to support the thinking skills and processes that instructors are required or seek to foster in their students. To guide the development of design objects, then, we should work from the forms of thinking most desirable to support. Most educators agree that students of the information age require a robust skill set to process and utilize an ever-growing body of resources, with thinking skills widely held as some of the most important (Partnership for 21st Century Skills, 2004). Presseisen (2001) observes there are a number of basic thinking subskills (i.e., qualifying, classifying, finding relationships, transforming, and drawing conclusions) that are combined in different ways and reused across a number of complex thinking processes (e.g., problem solving, decision making, critical thinking, creative thinking). Thus, a set of micro-level design objects might be created to help instructors foster basic thinking subskills in their students (e.g., Intel®, 2006). Or several micro-level objects might be combined into a macro-level design object to support a thinking process such as problem solving or inquiry (Williams et al., 2004).

A number of creative thinking tools are already available on the Web to support divergent student thinking (Frey, 2004). Several tools generate random words and pictures with note-taking capabilities to capture any associations the learner can make between their topic and the unrelated prompt. These tools lack management capabilities for the instructor to establish project spaces and student folders, and they are also limited like some learning objects by imposing random images rather than teacher-selected images. However, they serve to illustrate a potential micro-level design object that supports analogical reasoning, or attempting to map features of a known concept onto the less familiar target prompt. Instructors might start with one thinking subskill such as creating analogies and metaphors and assign a micro-level design object that allows students to describe how assigned concepts are similar or dissimilar to images the teacher has placed in a media library (e.g., "Tectonic earthquakes are like this image of a jagged piece of glass, because ..."). The instructor could gradually build to more open-ended problems through which students make more decisions and select their own design objects from a toolbox based on relevance to the task. Future design object research might focus not only on student usage of individual design objects and subsequent learning, but also on emergent metacognition and evidence that students can learn to self-manage their own thinking by selecting from among multiple design objects.

Some have already created systems that prescribe instructional strategies or models for teachers based on their inputs about the instructional environment (e.g., jigsaw cooperative learning) (Kang et al., 2004). As discussed previously, these systems might be used as one basis for creating design objects by taking all of the strategies/models in the prescriptive database and developing related design objects to support them. Providing teachers with a system that not only prescribes or recommends strategies, but also embeds the functionality to implement the strategies would enhance overall system usability. Future design object research could focus on the type of teacher most likely to utilize stand-alone design objects successfully and the prescriptive or embedded supports required for other teachers who may struggle to select or utilize tools appropriately (e.g., preservice, first-year teachers). Further, what models of teacher training can be utilized to promote the best use of design objects (see, for example, Intel®, 2006).

Other strategies that could be readily deconstructed and applied to the development of design objects include the numerous games and tools used by trainers in the training community (Michalko, 1991; Pickles, 1996). For example, a micro-level design object might be created to foster the "six thinking hats" strategy for thinking divergently about problems rather than jumping to conclusions (deBono, 1999). Through this object, instructors or trainers would specify a problem and related resources, then provide virtual rooms or "hats" for student groups to post analyses of the problem from six divergent perspectives—thinking objectively about it, emotionally, cautiously, creatively, and so forth. Students could attach instances of certain resources in the virtual rooms to help justify their ideas.

Micro-level design objects might also be created to enable a wider selection of classroom assessment strategies in courses (Angelo & Cross, 1993). For example, an instructor might quickly employ a "defining features matrix" that allows student groups to compare two or more items and mark which features are present in each.

Several constructivist learning theories are particularly well suited to inform the development of future learning object systems, as they are for design objects (Bannan-Ritland et al., 2002). Learning environments that stress context and communication are often referred to as situated learning environments (Brown, Collins, & Duguid, 1989). Situated learning environments take many forms with one premise being, "students carry out tasks and solve problems in an environment that reflects the multiple uses to which their knowledge will be put in the future" (Collins, Brown, & Newman, 1990, p. 487). Proponents of situated learning suggest schools too often decontextualize instruction into chunked units removed from natural activities, contexts, and cultures (Lave, 1988), which sounds alarmingly like the core problem associated with learning objects. To retain an emphasis on authentic context then, future design objects could allow instructors to create anchored instruction (Cognition and Technology Group at Vanderbilt, 1990) or goal-based scenarios (Schank, 1992), two well-known situated learning models. Further, cognitive flexibility theory (CFT) suggests knowledge is ultimately interrelated across a number of contexts, thus presenting information in one static form will not help learners develop flexible knowledge structures that allow information to be retrieved and used in new situations encountered (Jacobson & Spiro, 1995). A design object in line with CFT would allow the instructor to structure hypermedia to provide the learner with multiple representations of knowledge (i.e., audio, visual, spatial); alternative points of view; case studies to demonstrate a variety of applications of the same knowledge; and cross-associational content to promote the development of cognitive flexibility. Detailed macro-level design objects that support these learning theory frameworks might require more time for lesson development than concise micro-level design objects, pointing to a need for future research on teacher preferences and situation-specific usage data. Do teachers prefer the easily-deployed micro-level design objects? Under what conditions are macro-level objects employed?

Future design object research could focus on the most appropriate procedures for developing new objects. A task analysis process of the sort described by Smith and Ragan (2005), for example, could be employed to translate the necessary teacher procedures required in designing a lesson by a teaching strategy, learning model, or learning theory framework. This specification would then be used to develop the design object in support of the requisite instructor steps. Likewise, student steps in carrying out activities tied to specific strategies could be studied to build embedded support tools.

Developing new design objects is only one step, however. To increase their usability by various audiences, existing design objects should also be aligned with national and state standards for a subject area, or with subject-specific curricula. We have databases to search for instructional materials and learning objects (Joint Information Systems Committee, 2006; National Learning Network, 2006), but there is not a standard database through which instructors can search for relevant design objects according to the desired thinking activities or processes they wish to support (e.g., tools for analogical reasoning) or by the teaching strategy of interest (e.g., case analysis). In his study of the degree to which teachers practice different instructional design tactics, Branch (1994) found teachers most frequently define goals and relate lessons based on a set curriculum, and also organize content around themes. If a number of student thinking processes are recommended from a state's sixth grade science curriculum, then, it would be helpful if teachers could quickly identify design objects to help teach to these skills. Future design object research should focus not only on the overall usability of tools from a technical standpoint, but also in a practical/applied sense based on their overall "fit" with the teacher's daily classroom needs.

Conclusion

In this chapter, tools referred to as "design objects" have been presented for both teachers to develop lessons around effective teaching frameworks and students to actively process connected content resources. The term "design" is taken literally from helping teachers practice instructional design by employing effective strategies and models and their students create original knowledge designs by manipulating information. Given the concerns associated with segmented and decontextualized learning objects, design objects are recommended for the ease with which a teacher's own context or resources can be applied to a customized lesson, including but not limited to learning objects. Like a traditional learning object, the design object's instructional design shell which promotes a specific teaching strategy or learning model can be replicated and reused multiple times, however the content embedded through design objects remains locally defined to mitigate decontextualization issues associated with learning objects.

Design objects that support relatively concise and bounded teaching strategies may be considered micro level (e.g., mind mapping), while design objects that support more complex and detailed learning models may be considered macro level (e.g., case analysis). Both types emphasize the layering of original content resources into a specified teaching framework, and both include tools for students to process information in a manner consistent with the strategy/model framework and tools for teachers to manage student work (e.g., project folders, mark-up/critique).

Several development systems are available that liken to design objects by emphasizing lesson design around effective teaching frameworks, but differ in focus with an emphasis on packaging content for reuse by others rather than teaching to one's own students. Concerns with development systems are substantial and interrelated, including: lack of a learning object economy and core resources for import into the systems, teacher conceptions regarding teaching materials that may not align with developing "objects" for reuse, technical issues associated with using development systems, and the lack of control given to teachers and students through some systems. Good learning design systems based on the import and packaging of learning objects around effective teaching frameworks are feasible, but lack a current practicality for many teachers based on these constraints. Each of the constraints provides a potential line of research in terms of variables that can be manipulated to potentially improve or detract from overall system usability. A hybrid system may be one of the more usable structures, taking the best prescriptive features from development systems, and combining those prescriptions with design objects for immediate application to a classroom and a teacher's contextualized resources.

More design objects and refinements are needed to ensure their practicality for teachers. Design objects are needed to support core thinking skills and processes that many teachers are required to foster among students. Design objects that allow teachers to employ effective teaching models or learning theories in the classroom are also needed. Complete sets or toolboxes with multiple design objects might increase overall applicability (e.g., a set of design objects for promoting classroom assessment strategies), as would alignment of design objects with state standards and curricula for different grade-levels and subjects. Sources of future research on design objects cross from developers to teachers to students: appropriate analytic procedures for translating the embedded steps in teaching strategies and learning models into teacher and student tools; training, embedded/prescriptive support, and/or curricular ties required for different teachers to utilize design objects successfully; types of design objects most frequently utilized by teachers and the classroom environment conditions that lead to this choice; and student learning and metacognition when using individual or combined design objects.

Design objects provide many teachers with effective frameworks for structuring content resources and engaging their students in constructive activities. Their flexibility for contextualizing original lessons with any available resource makes them a practical option for teachers wishing to leverage the growing body of online information in the classroom.

References

Ainsworth, S., & Fleming, P. (2005). Evaluating authoring tools for teachers as instructional designers. *Computers in Human Behavior, 22*(1), 131-148.

Angelo, T. A., & Cross, K. P. (1993). *Classroom assessment techniques: A handbook for college teachers* (2nd ed.). San Fransisco: Jossey-Bass.

Bannan-Ritland, B., Dabbagh, N., & Murphy, K. (2002). Learning object systems as constructivist learning environments: Related assumptions, theories, and applications. In D.A. Wiley (Ed.), *The instructional use of learning objects* (pp. 61-97). Bloomington, IN: Agency for Instructional Technology and Association for Educational Communications and Technology.

Baruque, L. B., & Melo, R. N. (2004). Learning theory and instruction design using learning objects. *Journal of Educational Multimedia and Hypermedia, 13*(4), 343-370.

Bradley, C., & Boyle, T. (2004). The design, development, and use of multimedia learning objects. *Journal of Educational Multimedia and Hypermedia, 13*(4), 371-389.

Branch, R. C. (1994). Common instructional design practices employed by secondary school teachers. *Educational Technology, 34*(3), 25-34.

Brown, J. S., Collins, A., & Duguid, P. (1989). Situated cognition and the culture of learning. *Educational Researcher, 18*(1), 32-41.

Center for Internet Imaging and Database Systems. (2005). *IThink: A case analysis tool.* Retrieved February 13, 2007, from http://www.ciids.org/index. cfm?show=ithink

Cognition and Technology Group at Vanderbilt. (1990). Anchored instruction and its relationship to situated cognition. *Educational Researcher, 19*(5), 2-10.

Cognition and Technology Group at Vanderbilt. (1993). Anchored instruction and situated cognition revisited. *Educational Technology, 33*(3), 52-70.

Collins, A., Brown, J. S., & Newman, S. E. (1990). Cognitive apprenticeship: Teaching the crafts of reading, writing, and mathematics. In L. B. Resnick (Ed.), *Knowing, learning, and instruction: Essays in honor of Robert Glaser* (pp. 453-494). Hillsdale, NJ: Lawrence Erlbaum.

deBono, E. (1999). *Six thinking hats*. New York: Back Bay Books.

Dodds, P., & Fletcher, J. D. (2004). Opportunities for new "smart" learning environments enabled by next-generation Web capabilities. *Journal of Educational Multimedia and Hypermedia, 13*(4), 391-404.

Duval, E., Hodgins, W., Rehak, D., & Robson, R. (2004). Learning objects symposium special issue guest editorial. *Journal of Educational Multimedia and Hypermedia, 13*(4), 331-342.

Earle, R. (1998). Instructional design and teacher planning: Reflections and perspectives. In R. Branch & M. Fitzgerald (Eds.), *Educational media and technology yearbook* (23rd ed., pp. 36-45). Englewood, CO: Libraries Unlimited.

Frey, C. (2004). *Free creative thinking tools on the Web*. Retrieved March 19, 2007, from http://www.innovationtools.com/Article/ArticleDetails.asp?a=155

Garrison, J. W. (1995). Deweyan pragmatism and the epistemology of contemporary social constructivism. *American Educational Research Journal, 32*, 716-740.

Hannafin, M. J., Land, S., & Oliver, K. M. (1999). Open learning environments: Foundations, methods, and models. In C. Reigeluth (Ed.), *Instructional-de-*

sign theories and models: Volume II (pp. 115-140). Mahwah, NJ: Lawrence Erlbaum Associates.

Heinich, R. (1995). The proper study of instructional technology. In G. J. Anglin (Ed.), *Instructional technology: Past, present, and future* (2nd ed., pp. 314-321). Englewood, CO: Libraries Unlimited.

Intel®. (2006). *Intel® Teach to the Future Workshop on Teaching Thinking with Technology.* Retrieved February 13, 2007, from http://www97.intel.com/education/teach/workshops/index.asp

Ip, A., Linser, R., & Naidu, S. (2001, April). *Simulated worlds: Rapid generation of Web-based role-play.* Paper presented at the 7th Australian World Wide Web Conference, Coffs Harbour, New South Wales. Retrieved February 13, 2007, from http://ausweb.scu.edu.au/aw01/papers/refereed/ip/paper.html

Jacobson, M. J., & Spiro. R. J. (1995). Hypertext learning environments, cognitive flexibility, and the transfer of complex knowledge: An empirical investigation. *Journal of Educational Computing Research, 12*(4), 301-333.

Joint Information Systems Committee. (2006). JORUM. Retrieved February 13, 2007, from http://www.jorum.ac.uk/

Jonassen, D., Peck, K., & Wilson, B. (1999). *Learning with technology: A constructivist perspective.* Upper Saddle River, NJ: Prentice Hall.

Kang, M., Lim, D. H., & Kim, M. (2004). Learning designer: A theory-based SCORM-compliant content development tool. *Journal of Educational Multimedia and Hypermedia, 13*(4), 427-447.

Koppi, T., Bogle, L., Hodgson, N., & Lavitt, N. (2004). Institutional use of learning objects: Lessons learned and future directions. *Journal of Educational Multimedia and Hypermedia, 13*(4), 449-463.

Lave, J. (1988). *The culture of acquisition and the practice of understanding* (IRL Report #88-00087). Palo Alto, CA: Institute for Research on Learning.

Liber, O. (2005). Learning objects: Conditions for viability. *Journal of Computer Assisted Learning, 21*(5), 366-373.

Longmire, W. (2000). A primer on learning objects. *Learning Circuits, 1*(3). Retrieved February 13, 2007, from http://www.learningcircuits.org/2000/mar2000/Longmire.htm

Lukasiak, J., Agostinho, S., Burnett, I., Drury, G., Goodes, J., Bennett, S., et al. (2004). A framework for the flexible content packaging of learning objects and learning designs. *Journal of Educational Multimedia and Hypermedia, 13*(4), 465-481.

Merrill, M. D., & Thompson, B. (1999). IDXelerator: Learning-centered instructional design. In J. V. D. Akker, R. M. Branch, K. Gustafson, N. Nieveen, &

T. Plomp (Eds.), *Design methodology and development research in education and training* (pp. 265-277). Boston: Kluwer Academic Publishers.

Michalko, M. (1991). *Thinkertoys: A handbook of business creativity for the 90's.* Berkeley, CA: Ten Speed Press.

National Learning Network. (2006). Retrieved February 13, 2007, from http://www.nln.ac.uk/index.asp

Northrup, P. T., Rasmussen, K. L., & Pilcher, J. K. (2001). Support for Teachers Enhancing Performance in Schools (STEPS): An EPSS professional development tool. In B. H. Khan (Ed.), *Web-based training* (p. 469-474). Englewood Cliffs, NJ: Educational Technology Publications.

Oliver, K. M. (2001). Recommendations for student tools in online course management systems. *Journal of Computing in Higher Education, 13*(1), 47-70.

Parrish, P. E. (2004). The trouble with learning objects. *Educational Technology Research and Development, 52*(1), 49-67.

Partnership for 21st Century Skills (2004). *The road to 21st century learning: a policymakers' guide to 21st century skills.* Washington, DC: Author.

Pickles, T. (1996). *Tool kit for trainers: A compendium of techniques for trainers and group workers.* Tucson, AZ: Fisher Books.

Presseisen, B. Z. (2001). Thinking skills: Meanings and models revisited. In A. L. Costa (Ed.), *Developing minds: A resource book for teaching thinking* (3rd ed., pp. 47-53). Alexandria, VA: Association for Supervision and Curriculum Development.

Schank, R. C. (1992). *Goal-based scenarios* (Tech. Rep. No. 36). Evanston, IL: Northwestern University, Institute for the Learning Sciences.

Smith, P. L., & Ragan, T. J. (2005). *Instructional design* (3rd ed.). Hoboken, NJ: John Wiley & Sons.

Wiley, D., Waters, S., Dawson, D., Lambert, B., Barclay, M., Wade, D., et al. (2004). Overcoming the limitations of learning objects. *Journal of Educational Multimedia and Hypermedia, 13*(4), 507-521.

Williams, M., Linn, M. C., Ammon, P., & Gearhart, M. (2004). Learning to teach inquiry science in a technology-based environment: A case study. *Journal of Science Education and Technology, 13*(2), 189-206.

Chapter IX

Using Learning Objects for Rapid Deployment to Mobile Learning Devices for the U.S. Coast Guard

Pamela T. Northrup, University of West Florida, USA

William T. Harrison Jr., University of West Florida & U.S. Navy, USA

Abstract

This chapter introduces the use of a learning objects content development tool, the eLearning Objects Navigator, (eLON™) as a strategy for creating, classifying, and retrieving reusable learning objects and reusable information objects. The use of eLON™ provides a context for rapid deployment of these SCORM-conformant packages to mobile learning devices as well as to learning management systems for a beta test with the U.S. Coast Guard Institute. Presented in this chapter is the underlying theoretical framework for the development of eLON™ as well as the specific design decisions made regarding the deployment of PDA mobile learning devices to military personnel. Furthermore, initial results from the beta test yield positive results as well as a series of lessons learned.

Introduction

The field of distance education continues to grow as emerging technologies present new opportunities to distribute learning anytime, anywhere. As more students choose distance learning to achieve college and career goals, universities are now faced with challenges to distribute learning using a variety of strategies to accommodate student needs. Military students represent a large segment of many institutions in the United States through the Department of Defense off-duty voluntary education programs. Each year, approximately 300,000 service personnel enroll in voluntary education with universities making it one of the largest continuing education operations in the world (Department of Defense, 2003). As a result, universities with a strong military presence must be flexible to accommodate deployments, temporary duty, lack of Internet access, intermittent Internet access, and more. The level of flexibility required by military personnel pursuing educational degrees presents unique challenges to those who design distance learning instructional materials on university campuses. From creating blended learning opportunities to duplicative design across numerous delivery approaches, the time spent developing fully online programs and courses can easily exceed man-hours available on university campuses. Currently, the majority of higher education programs offered to the military are self-contained, nonflexible existing programs that may not meet the needs of individual service personnel that may be deployed, underway, or unable to access the Internet for an extended period of time. In an attempt to meet the need, the University of West Florida has partnered with the U.S. Coast Guard Institute and two community colleges, Florida Community College at Jacksonville and Coastline Community College to develop and beta test college level courses on a personal digital assistant (PDA). Given that few models currently exist for this mode of course development, the University of West Florida chose to develop all content using a learning objects content development tool, eLON™ for purposes of consistency and reuse across multiple delivery platforms.

Within the partnership, the community colleges agreed to offer a selection of general education courses, while UWF agreed to offer graduate level courses. For the beta test, UWF selected to offer a 12 semester hour graduate certificate in human performance technology.

The Beta Test with the U.S. Coast Guard

The U.S. Coast Guard Institute provided several specifications in the partnership to beta test the PDA as a viable mobile learning solution for Coast Guard personnel. The participants in the UWF study included those interested in the program area offered on PDA, including a graduate certificate in human performance technology (HPT). UWF students were recruited from several Coast Guard sectors including Key West, Islamorada, Miami, and the Yorktown Training Center. Students participating had to enroll at UWF to receive their tuition assistance or VA benefits. Students were then afforded access to all UWF student services. Since UWF is a SOCCoast Afloat institution, the programs offered had already been moved through the program approval process with other partnering institutions.

There were several restrictions placed on the selection and use of a mobile device that may be used on a Coast Guard cutter. All devices were required to have both Bluetooth and wireless disabled prior to use on a cutter for purposes of shipboard security. This presented some unique difficulties as most mobile devices offered these features with few companies or software applications in place at the time to disable both Bluetooth and wireless.

There were several design requirements that would ultimately affect the design models selected for development. We were asked to provide a bookmarking feature to enable users to pick up where they left off as many service personnel shipboard may have limited times available for study and may need to stop working at a moment's notice. With regard to access, we were required to design all materials for stand-alone use on the PDA in the event that Internet access was not available. For student assessment purposes, we were required to work with the educational services officer (ESO) to proctor and certify all exams. The ESO also served as the primary point of contact for the institution on behalf of the Coast Guard. The ESO received all shipments of PDAs, print materials, assessments, and directions for the return of materials. As an advocate for the Coast Guard personnel, the ESO in many cases also worked to assist students in receiving their tuition assistance or in filing any additional paperwork required.

Issues Faced

The Academic Technology Center is tasked with designing, developing, and implementing all distance learning endeavors at UWF and has been very successful in designing fully online courses, blended courses, and interactive distance learning classrooms using two-way interactive video. However, until this beta test, the opportunity to design instruction for mobile devices did not exist. Issues related to the overarching design needed to be made to compensate for the lack of Internet access and subsequent lack of interaction between students and the instructor. As well, the PDA operating system had limited software applications available to deliver best-fit instructional strategies. For example, the Pocket PC did not include a PowerPoint viewer, thus requiring conversion of the PowerPoint presentations to a compatable format for the PDA. Finally, issues of faculty and student use of this new model of learning took some time. Faculty learning how to design content as a subject matter expert and to include everything needed for individualized instruction required a great deal of work, even for faculty members with expertise in developing online learning. As well, the role of the faculty member and student shifted in this more individualized environment. The issue of providing feedback to students in a timely fashion became a major hurdle for faculty. For students, issues included how to seek advice, guidance and direction from the instructor when Internet access was limited or not available.

An additional issue faced included a change in the development process typically used in the Academic Technology Center. The reality of work effort required to develop courses on a PDA and provide flexible, duplicate courses available for those able to access on the Web through the learning management system required us to rethink our whole design process. With this change, two major issues emerged. First, the development of content for multiple delivery containers required a strategy to develop content systematically so that it could be exported and reused in a variety of ways. This required significant thought as design for a mobile device such as the PDA requirements may be different from the requirements used for designing Web-based instruction. This issue enabled us to think more broadly about learning objects, issues of granularity, consistency, and technical specifications for specific assets, such as sizing PowerPoint presentations or creating Flash applications. Considerations for using graphics, the amount of text and overall screen geography immediately became in an issue.

In line with the new considerations for design, not only did faculty and instructional designers collaborate on overall design, it was essential for faculty members to finish their efforts early enough to allow technical personnel the time needed to export the developed content from our learning objects content development tool, eLON™ to the secure digital (SD) chip, which at the time, could only be made one at a time.

Foundational Models

Without a body of research or best practice on developing mobile learning, there was extensive research and development work to be done before proceeding. The first step in this endeavor was to create a theoretical framework to serve as a guide for all design decisions made in the project. As a theoretical framework we chose Gagne's (1985) *events of instruction* as the major frame for *pre-instruction, instruction*, and *post-instruction* as a sound model representing the external events necessary to align to the internal processes of learning. These events should satisfy or provide the necessary conditions for learning and serve as the basis for designing instruction and selecting appropriate media (Gagne, Briggs, & Wager, 1992).

The flexibility of the model to align to a variety of learning outcomes and instructional tactics and strategies met the needs of this design effort. An additional benefit of using the events of instruction included its alignment to the Cisco model of creating reusable learning objects and reusable information objects. The Cisco model was constructed based on the foundational work of Merrill's (1994) component display theory and others. The linkage of Gagne's events of instruction and Cisco's model gave way to the inclusion of specific learning outcome specification templates that are embedded within eLON™. These eLON™ specifications include one template for each major learning outcome specified by Bloom's taxonomy enabling designers to select the most appropriate reusable learning object specification template.

Interaction and Feedback

With intermittent to no Internet access available, the instructional design and content development process required a complete reconsideration of the role of interaction in a distance environment. According to Moore (1989), typical online interaction includes: (1) peer-to-peer opportunities such as dialog in threaded discussions, small group assignments, and the theme of working with a partner; (2) student-to-instructor interaction including opportunities for assignment clarification, chat room events, threaded discussion with faculty participation to scaffold the process, and ongoing feedback on correctness of assignments; and (3) student-to-content interaction where the student interacts with the instructional materials by reading, participating in on-line simulations, and searching the Web for specific information. Since all possible interaction scenarios are not available in the mobile learning environment, design decisions were made to compensate for limited student-to-student interaction and student-to-instructor interaction, while designing strong processes for student-to-content interaction. Since we know that interaction is a key component in successful online learning (Northrup, 2002a), it is critical to make good decisions at this point to ensure student success in the mobile learning environment.

The feedback literature has long prescribed feedback models for purposes of learning and assessment. Kulhavey and Wager (1993) suggest that feedback on incorrect responses assists in further understanding specific concepts, which is the method designed into instruction. Mory's (1992) review of the feedback literature suggests that feedback has long been advocated as an important part of the learning process that historically has been used for purposes of reinforcement in behaviorist learning environments, but now being used more for error correction.

What We Know About Distance Learning

Distance learning has been around for quite some time, initially entering the main-stream of universities as correspondence courses. The correspondence model, an example of individual learning, was used nearly exclusively for the first 120 years of distance education in the United States (Moore & Kearsley, 1996). According to a recent Sloan Report (2005), over 2.35 million students in the U.S. participated in online education in 2004, which is up from 1.98 million in 2003. Most online program and course offerings use the Internet as the type of access for students through a learning management system such as Desire2Learn, WebCT, or Black-board. What has been found from years of research on distance learning are some guiding principles that became design requirements in the PDA course development model with the U.S. Coast Guard. There are many benchmarks that align to quality and distance learning (Kane, 2004) including the need for quality curriculum and student support. However, one of the most significant attributes for success in on-line learning has been the student's ability to interact with other students, in both a social and instructional environment. A recent study indicated that 90% of students cited interaction with the instructor and other students as one of the major reasons for staying in the course (Northrup, 2002a).

Interaction serves many purposes. First and foremost, it engages the learner with other students and the instructor and enables the instructor to provide the necessary scaffolding to achieve successful learning outcomes. When interaction is limited or not available, course retention and overall student satisfaction may be negatively impacted. Interaction also serves to assist in developing the students' social network. Distance students are isolated from others just by the nature of participating in a course remotely. In a campus-based course, students naturally form social groups by talking with one another after class, sitting together, or forming after class study groups. Each of these approaches help cement student success in college. Online, these social groups may not naturally emerge and it is essential to design experiences for getting to know one another into an online course. Student connection to other students remains a need, whether online or face-to-face.

Research also indicates that technical issues present a series of challenges to the student and the student's desire to stay engaged in school. Providing technical support such as a help desk, a student support center, an 800 number, or some type of FAQ repository will increase student success.

Another item that holds true across teaching and learning endeavors includes early success. Students with early, incremental success will build confidence and to continue with their schooling.

Finally, designing instruction that includes significant student engagement will increase opportunities for deeper processing of knowledge and ultimately remembering and hopefully applying what is learned.

Figure 1. eLON™ learning objects export architecture

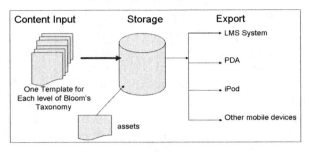

Learning Objects

Learning objects have been a major topic of discussion for the past several years with heated debates focusing on data standardization, interoperability, metadata, and SCORM. Most absent in the discussion are those responsible for designing instruction using learning objects. As a result, less attention has been given to standardization and optimization of instructional elements to be included, used, and reused. In the effort to frame the role of learning objects in the development of mobile learning instruction, we adopted and modified Cisco's model (Barritt & Alderman, 2004) for developing reusable learning objects and reusable information objects.

UWF developed and is implementing a rapid learning objects content development tool called eLearning Objects Navigator (eLON™). eLON™ enables UWF instructional designers in the Academic Technology Center and content experts to create instructional content and learning objects within eLON™ and export it to the PDA Secure Digital (SD) chip as well as running a secondary export to the university's learning management system, Desire2Learn for a second section of the course to be offered fully online. A unique benefit is that students needing ongoing flexibility can take part of the course on the PDA and the remainder online as dictated by military duty assignments.

Learning Objects Framework

To accommodate a pedagogically sound framework and given the Coast Guard requirement to provide bookmarking and location identification, we also included an extensive menu system, classified into menu items by learning object title and type. We adopted a modified version of the Cisco model (Barritt & Alderman, 2004) to classify objects as reusable learning objects (RLOs) and reusable information objects (RIOs). The classification scheme enabled us to classify RLOs as complete sessions, with five to seven RIOs making up a complete RLO (see Figure 2).

Figure 2. Reusable learning objects

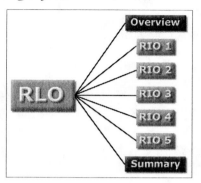

Figure 3. Mapping of knowledge models to learning object types

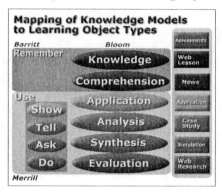

The classification scheme allowed us also to organize the menus around complete sessions making up an introduction, five to seven topics (RIOs), and a summary. This classification scheme was used to generate the menu system and subsequent bookmarking to the RIO level.

Additionally, we incorporated six templates, one for each learning outcome type specified by Bloom's (1956) Taxonomy as a way to establish explicit categories for each learning objects type. Each template represents a level of learning to accommodate the type of instruction that may be designed for specific learning outcomes. For example, for knowledge-level outcomes, selections may include tutorials, while higher order outcomes may include case studies. The templates provide an appropriate instructional strategy as well as maintaining consistency across reusable learning objects (see Figure 3).

Issues

Developing learning objects for a project using multiple instructional designers and faculty members presented challenges as many items needed resolution quickly. Major issues included decisions on metadata, granularity, context, and reuse.

- **Metadata:** Metadata was one of the first issues requiring resolution. *Metadata* is generally defined as "data about data." In some disciplines, this is translated to describe information about a set of data in a particular representation. However, in content management and information architecture, metadata generally means "information about objects," that is, information about a document, an image, a RLO, a RIO, an asset, or other object type. Dublin Core, as one well recognized standard for metadata was intended to support information retrieval or discovery of resources. However, it is now commonly agreed that the metadata are as useful for the management of content as they are for the discovery of them after publication, and so metadata in practice tend to be used for both purposes.

  Defining the level of metadata to provide at the beginning of the development process proved challenging. Faculty resisted completing all metadata fields, and when they did complete, there were major inconsistencies in keyword identification and object descriptions. When course content was similar, keywords were so similar that it was difficult to differentiate from the titles, thus creating an ineffective strategy for resource discovery or management. In our lessons learned, in the next effort, we will assign one person to develop the keywords from an index of course-related topics.

- **Granularity:** Although granularity is routinely an issue when developing learning objects, in this effort, with a commonly defined template and agreement to use the guiding principles that specify limitations on text, large graphics, and PowerPoint, there were not as many issues. It was our decision to create RLOs with accompanying RIOs and couple them as intact reusable learning objects, translated in the PDA course to a complete session. In later situations, if RIOs are reused, the architecture of the RIO as defined by some as a sharable courseware object (SCO) will allow consumers to use more granular RIOs, or even select to use the assets embedded within the RIOs themselves. Although the RLO with accompanying RIOs were intact for this effort, we have intentionally left the option available to drill down to the asset level in the eLON™ tool as well as providing the ability to create subsequent versions while retaining the original version of the asset or RIO. At any point, the RLOs could be reconfigured with other existing RIOs as well.

- **Context:** The context issue is resolved when this decision is made as introductions and summaries can be tied to the specific topics at hand. The issue with context was more tied to reuse on multiple delivery platforms. For example, descriptive information on what to do in the online version of the courses was a bit different from descriptive information on the PDA version of the course.

- **Reuse:** In many articles on learning objects, the focus is on initial development using highly defined specifications and metadata. What is not addressed as well in the literature is the capacity of learning objects to be reused. Initially eLON™ was designed with four major goals:

  o   To promote *consistency* across a single course and among a group of courses in a program

  o   To promote *efficiency* in the process of designing and developing Web-based courses

  o   To promote *reuse* and *content sharing* across courses and between faculty members if chosen by content owners

  o   To improve *overall course quality* by providing a series of pedagogically sound *templates* aligned to specified learning outcomes that *store* instructional *content*

For this project, an additional goal was included to reuse content across learning platforms. This has in effect been the major outcome of our investigation with the Coast Guard that we can successfully design high quality content once, thus increasing design efficiency and rapid deployment of content to multiple delivery containers. In working with the military, there are numerous available learning technologies; therefore our goal is to export learning objects across these major platforms using robust metadata tied to specifications within stylesheets and hooked through the manifests available in the export function of eLON™. Our design decision to export the RIOs together with the RLOs as a complete SCORM package will encourage reuse across major platforms but reduces the granularity of the object. However, the objects can be separated into discrete reusable information objects and assets, thus increasing the level of granularity and ultimately the capacity to reuse in other learning environments.

Guiding Principles for PDA Development

From this brief knowledge base, a set of guiding principles have been developed in an attempt to address the specifications identified by the U.S. Coast Guard Institute.

Considerations included the issues faced initial research and development of mobile learning, the constructed theoretical framework along with what is known about distance learning and translate to practice in a mobile learning environment using the following guiding principles for PDA development:

1.   All course materials designed will use an RLO template available in eLON™ for purposes of consistency.

2.   All course materials will be cataloged for retrieval using common identifiers that will export to the menu.

3.   All cataloged RIOs will be hooked to a larger RLO for purposes of export and to maintain state with the menu specifications allowing for bookmarking.

4.   Each session will include a brief video to personalize the instruction and to motivate students.

5.   Each session will select multiple media approaches to deliver instructional content, limited text and capitalizing on audio narrated PowerPoint short lectures, video, and Flash simulations and animations.

6.   PowerPoint presentations will be focused on individual topics or RIOs, will minimize text and bullets, and will be no longer than 10 minutes in length.

7.   PowerPoint presentations will attempt to tell stories to align bullets to real experiences.

8.   Each session will have minimal use of detailed graphics due to the size of the screen display. Detailed graphics should be placed in print materials.

9.   Each session will use self-check questioning to accommodate for limited interaction.

10.   Each self-check question should provide corrective feedback enabling the learner to continue learning while participating in the self-check portion of the session.

11.   Multiple choice assessments will be administered and proctored by a designated education services officer (ESO).

12.   All content for a single course will be placed on a SD chip, duplicated and sent to students via surface mail.

13.   All course materials will have an accompanying print-based guide and textbook to support the course.

14.   All course materials will be packaged and sent to the ESO contact for distribution to students on base.

Figure 4. Overarching framework for PDA session design

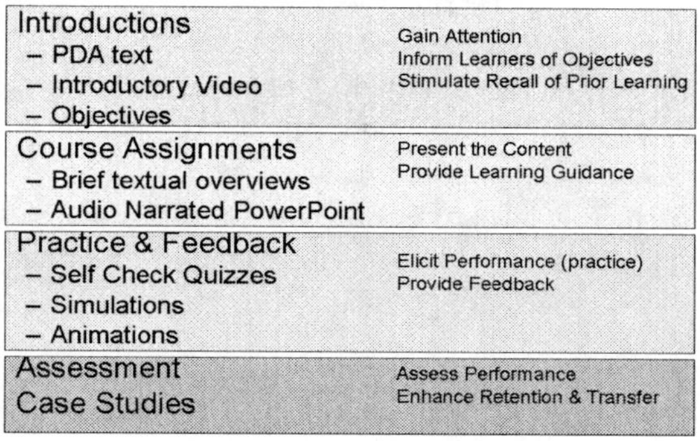

Introductions – PDA text – Introductory Video – Objectives	Gain Attention Inform Learners of Objectives Stimulate Recall of Prior Learning
Course Assignments – Brief textual overviews – Audio Narrated PowerPoint	Present the Content Provide Learning Guidance
Practice & Feedback – Self Check Quizzes – Simulations – Animations	Elicit Performance (practice) Provide Feedback
Assessment Case Studies	Assess Performance Enhance Retention & Transfer

The PDA Learning Environment

The PDA learning environment incorporates the foundations of learning and considerations for learning objects design while maintaining a simple interface and set of materials. Included in the materials sent to the student is a bag containing instructions for using the PDA and taking the course, the SD card containing the course materials, a textbook and a print packet including all PowerPoint lecture handouts, project assignment descriptions, and any worksheets required for class practice. As well, all additional readings are included given the fact that some students will be deployed, underway, or on temporary duty at some other location and do not have Internet access.

As noted in Figure 4, each session includes an introduction that is intended to provide a motivating anchor for the session that includes text, video, and written session objectives. The actual course assignments include course content presented with minimal text and supported fully by audio narrated PowerPoint presentations. Course assignments may have several topics all tied to the major session topic and is fully documented through metadata when the content is developed.

Course practice and feedback is achieved within each session by offering a series of self-check questions to allow students to determine the level of understanding achieved at that point. If students succeed on the self-check questions, they are ready to move forward to the next session. If not, corrective feedback is intended to guide students to the correct response, or students can repeat the session. This section was incorporated due to the lack of student-to-student and student-to-instructor interaction. This effort, at a minimum, allowed students to judge whether or not they were on track and gain immediate feedback on their responses to self-check items. Additional strategies used within the course practice and feedback section included short Flash-based simulations, a study guide, and encouragement to partner with another student in collaboration on course-based issues.

Assessing retention and transfer was encouraged through the use of standard multiple choice assessments, papers, projects, and field work. Standard closed-book assessments were paper-based and proctored by the U.S. Coast Guard's ESOs and returned to UWF via surface mail. Papers, projects, and field work were returned to us either electronically (through e-mail or the learning management system drop box) or delivered via surface mail. To encourage transfer, one major case study was embedded in each course. Case studies are intended to engage students fully in a real-world case and apply newly learned information immediately.

Components of the PDA Course

Each PDA delivered course is developed in 12 complete sessions. Each session is equal to one reusable learning object. Each RLO contains an introduction, five to seven RIOs, and a summary. Evidenced in the following examples are the components of a session RLO. Students enter the course through a main menu that provides them with basic information about the instructor, the course syllabus, the course assignment sheet, about the class, and the course content materials.

Each section is intended to align to items a student would need to be successful in class and to encourage and personalize the content as much as possible. Another significant variable while maintaining a strict representation of the events of instruction, Keller's (1987) ARCS model was woven throughout each session by presenting a motivating introduction, embedding video, promoting opportunities for successful small steps, and provided relevant case studies to apply newly learned knowledge.

- **Session introduction:** The session introductions include a brief video by the instructor talking about the upcoming session. The video is typically two to three minutes and provides the hook for each session. Students have noted that this short clip provides a connection to the instructor and to provide them with a sense of connectedness to the course. So, the brief videos as well serve as a motivational segment and a layer of interaction, albeit a small one. Also in the session introduction is the goals for the session and a paragraph or so describing upcoming events. Within the RIO, the introduction is tied to the content and the practice as a complete reusable information object package.

- **Content presentation:** The content RIOs include several "topics" that are further classified into small content objects to align to the Cisco model. The presentation of content presented some unique challenges as we tried to balance the media to limit the amount of text scrolling on the PDA, to take advantage of the outstanding video and audio available on the PDA, and to ensure multiple modes of media are presented to the learner. Within this section, audio nar-

Figure 5. Content presentation example

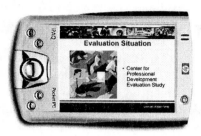

Figure 6. Immediate feedback example

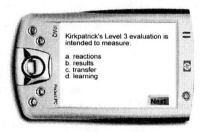

rated PowerPoint presentations were used consistently as the course lecture, while limited text extended the presentations providing further descriptions as needed (see Figure 5).

- **Immediate feedback:** As a major strategy for interaction, students are presented with self-check questions and feedback at the end of each instructional session. The self-check questions are tied to each RIO although they receive the items at the end of a session. If students do not perform well on the RIO, they can go back into the individual sections to review and retake the self-check. The self-check is not graded, but is used as an embedded cognitive strategy for students to self-assess and self-regulate their learning (see Figure 6).

- **Case studies:** During the second half of each 12 week course, students are presented with a case study of a real-world situation in an attempt to apply newly learned information to encourage retention and transfer. Case studies provide relevance to the course by engaging students in real-world practice, discussing real-world issues that are typically ill-structured and not always completely defined with one accurate, correct response. Cases cut across a range of fields including the military, financial management, corporate training, and the information technology industry. Case studies done online or face to face can be easily scaffolded by the instructor. In a mobile learning environment, this was a challenging task. Much scaffolding had to be pre-prescribed rather than guiding students to "ah-ha" moments. Much data are provided, worksheets, surveys, schematics, notes, and whatever else is required to filter through the information to discuss and ultimately make a decision. For students with Internet access at some point in the course, clarification and communication with others could be provided in that manner. For the full PDA courses, students had to make some of their own assumptions and describe their positions in their final analysis and case study reports.

Initial Findings

The beta test of U.S. Coast Guard students is complete with 20 of 20 students finishing their certificates in human performance technology. The HPT is a graduate level certificate and most of the completers were midcareer military and civilian professionals or retired military. The experience and age range of students participating in the beta test allowed us to look at the midcareer student, in contract with students served by the community colleges. As students mature, their experiences with the technology would be different than students who are undergraduate, 18 to 21 year olds.

As an incentive, each student was allowed to keep the PDA for participation in the effort. Overall, students participating in the beta test were satisfied with their experience and achieved equivalent grades to students participating in UWF's fully online HPT program. Reported will be student satisfaction comments as measured through a self-report survey and a focus group interview, test score comparisons, and their issues and suggestions for change.

Satisfaction

Overall, 100% of students completing the survey indicated satisfaction with the PDA course, with 83% indicating they would take another course in the program. Ironically, not only did 100% of the students participating in the beta test complete the program, more students joined as a result. Once students became comfortable with the technology, the fears of learning on a PDA virtually disappeared. 83% of the students reported that the courses met their goals and that it was relevant to them.

With regard to media usage, 100% of the students indicated satisfaction with the audio-narrated PowerPoint presentations and the self-check questions. Both were perceived to be very practical and usable for their course experience. The introductory course video that we incorporated for motivation was reported by 91% of students to align to their course needs. The bookmarking feature was successfully used by 83% of the students.

Eighty-four percent of students reported the overall course structure to work for them incorporating the menus, the cookie crumb trail as a notation of location information such as "where you have been" and "current location." Seventy-five percent of students reported that the directions were clear and understandable. The 12 week timeframe was reported to be just the right amount of time for 92% of the students. In focus group sessions, discussion focused on the amount of work required for the course. In later courses, more rigorous course requirements existed with less specific instructions requiring students to think more deeply about course direction. Students indicated that possibly later courses may need to be lengthened to provide time for reflection and completion of course materials.

Interaction

Recalling that interaction is a key component in successful online learning (Northrup, 2002b), there were three types of interaction described by the literature including student-to-instructor, peer-to-peer, and student-to-content. The PDA environment lent itself well to the student-to-content interaction, but was less able to design a robust system for peer-to-peer and student-to-instructor interaction. However, students who had Internet access at any time during the course were highly encouraged to log on and participate with the group. As well, students were encouraged to check in with the instructor for any clarification needed on assignments and projects.

In an attempt to find out how students interacted with the instructor, a series of questions were asked about the frequency of both peer-to-peer and student-to-instructor interaction through e-mail, online through the learning management system, or through phone calls. An additional question was posed asking how many students requested feedback from the instructor. Students reported interaction with the instructor as follows: 91% of students had the opportunity to interact via e-mail, 78% through the LMS, and 27% of students had the opportunity to interact via phone call.

An additional line of questioning attempted to determine how students interacted with peers throughout the course. Ninety-two percent of students had the opportunity to interact with peers throughout the course. The beta test provided strong cohorts where several students from single locations would participate together. In some cases, the social interaction evidenced through the course included students riding in to work together while one drove the other would be playing the lectures on the PDA, and then talking about the assignments together. In other cases, students collaborated in the office and online via the threaded discussions when possible. At no time during this test was Internet participation a requirement, but it was encouraged when available to encourage camaraderie and the community of learners that form in cohort environments. One hundred percent of students reported that they were able to discuss course content with peers at some level with 42% of students indicating that they interacted with peers through e-mail while 58% of students interacted through the learning management system's threaded discussions.

Open-Ended Comments

Course comments related specifically to the level of access and flexibility provided to empower students to continue learning where ever they may be. In some cases, the ability to take the course materials to little league fields and on the road for traveling encouraged students to continue learning and afforded them the opportunities they would not have had if having to sit in a classroom at a designated time and place. Overwhelmingly positive statements about convenience, access and flexibility were provided.

Suggestions for Change

Students did make several suggestions for change; however, most of them were directly related to the technology itself. Some of the issues included the fact that the screen was too small and the battery life was not as long as hoped. Of course, newer technologies will likely assist with both screen size and battery life. One of the suggestions was to include an additional battery or a car charger cable. Another suggestion was to include a keyboard attachment so that responses could be generated directly on the PDA. In the courses offered by UWF, we purposefully did not have a great deal of writing requirements, however, had a keyboard been included, we likely would have included some additional assignments and is under consideration for future courses.

Summary

In conclusion, the U.S. Coast Guard beta test did suggest that mobile learning devices such as PDAs could successfully be used for voluntary education. Given the lack of research in the field of mobile learning design, this chapter presented a framework for consideration using learning objects defined as reusable learning objects and reusable information objects to align to pedagogically sound instructional practice. Embedded as well were instructional strategies most appropriate to achieve educational learning outcomes. The use of learning objects accomplished several tasks including design efficiency and consistency across designers. The most significant aspect of using learning objects for the design of mobile learning instruction is the ability to export the same instruction to other mobile devices and to learning management systems for online learning.

References

Barritt, C., & Alderman, F. L. (2004). *Creating a reusable learning objects strategy: Leveraging information and learning in a knowledge economy.* San Francisco: Pfeiffer.

Bloom, B. S. (1956). *Taxonomy of educational objectives* (Handbook I: The cognitive domain). New York: David McKay.

Department of Defense. (2003). *DoD voluntary education.* Retrieved on February 10, 2007, from http://www.voled.doded.mil/voled_web/VolEdProgramScope.htm

Gagne, R. (1985). *The conditions of learning* (4th ed.). New York: Holt, Rinehart & Winston.

Gagne, R., Briggs, L., & Wager, W. (1992). *Principles of instructional design* (4th ed.). Fort Worth, TX: HBJ College Publishers.

Kane, K. (2004). *Maryland online. Quality matters.* Sponsored in part by the Fund for the Improvement of Postsecondary Education (FIPSE), U.S. Department of Education. Retrieved on February 10, 2007, from http://www.qualitymatters.org/index.html

Keller, J. M. (1987). Development and use of the ARCS model of motivational design. *Journal of Instructional Development, 10*(3), 2-10.

Kulhavey, R. W., & Wager, W. (1993). Feedback in programmed instruction: Historical context and implications for practice. In J. V. Dempsey & G. C. Sales (Eds.), *Interactive instruction and feedback.* Englewood Cliffs, NJ: Educational Technology Publications.

Merrill, M. D. (1994). *Instructional design theory.* Englewood Cliffs, NJ: Educational Technology Publications.

Moore, M. G. (1989). Three types of interaction. *The American Journal of Distance Education, 3*(2), 1-6.

Moore, M. G., & Kearsley, G. (1996). *Distance education: A systems view.* Belmont, CA: Wadsworth Publishing.

Mory, E. H. (1992). The use of informational feedback in instruction: Implications for future research. *Educational Technology Research and Development, 40*(3), 5-20.

Northrup, P. T. (2002a). An initial investigation of online learners' preferences for interaction. *Quarterly Review of Distance Education, 3*(2), 219-226.

Northrup, P. T. (2002b). A framework for designing interactivity into Web-based instruction. In A. Rossett (Ed.), *ASTD's e-learning handbook: Best practices, strategies and case studies for an emerging field.* Upper Saddle River, NJ: McGraw-Hill.

Sloan Consortium. (2005). *Growing by degrees: Online education in the United States.* Retrieved February 10, 2007, from http://www.sloan-c.org/publications/survey/pdf/growing_by_degrees.pdf

Chapter X

Learning Objects for Employee Training and Competency Development

Anne-Marie Armstrong, Wayne State University, USA

Abstract

Learning objects are being used more and more by the corporate training world. Their acceptance by corporate training can be attributed in part to the fact that they provided those departments with a system and tools that they could present to their decision makers—a system that aligned with corporate goals. Some of those goals included the need to train a global workforce and the need to do it in an effective, competitive, and efficient manner. The examples provided demonstrate how and why learning object systems have found success in different corporations. First content was chosen that could be developed, parsed, stored, and retrieved. The content was both reusable and migratory. Next robust systems that allow the various learning audiences to access the content and use it for various purposes were built. And finally, the benefits to the various stakeholders were successfully marketed and accepted.

Introduction

The corporate training world has for the most part embraced the concept of learning objects in one form or another. This was partly the result of the fact that the government and the military led the way and established standards and duplicable processes. But also because corporate training managers found that the inclusion of a database driven system of reusable learning objects either as a learning management system (LMS) or as a learning content management system (LCMS) was an easy sell to their upper management. The LMS and LCMS were readily accepted because the proponents were able to verify its cost-cutting potential and to tie it to the corporations' business goals. In this chapter, two case studies of the use of learning objects by training management in the corporate world are presented. The first study describes how employees and supervisors use a LMS that is tied to individual development plans to identify and verify self-paced competency development. The second study describes a LCMS that allows courses to be built, searched, modified, and repurposed with a minimum of redesign and redevelopment. However in order to understand the context within which these systems operate there is a discussion of learning objects, learning, training, and business goals.

The single laudable goal of learning objects is the use of modern information technology to make the ideas in information and learning programs accessible, useful and reusable. Think of it. What if all ideas, facts and knowledge was coded and classified in such a way that you could simply specify a few parameters, such as your current level of knowledge and your future goal, then press a button, and out of a database comes a fully formed learning sequence that guides your learning from its present state are to where you want it to be. It would be cheap too, because of the economies of scale and efficiency coming from the intelligence applied to reusing parts and pieces over and over again. It would be a philosopher's stone, created from intelligence and silicon dioxide and it is here now at least it is here for the purposes of corporate training (deSousa, in press).

Training that is deployed to tens of thousands of employees across the globe with millions of dollars of impact at stake has been implemented. And a system that captures, slices, dices, and codifies a complex corporation's knowledge exists. The problem of integrating the system into the culture of the corporation is being addressed and progress has been made.

The hope and promise of training curricula spun out of a database on the fly has been hindered by at least two significant constraints. First is the complexity of both the technology infrastructure and the classification system that permits the information to be chunked and stored in a database. This was not so much a problem as it was a fight for resources both technological and monetary within corporations. It was a fight that was won by presenting a business case that justified its expense.

The second issue was and is perhaps more difficult: corporate resistance, inertia. Contemporary corporate knowledge is easily so detailed and complex that it is difficult to believe the body of knowledge can be reduced to bite-sized chunks and bits that can be served up by a browser or some equivalent technology du jour. We do not question the value of being able to access and share, say, accounting data. But many do not believe that the rich tapestry that comprises the aggregated knowledge of a corporation can be funneled into fields in a database. So they do not begin the process of making it happen.

Requirements for Developing Learning Objects

Cisco Systems in 2000 published a white paper, "Reusable Learning Object Strategy," which is an excellent model for discussion (Cisco, 2000). In this paper they outline the steps in designing, and developing RLOs, reusable learning objects from RIOs, reusable information objects:

The RIO Strategy is built upon the Reusable Information Object (RIO). An RIO is granular, reusable chunk of information that is media independent. An RIO can be developed once, and delivered in multiple delivery mediums. Each RIO can stand alone as a collection of content items, practice items and assessment items that are combined based on a single learning objective. Individual RIOs are then combined to form a larger structure called a Reusable Learning Object (RLO).

Figure 1. Reusable information object

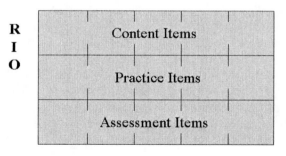

Figure 2. Reusable information object

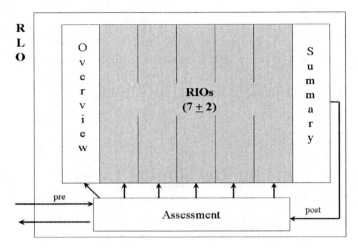

Leveraging the concepts of Bloom (1994), Clark (1999), Merrill (2000), Mager (1984), and Kirkpatrick (1996), Cisco presents a systematic template approach for the creation of chunks of learning such that:

The learner can drill into an RIO as a stand-alone performance support tool, job-aid, or just-in-time training coach. A RIO can be titled in any manner that is intuitive to the Learner given corporate style considerations. The terms "page" or "job aid" may be used generically but must fit in several delivery contexts. The learner may choose to take the entire RLO, which could be called a "lesson." As in any traditional lesson, the RLO gives the learner the needed learning context, the knowledge and skills they need to perform the given objective, and a method to assess mastery.

As with any kind of knowledge or communication, the cultural context in which it occurs has a major impact on how learning objects are used, and valued. In the development of reusable learning object delivery systems, the work of adapting delivery schema to cultural context remains substantially undone.

Cultural Variables for
Learning Objects-Based Programs

Moreover, little if any, research has been done on the requirements for delivering learning objects into multiple cultural environments. Common sense and the anecdotal recommendations of Web usability experts such as Jacob Nielsen (2000) call for testing of learning interventions by the specific intended audience, wherever and whoever they may be. Inferences for developing learning objects can be made from research such as that by Néstor Trillo (1999) who investigated the impacts of usability design on commercial automobile Web sites in various different cultural environments. As interesting as it is, his research did not result in postulates to guide development. "In other words, a developer is left unguided on how to select an appropriate cultural model, identify salient variables, collect empirical data and apply the resulting user/task/environment profile to standard design and evaluation techniques" (Trillo, 1999). There is no reason to think that the requirements of multicultural users of educational content are less demanding than the requirements for commercial Web sites. So in the end the advice of usablility experts is certainly practical and intuitively valid—test it!—but the advice has yet to be prescriptive; the research does not tell us how to make learning objects maintain meaning across multicultural boundaries.

There are many models for the evaluation of cultural variables that could serve as a lens through which to examine learning object based programs, and to estimate whether or not they are being delivered appropriately into a given culture. One example is (as described in Sánchez & Curtis, 2000) Geert Hofstede, who posits that culture is formed by values. He names four forces that distinguish cultures, and presumably the learning processes of the members of the culture: power distance, avoidance of uncertainty, individualism vs. collectivism, and masculinity vs. femininity. Power distance refers to the assumptions that a person makes about inherent inequalities in the culture; that is, is the culture hierarchical in nature or more egalitarian? Avoidance of uncertainty refers to the relative desire for structured over unstructured situations. Individualism vs. collectivism refers to the predisposition to individual initiative. And, masculinity vs. femininity refers to a cultures valuing of "tough" values vs. softer "feminine" qualities such as warmth and service.

With this model of cultural differences in mind we might imagine a Web-based training (WBT) program on safety, designed for training factory workers based in both Mexico and Austria. In our example, Mexico and Austria are chosen *for* their differences; they are polar opposites in the four dimensions of Hofstede's model (1997).

Let us say in our safety program there is a section that relates to the proper procedure for escalating safety issues to a superior or supervisor. All the required content and information has been selected and it has been properly developed using the Cisco model for creating reusable information objects. It has been properly metatagged. The quizzes' scoring systems comply with SCORM and AICC.

Clearly the goal of the program would be the same for both countries: safety. And we can suppose that most of the actual technical safety standards would be the same. Would a "safety issue" be perceived as being the same in each country, given the differences in the "masculinity" quotient for each country, where safety and toughness are likely to be differently viewed? Is there likely to be a single way that a worker should be taught to address their supervisor in both Mexico and Austria, given the different postures for power/distance in each country? Do you suppose the written procedures would even be the same, with the same amount of detail and precision given to each? It is difficult to imagine that the standards for safety could be presented in a single way that would be meaningful and persuasive in both of these two cultures, no matter how many metatags are applied. This subject, for an audience situated in places as different as in Mexico and Austria, would not be a good candidate for a single Web-based training program, no matter how smartly metatagged it might be. And while one could imagine that the basic component "objects" would be properly contextualized, it is difficult to imagine that the effort would be worthwhile in this case.

Using the examples of Austria and Mexico is deliberately extreme to make the point that cultural differences are a significant potential hurdle in the efficient and economical development of corporate knowledge sharing programs based on reusable learning objects. Most executives would perceive this issue immediately, even if only at an intuitive level. Fear of overcoming these differences is a major disincentive to launching initiatives to use these emerging technologies. Even minor differences in geographic location (one plant in the Seattle, one plant in Charlotte) can introduce cultural elements that threaten the viability of large scale technology-based training (TBT) programs.

Types of Knowledge for Learning Objects Systems

Another aspect of the more developed corporate training learning objects systems is the defining of the types of knowledge best suited for the systems. In 1991, Joseph L. Badaracco, Jr., wrote *The Knowledge Link: How Firms Compete through Strategic Alliances* (Badaracco, 1991). In his book Badaracco defines and describes at length the concepts of "migratory knowledge" and "embedded knowledge."

Migratory knowledge can move from place to place quickly—in fact more quickly all the time. It has four basic properties: (1) it resides in "packages," (2) a person or group must be capable of opening the package—of understanding and grasping the knowledge, (3) a group must have sufficient incentives to do so, and (4) no barriers must stop them. It can exist in multiple places simultaneously, and migrate in numerous directions at once. There are three basic categories of migratory knowledge: (1) designs, formulas, engineering specifications, and data; (2) knowledge contained in machines—even simple machines "know how" to do certain tasks; and (3) knowledge contained in individual minds.

Embedded knowledge "moves very slowly, even when its commercial value is high and firms have strong incentives to gain access to it" (Badaracco, 1991). Craftsmanship is his first example of embedded knowledge. He cites the example Antonio Stratevari, stringed instrument maker, as an individual who embodied heroically unique abilities and skills. Badaracco argues that companies are full of these unique sets of highly personal abilities, and that this level of knowledge is quite above the information contained in blueprints.

The next kind of embedded knowledge is the knowledge inherent in teams and groups, each of which include unique combinations of skills and abilities. This knowledge is elusive and perhaps impossible to describe completely and quantify. The firm itself is a set of knowledge and knowledge skills— "it can learn, remember and know things that none of the individuals or teams within it know. ...it is in essence a very large team, or a confederation of teams, in which enormously complex skills and knowledge are embedded in the minds of its members and in the formal and informal social relationships that orchestrate their efforts" (Badaracco, 1991).

Further, embedded knowledge and capabilities exist outside the firm—they live in relationships and interaction processes that go between firms. Similarly, there are group affiliations, relationships among trade group members, even competitors, which embody a certain kind of embedded knowledge.

Finally, he discusses geography and knowledge, the impacts of proximity and physical location. These are all examples of knowledge that does not move quickly, if at all.

Knowledge, then, can be seen as either embedded or migratory. Corporations today need to consider cutting through the staggering complexity of implementing learning systems based on knowledge objects by realizing first *what these systems perhaps cannot do very well.* When discussing *embedded* knowledge, Badaracco includes a huge percentage of total corporate knowledge. It is vastly more difficult to transmit, communicate, teach, and learn. This is the kind of knowledge that includes the corporate cultural obstacles discussed, that executives instinctively fear cannot be managed effectively through learning objects.

Corporations need to focus on migratory knowledge when first implementing a system of learning objects. It is vastly simpler to begin with migratory knowledge. At this time most corporations will, at least temporarily, suspend the notion that even a complex and comprehensive knowledge or learning management system can be built to deal effectively with the issues of culture, personal craftsmanship, and so on.

Getting into motion is essential for survival. The notion that the ability to learn quickly is the only sustainable advantage is at this point a cliché. Distributed knowledge and learning objects *are* the future. Firm standards, at least in the 1.0 release version, are virtually complete. The computers are ready and networks—even bandwidth—is just around the corner. It is better to light a candle by beginning the process of creating standards based objects dealing with "migratory" type knowledge than curse the darkness of complexity.

Obstacles for Learning Objects Stragedies

There are two significant issues that dampen wide spread enthusiasm for fully developed learning object strategies—issues which are beyond the realm of the significant technical obstacles (network bandwidth, security, etc.) that are well defined and described in the literature and the press.

The first obstacle is the challenge described previously, the struggle to deal with the "intercultural" issues faced by corporations doing business on a global stage. How do you write a program that accounts for the cultural differences that exist one place to another?

The second obstacle is subtler, the challenge of taking on what we will call the "intracultural" issues. Virtually every manager or executive "knows" that a major part of the "knowledge" that exists in a corporation on a given day cannot be written down, much less communicated through a learning object, no matter how well crafted and coded. This knowledge class includes not only what to do but how to do it, in the sense that corporate actions are inevitably political in nature and rooted in the unique style and culture of any specific company.

The sum of these two obstacles, in the presence of the relatively high costs of development for technology based training, is a hidden disincentive to enthusiastic adoption to these systems. We think upper management does not believe that these obstacles can be overcome in any way that is remotely economical. Perhaps they are correct, but several attempts are being made. In this chapter we describe two different usages of learning objects being made in two different industries. The first describes a system of learning objects in which learners identify competencies that they need for their job responsibilities and then seek sources for their own training. The second describes development system that instructional managers and designers use to populate content that can then be searched and retrieved in order to build, modify, or repurpose existing courses.

Usage of Learning Objects in Industry

The first step that the first company took was to redefine their system's goals from learning to training. This redefinition did not preclude learning but only reframed the objectives in such a way that the knowledge and competency needed to meet their business objectives could be articulated. This was vital because the company wanted to both justify the resources being expended but it also wanted to pull as much information on the needed knowledge and competencies from the performers. This knowledge was further restricted so that it represented migratory knowledge and not embedded knowledge.

The company began with the company's major goals and mission, what was required to reach the goals, and some broad headings that defined the paths for reaching those goals. Then a role and responsibility taxonomy was integrated (Table 1). This taxonomy defined, described, and explained the competency and its relationship to the individual career goals or position within the company's business requirements. Finally the levels of the competency (know about, apply and use, guide others) were selected for each role and/or responsibility.

Table 1. Position and competency level requirements

POSITION / COMPETENCY	Customer Satisfaction	Market Representation	Brand @ Retail	Sales Program'g & Inventory Mgt.	Dealership Operations	Remarketing	Managing the Marketing Mix	Brand Positioning	Marketing Launch	Revenue Management	Vehicle Personalization
Vice President – Sales	S	S	S	S	G	S	AP	AP	AQ	AP	AP
Dealer Development Director	G	G	G	G	G	G	AQ	AP	AP	AP	AP
Dealer Affairs Manager	AQ	AQ	AP		G	AP	AQ	AQ	AQ	AQ	AQ
Sales Director	AP	AQ	AQ	G	G	G	AQ	AQ	AQ	AQ	AQ
Sales Process Manager	AQ		AQ	G	G	AP	AQ	AQ	AQ	AQ	AQ
Account Manager	AQ		AQ	AP	AQ					AQ	AQ
Distribution Planner	AQ		AQ	AP	AP						
Sales Analyst	AQ		AQ	AP	AP					AQ	
Distribution Coordinator	AQ		AQ	AP	AQ					AQ	
Distribution Scheduler	AQ		AQ	AP	AQ					AQ	

Note: G = Guide, AP = Apply, AQ= Aquire

Figure 3. Learning object manager

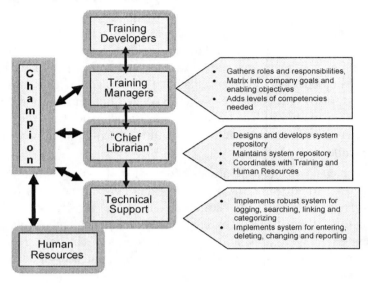

This was a time-consuming process and it involved many different inputs from a variety of levels within the company. The champion had to include all the stakeholders including the human resources department in the process. It also required that the champion keep the goals intact and the details up-to-date through the different business cycles. This champion also empowered others including the training managers, the "chief librarian" and the technical support personnel who were needed to leverage present and future technology. None of this was easy. It involved years, not months. Therefore it was imperative that the champion included the system's goals as part of the company's goals in a specific way. At the same time, though the goals were large, the system's implementation was completed in stages (see Figure 3)

The benefits for stakeholders were articulated and made transparent in the LMS that was designed and developed. Employees were automatically routed to the list of competencies previously selected and structured to apply to their present role. Those competencies were in turn linked to resources that could be used to learn, practice, and demonstrate the competency. An individual development plan was automatically generated and a copy could be sent to the employee's supervisor. Additionally, employees who were interested in the competencies needed for other positions could access those as well (see Figure 4).

Figure 4. Electronic individual employee assessment process

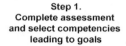

| Step 1. Complete assessment and select competencies leading to goals | Step 2. Develop plan for attaining competencies | Step 3. Utilize resources for developing competencies and assess completion | Step 4. Complete assessment and share with supervisor |

Supervisors not only received the individual development plans filled out by their employees, they were also able to generate reports on their entire staff regarding their progress in completing and reporting on competencies achieved and competencies that needed to be developed.

The training manager and developers received requests from managers concerning the need for competency training along with a list of potential learners, the learner's own assessment of their competency level, and the specific competencies needed according to the roles and responsibilities of the learners.

The chief librarian and technical support personnel produced a system that was not only well-received, but also used by the employees.

Human resources ended up with an automated employee development program that produced individual and group reports on the achievements and gaps of the company's employees and their relationship to the mission and goals of the company.

RLOs used in training and career development can also be utilized in design and development. They can then be connected so that the instruction is designed and developed with the learning, the learner, and learning environment in mind.

An interesting example of such a use of RLOs is found in the National Automotive Technicians Education Foundation's (NATEF) (2005) training curriculum. The NATEF certifies eight automobile areas. Similar programs exist for automobile technicians in other countries. The curriculum is part of a certification process that is applicable not only for individual technicians and their employers but is also used as the basis for community college and corporate training programs. An iterative process was used to breakdown the knowledge and skills needed by different levels of automotive technicians and to classify the results into learning objectives. The learning objectives are then categorized into academic areas, general subject areas, and specific knowledge points.

- **MA232:** Solves Problems (Proportion, Volume)
  - o   The technician can solve problems that involve determining whether the proportion of the existing volume is within recommended tolerance when compared to the manufacturer's specifications.

- **MA238:** Solves Problems (Trial and Error)
  - o   The technician occasionally solves problems by trying a suggested solution and observing the results.

- **MA239:** Understands (Conditionals)
  - o   The technician understands that if the described problem has certain conditions (symptoms), then there are a limited number of probable solutions to the problem.

- **SC212:** Describes/Explains (Electrochemical Reactions Activity of Metals)
  - o   The technician can explain the conductivity problems in a circuit when connectors corrode due to electrochemical reactions.

- **SC213:** Describes/Explains (Electrochemical Reactions Oxidation/Reduction)
  - o   The technician can explain the effect of oxidation on electrical connections.

- **LA134:** Comprehends Information (Written, Cause/Effect Relationships)
  - o   The technician interprets charts/tables/graphs to determine manufacturer's specifications for system operation to identify out of tolerance shift points and linkage adjustments.

The various training companies who contract with original equipment manufacturers (OEMs), dealerships, and after market contributors can then use both the NATEF's academic categories and the automobile as an organizing principle to produce content for their many different requirements. The content is customized by these training companies and decomposed into learning objects that populate a LCMS.

The benefits of use of RLOs for this industry include:

1. The training companies do not reinvent the wheel.
2. The lessons and topics developed allow just-in-time learning.
3. Learners can freely explore the curriculum whether the objective is career development, problem solving, or just plan curiosity.
4. Learners can explore the lessons and topics to the depth of understanding required and individually wanted.
5. Customized learning paths are developed.
6. Repurposing of material is facilitated.
7. Development time is shortened.
8. Courses, lessons, and topics can be integrated and accessed in a variety of ways.

RLOs that have been cut, parsed, and classified can then be input and accessed in a searchable database. Delivery methods are chosen and templates completed. Elaboration and examples contextualize the content for the selected learners.

Figure 5. Individual learning object file structure

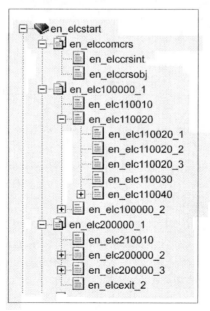

This explanation sounds much simpler than the actual practice. The process of storing and classifying this migratory information according to a system that can be used across companies, platforms, and instructional designers can be tedious. The ramping up of participants into the system is time consuming and frustrating to some. Since the goals require that the learning objects not only be independent and effective but also classifiable and searchable; the LCMSs usually look a lot like Figure 5. In this particular case the learning curve for translating the files names can be steeper for some than others. But the originating group tried to compensate for future uses and for some modicum of logic in the assignments. Even with this upfront planning the inability to go beyond the numerals 0 to 9 can result in creative structuring of courses, lessons, topics, practice, and reviews.

Summary

Our purpose was to present some examples of the use of learning objects in career development and training within corporate environments. The lesson for instructional designers who want to design and develop in the corporate training world is to develop and use systems that fit the needs of the corporate systems, that is, are aligned with their goals and that provide direct links to their bottom line. In other words, look beyond and in addition to the needs analysis, the learner analysis, and the task analysis to a systems analysis. The corporate decision makers are looking for those links to their goals from the training departments and using learning objects as described can mean that training can fulfill its potential for their systems.

References

Automobile Technician Training Programs. (2005). Leesburg, VA: National Automotive Technicians Education Foundation (NATEF).

Badaracco, J. L., Jr. (1991). *The knowledge link: How firms compete through strategic alliances.* Boston: Harvard Business School Press.

Bloom, B. S., & Krathwohl, D. R. (1994). *Taxonomy of educational objectives* (Handbook 1: Cognitive Domain). Addison-Wesley.

Cisco Systems, Inc. (2000). *Reusable learning object strategy: Version 3.1.* Retrieved February 10, 2007, from http://www.cisco.com/warp/public/10/wwtraining/elearning/implement/rlo_strategy_v3-1.pdf

Clark, R. (1999). *Developing technical training: A structured approach for the development of classroom and computer-based instructional materials.* Silver Springs, MD: Society of Performance Improvement.

deSousa, P. (in press). *Learning to love learning objects.*

Feldstein, M. (2001). Back to the future: What's after learning objects? *eLearn Magazine.* Retrieved February 10, 2007, from http://elearnmag.org/

Hofstede, G. (1997). Cultures and organizations: Software of the mind. In *Handbook of human performance technology.* New York: McGraw-Hill.

Kirkpatrick, D. L. (1994-1996). *Evaluating training programs: The four levels.* San Francisco: Berrett-Koehler Publishers.

Mager, B. F. (1984). *Measuring instructional results, or got a match* (2nd ed.). Belmont, CA: David S. Lake Publishers.

Merrill, M. D. (1983). Component display theory. In C.M. Reigeluth (Ed.), *Instructional design theories and models.* Hillsdale, NJ: Lawrence Erlbaum.

Merrill, M. D. (2000). Knowledge objects and mental models. In D. A. Wiley (Ed.), *The instructional use of learning objects.* Retrieved February 10, 2007, from http://reusability.org/read/chapters/merrill.doc

Nielsen, J. (2000). *Designing Web usability.* Indianapolis, IN: New Riders Publishing.

Sánchez, C. M., & Curtis, D. M. (2000). Different minds and common problems: Geert Hofstede's research on national cultures. *Performance Improvement Quarterly, 13*(2), 9-19.

Trillo, N.G. (1999). The cultural component of designing and evaluating international user interfaces. In *Proceedings of the 32nd Hawaii International Conference on System Sciences.* IEEE.

Chapter XI

Developing Learning Objects:
Implications for Course Content Strategies

Christine H. Olgren, University of Wisconsin-Madison, USA

Patricia Ploetz, University of Wisconsin-Stevens Point, USA

Abstract

This chapter examines the issues and concerns of faculty regarding the development and use of learning objects as instructional resources. It describes the characteristics and benefits of learning objects, barriers to adoption, and strategies to increase learning object use. Included are communication and support strategies for working with faculty. Concerns about quality and effectiveness are also discussed, and a comprehensive set of criteria is presented to guide learning object design and evaluation. The chapter concludes with ten recommendations to help overcome barriers to faculty adoption of learning objects. The chapter is based on the authors' personal experiences in using learning objects, current literature,[1] and their involvement in the Fund for the Improvement of Post Secondary Education (FIPSE) Grant entitled "An Investigation of the Pedagogical and Economic Effectiveness of Sharable Content Objects, Using Standards, in Online Instruction." The work of the grant was conducted from November 2002 through December 2005.

Introduction

In 1992, Wayne Hodgins, Director of Worldwide Learning Strategies at Auto Desk, Inc., was credited with both the term and the concept of reusable learning objects, mini reusable programs that provide instruction over the Internet. According to Hodgins (2002), these small digital lessons are mixed and matched to meet individual learner needs at a time and place that is convenient for the learner. This suggests that learning object use is dependent upon the learner engaging with the content outside the normal instructional environment. When students have the opportunity to determine when and how they learn, they begin to move toward a learner-centric model of learning that benefits both learners and instructors alike. This is but one of the benefits that reusable learning objects bring to the learning environment. While learning objects have been around for some time, their use in instruction in higher education is limited.

In order to understand why learning objects are on the periphery of higher education, it is important to identify issues and concerns related to their adoption. Thus, after a brief introduction that includes a definition, history, and the characteristics and benefits of learning objects, this chapter will focus on the following four areas: barriers to faculty adoption of reusable learning objects, strategies to increase reusable learning object use, achieving quality and effectiveness with reusable learning objects, implications for teaching and learning, and recommendations for practice.

Definition

Reusable learning objects have their roots in information technology and object oriented programming, "representing a combination of the concept of learning and the paradigm of object orientation" (Oakes, 2002, p. 1).

Simply put, object oriented programming supports the creation of individual objects (programs) that can be used repeatedly in different contexts to perform specific tasks. For example, instead of recreating a program to add numbers over and over again, object oriented programming uses an "add numbers object" to perform the "add numbers task" in multiple contexts. Reusable learning objects use the same concept only instead of adding numbers, learning objects provide stand alone guided instruction on a specific topic that can be used over and over again in a variety of contexts.

Adhering to the idea of reusable learning, a learning object for this chapter is viewed as an individual lesson, which includes a learning objective (a single objective is preferred), content to support students in reaching the learning objective, one or more activities in which learners interact with the content, and an assessment to determine whether or not the learner has met the learning objective.

Images, audio, video, and simulations, often referred to as assets, are not considered learning objects for our discussion. While assets have the potential for providing meaningful instruction and may be reusable, they usually do not include an identifiable learning objective or an assessment strategy to measure student learning.

History

In the early 1990s public and private colleges and universities turned to online technologies to replace and/or enhance the traditional classroom experience through distance education courses and programs. As online instruction grew, organizations already invested in teaching and learning with technology jumped on the learning object bandwagon (Jacobsen, 2002).[2] During this same period of time, educators saw both the proliferation of learning management systems (LMSs), and a growing need to move early learning object content between propriety systems. The need to share learning objects prompted Executive Order 13111 charging the Department of Defense and consequently the Advanced Distributed Learning Co-Laboratory (ADL Co-Lab) with the task of leading the development of a common specification and standard for technology-based learning across both federal and private sectors (Advanced Distributed Learning, 2005). This tasking brought together existing e-learning specification/standard groups and other interested users to develop a standard for sharing e-learning content that resulted in the development of the sharable content object reference model (SCORM), the de facto standard for sharing learning objects across learning management systems.[3]

Major Characteristics and Benefits of Learning Objects

Characteristics

Reusability, accessibility, interoperability, and durability (RAID) are the four major characteristics of reusable learning objects.

- **Reusability:** A learning object is reusable when it conforms to the SCORM from a technical perspective and when the content itself promotes reusability. When developing reusable learning objects, content developers (faculty) need to take reusability into consideration. In order to be reusable a learning object must stand alone; that is, content within the learning object must not link to content outside the learning object; in addition, content cannot reference earlier or later content that may be found in a related series of learning objects. Content developers also need to "chunk" content to a level that promotes learning yet is granular enough to be used across multiple disciples.

  The design of the learning object must also be such that it "fits" with other learning objects. While there are no "standards" for designing learning objects, developers schooled in instructional design concepts are familiar with best practices in developing digital learning environments that support reusability.

- **Accessibility:** In order for electronic learning content to be accessible, metadata are required. Internet and repository search engines search learning object metadata, returning content based on learner search criteria. Metadata is a file that contains, but is not limited to, the title of the learning object, a description of its content, the intended audience, requirements for use, copyright restrictions, and other important information including keywords that appropriately identify the content. Metadata help potential users determine whether or not a learning object will meet the learning needs of specific learner/s and provides a method for accessing the learning object.

- **Interoperability:** Interoperability requires a learning object to be packaged according to the SCORM, the standard for sharing content between learning management systems that describes how the learning content is organized and how to present the content to the learner. Learning objects that have been standardized are also known as sharable content objects or SCOs.

- **Durability:** Durability is the ability of a learning object to stand the test of time both technically and contextually in order to be meaningful and usable next year, 5 years or even 10 years from now. A learning object designed for durability takes into consideration content that is "timeless." Timeless content focuses on one learning objective, contains content that changes little over time, refrains from using information that dates the content, and is developed with a global audience in mind. Technically, durability supports learning object usability across evolving versions of operating systems, a well known barrier to both information technology specialists and personal computer users alike.

  While RAID outlines the characteristics of a learning object that promotes technical reusability, it is the quality of the content that ultimately determines whether or not a learning object will be reused.

Benefits

The characteristics of reusable learning objects, reusability, accessibility, interoperability, and durability provide added value to the learning content. That value is realized through savings in time and money, and benefits to the educational process. The following table presents a limited list of benefits found in reusable learning objects (Degen, 2001; Robson, 2001; Seimens, 2003)

What is even more important, however, is the potential for changing the existing model of learning from an instructor-centric model to a learner-centric model. In instructor-centric learning environments instructors control the content, the learning process, the conditions for learning and the assessment, which may lead to dependent unmotivated students (Weimer, 2002). Moving to a learner-centric model supports students' ownership of the learning process, where the instructor facilitates learning by guiding students in their search for knowledge and enabling them to become partners in the learning process.

Table 1. Benefits found in reusable learning objects

Added Value in Time and Resources	Added value to Education
Reusability	
Reduced production costs are realized when content is reused for multiple purposes, markets, and devices. As demonstrated by Conceico, Olgren, and Ploetz (2006) learning objects can be adapted to different learning needs and contexts, saving time and resources.	Reusable learning objects allow educators to easily share their content with their peers. This sharing of content opens the door for feedback that supports ongoing assessment and revision of the learning content.
Accessibility	
Easily locatable content; finding and retrieving the right content at the right time saves both time and effort. Educators no longer need to take the whole book when they want one or two chapters (Seimens, 2003).	Easily accessible learning objects allows for the customization of content. The power of reusable learning objects is harnessed when learners are able to get the right information at the right time.
Interoperability	
The ability to use content developed by multiple proprietary software programs across a variety of proprietary platforms without having to rebuild the same content in each software package for each learning management system saves an enormous amount of time and money.	Interoperability assures educators that they will be able to use any standardized learning object that meets their individual instructional needs. Educators no longer have to worry if they have the needed software to view a specific piece of learning content.
Durability	
Content that transcends changes in hardware and software over time, results in increased reusability and decreased production costs.	Durable learning objects allow faculty to easily move content from one institution or system to another; whereas, institutions can change from one LMS system to another without jeopardizing faculty content.

Barriers to Faculty Adoption of Learning Objects

Accessibility

Accessibility is a key issue in faculty adoption of learning objects. Faculty's first introduction to learning objects is often brought about by the need to solve an instructional problem. When trying to locate resources to help their students better understand a concept or idea, they search the Internet looking for the learning objects they've heard about. Unfortunately, locating a specific learning object can be very frustrating. While we are beginning to see growth in learning object libraries (repositories), the growth needed to support accessibility is still in its infancy. If faculty cannot easily locate a reusable learning object that meets their instructional needs the first time around they are bound to "pass" on the new technology until they are convinced to try again.

Time

In almost every instance involving the implementation of a new technology in higher education, lack of time is consistently identified as a barrier in engaging faculty. While reusable learning objects may ultimately save time, the time expended to retrieve or develop a reusable learning object is still prohibitive enough to prevent faculty from fully utilizing reusable learning objects. The extra time needed to search, edit, and/or develop reusable learning objects takes away from faculties first priority, teaching. Until accessing and using a reusable learning object requires less time than finding just the right book, or hyperlinking to just the right article it is understandable that busy faculty will not be inclined to change their way of working or teaching.

Language

Educators attempting to develop learning objects face many challenges. Of these challenges, the language of learning objects can be the most difficult as users outside the discipline must become literate in the language of information technology in order to be successful in the development process. "Faculty think and speak in the world of courses and lessons, the classroom environment, and discipline specific rhetoric, not in the world of learning objects and learning object technologies" (Ploetz, 2003, p. 11). For faculty "the term learning object suggests neither simplicity, compatibility nor any other obvious relative advantage over prevailing teaching practice" (Friesen, 2003, p. 2). Educators are content experts, not technologists, and most are not interested in becoming technology experts. Yet the language used to describe, use, and develop learning objects is firmly situated in information technology.

Tools

The tools for developing learning object content range from very sophisticated programming software to simple Word templates. With direction and guidance, storyboards and templates can be used to develop quality content for use in reusable learning objects. The more sophisticated the reusable learning object, the more "tools" are required. While quality learning content does not require sophisticated design elements that involve the use of software other than html, including images, interactions, and simulations adds to the users' learning experience. In order to use graphics and simulations effectively content developers need to be familiar with other programming tools such as image editors and simulation software. While most faculty are proficient in html, many are not familiar with PhotoShop and Flash development programs, the software needed to edit images, and create interactions and simulations.

Content Chunking

Historically content developed in higher education begins with the course. While educators routinely "chunk" their content into lessons, the focus is often on the course or content to be covered rather than the individual lesson. When developing learning object content the focus is on one learning objective, a small chunk of content that is often one part of a traditional lesson. Transitioning from the course perspective to a learning object viewpoint requires a paradigm shift; as learning object development begins where course development typically ends.

Design

For the most part, higher education faculty receive minimal instruction in developing content for the online environment. Designing quality learning experiences for digital learning environments requires knowledge of elearning design principles that are quite different from the design of the face-to face lecture format. Many of us can easily recall a Web site that had great content with bad design. Unfortunately, bad design can have a negative impact on learning.

Packaging Issues

Packaging content to meet SCORM specifications is a process that requires an intimate knowledge of SCORM and the standards. While recent updates in development software (Dreamweaver, Flash, etc.) and new products dedicated to packaging (Reload) include a push button approach to packaging learning object content, there is still a great deal of underlying knowledge that is required.

Strategies to Increase
Learning Object Development and Use

The barriers to faculty adoption of reusable learning objects are many; however, they are not insurmountable. We begin by communicating with faculty in their language.

Importance of Communicating on Faculty's Own Terms

Faculty support personnel can help faculty understand the language of learning object technology by creating bridges to faculty content developers prior knowledge and experience. Table 2 illustrates how instructor language can be used to introduce learning object content development.

Content Chunking as a Design Approach

One of the lessons learned in developing learning object content has been the need to look at course content from the perspective of a mini-lesson rather than the course. In *Understanding by Design*, Wiggins and McTighe (1998) suggest that educators use the backward design process to develop their curriculum. In the backward design process, educators look at the intended outcomes of the instruction to guide and direct curriculum development. This approach leads to the natural chunking of content into highly granular pieces of learning that fits nicely with the learning object approach.

Table 2. Bridging the gap

Bridging the Gap: A Conversation		
Faculty support asks:	**Faculty responds with:**	**Results in:**
→	→	
What do you (the faculty member) want your students to know or be able to do as a result of the course you are teaching? What are the ideas or concepts that seem to be most difficult for the majority of your students?	• List of instructional goals for the course that are or will be broken down into discrete learning objectives	The most difficult learning objective becomes the focus of the reusable learning object. ↓
How will you (the faculty member) know if the required learning has occurred?	• List of current assessment strategies • Assessment strategies that would be most beneficial to students learning on their own in the online environment	Quizzes, puzzles, simulations, and so forth, that will be used in the learning object to demonstrate the achievement of desired results. Usually some kind of self-assessment. ↓
What learning content will you (the faculty member) need to provide the students to help them move from where they are now to the identified end result?	• Resources that will help students learn what they need to know in order to meet the learning outcomes	Resources to support student learning. ↓
What learning activities will develop cognitive, affective or psychomotor abilities that support learner acquisition of required knowledge?	• Learning activities to support knowledge acquisition	Games, puzzles, simulations, audio, video, etc. ↓
		Learning Object Content

Templates and Tools for Content Development

The use of templates for both content and graphic development gives faculty a head start in the reusable learning object development process. Content templates are used to guide faculty from the big picture or course level approach to a single learning objective, the point at which they begin developing learning objects. Use of design templates for navigation, and the overall look and feel of an institution's learning objects, provide consistency while giving faculty a preview of the context for the content being developed.

Providing Help with Process, Procedures, and Approach

In an Educause Center for Applied Research survey completed in 2002, Metros and Bennett claimed that instructional technologists were partnering with educators in the development of learning objects, this partnership "allows educators in higher education to concentrate on what they do best—research, creative activity, teaching, and service—without having to focus heavily on technology" (p. 6). Experience has shown that using a team approach to learning object development meets the needs of higher education faculty while eliminating many of the barriers to faculty development discussed earlier.

The team development process revolves around a series of meetings between a development team and the faculty member. Project meetings can be held in the traditional face-to-face format or through online discussion forums. The team consists of a project leader, content developer (faculty), instructional designer, graphic artist, and Web/Flash developer. After content goals and objectives have been identified the team begins the development process:

- The faculty member works with an instructional designer to develop the learning object content using a storyboarding template.

- Once the content has been developed it is reviewed by content experts for clarity, application, and instructional fidelity. Suggested changes and edits are made at this time.

- The graphic designer then develops a visual look and feel for the content through the addition of graphics.

- The Flash/Web developer designs and develops simulations and other interactive components as identified by the content developer.

- The content with graphics and interactions is reviewed a second time.

- The faculty member reviews and accepts or rejects the completed learning object. The learning object goes back to the development team for editing or is marked as complete.

- When the learning object is complete a technologist creates the metadata file using keywords provided by the faculty content developer and "packages" the content to conform to SCORM guidelines.

- The reusable learning object is then run through the SCORM test suite to assure the accuracy and completeness of the packaging process.

With limited personnel and resources, it is difficult to put an entire team together. However, that does not mean that an institution cannot begin the development process, it just means that the scope of the project is limited by the time and resources available. Using students as graphic artists, Web developers, and metadata and packaging support not only helps the institution, it provides students with practical experiences that will assist them in getting that first job after graduation. In addition, students bring important information to the process that aids in the development of quality learning objects.

Quality and Effectiveness Issues

Quality and effectiveness are two central issues in the development and use of learning objects. Quality involves concerns about whether or not learning objects can meet expectations or standards of excellence as instructional resources. Effectiveness involves concerns about how well learning objects function in meeting learning goals and objectives. In both cases, decisions about the value of learning objects are made in relation to the instructional context or their use within a lesson, module, course, or program.

It may be helpful to use the terms "objects-in-theory" and "objects-in-use" as shorthand expressions that distinguish between theory and practice, or the conceptualization of learning objects compared to their actual application for instruction. Although theory should inform practice, problems develop when theory lacks clarity, as in the case of learning objects. Quality and effectiveness relate mainly to objects-in-use where questions of value, worth, and utility are grounded in the teaching context. The technical terminology surrounding objects-in-theory tends to obscure the practical usefulness of learning objects. As Haughey and Muirhead (2005) emphasize, the basic purpose of a learning object is to aid teaching and learning. A focus on objects-in-use reminds us that learning objects should help faculty to perform various teaching functions, such as introducing new topics or skills, reinforcing existing knowledge, or supporting new kinds of learning opportunities.

The notion of the practical functionality of objects-in-use circles back to a major barrier to faculty adoption of learning objects: questions about their instructional value and utility. That is, how can the quality and effectiveness of learning objects be determined within an instructional setting?

Defining Learning Object Standards

An important step in clarifying the concept of learning objects is the development of criteria that define the major characteristics. A set of clear criteria would help to:

- Provide measurable quality standards
- Communicate the features of learning objects in relation to instructional value
- Guide the instructional design and development of new learning objects
- Review and select existing learning objects for reuse
- Evaluate the quality and effectiveness of objects-in-use within instructional contexts

A set of defining criteria, then, could provide a methodology and a set of standards or guidelines for creating, using, and evaluating learning objects.

Sources of Learning Object Standards

A number of projects have worked to develop quality criteria or standards for designing and evaluating learning objects. Most of the projects have centered on establishing online repositories, where standards play an essential role in assessing reusable learning objects stored in a digital content library. However, as Polsani (2003) observes, existing repositories may use different definitions and standards, resulting in a wide array of digital content being classified as learning objects. Anything from a brief video clip to a lengthy article or tutorial may be referred to as a learning object. The wide range of digital content contributes to some of the confusion and uncertainty about the definition of learning objects (McGreal, 2004; Polsani, 2003).

Of the projects that have developed learning object criteria, MERLOT and LORI have emerged as the two most commonly referenced:

- **Multimedia Educational Resources for Learning and Online Teaching (MERLOT):** MERLOT is an international consortium of partners in higher education that was formed in 1997 to help faculty and instructors overcome one of the major barriers to using digital library materials: finding high quality, effective materials that meet their teaching objectives (McMartin, 2004). Merlot established a set of 20 criteria for peer review of digital materials intended for acceptance in its repository. The criteria relate to three broad areas: (1) quality of content, (2) potential effectiveness as a teaching-learning tool, and (3) ease of use.

  1. **Quality of content:** The content is professional, clear, and accurate. The use of technology is appropriate for the content, and the learning object is provided with academic references and credits to the creators.

2. **Effectiveness as a teaching/learning tool:** The learning object is able to function as a learning tool in different types of learning environments. The prerequisite knowledge or skills is identified and the author provides evidence that the learning object enhances student learning. The learning object has clear learning objectives and the target learners are identified. There are clear instructions on how to use the learning model. It must also provide an opportunity for students to get feedback within or outside the learning object.

3. **Ease of use:** There are easy to use navigation tools and user control. The author indicates if the learning object can be accessed by learners with various needs. Technical requirements to run the learning object are stated.

Although the MERLOT criteria were developed for digital materials in general, the criteria have been adopted by several projects as quality standards for learning objects. Those projects include the Technology Enhanced Learning and Research (TELR) project at The Ohio State University and the collaborative learning object exchange (CLOE) at the University of Waterloo.

•   **Learning Object Rating Instrument (LORI):** The LORI is based on a set of nine criteria drawn originally from the literature on instructional design, multimedia development, and educational psychology. The instrument is intended for peer review of learning objects and uses a five-point rating scale to evaluate the following nine dimensions of quality:

1. **Content quality:** Veracity, accuracy, balanced presentation of ideas, and appropriate level of detail

2. **Learning goal alignment:** Alignment among learning goals, activities, assessments, and learner characteristics

3. **Feedback and adaptation:** Adaptive content or feedback driven by differential learner input or learner modeling

4. **Motivation:** Ability to motivate, and stimulate the interest or curiosity of, an identified population of learners

5. **Presentation design:** Design of visual and auditory information for enhanced learning and efficient mental processing

6. **Interaction usability:** Ease of navigation, predictability of the user interface, and the quality of UI help features

7. **Accessibility:** Support for learners with disabilities

8. **Reusability:** Ability to port between different courses or learning contexts without modification

9. **Standards compliance:** Adherence to international standards and specifications (Nesbit, Belfer, & Leacock, 2003).

A potential problem with the LORI is the broad nature of the nine items, where an item typically comprises several characteristics or attributes rather than a single one. The use of compound items in evaluation instruments raises issues of validity, reliability, and interpretation. The LORI user manual includes a rubric and examples as background to using the nine-item scoring sheet (Nesbit et al., 2003). However, the scoring sheet by itself does not provide sufficient detail for interpreting results and improving specific features of the learning object. As recommended by Nesbit et al. (2002), using the LORI for a convergent participation model of peer review would enable a panel of reviewers to explain and discuss their ratings. However, using the LORI as a scoring sheet for individual reviews raises methodological issues.

Another instrument, the Learning Object Evaluation Instrument (LOEI) drew upon several sources of criteria, including CLOE and LORI, to tailor a review process to the special concerns of K-12 environments (Haughy & Muirhead; 2005). The LOEI has 14 criteria related to the integrity, usability, learning, design, and values focus of a learning object. An advantage of the LOEI compared to LORI is that each criterion is more specific in referring to a single attribute. In addition, the LOEI is directed to the quality, utility, and pedagogical concerns of K-12 teachers in using learning objects for school-level content.

An Integrated Set of Learning Object Criteria

A comparison of the learning object criteria found in the literature and repository projects reveals similarities and differences. The criteria are similar in emphasizing features related to content, design, and ease of use or accessibility. However, the sources differ in some of the specific characteristics used as indicators, and they do not clearly differentiate quality in terms of content and design considerations.

Table 3 lays out an integrated set of learning object criteria (LOC) that synthesizes the similarities found in the literature, especially the commonalities between MERLOT and LORI. The LOC table is presented as a classification matrix that clarifies the differences between content criteria and design criteria. The content criteria comprise characteristics that define content quality and effectiveness. The design criteria comprise characteristics that specify quality in relation to usability, interactivity, and reusability. The result is a set of 25 criteria that can serve as either instructional design guidelines or as indicators for evaluating quality and effectiveness. In addition, the criteria are informed by pedagogical principles for providing content and interactivity.

Table 3. Learning object criteria

Content Criteria	Design Criteria
Quality of the content	**Quality of the design**
• Clarity of the information	**Usability**
• Accuracy of the information	• Ease of use or navigation
• Relevance to the learning objectives	• Clarity of instructions for using the object
• Appropriate level of difficulty	• Aesthetic appeal in use of fonts, colors and images
• Appropriate amount of information	• Readability in text size and formatting of information
Potential effectiveness for teaching/learning	**Interactivity**
• Identifies learning objectives	• Uses activities or quizzes to practice, apply or check learning
• Identifies prerequisite knowledge	• Uses graphics, audio, or video for variety and interactivity
• Engages the learner to interact with the content or activities	• Provides feedback to learner
• Stimulates interest or motivation to learn	
• Explains the concepts and relationships between concepts introduced in the object	**Reusability**
• Uses examples, analogies, or other devices to help learners to understand the concepts	• Object stands alone as independent learning element
• Requires higher-order thinking processes to learn the material (beyond memorization)	• Object can be used in different instructional contexts
• Uses reviews or summaries to reinforce learning	• Appropriate level of granularity
	• Conforms to technical standards for interoperability, such as SCORM
	• Conforms to universal design standards for accessibility, diversity, and disability

The Role of Criteria for Quality Assurance

An important use of learning object criteria is to ensure quality and effectiveness. In addition to establishing quality standards for learning objects, the criteria also promote faculty adoption by clarifying quality. As Christiansen and Anderson (2004) note, a major barrier to faculty adoption of learning objects is a perceived lack of quality, or variations in quality, along with the time-consuming nature of locating and assessing objects for instructional use.

As part of a quality assurance process, criteria serve as a source of indicators or items that can be incorporated into either formative or summative evaluation processes. A formative evaluation, which is conducted during the development of a learning object, provides quality control by identifying strengths, weaknesses, and elements needing improvement. A summative evaluation, conducted after development, assesses how well a learning object meets quality standards and effectiveness measures.

The evaluation of learning objects through peer or expert review promotes reusability by providing quality assurance and by helping faculty to assess and locate learning objects in searching a repository. A peer review process, such as that used by MERLOT or recommended for LORI, may also encourage adoption by involving faculty in the review process and by mirroring a familiar academic culture (Nesbit et al., 2002).

The 25 learning object criteria listed in Table 3 can be used for either formative or summative evaluation. The evaluation could incorporate all of the criteria, or it could use only some, depending on the evaluation's purpose and scope. The criteria could be built into evaluation checklists, rubrics, Likert scale questions, or qualitative questions. In other words, the LOC provides some flexibility in deciding how the criteria will be used in evaluation methodology. An approach that incorporates both formative and summative evaluation would be recommended for a comprehensive assessment, but simpler methods using checklists or rubrics could also provide some quality control measures.

All 25 criteria were used in a recent FIPSE project to develop and evaluate nearly 70 learning objects for online instruction (Meachen, Olgren, & Ploetz, 2005). The learning objects were developed by faculty, with assistance from an instructional designer and a graphics designer. The evaluation involved a two-stage expert review process conducted at two points during the development process. As show in Table 4, the first review was done at the storyboard stage and focused on content criteria. The second review was done after graphics development to assess design quality. Each learning object was evaluated by two peer reviewers who were faculty experts in the subject matter. The reviews were conducted online using electronic tools for rapid feedback and access to data, with findings tailored to the needs of different team members. Evaluation, then, played an integral role in involving faculty in developing, reviewing, and improving the learning objects.

For the FIPSE project, the expert review process used two evaluation instruments that incorporated the 25 criteria along with open-ended questions and overall ratings:

- **Expert Review Stage 1:** A 28-item online questionnaire to gather data on content quality and effectiveness in relation to: (a) the content clarity, accuracy, relevance, and appropriateness; and (b) its potential effectiveness in relation to learning objectives, learner engagement, conceptual relationships, higher-order thinking, and learning process reinforcements.

- **Expert Review Stage 2:** A 20-item online questionnaire to gather data on design quality in relation to: (a) usability or the aesthetic appeal, readability, and ease of navigation; (b) interactivity or the expectation of using higher order thinking skills to respond to questions or generate new applications of information through the use of activities, quizzes, graphic treatments, and feedback responses; and (c) reusability or the potential to be applied across disciplines and contexts, to run on different platforms, serve diverse learners, and demonstrate an appropriate level of granularity.

In both review stages, the questionnaires provided useful and comprehensive data for evaluating the learning objects. Both questionnaires used Likert scale responses to provide quantitative data on how well a learning object met each quality standard. In addition, the qualitative responses to open-ended questions were especially useful for identifying specific elements needing improvement and for providing insights to help interpret the numerical ratings.

An unanticipated benefit of using a comprehensive set of criteria as a source of evaluation items is the educational value it has in helping faculty to understand the nature of learning objects. Faculty who served as the content developers and the expert reviewers for the FIPSE project found the criteria helped them to grasp the major features that needed to be included in a learning object in order to meet content and design considerations (Meachen et al., 2005).

Table 4. Example of two-stage expert review for learning object development

Learning object content development and review process:

1. Content submitted by content developer
2. Instructional designer reviews content
3. Content developer submits storyboard
4. Instructional designer reviews storyboard
5. Storyboard is revised, if needed
6. **Expert Review of storyboard (Stage 1 review of content criteria)**
7. Storyboard is revised and finalized
8. Storyboard is edited by editor
9. Learning object (LO) is developed for the Web (graphic design)
10. **Expert Review of developed LO (Stage 2 review of design criteria)**
11. LO is revised and re-edited
12. LO is tagged and packaged for SCORM compliance

Conclusion

Experience in working with faculty in developing and evaluating learning objects has provided insights into some of the challenges involved in faculty adoption. Some challenges are due to the concept itself, or to objects-in-theory, where there are problems with conceptual ambiguity and technical terminology that create confusion and uncertainty about the nature of learning objects. Objects-in-theory also lack a clear conceptual model showing the relationships to pedagogical principles and learning theory.

Confusion about objects-in-theory contributes to uncertainty about objects-in-use. When it comes to applying learning objects for teaching, faculty are often skeptical about their instructional value and utility. Faculty are also apt to view learning objects as foreign to their customary approach to teaching, as time-consuming to locate, and as questionable in terms of their effectiveness in achieving instructional objectives.

What strategies might help to overcome barriers to adoption? There are several "lessons learned" or recommendations we can draw from faculty experiences with learning objects:

- Introduce learning objects in language commonly used and understood by faculty; avoid the technical jargon common to learning object discussions.

- Help faculty to understand the concept of "chunking" or the notion that people remember information better when it is presented in short segments or groupings of five to seven units.

- Show how learning objects serve as content resources similar to the ways faculty make use of ideas, concepts, examples, or other "chunks of content" found in textbooks or journal articles.

- Emphasize the link between learning objects and pedagogy, where learning objects can be used for a variety of teaching functions, such as introducing new concepts, explaining abstract models, reinforcing conceptual understanding, or providing strategies for applying ideas to problem solving.

- To help faculty develop learning objects, provide a template or storyboard that walks faculty through the steps of designing simple learning objects to start; add advanced templates as faculty gain practice. Provide at least some assistance for instructional design, graphics design, and packaging.

- To help faculty locate learning objects, create a Web page with links to learning object repositories, search strategies, shared tips, and a list of criteria to consider in evaluating objects, and other information that makes finding and retrieving objects less time-consuming.

- Provide faculty with a set of learning object criteria that help them to understand the major characteristics defining quality and effectiveness.

- To provide consistency in design and evaluation, use the learning object criteria as a source of guidelines for designing, developing, and reviewing learning objects.

- Use learning object criteria as a source of quality standards and instrument items to evaluate the use of learning objects within instructional contexts (e.g., checklists, rubrics, questionnaires, interview questions).

- Involve faculty in reviewing the learning objects created by others to give them hands-on experience in understanding learning objects and assessing the characteristics that contribute to content and design quality.

We have found that the best adoption strategy is to involve faculty in hands-on practice, starting with simple templates, storyboards, checklists, rubrics, and other tools that help them to gain experience with learning objects. By incorporating appropriate criteria or quality standards, those tools would also introduce the key elements involved in designing and evaluating learning objects. As faculty gain experience with objects-in-use, they may see new ways to incorporate them into their teaching and to draw upon learner-centered principles in using learning objects to customize content in response to individual student needs. As the saying goes, "the proof is in the pudding" or in providing faculty with the practical tools they need to create, use, and evaluate learning objects as teaching resources.

References

Advanced Distributed Learning. (2005). *SCORM history.* Retrieved February 10, 2007, from http://www.adlnet.gov/scorm/history/index.cfm

Christiansen, J., & Anderson, T. (2004). Feasibility of course development based on learning objects. *International Journal of Instructional Technology and Distance Learning, 1*(3). Retrieved February 10, 2007, from http://www.itdl.org/Journal/Mar_04/article02.htm

Conceico, S., Olgren, C., & Ploetz, P. (2006). Reusing learning objects in three settings: Implications for online instruction. *International Journal of Instructional Technology and Distance Learning, 3*(3), 3-14.

Degen, B. (2001). *Capitalizing on the learning object economy: The strategic benefits of standard learning objects.* Retrieved February 10, 2007, from Learning Objects Network, Inc., http://www.learningobjectsnetwork.com/resources/LONWhitePaper_StrategicBenefitsOfStandardLearningObjects.pdf

Friesen, N. (2003). *Three objections to learning objects.* Retrieved February 10, 2007, from http://phenom.educ.ualberta.ca/~nfriesen/

Haughey, M., & Muirhead, B. (2005). Evaluating learning objects for schools. *E-Journal of Electronic Science and Technology, 8*(1). Retrieved February 10, 2007, from http://www.usq.edu.au/electpub/e-jist/docs/vol8_no1/content.htm

Hodgins, H. (2002). *The future of learning objects.* Paper presented at the 2002 ECI Conference on e-Technologies in Engineering Education, Davos, Switzerland.

Jacobsen, P. (2002, November 1). History and definition of RLOs. *e-Learning Magazine.*

McGreal, R. (2004). Learning objects: A practical definition. *International Journal of Instructional Technology & Distance Learning, 1*(9). Retrieved February 10, 2007, from http://www.itdl.org/Journal/Sep_04/index.htm

McMartin, F. (2004) MERLOT: A model for user involvement in digital library design and implementation. *Journal of Digital Information, 5*(3). Retrieved February 10, 2007, from http://jodi.tamu.edu/Articles/v05/i03/McMartin/

Meachen, E., Olgren, C., & Ploetz, P. (2005). *Final report: An investigation of the pedagogical and economic effectiveness of sharable content objects, using standards, in online instruction.* Fund for the Improvement of Postsecondary Education (FIPSE). U.S. Department of Education. Grant No. P116B020126. Retrieved February 10, 2007, from http://www.fipse.aed.org/grantshow.cfm?grantNumber=P116B020126

Metros, S. E., & Bennett, K. (2002). *Learning objects in higher education* (Bulletin): Educause Center for Applied Research.

Nesbit, J. C., Belfer, K., & Leacock, T. (2003). *Learning object review instrument (LORI).* E-Learning Research and Assessment Network.

Nesbit, J., Belfer, K., & Vargo, J. (2002). A convergent participation model for evaluation of learning objects. *Canadian Journal of Learning and Technology, 28*(3). Retrieved February 10, 2007, from http://www.cjlt.ca/content/vol28.3/nesbit_etal.html

Oakes, K. (2002). An objective view of learning objects. *Training & Development, 56*(5), 103-105.

Ploetz, P. (2003). *Faculty experiences with learning object development: A case study of proof of concept grant applying advanced distributed teaching and learning to pre-calculus mathematics.* University of Wisconsin System Administration, Office of Learning and Information Technology.

Polsani, P. R. (2003). Use and abuse of reusable learning objects, *Journal of Digital Information, 3*(4). Retrieved February 10, 2007, from http://jodi.tamu.edu/Articles/v03/i04/Polsani/

Robson, R. (2001). *Learning object tutorial*. Retrieved February 10, 2007, from http://www.eduworks.com/LOTT/tutorial/index.html

Seimens, G. (2003). *Why we should share learning resources?* Retrieved February 10, 2007, from http://www.elearnspace.org/Articles/why_we_should_share.htm

Weimer, M. (2002). *Learner-centered teaching*. San Francisco, CA: Jossey-Bass.

Wiggins, G., & McTighe, J. (1998). *Understanding by design*. Alexandria, VA: Association for Supervision and Curriculum Development.

Endnotes

1   For detailed information on the FIPSE Grant, An Investigation of the "Pedagogical and Economic Effectiveness of Sharable Content Objects, Using Standards, in Online Instruction," see the final report at http://www.academiccolab.org/resources/documents/FIPSEFinalReport-013006.pdf

2   AICC, IEEE, IMS, and ADRIADNE

3   The AICC, Aviation Industry CBT (Computer-Based Training) Committee, the IEEE, a professional association for the advancement of technology, the IMS/GLC a global, nonprofit, member organization that provides leadership in shaping and growing the learning industry through community development of standards and ARIADNE a European organization devoted to the sharing of knowledge in learning and technology were involved in the early SCORM development process.

Chapter XII

Learning Objects:
A Case Study in
Teacher Education

Charlotte J. Boling, University of West Florida, USA

Abstract

This chapter presents a case study of a teacher education faculty member as she researches learning objects and integrates the concepts into her curriculum. The case unfolds as the instructor begins to plan the curriculum for the upcoming semester. The planning process leads to questions where the instructor investigates: why learning objects should be used, how learning objects should be used, where learning objects can be found, how learning objects should be integrated, and how learning objects should be evaluated. The investigation concerning learning objects and the course continue simultaneously. Throughout this journey, the author provides examples from the course as she strives to: (1) create an awareness of learning objects among her students and (2) provide an experience where students are afforded opportunities to determine the value of using learning objects as an instructional tool.

Introduction

While planning the curriculum for next semester's reading theory course, I chose to integrate Internet-based learning objects into several lessons. I did this for a couple of reasons. First, I wanted to teach my students about learning objects. I wanted my students to know what learning objects are, how they can be used, where to find them, and how to determine if the learning object is a quality learning tool or not. Second, I wanted my students to have an opportunity to experience using learning objects and determine the value of the experience. By creating this personal learning experience, my students would have firsthand knowledge of a learning object experience. They would not read about it or observe me in demonstration; they would experience the learning object themselves. In that way, each would determine the value of using learning objects to teach specific content or skills. My prediction was that students would place high value on the learning objects; they would value learning objects as instructional tools and discover many ways to use the objects to teach and learn.

However, before I created this experience, I needed to carefully research learning objects and determine how my instruction could be enhanced using them. The situation was precarious. Not only do I have the responsibility of producing knowledgeable teachers but I must also ensure that I have provided comprehensive content information for them. Specific to this course, these future teachers must understand educational and reading theory as well as how to use instructional strategies, integrate technology, address multicultural and special needs students, and differentiate between information that is useful and distracting. Therefore, any tool used, any content presented, or techniques demonstrated must contribute to the overall enhancement of my instruction.

As I continued planning the curriculum for the methods course, I identified several learning objects that could be used in my instruction. I also made deliberate changes in the types of assignments that had been previously required in this course. Students from previous semesters were encouraged to create original material for the course assignments and were discouraged from using Internet-based materials. Changes made for this class included required Internet-based materials and no teacher-made materials.

With the preparation phase complete and the course ready to begin, I stood before my students on the first day of class. I discussed goals for the course, specific objectives required for student learning outcomes, and then, fielded questions. *Are you saying that you want me to use the Internet to find activities for my assignments? What about the idea of using original or teacher-created materials? What are learning objects? How do I find learning objects? How do I know if it is a good learning object?*

These are typical reactions and good questions. Students want reassurance of a variety of resources and high quality materials. For this reason, many teacher education programs require students to create their own resources. With student-created materials, the student is responsible for the quality of content, accuracy of information, and presentation of material. The materials are then custom-made and specifically address the learning goals and objectives. However, this process is time consuming and many times, unproductive.

Today's preprofessional teacher has a plethora of information and educational materials readily available through the Internet. The need to create original materials is quickly diminishing. It is more efficient for preprofessional teachers to know how to find and use learning objects than to create their own each time materials are needed. The challenge for teacher education programs is to teach preprofessionals and practicing teachers why learning objects should be used in instruction, how to integrate learning objects seamlessly into instruction, ways to evaluate individual learning objects, and how to assess the successfulness of the instruction when learning objects are used.

Teacher Education Learning Objects Defined

Learning objects are "chunks" of instructional media that are multifunctional. In teacher education programs, learning objects can be defined as multimedia objects that are used to promote an intellectual experience. A learning object may be an illustration, simulation, or a complete lesson. The type of object varies almost as much as its potential uses (Brown, Miller, & Robinson, 2003).

Learning objects are not new to teacher education. In fact, instructors have been using instructional objects for years in an effort to stimulate interest, simulate authentic instructional situations, and provide materials that could be used for a variety of purposes. A prime example is the world map found rolled and hanging above the chalkboard in most classrooms. This object can be used to identify continents and countries, longitudinal degrees or positions, and define characteristics of a culture. The map can be used when teaching geography, math, or sociology. While the learning object (map) is important to the instruction, the teacher serves as the pivotal component. It is the teacher who decides how to use the learning object so that instructional needs are met and intellectual experiences created.

Using Learning Objects in Teacher Education

The focus of teacher education programs is to provide intellectual experiences so that preprofessional and practicing teachers are successful educators. These teachers must know how learning occurs and facilitate learning in a variety of ways. Teachers must also possess content knowledge and pedagogical skills. The teacher must be prepared to make informed instructional decisions that will lead to student learning. It is in this mode that learning objects should be used in teacher education—the teacher as the instructional decision maker using learning objects to meet a specific learning goal.

Why Should Learning Objects be Used in Teacher Education?

The benefits of using learning objects in teacher education are numerous. They are powerful learning tools that can be used to promote teaching and learning in a variety of ways. One of the many strengths provided by learning objects is the ability to provide customized learning. Learning objects are just enough, just in time, and just for you. This means that learning objects are modular (just enough), searchable (just in time), and customizable (just for you) (Wisconsin Online Resource Center, 2005).

Another benefit is the ability to use learning objects in a variety of instructional settings. Teachers may require a learning object for an independent research topic, a group project, or as a class assignment. Additionally, the learning object can be used to accommodate a variety of learning styles. Some students learn best in independent environments while others need the opportunity to discuss with others in a group or classroom setting. Learning objects provide another avenue of assisting students as they learn best.

Many learning objects have been designed using a multisensory approach. This benefits those in teacher education by providing examples of how a multisensory approach can be used in the instructional process. By incorporating texts, colors, graphics, sound, and interactions, the likelihood of students processing the information has increased greatly. Research demonstrates that a multisensory approach leads to a deeper understanding of content knowledge. A deeper understanding will yield students with greater knowledge.

As with any instructional technique or learning tool, the teacher should carefully examine the new item before committing to use it. The teacher should critique the learning object and evaluate the benefits that using it will bring to the intellectual experience. In short, the learning object should aid in the process of enhancing content knowledge and developing skills.

Figure 1. Sample learning object

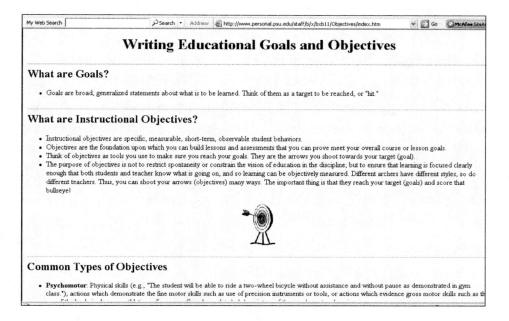

For example, in previous semesters of my undergraduate reading theory course, I found that students were having difficulty writing behavioral objectives correctly. As I planned for this semester, I sought a learning object that might provide additional reinforcement for those skills. With a quick search through a couple of learning object repositories, I found a learning object, "Writing Educational Goals and Objectives" (Bixler, 2006) that fit my needs perfectly (see Figure 1).

The learning object had correct information, was relatively short, used font emphasis to highlight pertinent text, and was interactive. This learning object met my needs of being "just enough, just in time, and just for [me]." Simultaneously, the object reinforced the concepts that I taught in class and presented the information in an interactive format.

How Should Learning Objects be Used in Teacher Education?

The purpose for designing and using learning objects is instruction. Learning objects are used to help instructors teach and students learn. Haughey and Muirhead (2005) suggest that the value of a learning object is in the "application to classroom settings and to online environments where teachers may or may not be present." In teacher education settings, some courses are campus-based while others are Internet-based. Learning objects are instructional tools that can be used in either setting.

Learning objects can be used for many functions. The teacher, as the instructional decision-maker, gathers many types of instructional resources to organize the lessons. Picture books, novels, textbooks, pictures, Web sites, games, and activities are just a few of the many items teachers use to develop curriculum. Similarly, preprofessional and practicing teachers must be taught how to use learning objects as they develop curriculum. According to Haughey and Muirhead, learning objects are used primarily to:

1.   Introduce new topics and skills
2.   Provide reinforcement to existing skills
3.   Extend learning by providing new means for presenting curricular material
4.   Illustrate concepts that are less easily explained through traditional teaching methods
5.   Support new types of learning opportunities not available in a classroom environment
6.   Provide enrichment activities for gifted and highly motivated students. reinforce concepts taught in the teacher education program as well as a resource for preprofessional teachers (Haughey & Muirhead, 2005)

While this list is not exhaustive, it supplies practical methods that teacher education instructors might use when introducing learning objects to preprofessional and practicing teachers. The topics presented in this list include many concepts associated with the learning process and comprehensive instruction that teachers may use when teaching. It also allows for individualized instruction for those students needing additional reinforcement or enrichment activities.

- **Introduce new topics and skills:** Learning objects can be used to create interest and motivate students to learn complex subjects or unfamiliar topics. By using the object, the teacher builds background information concerning the particular topic and activates prior knowledge. The learning process begins for the student as soon as the student begins using the learning object.
- **Provide reinforcement to existing skills:** Reinforcement is critically important to the learning process. Logan's (1990) research found that the average student needed 16 experiences with a concept before it could be committed to long term memory. Therefore, activities that provide additional practice with a concept promote the likelihood that the information will be processed as a long

term memory concept. The variety of learning objects increase the probability that students can receive the reinforcement and adds to their knowledge.

- **Extend learning by providing new means for presenting curricular material:** Quick simulations and informational learning objects are motivational activities I use to extend my classroom lessons. For example, in my reading methods course, I teach a lesson on educational objectives and require my students to develop an objective and subsequent lesson that addresses the identified objective. After the campus-based lesson, I require my students to log onto the "Writing Educational Goals and Objectives" learning object Web site for a homework assignment. This assignment requires students to review the website, read the information, check out the links, and take the quiz. The learning object helps me maximize the learning for my students. While this homework assignment requires no more than 20 minutes of the student's time, I achieved a great deal. By using this learning object, my students have enhanced their knowledge concerning educational goals and objectives, found a resource for writing objectives, viewed several correctly written examples, and tested the extent of their knowledge concerning educational goals and objectives.

- **Illustrate concepts that are less easily explained through traditional teaching methods:** Sometimes a "picture is worth a thousand words". When you are teaching a complex concept, the picture may be worth more. Teachers often use graphics, photographs, and movies in their instruction to explain abstract ideas such as persecution, slavery, success, fulfillment, and so on. Learning objects can be used in a similar fashion. The graphics, simulations, and interactive characteristics of many learning objects create engaging learning environments. Students working with unfamiliar or complex concepts may need the multisensory approach offered through learning objects in order to comprehend the concept and achieve the intended learning goal.

- **Support new types of learning opportunities not available in a classroom environment:** A virtual field trip to the Amazon Forest, racing on the *Iditarod*, a tour of the White House, and observe chemical changes in an atom are all learning opportunities made possible through the Internet. The teacher, as the instructional decision maker, must peruse the learning objects and select the one that best meets the teacher's needs. Teachers have the opportunity to build background knowledge and develop positive learning environments like never before in educational history.

- **Provide enrichment activities for gifted and highly motivated students:** Advanced learning opportunities abound in the learning object world. Students interested in particular topics may research, read, participate in simulations, and add to their knowledge bank. Teachers may facilitate this knowledge acquisition by organizing individualized instruction for a student. Students may then revisit concepts not fully acquired or enhance their knowledge by moving on to more complicated skills within the concept.

Where Do I Find Learning Objects?

Learning objects are found primarily in learning object repositories (LOR). The repositories contain quite an array of learning objects. Some are free resources; some are not. Some are text driven while others are interactive graphics. Most include categories and a search engine so that the teacher may select the learning object that best meets the teacher's needs. Below is a listing of a few repositories that are used by education instructors and students.

- **Multimedia Educational Resource for Learning and Online Teaching (MERLOT) (http://www.merlot.org/):** MERLOT is a free and open repository that primarily serves higher education faculty and students. MERLOT's Teacher Education Portal contains resources specifically for teachers. Teachers can find advice concerning how to use learning objects in instruction, join professional organizations, or view the learning objects under the Education materials link.

- **Co-operative Learning Object Exchange (CLOE) (http://cloe.on.ca):** CLOE is a learning object database developed in a collaborative project between Ontario universities and colleges. CLOE provides a way for colleges and universities to develop, share, and reuse multimedia-rich learning resources.

- **Apple Learning Interchange (http://ali.apple.com/ali/resources.shtml):** The folks at Apple have organized a free repository of thousands of Internet resources that can be use in teaching and learning.

- **Educational Software Components of Tomorrow (ESCOT) (http://www. escot.org/audiences/classroom-user.html):** ESCOT is a resource that challenges teachers and students in a feature "online problem of the week" or EPoW. The database was developed to "accumulate, integrate, and scale up" K-12 mathematics and science education to meet the needs of systemic reform.

- **Campus Alberta Repository of Educational Objects (CAREO) (http://careo. ucalgary.ca/cgi-bin/WebObjects/CAREO.woa):** CAREO is a searchable collection of teaching materials that educators may use. It is supported by Alberta Learning and CANARIE (Canadian Network for the Advancement of Research in Industry and Education).

- **Wisconsin Online Resource Center (WISC-ONLINE) (http://www.wisc-online.com/):** WISC-ONLINE contains numerous learning objects in their repository. Teachers may select one of the subjects, use a keyword search, or select the General Education tab to locate learning objects for their instruction. WISC-ONLINE learning objects are free when used online.

How Should Learning Objects be Integrated into Instruction?

Teachers use learning objects to enhance their curriculum and create meaningful lessons for their students. Integrating learning objects should be part of a total learning experience not a separate "stand alone" activity. To illustrate this process, I integrated multiculturalism, technology, and lesson planning objectives into one assignment.

The learning objectives for this lesson were threefold: (1) to develop ways to incorporate multicultural concepts into instruction; (2) to increase the student's awareness of learning objects; and (3) to perform basic Internet-based skills of surfing and posting a response to a discussion Web. To accomplish these tasks, students were required to explore a multicultural learning object and then identify instructional topics that could be developed into a lesson for second graders.

The procedures for this task were to log on and investigate "Chickens Around the World" (Kirsch & Bodoh, 2006). This interactive learning object informs the reader of a variety of ways that meals can can be prepared and cooked in a variety of countries and cultures.

After reviewing the site, preprofessionals were charged with identifying ways that this learning object could be used in instruction. Ideas were posted and discussed on

Figure 2. Interactive learning object

an Internet-based discussion board. Gleaned from the discussions for this assignment were issues concerning ethnic cultures, geographic locations, instructional design, memory skills, reading skills, and others.

In a later assignment, I combined the skills of "Writing an Educational Objective" with the use of a learning object. In this assignment, preprofessional teachers were required to identify a subject area (social studies, science, math, language arts, reading, etc.), write an educational objective, and find a learning object that would meet the learning goal(s) of the objective. For this exercise, I provided a list of learning object repositories and encouraged the students to explore the repositories completely. By expanding the concept and requiring students to match additional educational objectives with learning objects, I increased their awareness of learning object repositories and the educational opportunities that exist.

Preprofessional teachers are most likely to integrate instruction and transfer knowledge and skills from the university classroom into classroom curriculum when the following characteristics are evident:

- **Relative advantage:** Preprofessionals understand the benefits of using learning objects in their classroom curriculum.
- **Compatibility:** Learning objects are viewed as tools that support the curriculum.
- **Complexity:** Preprofessionals view learning objects as tools that they can use without advanced training.
- **Trialibilty:** Preprofessionals experience learning objects in an authentic yet nonthreatening manner.
- **Observability:** Preprofessionals develop a supportive community where learning objects are used in a variety of ways and ideas are shared (Rogers, 1995).

Learning objects were integrated in the examples described above by requiring preprofessional teachers to investigate and respond to the learning objects (relative advantage). Students learned that there are many learning objects that can be used to support their curriculum (compatibility) without spending large amounts of time learning how to use them (complexity). These preprofessional teachers also had the opportunity to engage with (trialibility) and discuss ways to use (observability) learning objects.

As preprofessional teachers continue to investigate learning objects and explore different ways to use them, each will acquire a knowledge base on how to integrate learning objects. These experiences should lead to a transference of knowledge and skills as the preprofessional teachers move from the university setting to a classroom environment. The intended result will be that preprofessional teachers enter the educational workplace with information and skills that enhance student learning without spending a lot of time or money on the experience.

How Should Learning Objects be Evaluated in Teacher Education?

The purpose of using learning objects in teacher education is to teach. Without an instructional purpose the value of the learning object diminishes. Therefore, learning objects are evaluated in two distinct ways. First, learning objects are evaluated as individual tools to determine if the object is, indeed, a quality learning tool. Second, the instruction in which the learning object has been embedded is evaluated to determine the effectiveness of the learning outcomes using the learning object.

Evaluating the Learning Object

Most learning object repositories have some form of evaluation process to ensure that the resource provided is of high quality. The purpose of the review is to assist non-users as he or she determines the usability of the learning object. Several repositories have a peer review while others include a user-rating and review. The review process used by several popular learning object repositories as described on their respective websites is described below.

MERLOT provides a peer-review evaluation process to assist educators in selecting high-quality learning objects. The peer-review process evaluates three areas: quality of content, potential effectiveness as a teaching-learning tool, and ease of use. These broad areas of evaluation are reported on the learning object page. The review alerts the user to the evaluation findings by posting specific information on the learning object's page. Information includes such items as a description of the object, cost involved, dates added and modified, special technology requirements, Language, Copyright status, and 508 compliance status.

CLOE uses a peer-review process to evaluate their learning objects (CLOE, 2006). The evaluation process is termed CRAFT and requires an evaluation of an instructional designer and content expert. CRAFT is a mnemonic devise that includes the following criteria:

- **C**lear (consistent with author guidelines)
- **R**ecognized (being a reviewer is institutionally valued)
- **A**utomated (neither onerous nor a disincentive for reviewer or reviewed;

automation of certain tasks should occur)

- **Familiar** (like other forms of scholarly peer review in the disciplines)
- **Thorough** (capacity to evaluate the form and the content of a learning object)

WISC-ONLINE includes a user-review where the learning object is rated using a star system. Users rate the object from one-star to five-stars where one star equates to a poor rating while five stars equates to an outstanding rating. WISC-ONLINE users can also submit a review where information concerning the object is shared with others.

In reviewing information concerning learning object evaluations (Cafolla, 2006; Haughey & Muirhead, 2005; Williams, 2002), I discovered a variety of criteria used in the evaluation process. In an attempt to synthesize this information and organize a straight-forward list of criteria that could be used in determining the value of a learning object for instruction, I developed a checklist (Appendix A). This checklist is based on the criteria set forth in the documents mentioned earlier and is based around four specific criteria. The criteria include design, usability, content integrity, and the learning process.

- ***Design* of the learning object:** When considering the design of the learning object, I specifically investigated the aesthetic qualities of the object. I looked specifically at the font, text color, background color, readability of text of the page, appropriateness of the graphics, and placement of objects on the page. Questions added to the checklist include:
  - o   Is the font appropriate for the audience?
  - o   Were the text and background colors complimentary to maximize readability?
  - o   Do the graphics facilitate comprehension of the content topic or learning process?
  - o   Are the graphics placed appropriately on the page in a nondistracting format?
  - o   Is the learning object visually appealing?
  - o   Is there an appropriate amount of text on each page?
- ***Usability* of the learning object:** When students use a learning object, they depend on the designers to include clear directions so that each will know what to do. The functions of the learning object should be intuitive so that learning is focused on the content and not spent frustrated by technology. Specifically, I looked for the following criteria when assessing the usability of the learning object:
  - o   Are clear and concise directions posted on the learning object?

- o Is the readability of the directions appropriate for the audience?

- o Do all links work?

- o Are the functions of the learning object intuitive? (Do students know what to do?)

- o Does the learning object provide for active engagement with the concepts or skills?

- *Content integrity* **of the learning object:** Information presented on a learning object should be accurate and professional. The content should be well-researched with appropriate credit given to deserving individuals. The text should be written using a professional manner and demonstrate appropriate grammar, spelling, and mechanics of writing. A high quality learning object should also contain accurate information at a level appropriate for the intended audience. Criteria important to this category are:

- o Is the content information accurate?

- o Is the level of content information appropriate for the intended audience? (not too easy; not too challenging)

- o Is the text written using a professional format?

- o Is the text free of grammatical and spelling errors?

- o Has credit been given to creators?

- o Are appropriate academic references provided?

- *Learning process* **incorporated in the learning object:** The purpose of learning objects is to teach a concept. Therefore, this evaluation must also verify that the learning object has the potential to teach the intended concept or skill. In order to accomplish this, the learning object must address components of the learning process making certain that the necessary items are included.

- o Are there clear learning objectives?

- o Does the learning object reinforce concepts progressively?

- o Does the learning object provide an opportunity to receive feedback on the intended knowledge or skill?

- o Does the learning object meet the stated learning objective(s)?

The categories identified in this checklist design, usability, content integrity, and the learning process, are not intended to be exhaustive but rather a place to begin evaluating quality learning objects. This checklist provides a prompt that preprofessional and practicing teachers may use to determine whether or not an identified learning object meets their instructional needs. Additionally, teachers will be able to determine if the learning object is of high enough quality to be used in their instruction.

How are Preprofessional Teachers Responding to Learning Objects?

The preprofessional teachers are responding to learning objects and in a most favorable manner. After using the "Writing Educational Objectives" learning object, my undergraduate students provided the following unsolicited comments:

I like those integrated links because they make the content/reading more interesting. That particular link was informative and simple. The quiz was short and to-the-point. (Roger)

Thanks for including the LO link. It helped me a lot. I am a very visual learner, so seeing the explanation and examples really helped. (Sue)

In regards to the learning object in lesson 5, I found it to be informative. It helped break the objectives down into parts so you understand what all needs to be included when writing your objectives. I know when I wrote my objective I made sure I had each of the 4 parts. I think this helps make your objectives clear to not only yourself, but to your students, and anyone else reading your lesson. (Tonya)

I found this page to be very beneficial when I was writing my objective; it gave me examples of ways that I could write the educational objective. (Becky)

Many students commented that they have a deeper understanding of the concept. That is, the students feel more confident when writing learning objectives. When compared to previous student performances, I feel this class demonstrated mastery of the skill and wrote accurate learning objectives at a faster rate than their peers from earlier semesters.

Evaluating the Instruction When Using a Learning Object

In my undergraduate methods course, I used learning objects to reinforce educational concepts and promote intellectual experiences. As my students began to use the learning objects, there were questions I asked concerning my instruction. The two questions guiding my instructional evaluation were:

- Did the learning object meet and/or enhance my curricular goals and objectives?

- Did the use of the learning object increase student knowledge?

The answer to both questions is *Yes!* While similar information was provided in the textbook as well as classroom discussions, the learning object offered an interactive approach to the content information. The learning object reinforced the concepts I presented in class.

In order to determine if the learning object meets the curricular goals, the teacher must be diligent in determining the specific goals and searching to find a learning object that meets those goals. For example, "Writing Educational Goals and Objectives" provided an additional experience for my students in their quest to understand the components of an educational objective. While the learning object could be used for a variety of purposes and classes, it met my needs perfectly and my students benefited from the experience.

The use of learning objects should also be evaluated to determine if student knowledge is increased due to the experience. Student achievement may be measured using a general knowledge test, performance-assessment, problem-based assessment, or self-assessment. For my undergraduate students, specific improvements were evident on midterm and final exam questions as well as an application assignment where students were required to develop a lesson based on their learning objective.

Benefits for Using Learning Objects in Teacher Education

As I began this journey of discovering more about learning objects and integrating them into my own instruction, I had two goals. First, I wanted to increase my students' awareness concerning learning objects. Second, I wanted students to have an opportunity to experience a learning object and determine the value of learning objects in education.

My students accomplished these goals. They explored learning objects, reflected on the purposes and usefulness, and evaluated the effectiveness. Additionally, my students know what learning objects are, where to find them, how to use them, and how to determine if the learning object is worthy of instructional use. My students were successful learners.

The benefits for using learning objects in teacher education are endless. Teachers have the possibility of logging on to the Internet and finding multi-functional tools that can lead to enhanced student learning. Internet-based learning objects provide teachers with a way to integrate traditional textbook curriculum with multisensory, interactive learning. It is a powerful mix. Using learning objects requires that the teacher leads the curriculum. The teacher is the instructional decision-maker selecting learning objects that enhance his or her learning goals. The teacher is not bound by a "script" but rather encouraged to make informed curricular decisions based on knowledge, skills, and experience.

Many of the learning objects currently available have been developed for faculty and students in higher education institutions. With the integration of learning objects into teacher education curriculum, teachers will continue to benefit. Learning objects provide new teachers with resources and best practice activities that will enhance their teaching and provide meaningful activities for their students. New teachers will complete their teacher education programs equipped with knowledge of current educational resources and the ability to integrate meaningful objects into their curriculum.

References

Bixler, B. (2006). *Writing educational goals and objectives*. Retrieved February 9, 2007, from http://www.personal.psu.edu/staff/b/x/bxb11/Objectives/index.htm

Brown, A., Miller, D., & Robinson, L. (2003). Teacher-directed software design: The development of learning objects for students with special needs in the elementary classroom. *Information Technology in Childhood Education,* 173-186.

Cafolla, R. (2006). Project MERLOT: Bringing peer review to Web-based educational resources. *Journal of Technology and Teacher Education, 14*(2), 313-123.

CLOE. (2006). *Co-operative learning object exchange: Peer review*. Retrieved on February 9, 2007, from http://cloe.on.ca/peerreview.html

Haughey, M., & Muirhead, B. (2005). The pedagogical and multimedia designs of learning objects for schools. *Australian Journal of Educational Technology, 21*(4), 470-490.

Kirsch, V., & Bodoh, A. (2006). *Chickens around the world*. Retrieved on February 9, 2007, from http://www.wisc-online.com/objects/index_tj.asp?objID=SOC2402

Logan, G. (1990). Repetition priming and automaticity: Common underlying mechanisms? *Cognitive Psychology, 22,* 1-35.

Rogers, E. (1995). *Diffusion of innovations*. New York: The Free Press.

Williams, D. D. (2002). *Evaluation of learning objects and instruction using learning objects*. Retrieved February 9, 2007, from http://reusability.org/read/

Wisconsin Online Resource Center (2005). *Wisc-Online*. Retrieved on March 26, 2007 from http://www.wisc-online.com/

Appendix: Evaluating a Learning Object Checklist

Design of the Learning Object

- Is the font appropriate for the audience?
- Were the text and background colors complimentary to maximize readability?
- Do the graphics facilitate comprehension of the content topic or learning process?
- Are the graphics placed appropriately on the page in a non-distracting format?
- Is the learning object visually appealing?
- Is there an appropriate amount of text on each page?

Usability of the Learning Object

- Are clear and concise directions posted on the learning object?
- Is the readability of the directions appropriate for the audience?
- Do all links work?
- Are the functions of the learning object intuitive? (Do students know what to do?)
- Does the learning object provide for active engagement with the concepts or skills?

Content Integrity of Learning Object

- Is the content information accurate?
- Is the level of content information appropriate for the intended audience? (not too easy; not too challenging)
- Is the text written using a professional format?
- Is the text free of grammatical and spelling errors?
- Has credit been given to creators?
- Are appropriate academic references provided?

Learning Process incorporated in the Learning Object

- Are there clear learning objectives?
- Does the learning object reinforce concepts progressively?
- Does the learning object provide an opportunity to receive feedback on the intended knowledge or skill?
- Does the learning object meet the stated learning objective(s)?

Chapter XIII

Bridging the Academic Divide:
A Collaborative Production Model for Learning Objects in Workforce Development

Tom Cavanagh, Embry-Riddle Aeronautical University-Worldwide Campus, USA

Abstract

There is a commonly held perception in industry that the academic community is out of touch and irrelevant. Surely, there must be a way to bridge this perception gap and leverage academe's disciplinary and instructional expertise to benefit the commercial workforce. This chapter presents a collaborative development model that accomplishes this goal, specifically relating to the production of self-paced, Web-based learning objects, catalogued within workforce development curricula. The model provides a roadmap that maximizes the expertise of college faculty, industry managers, and multimedia production specialists to meet the needs of government sponsors, commercial corporations, nonprofit postsecondary institutions, and individual learners.

Introduction

There is a commonly held perception among many in industry that the academic community is out of touch and not particularly relevant; although there are many cases where academics work well with industry partners. As a result, industry many times chooses to collaborate with non-academic partners for their training needs. The vast majority of commercial workforce training and development activity is performed by for-profit vendors and contractors, comprising the bulk of an economic sector worth more than $50 billion annually in the United States alone (Galvin, 2002). When considered in comparison to their larger academic missions, postsecondary institutions conduct very little of what is traditionally considered workforce development. Yet, paradoxically, it is the academic community that provides industry with its most important resource: employees. Surely, there must be a way to bridge this perception gap and leverage the academic community's disciplinary and instructional expertise to benefit the commercial workforce.

This chapter presents a development model that accomplishes this goal, specifically as it relates to the production of self-paced, Web-based learning objects, catalogued within targeted workforce development curricula. This collaborative development model provides a roadmap that maximizes the expertise of college faculty, industry managers, and multimedia production specialists to meet the needs of varying stakeholders which include: government sponsors, commercial corporations, nonprofit postsecondary institutions, and individual learners. By applying this collaborative development model, almost 100 learning objects were successfully developed during a two year period, representing more than eighty hours of student contact time across three distinct curricula.

Context

While recognizing that there is ongoing debate in the academic and commercial discourse regarding the precise definition of a learning object, the learning objects produced as a result of the collaborative development model described in this chapter conformed to many generally-accepted definitions of learning objects. From a macro perspective, they are consistent with the often-cited definition provided by the IEEE Learning Technology Standards Committee: "any entity, digital or non-digital, which can be used, re-used or referenced during technology supported learning" (IEEE, 2005). To narrow the definition a bit, the learning objects were further consistent with Wiley's contention that learning objects should be "small (relative to the size of an entire course) instructional components that can be reused a number of times in different learning contexts," and "be digital entities deliverable over the Internet, meaning that any number of people can access and use them simultaneously" (Wiley, 2001). Hamel and Ryan-Jones (2002) echo Wiley's definition of learning objects "as small but pedagogically complete segments of instructional content that can be assembled as needed to create larger units of instruction, such as lessons, modules and courses."

This repeated notion of being small is critical. Because the curricula being produced were for an adult workforce audience, smaller, "bite-sized" instructional units not only supported object reusability but were a conscious strategy for learner completion. Many of those in the target populations were working adults with job, family, and other responsibilities. The learning objects needed to be presented as discrete elements that could be launched and completed during short windows of availability, "ideally completed in a single sitting (such as during a lunch hour)" (Cavanagh & Metcalf, 2002). Indeed, this notion is central to Morris' (2005) very definition of a learning object, which, among other aspects, "encapsulates learning activities that are standalone and achievable in a single sitting" (p. 40). While the actual object duration varied according to the particular needs of the content and the individual learner, the target length for each learning object in all three curricula was thirty minutes. Over a longer period of time, perhaps weeks, an individual student could complete a large, comprehensive curriculum one thirty-minute object at a time.

A key strategy for achieving this 30-minute learning object duration was to ensure that each object had a single terminal learning objective. Boyle (2002) argues that not only should each learning object be based upon a single objective for pedagogical reasons, but from a programming perspective, each object should do only one thing and have minimal linkages to other objects, thus enhancing reusability. Similarly, Hamel and Ryan-Jones (2002) state that "learning objects should be stand alone, and be built upon a single learning objective, or a single concept." This theoretical foundation was the basis for later curricular design.

The general metric for a learning object in this curricula was approximately one minute of learner contact time per Web-based page (or screen). The learning objects were structured as sequentially-presented pages in a self-paced tutorial format. Pages contained text, graphics, animations, interactions, game-style challenges, audio narration, video, or other media as required to accomplish the learning objectives. A typical user could expect to spend approximately one minute on each page of the tutorial. Thus, for an object that met the target duration of 30 minutes, a learner could expect to interact with approximately thirty screens in the tutorial. Strict text, graphic, and other media guidelines were employed to ensure that each page (and, by extension, each completed learning object), was "right sized" for learner delivery. Likewise, to preserve the aesthetic presentation of the material and support instructional integrity, the browser window size was locked and scrolling (horizontal and vertical) was not permitted, nor even necessary.

Each learning object had an associated pretest and post-test, although they existed separately from the instructional elements as pure assessment objects. This separated-but-linked relationship between instructional and assessment elements allowed much greater flexibility in learning object reuse. Objects could be extracted or repackaged for presentation either with or without the tests, depending upon the particular *in situ* needs of the deployment. To further enhance reusability, all learning objects were developed in accordance with the shareable content object reference model (SCORM).

Apples and Oranges

Developing a semester-length course for a traditional classroom environment is a very different proposition from developing a self-paced, Web-based curriculum of interactive learning objects for workforce training. While the overarching instructional strategies and models may be the same, the tactics that are used to act on those strategies vary widely. For example, a traditional, classroom-based academic course may require extensive preparation that includes the development of a course outline, a syllabus, a schedule, lecture notes, assessments, visual presentation aids, and other support materials. However, a traditional classroom course does not require the precise scripting of every word of instruction to be delivered to students. Because the instruction within a self-paced learning object is computer-facilitated, with no external human intervention, there is an extra burden on the development team to precisely capture the subject matter expertise of the academic authority. In this self-paced, technologically-mediated construct, the computer functions in an *in loco professor* capacity for the student.

Even the development of an Internet-based academic course is very different from a Web-based training (WBT) curriculum comprised of short, 30-minute self-paced learning objects. For example, the learning management systems (LMSs) used to deliver the instruction are very different (academic-oriented LMSs such as Blackboard, WebCT, Desire2Learn, and Angel vs. industry-oriented LMSs such as Saba, Docent, and Plateau); the length of the curriculum rarely aligns (an established academic term vs. any duration required to complete the training); the selection of instructional activities is driven by the platform (required online discussions in an academic course vs. no peer/instructor interaction in a self-paced WBT curriculum); and the educational outputs are in disparate formats (LMS-driven presentation in an academic course vs. custom interfaces and navigational schema in WBT courseware). Clearly, while both academic instruction and industry training have the same roots in instructional design and learning theory, the executions of the educational interventions are very different, even when both are technologically-mediated.

Figure 1. Collaborative learning object development

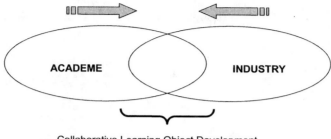

Collaborative Learning Object Development

It is no wonder, then, that there is a perceived disconnect between the academic community and commercial industry. In some respects, they are speaking different languages. The situation is similar to translating between Spanish and Portuguese. The languages are close enough to have some overlap, but they are undeniably separate and distinct in their own rights.

To use another common metaphor, it's the difference between apples and oranges. Academe is growing apples and industry is growing oranges. While the care and nurturing of both have common elements (plenty of water, sun, and nutrients), the specific requirements to be successful with each are quite different (a colder climate with seasonal change for apples vs. a consistently warm climate for oranges). Yet, they are each fruit. Surely an apple farmer could be taught the specific requirements for growing oranges without having to start from a completely blank knowledge base. The key to facilitate such a skill transfer is to identify those common knowledge areas and use methodological tools (i.e., job aids, mentoring, formal training, just in time support, etc.) to ease the transition. This concept is the foundational context for the collaborative production model described in this chapter (see Figure 1).

During a two-year period, this collaborative production model was successfully applied in the development of three distinct self-paced, Web-based training programs, with combined budgets of approximately $2 million. All three programs were produced and delivered to large statewide audiences and all three used academic expertise from postsecondary institutions as the basis for Web-based workforce-oriented training. The largest application was a 42-hour curriculum developed to prepare biotechnology technicians to enter the workforce. It consisted of 57 discrete learning objects covering a wide variety of topics relating to laboratory technology, biomanufacturing, and regulatory affairs. Another program was a 10-hour curriculum designed to prepare workers with no background in education to become successful K-12 classroom teachers (see Figure 2). The curriculum contained 15 discrete learning objects and was a key workforce initiative designed to help address a criti-

Figure 2. Screen capture from a Web-based learning object for workforce development

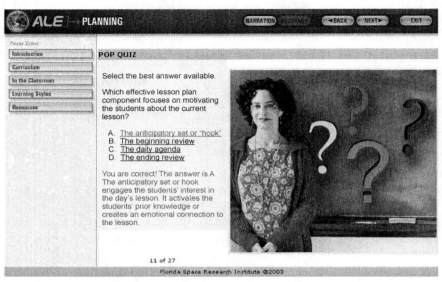

cal statewide teacher shortage. The courseware was not designed as an alternative teaching certification program; rather, it was created solely to re-skill professionals from non-academic disciplines to enter the classroom and be productive until they could complete an approved/accredited alternative certification. The third program also prepared K-12 educators, except it was focused specifically on the preparation of math and science teachers. The 30-hour curriculum consisted of 24 discrete learning objects and covered both discipline-specific (i.e., marine biology) and pedagogical (i.e., how to teach middle-school math) content areas.

The Collaborative Production Model

Grounded in established instructional methodology, the collaborative production model for workforce-oriented learning object development follows the traditional ADDIE process of analysis, design, development, implementation, and evaluation. However, several key enhancements have been incorporated into the ADDIE process that specifically function as translational support between the academic community and commercial industry. Each step in the process will be described in the subsequent sections. The following is a high-level overview of the system:

1. Align with industry needs
2. Describe competencies
3. Train faculty developers
4. Draft learning object storyboards
5. Conduct peer review
6. Deliver draft learning object courseware
7. Conduct multipurpose review
8. Implement into LMS
9. Evaluate courseware

Align with Industry Needs

One of the best ways to counter the argument that academe is out of touch with industry is for industry to actively participate in the curricular analysis. When employers can specifically define their workforce requirements, with a particular emphasis on projected future needs, then the training intervention can be targeted on the most critical areas. There are a variety of methods that can be employed to capture this information from industry participants, including formal job analysis, task analysis, needs analysis, and facilitated "developing a curriculum" (DACUM) processes. The K-12 general teacher preparation curriculum involved a customized analysis of the state's published 12 "accomplished practices" for teachers in the 21st century. These accomplished practices outline the knowledge and performance standards that the state department of education expects from all K-12 teachers in all subject areas. By analyzing these published competencies the program management team was able to prepare a learning object-based curriculum for Internet delivery that met the required workforce needs.

The biotechnician workforce development program used a hybrid approach involving a series of focus group meetings around the state, culminating in a modified performance criteria analysis (PCAL), a systematic process developed by Richland College in Texas. Program management team members used an iterative approach, first presenting an unedited list of key jobs, tasks, and skills in the biotechnology industry gleaned from various primary and secondary sources. Over the course of three separate focus group meetings (each meeting involved different participants), this list was refined until consensus was reached. Then participants in the final focus group meetings used the PCAL process to rate each skill on a 1 to 4 scale according to its *importance* (how critical is it for entry-level biotechnicians to know?), its *level* (how good is "good enough" for entry-level biotechnicians to know or do?), its *time* (how frequently will entry-level biotechnicians have to know or do the skill?), and its *difficulty* (how hard will the skill be for an entry-level biotechnician to master?).

The development team then used the industry ratings to prioritize the workforce skills. Because resources are always limited, especially in the development of a costly, media-rich, technology-enabled curriculum, this priority list ensured that the industry's most critical workforce needs were addressed in the resulting training program.

Describe Competencies

Building upon the results of the focus groups and PCAL process, the program management team prepared a matrix of skills and competencies that served as an over-arching curriculum map for later learning object production and delivery. The matrix organization structured competencies as goals that are supported by individual skills. The intention in the preparation of the competencies and curriculum map was to identify a one-to-one relationship between a skill and a discrete learning object. Each Web-based learning object that a trainee would later launch from within an LMS was directly correlated to a specific skill, which in turn was correlated to a larger job competency. The matrix further described specific teaching topics to be addressed within each learning object. These were captured as enabling learning objectives within each skill and were eventually presented as individual Web page (or multipage) level information within a learning object. Thus, to summarize the curricular structure: a curriculum is comprised of competencies, which is comprised

Figure 3. WBT curricular structure

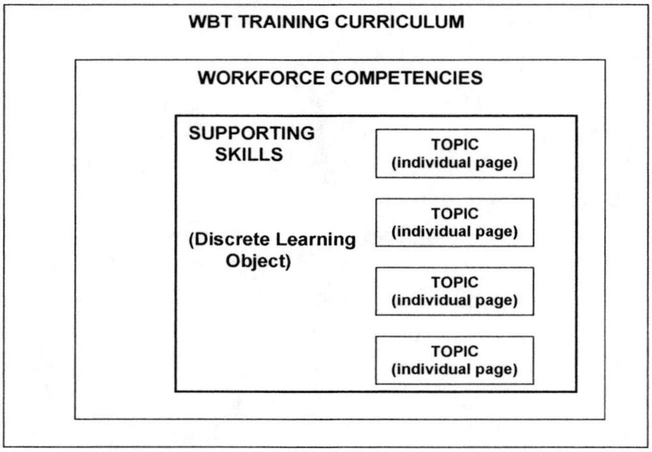

of various skills, which is comprised of instructional topics (see Figure 3). The level at which the discrete object is produced is at the skill level.

By aggregating a collection of short, skill-based learning objects, the curriculum uses a constructivist organization to achieve much larger and more comprehensive instructional goals. The same aggregated structure is used in the K-12 WBT programs. For example, there is a direct one-to-one correlation between each of the 12 accomplished practices and a discrete, "launchable" learning object (in addition to supplemental objects). To keep learning objects within the targeted window of student contact time, some skills needed to be subdivided into parts, such as Marine Biology 1 and 2. This was also true in the biotechnology curriculum.

Train Faculty Developers

Where the previous two steps attempted to bring industry towards academe, this step brings the academic community closer to industry expectations. After the general curricular structure was established (although later revisions certainly occurred), the faculty experts entered the process. While several academic experts participated in the front-end analysis and curricular planning, the overall sizes of the curricula in question required an extensive network of academic experts. These experts were primarily fulltime faculty members of partner institutions, although additional supplemental experts were found in industry and as specialized consultants.

Once the broad cadre of subject matter experts was identified, they were gathered together for a half-day conference (although, in practice, several sessions were also conducted individually for those unable to attend the general conference). During this conference, the faculty developers were given a primer for writing industry-oriented Web-based training. Because many of the faculty involved had never been exposed to this type of workforce instruction, they were shown several examples of workforce-oriented learning objects. They were also provided with a "toolkit" of templates and examples. Each element of the toolkit was explained in detail, with particular emphasis placed on the script template. These templates not only provide a model for the actual writing of content, but they also ensure that the material produced is the proper duration, contains appropriate media, and conforms to established instructional design best practices. They allow the subject matter experts to concentrate their efforts on discipline-specific activities and not waste their time trying to understand the courseware's production mechanics.

The templates and samples are based upon an industry training paradigm and, once the requirements were explained, most faculty members fully grasped the developmental expectations. The biggest challenge was a shift from a semester-based or even a class-based instructional unit to a 30-minute object-oriented instructional unit. The granular nature of a curriculum made up entirely of single-subject learning objects was foreign to some faculty experts. Describing the learning objects in familiar terms—such as referring to them as Web-based "lessons"—helped to facilitate understanding. The templates defined the boundaries for courseware production and "translated" between industry and academic frames of reference.

Draft Learning Objects Storyboards

A critical guide for faculty to actually write their material was the script template. Again, using familiar terminology to "translate" between academe and industry, the script template was described as "lecture notes" for the learning object. With both a completed sample and a blank template, the faculty expert could clearly understand how to write material for eventual learning object production. For example, the template explained how to chunk textual information into paragraphs that would fit within the learning object interface without vertical or horizontal scrolling. Additionally, the template provided a target range for the total page count, ensuring that each produced learning object would be the proper duration. When properly written, including pre/post-test assessments, an 8-10 page templated script usually turned into approximately 30 minutes of learning object student contact time.

Completed scripts ("lecture notes") were then delivered to instructional designers who converted them into storyboards. A storyboard in this context acts as a blueprint for further development and production of the final courseware. Storyboards fully document training content, program functionality, and multimedia assets to be used. Subtasks involved in storyboard creation can include the following:

- Write instructional text
- Write audio/video scripts
- Define interactions/other media
- Define graphics
- Define branching
- Provide feedback and remediation
- Detail programming interactions

Faculty experts were instructed not to modify the instructional topics or enabling objectives of their assigned learning objects without prior approval from the program management team. While changes were typically accommodated, a change in one object could adversely impact another object elsewhere in the curriculum. If the curriculum development could be compared to a film production, then each faculty expert was responsible for writing an individual scene in the story. Changing what happens in that scene could alter its relationship with the rest of the film and jeopardize the entire project's cohesion. In this case, an unauthorized revision to the content being taught in each object opens the program up to the risk of wasteful redundancy between objects or, even more critically, an important topic being omitted from the final program.

It is during the storyboarding stage in the process that a prototype object is typically developed, based upon preliminary content. Different programs require various types of prototypes. Typically, prototypes fall into one of two broad categories: the excerpt and the sampler. With an excerpt prototype, a coherent piece of instruction is "lifted" from the curriculum and built as an example of the flow between screens, the instructional design, the graphical look and feel, and the content presentation style. Because it is a sequential, excised chunk of instruction, it does not necessarily demonstrate all of the various screen types and interaction strategies that will be utilized in the wider curriculum. In contrast, the sampler prototype does not even attempt to be a sequential, coherent piece of instruction. Instead, its purpose, in addition to presenting the graphical look and feel, is to showcase an assortment of interaction strategies, screen types, and media. The sampler is intended to portray the range of elements that will be used throughout the curriculum and is of little value when considering writing style, content flow, and object-level instructional design. Each type of prototype has benefits and disadvantages and both of these types of prototypes were developed for the programs described in this chapter.

Conduct Peer Review

The first draft storyboards were reviewed for instructional soundness, completeness, and accuracy. The primary review was conducted by a peer with an equal level of expertise in the subject area. The purpose of this review was to guarantee the accuracy of the material. It was imperative that no wrong information be presented to the eventual student, even if might be deemed a minor error. Because of the high-stakes nature of the workforce being trained—biotechnology and K-12 teaching—the content had to be rigorously accurate. Not only could wrong information have dire consequences, it would also undermine the authority of the curriculum as a whole. Instructional validity was of paramount importance. Each peer reviewer was provided with specific instructions and a form containing evaluation criteria to be examined. The feedback on this form was used to revise the storyboards prior to production.

Occasionally, the peer reviewer would contradict the original author of the learning object. When such disagreements were stylistic in nature, the original author's preference would usually prevail. However, in some cases, the contradiction was substantive relative to the technical accuracy of the learning object's instruction.

When this occurred, and the two experts could not agree, a third peer expert from the program management team would make a final ruling for the ultimate curriculum. Catching and correcting an error during the storyboard phase is extremely important from a program management perspective, since it is far more cost effective to make a revision within a document than after media is produced.

Concurrent to this review, an instructional design and editorial review also occurred. This review not only confirmed instructional issues (e.g., *Does the material align with the learning objectives? Is the learning object an appropriate length? Is there sufficient interaction and media?*), it also ensured that the written material did not contain spelling or grammatical errors. Furthermore, this editorial review maintained consistency in style and conventions, especially regarding specialized terminology, acronyms, and abbreviations. In some cases, an extra, specialized review also occurred. For example, during the K-12 math and science teacher workforce program, certain learning object storyboards were reviewed by an educational expert to ensure conformance with critical state standards tied to high stakes testing requirements. Within the biotechnology program, selected learning object storyboards were reviewed by research scientists at partner universities to determine if the subjects and/or treatment were at risk of being obsolete in the near future due to forecasted developments. After the peer and instructional/editorial reviews were complete, the storyboards were revised in preparation for online production.

Deliver Draft Learning Object Courseware

After the storyboards were revised, the development phase began. The purpose of the development phase is to produce and integrate all elements described in the revised storyboards. The updated storyboards from the design phase are used as guides to generate the related graphics, audio, video, and HTML programming elements of the curriculum. The development phase can consist of the following:

- Creating all graphics/media/animations/interactions
- Producing video and audio files (if applicable)
- Incorporating textual content
- Finalizing the graphical user interface
- Programming the product
- Compiling the courseware with all required media (graphics, video, audio)
- Continual quality assurance (formative evaluation)
- Production of final curriculum elements
- Addition of SCORM programming requirements

If the storyboard document is analogous to a blueprint, then the development phase can be compared to the physical construction of the building. This is where the actual instructional media are created and assembled for the learning object, in the format that the student will eventually see. With a few exceptions for explanations and extra clarity, in most cases, the development phase was conducted by multimedia professionals without a significant amount of interaction with the faculty experts. The storyboards should provide the necessary guidance for production. Just as the templates and samples allowed the faculty experts to concentrate their efforts on their specific areas of expertise without concerning themselves with production logistics, the completed/revised storyboards should contain sufficient subject matter expertise to allow the multimedia professionals to concentrate their efforts on programming and media production.

Conduct Multipurpose Review

Once the draft learning object was completed, it underwent another, rigorous formative evaluation. The multimedia production members of the team posted a draft version of the courseware to a private Web site for review. The draft courseware did not include the audio narration, since that required the text for each screen to be absolutely final to avoid costly re-recording. In addition, the courseware ran as a simple Web site without any of the SCORM-related data transfers required for the LMS. Those would be added once the learning objects were reviewed and revised.

From a content accuracy perspective, both the original faculty developer and the independent peer reviewer were asked to assess each learning object. They were each responsible for ensuring the technical correctness of the courseware and, as such, had equal voices in the review process. A key element that the content review focused on was ensuring that there were no errors resulting from the translation between the paper-based storyboards to the Web-based learning object. An area of particular emphasis was to verify that the textual descriptions of requested graphics, animations, interactions, and other media were properly interpreted and produced. In highly technical content such as biotechnology, even a seemingly minor mistake in a graphic could be considered a significant error.

Concurrent with the content accuracy review was another instructional/editorial review. While this second instructional design review was not conducted from an overarching strategic point of view (since that was addressed in previous reviews), this was an opportunity to confirm that the objectives were adequately met, that the pre/post assessments addressed the learning objectives, and that there was a sufficient level of interactivity. The editorial review checked spelling, grammar, transitions, conformance to style conventions, graphic quality, and other areas related to the presentation of the content. Because the storyboards were previously approved, textual revisions were typically discouraged during the draft courseware review, as were structural changes such as the reordering of screens. In some cases these types of changes were unavoidable. However, to control the project scope (both schedule and budget), the importance of a thorough review at each stage of the formative evaluation process was stressed. The farther the learning object moved along the development continuum, the more expensive and time consuming it became to make changes.

Finally, the learning object was subjected to a functional review. Also known as a "crash test," the functional review assessed the technical performance of the courseware. Button functionality, links, interactions, and other programmatic elements were verified to ensure they functioned as intended. All "Next" and "Back" buttons were checked, as were glossary terms, supplemental documents, and embedded questions (including remediation and feedback). Once all of these concurrent reviews were completed and their associated review forms turned in, the courseware was revised accordingly.

Implement into LMS

One of the critical tasks associated with revising the courseware was the addition of audio narration and the incorporation of SCORM-related application programming interfaces (APIs). These APIs facilitated the transfer of data from the student/client to the LMS/server, where it was stored for later reporting. Data captured included the enrollment date, the completion date, pretest scores, and post-test scores. As they were revised, each learning object was placed into an industry-oriented LMS and learners were enrolled. A basic post-implementation functional review was conducted to ensure that each object properly launched and correctly recorded student performance data. Once an entire curriculum of learning objects was completed, revised, and implemented into the LMS, a summative evaluation was conducted.

Evaluate Courseware

The requirements of each program differed regarding the rigor of the summative evaluation. Typically, however, all summative evaluations addressed at least the first two levels of Kirkpatrick's (1994) taxonomy of assessment. According to Kirkpatrick, Level 1 evaluation solicits student reaction to instruction and typically is conducted with questionnaires or interviews at the end of the training program. This type of data is used to determine whether the students consider the instruction relevant to their jobs and suited to their needs and learning styles. Level 2 evaluation determines whether the students have mastered the specified performance objectives. Through the comparison of baseline pretest data with terminal posttest performance, the training validity can be assessed. These results should answer the questions: *"Does the instruction properly teach the objectives? Did the students learn what was intended?"*

The LMS used to deliver all three workforce curricula provided the capability to generate individual and aggregate student test performance results, including the ability to perform specific test item analysis. By reviewing student performance statistics, trends could be identified (e.g., all students missed a particular question on a particular test) and mitigation strategies could be implemented (e.g., revise the

Figure 4. High-level illustration of learning object development evaluation strategy employed in the biotech curriculum development project

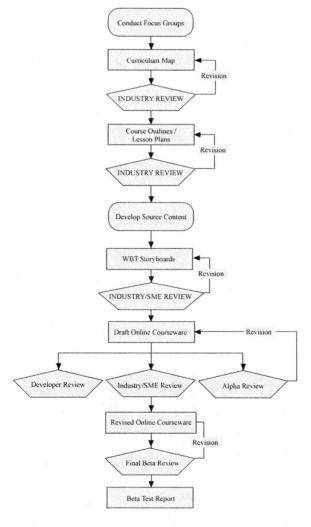

question if it is a poor question or revisit the training content, if it was inadequate to prepare the learner for the test).

The biotechnician curriculum development project employed a fairly comprehensive formative and summative evaluation strategy (see Figure 4), including milestone reviews by industry representatives, subject matter experts (SMEs), academic experts in the disciplines, members of the target audience, and formal beta testing. In addition, both alpha and beta tests were conducted and were integral components to the overall development process, helping to ensure that the delivered curriculum met the specified needs of the state's biotechnology industry.

Two separate formal evaluations (alpha and beta) were conducted with members of the target audience to validate the effectiveness of the biotech learning object curriculum.

1. During the initial alpha test, 29 of the 57 total modules were reviewed, resulting in 65 completed surveys. This initial test was considered "formative" since the curriculum was still in production. Results of this testing were used to guide revisions to the courseware.

2. During the beta test, all Web-based learning objects were reviewed. Between both tests, all 57 learning objects were reviewed with a minimum of 5-7 testers per learning object, resulting in 424 learning object completions across the entire curriculum.

Highlights from the Level 1 evaluation data included the following:

•   94% rated the online biotech curriculum as a positive experience (with 55% rating it in the highest category)

•   95% found the e-learning format to be an engaging instructional experience.

•   97% would recommend the online curriculum to friends or colleagues interested in a biotech career

Table 1. Aggregated Level 2 student performance data

CALCULATION	PRETEST SCORE	POSTTEST SCORE
MODE (most commonly occurring value across all 424 learning object test instances)	50%	80%
AVERAGE (the arithmetic mean of all aggregated values across all 424 learning object test instances)	51.4%	72.2%

Figure 5. Aggregated Level 2 student performance data

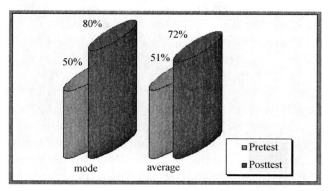

These conclusions were among nineteen total questions asked via an electronic survey and were representative the general student impression of the learning object-based curriculum. The number of respondents for each question ranged between 350 and 364 (not all respondents answered every question).

Level 2 assessment data are summarized above (see Figure 5), validating that learning did indeed occur as a result of the instructional intervention. When comparing aggregated learning object pretest and posttest scores, there was a 30-point improvement in the score mode and a more than 20-point improvement in the score mean.

Only by assessing the learning that occurred could the program sponsor and development team be confident that the workforce development objectives were met. Regardless of the sophistication of the media, the quality of the graphics, or the complexity of the interaction strategies, ultimately each learning object must teach something and the quality of that instruction must be evaluated.

Conclusion

As is clear, the process used to build the three learning object curricula described in this chapter is the long-established instructional systems design process. However, by inserting key customized elements into that proven process, the collaborative production model can effectively mediate between disparate academic and industrial participants. In addition, the importance of strong program management cannot be overstated. Each project had the potential to veer off into inappropriate areas and suffer what is commonly referred to as "scope creep," where the production team loses control of the budget and schedule. With each project, these risks were mitigated with strong, proactive program management. In fact, in each project, additional learning objects were delivered beyond what was proposed without modifying the project budgets or schedules.

Interestingly, while the learning object curricula were each developed by academic experts for a workforce development constituency, their post-implementation utility extends recursively back into academia. Driven by the same academic experts involved in development, the finished learning objects are now being individually cherry-picked from the workforce curricula and integrated back into academic, for-credit courses, both online and on-ground, as interactive, Web-based lessons. That this is not only possible but being actively done speaks to the stand-alone reusability of each learning object. This, ultimately, may be the true test of the collaborative production model's ability to translate between academe and industry: a curriculum developed by academic experts for industry is being successfully used by both satisfy their own unique learning requirements.

References

Boyle, T. (2002). Design principles for authoring dynamic, reusable learning objects. In A. Williamson, C. Gunn, A. Young, & T. Clear (Eds.), *Winds of Change in the Sea of Learning: Proceedings of the 19th ASCILITE Conference* (pp. 57-64). Auckland, New Zealand: UNITEC. Retrieved February 9, 2007, from http://www.ascilite.org.au/conferences/auckland02/proceedings/papers/028.pdf

Cavanagh, T. B., & Metcalf, D. (2002). An advanced learning environment for the aerospace industry. *The Interservice/Industry Training, Simulation & Education Conference,* Orlando, FL.

Galvin, T. (2002). 2001 industry report. *Training, 38*(10), 40-75.

Hamel, C. J., & Ryan-Jones, D. (2002). Designing instruction with learning objects. *International Journal of Educational Technology, 3*(1). Retrieved February 9, 2007, from http://www.ed.uiuc.edu/ijet/v3n1/hamel/index.html

IEEE. (2005). *The Learning Object Metadata standard.* Retrieved February 9, 2007, from http://ieeeltsc.org/wg12LOM/lomDescription

Kirkpatrick, D. L. (1994). *Evaluating training programs: The four levels.* San Francisco: Berrett-Koehler.

Morris, E. (2005). Object oriented learning objects. *Australasian Journal of Educational Technology, 21*(1), 40-59. Retrieved February 9, 2007, from http://ascilite.org.au/ajet/ajet21/morris.html

Wiley, D. (2001). Connecting learning objects to instructional design theory: A definition, a metaphor, and a taxonomy. In D. Wiley (Ed.), *The instructional use of learning objects.* Retrieved February 9, 2007, from http://www.reusability.org/read/

Section III

Tool-Based Solutions for the Development and Implementation of Learning Objects

This section presents three tools that can effectively bridge theory to practice in the creation, catagorization, and reuse of learning objects.

Chapter XIV

Being a Content Expert is Fun Again with Pachyderm

Tom Hapgood, University of Arkansas, USA

Abstract

This chapter discusses the reasoning behind the lack of the expected authoring of digital learning objects. It argues that the creation and dissemination of learning objects by university faculty have not occurred as a result of technical hurdles and frightening acronyms, lack of organizational procedures, unclear legal and ownership issues, and the ineffectiveness of "selling" the idea to faculty as part of the promotion and tenure process. The technology, interfaces and storage devices have been in place for some time, waiting for the learning object authors to publish their work. The Pachyderm 2.0 software is discussed as a tool for faculty to utilize. The author hopes that discussing and enumerating the obstacles to learning object authoring and dissemination, combined with the proposal of using the Pachyderm software along with a model of working with organizational information technology (IT) staff, will assist all involved in circulating successful digital learning objects.

Introduction

Well-made digital learning objects are an exceptional supplement to good teaching. But, who is actually creating and disseminating them? For all the buzz and hype over the past few years, it does not seem that we are witnessing the predicted explosion of learning objects at the campus level. Why is this still the case? The technology exists, the computer file servers blink and hum in anticipation, the content experts engage in new research, the learning system software provides the navigation structure, and the helpful support staff stands at the ready. The overall answer is that for content experts, producing and sharing learning objects just has not been any fun. In this case, fun is defined as sitting down to create something, doing it easily and sharing it quickly with the world.

Educators and museum curators have always thrived on being experts in their field. They enjoy researching, teaching and taking any opportunity to publish their findings and circulate their passion. Coupling this zeal of discovery with the world of brightly colored pixels and a network connection to the world's computers seems like the perfect combination.

Why then does any discussion of "authoring learning objects" cause these accomplished people to scurry back to their labs and vaults, shunning the nearby group of mammoth Web servers that are aching to disseminate their work?

Indeed, if it is true that a "learning object" is "any digital resource that can be reused to mediate learning" (Wiley & Edwards, 2002, p. 3), why is it that there have been very few avenues to ameliorate the actual creation of learning objects into cohesive and successful presentation formats? What would happen if faculty needed to understand the intricacies of paper absorption, inks, binding methods, and how to run a printing press in order to publish their findings in a book format? A similar situation would occur in our libraries with shelves and librarians standing at the ready with very few books.

Issues with Learning Object Creation

What is at the root of the problem with widespread adoption of learning object creation? It is probably because publishing research, lectures, or exhibits in an engaging, multimedia form has not been the fulfillment it sounds like. It has been intimidating and time-consuming, and too often devolves into a cryptic discussion of "interoperability" or "metadata". Where's the fun in that? What faculty member or curator has time to delve into the sharable content object reference model (SCORM) or clearing up the ambiguities of the "fair use" argument? Then, after all that mysterious work is complete, the author discovers he or she may not even own the piece anymore? It's enough to make a content expert not feel like one.

The solution lies in the remarketing of these collections of digital goodness and helping educators and curators feel smart and popular again. In other words: make it easy, make it flow, and make it easy to share. They need easy, quick Web pages that enable them to create or compile digital files into rich media presentations, and then watch them revel in the praise of colleagues. There should be no use of words like "metadata".

Thankfully, many obstacles to fashioning successful learning objects are starting to be better understood or are disappearing. In fact, we are firmly entrenched in what many call the "Web 2.0, Era," where the Web is an open and collaborative place, even "alive" and many nontechnically-trained people are sharing methods and notes, creating a compelling and significant Web presence with the Web itself as the platform. "Normal" people have been uploading photographs to *flickr* (http://www. flickr.com) and "tagging" them with normal words like "beach" and "birthday" so that they are easily found by themselves and others. Weblogs (or "blogs"), many at http://www.blogger.com, have become a succinct way to have a professional, chronological way of publishing thoughts and research findings, and browser book-marks or favorites are now being shared among many Web users utilizing the del. icio.us (http://del.icio.us) Web program. "Metadata" is still there, except that it is now called "tagging" or adding a description. This is a much friendlier Web world with which to work.

Pachyderm: A Web 2.0 Solution

Firmly seated in this world of Web 2.0 is the Web-based Pachyderm software, created specifically for museum visitors and students to discover new principles through a stunning multimedia presentation, full of text, photos, videos, and sounds. Pachy-derm easily enables content experts to seamlessly communicate their knowledge of Rembrandt or robotics and supplement classroom time and gallery visits with self-paced interaction. Essentially, a series of Web-form screens are used to create a series of rich pedagogical Flash-based templates, with options to enter keywords and descriptions ("metadata") that assist in searches and collaboration. Such Pachyderm presentations are free to use, easy to create and update and run on the Web or kiosks. With Pachyderm available, suddenly being a content expert is fun again.

Figure 1. Published Pachyderm presentation

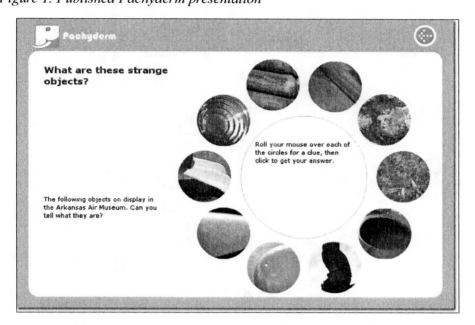

Pachyderm Presentation

A Pachyderm presentation can consist of one or many screens arranged in a nonlinear way that fosters exploration and discovery. It by no means solves all of the issues standing between a content expert and a sophisticated, polished Web presentation, but it offers a very straightforward way to make a compelling presentation.

Pachyderm can be used as a vehicle for bringing together learning objects into one presentation or lesson, and present them with a context, background or supporting examples. These learning objects can be videos or animations that help to describe the atmosphere and mood surrounding a work of art. In San Francisco Museum of Modern Art's "Ansel Adams at 100" Pachyderm presentation, video footage is shown of Ansel Adams and friends climbing the "Diving Board" in 1927, from which Adams would make the photograph *Monolith, the Face of Half-Dome*. In addition, a photograph of Adams with his tripod and burro is presented with a text description. Both of these learning objects enable the viewer to understand more fully the methods and circumstances surrounding the creation of the *Monolith* photograph, as opposed to merely viewing the photograph itself.

Pachyderm can provide a focus that will enable a content expert to prioritize and deal with the obstacles that have stood between the educator and the successful creation, publishing, and sharing of the learning object. These obstacles have amounted to

Figure 2. Ansel Adams at 100, San Francisco Museum of Modern Art

lack of time and interest to learn new technology, cryptic and frightening acronyms, large file storage requirements, learning assessment technology, and copyright and ownership issues. In addition, in terms of using others' work in instruction, faculty do not feel that they can steal, borrow, or even just use someone else's work, as it fundamentally conflicts with their job description, namely that of inventing "their own" new objects and methods.

The Pachyderm Team

An early version of Pachyderm was invented and used by the San Francisco Museum of Modern Art, with NEH and NEA support, for their presentations including "Making Sense of Modern Art," "Eva Hesse," and "Ansel Adams at 100." In 2002, Larry Johnson, CEO of the New Media Consortium and SFMOMA's John Weber and Peter Samis began a partnership, to be funded by the Institute for Museum and Library Services, that would create a new version of the Pachyderm software, "Pachyderm 2.0," which would be platform-independent, incorporate open-source components and new programming, and include a new friendly presentation-creation interface. The intention was also to keep intact the successful elements of the original

Pachyderm software, namely the use of pedagogically strong templates, ability for nonprogrammers to create presentations and the usage of multimedia components inside of rich Flash-animated screens.

The people who made Pachyderm, and who will continue to improve it through the months and years were mustered from all the requisite areas. These people were from universities and museums, were both faculty and staff, museum curators and technology staff, designers and programmers, pedagogy experts, and librarians. In addition to NMC and SFMOMA, several college, university, and museum partners took part in the project. Among them are California State University, Case Western Reserve University, Northwestern University, University of Arizona, University of Nebraska-Lincoln,University of British Columbia, University of Calgary, Berkeley Art Museum/Pacific Film Archives, Cleveland Museum of Art, Fine Arts Museums of San Francisco, Metropolitan Museum of Art and the Tang Teaching Museum of Art.

In order to ensure that all aspects of the target user group of the software were covered, the partners were organized into teams. These were the Requirements Team, the Pedagogy and Usability Team, the Programming Team, and the Metadata and Standards Team. The collective goal of these teams was to decide on and take care of as much of the decision-making as possible on the issues that have stopped content experts from successfully creating learning objects in the past. Through a process of discovery and research, the team needed to create a series of software requirements.

The process began with the creation of a series of personae, or character sketches representing the type of people who would be using the Pachyderm software in the

Figure 3. A few of the Pachyderm developers at work

university and museum setting. Four primary types were identified: students, faculty, museum personnel, and museum visitors. Two secondary types were also identified: support staff and librarians. Once enough personas were created to represent the main user group, they were placed into situations or scenarios that would allow the development team to work through any potential road blocks and authoring dead-ends. One of these personae and scenarios is presented in Box 1.

Such persona/scenario examples assisted the development team in planning a complete and accessible software package.

Box 1. Sample persona and scenario

Museum Personnel: Charles H., New Media Director

Charles is responsible for new media and works with curators who do not want to be Pachyderm authors but want to have him make projects for them. He needs to interpret the content delivered by the curator and convert it into something that will be easily understood and appreciated by the visitors. His technical skill level is high.

The museum Charles works for is hosting a major international exhibition 11 months from now. Charles is beginning to gather assets—photographs, QTVR 360s of sculpture, interviews with curators—but he knows that much of the actual physical assets of the presentation will not be available until just prior to the exhibition—when the funding will be made available for his team to go over to France and do blitzkrieg photography of the objects in-situ and the landscape.

Charles has physically storyboarded the entire Pachyderm experience—but needs to actually build the system on the promise of photographs and videos that may or may not be available at the 11 hour. To this end, he has actually crafted two different story-boards, one with assets he is sure he will be able to get in some form or other and a second with the images he hopes to be able to get.

Even though he may not get the assets until the last moment, the curator he is working with is absolutely certain about the text he wants associated with assets and with how he wants the experience structured. Thus even though Charles cannot get the assets until the last moment, the curator wants to see a functional working model and sign-off on the text prior to his extended vacation in the Bahamas. Using the authoring tool, Charles builds both structures, assigning placeholder images—clearly indicated as such in the structure of the tool (for example, sample.jpg, sample.gif, sample.mov, sample.ani). The resulting presentation includes all the appropriate text and layout, but the spaces for media have blank grey placeholders. When Charles gets the digital images later, it is easy for him to place them in the correct spots.

Box 2. Sample requirement

> 3.1.1.1 Persistent user accounts (#29)
>
> The system must support persistent user accounts, allowing users to log in (and out as needed) to access data tied to their account.
>
> *Rationale: Users will have basic data that should be "remembered" by the system so users don't have to look it up or enter it by hand each time they use Pachyderm.*
>
> *Notes: This refers to users of the Authoring Tool (not to users of completed modules).*
>
> *Volatility: stable*
>
> *Clarity: refine (We need a good definition of what data would be tied to their accounts.)*
>
> *Recorded by: Rachel Smith*
>
> *System Components: Authoring Tool*
>
> Stakeholders
>
> *Developers: Programmers, User Interface Designers*
>
> *End Users: Authors (Education), Authors (Museum)*
>
> *Official Priority: essential*
>
> *Desired Priority: useful*

As a result of these early exercises, over 300 requirements were delineated as being essential for the software to work successfully in the university and museum setting. These requirements were based on the strengths of the original version of Pachyderm, the needs of the user groups and the many years of collective experience of the expert development team. One of the requirements is presented in Box 2.

The team found that the process of collecting requirements was valuable in itself, because it provided a forum for everyone to think about and discuss what the end product would look like. In the beginning everyone had a different idea about what would be built; working through the process of capturing and refining requirements helped the team to come together with a shared vision (Howes, Shapiro, Smith, & Witchey, 2005, p. 11).

The Ideal Process for Using Pachyderm

When beginning a Pachyderm presentation, it is best if the content expert (instructor or curator) create the presentation through storyboarding and actual Web-based authoring, as only content expert can give the topic the personalized treatment needed for rendering the learning object a success. The information technology staff at the institution can be a great help in gathering and digitizing materials, but should not be the ones to create the actual presentation. Indeed, something is lost in the efficacy of the learning object or presentation if it is not constructed by the content expert.

Here is a map of an ideal process for faculty members or curators interested in creating a Pachyderm presentation, which should address two main obstacles, mainly those of lack of time and expertise to prepare the digital media assets:

1. Content expert creates and teaches, envisioning need for learning object to supplement teaching.
2. Content expert sketches-out ("storyboards") a presentation.
3. Content expert provides materials to IT staff for preparation.
4. IT staff prepares media assets (recording lectures, scanning, photographing, video footage gathering, file compression, and optimization).
5. IT staff imports media assets into Pachyderm and/or learning management system software.
6. Content expert reviews/revises storyboards of the presentation.
7. Content expert creates the presentation.
8. Content expert tests and publishes the presentation (loop back to #1).

Figure 4. Ideal process for faculty members or curators interested in creating a Pachyderm presentation

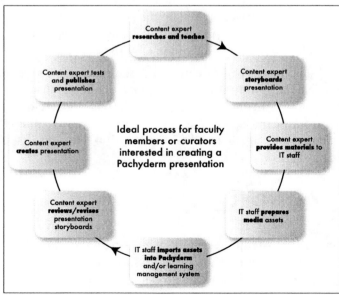

Pachyderm requires just as much noncomputer or nondigital planning time as the art of creation ever has, and this usually comes in the form of printing out and filling in storyboards, or planning documents. The storyboards are used to mock up how each screen of a presentation will link to other screens, what those links will be titled and in what order the links will be. In turn, the storyboards assist the user as a guide for other textual information on the screen, such as display titles, blocks of text, and media elements such as photographs and movies files. The storyboards, very similar to those used by SFMOMA in the creation of their Pachyderm presentations, are downloadable from http://www.pachyderm.org for use in presentation design.

Planning a Pachyderm Presentation

A Pachyderm presentation is like a plant, with twigs, layers, and leaves extending from a single trunk. But, like a plant, a Pachyderm presentation must be carefully controlled and pruned for greatest beauty and strength. It is easy and intuitive to put information into a template, and fun to play around with different templates to see what arrangement has the most visual impact, but unchecked growth can lead to tangled branches (and confused viewers) (Leonard, 2005, p. 4).

When planning a Pachyderm presentation, the author usually understands Pachyderm to be a combination of screens and media assets. A presentation consists of an unlimited amount of interlinked screens that are based on pedagogically tested template designs. When adding a new screen to a presentation, an author simply chooses a template design that he or she thinks would work best for the content, and then "populates" that template with media (images, movies, animations) and types in the content text.

According to Peter Samis and Larry Johnson, the interactive templates were the authoring tool's defining feature. Each of them embodied a distinct approach to the examination, contextualization, and modes of understanding objects and images. The *Formal Analysis* screen allowed close-up examination of salient parts of a graphic file and refreshed the text as you moused over each one. The *Slider Gallery* (named "Slider" in Pachyderm 2.0) enabled a diachronic reading of a set of images, or the establishment of variations within a typology. The *Zoom Screen* allowed for extreme close-ups and pans of graphic files accompanied by sound commentary. The *Onion Skin* (named "Layers" in Pachyderm 2.0) enabled multiple interpretations, or levels of approach, to a single work, movement, or idea (Samis & Johnson, 2005, p. 3).

Figure 5. Pachyderm "front" and "back" or creation and presentation screens

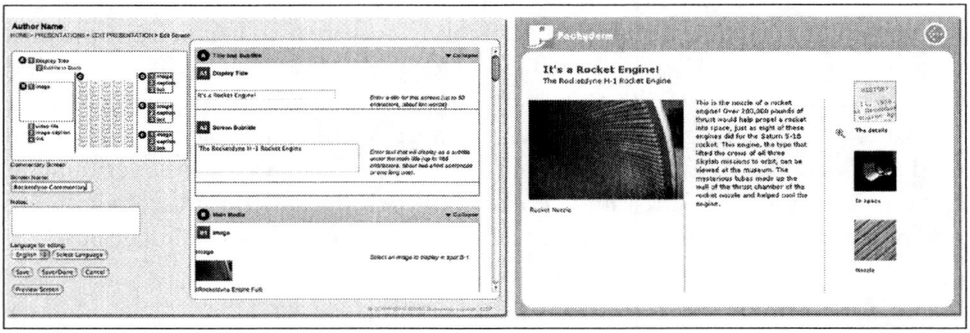

The Architecture

Pachyderm is not only a nifty way of pulling together and presenting digital learning objects on the Web, but can itself act as a learning object. A Pachyderm presentation can potentially contain only one simple screen with text and a photograph and function great on it's own as a learning object.

In terms of architecture, Pachyderm consists of a "front" and "back" or a set of creation screens and a set of presentation screens. In other words, the content expert, or "author," enters text and media files into the authoring screens and only the content expert interacts with these screens. This happens "behind-the-scenes," whereas the published presentation screens are available to anyone using a Web browser on the Internet or standing at a kiosk in a museum. The authoring screens area easy-to-use and accessible Web forms, with which even novice Web users are familiar, while the presentation screens with which students and museum visitors interact are compelling, animated screens with sound and video.

Assigning Tags

Pachyderm may not go into the philosophical and technological background as to effective metadata usage and assigning of tags, but it does request only the most pertinent and popular tags in order to help the author and others search for digital assets and completed presentations. When creating a Pachyderm presentation in the authoring area, a list of fields is presented when creating a new presentation or importing a new digital media file. For instance, when an author uploads a photograph of the Venus de Milo sculpture, Pachyderm simply asks for the requisite fields, based on the Dublin Core set of metadata tags, and the author does not need to worry about *which* fields would work best, only what information gets filled in.

These fields are *Title* (the name or title of the item), *Description* (a brief abstract), Rights (who owns the copyright), *Keywords* (descriptive terms such as media type or significant dates), Publisher (creator, publisher, or manufacturer of a work), *Contributor* (name of significant contributors other than the creator), *Coverage* (spatial, temporal characteristics of the resource, such as part of a building or a clip of a video), *Relation* (relationship to other resources), *Source* (unique number from which this resource is derived, such as a URL or an ISBN) and *Tombstone* (a caption that can be displayed with the media item). The author can, of course, skip that step of assigning any extra descriptive information to the uploaded file, and move ahead to dropping that file into a presentation screen. Unfortunately, not assigning any of this descriptive information to an uploaded file may render that file difficult for the author and other authors (if it is shared) to find for placement into a screen.

Finding and Evaluating Learning Objects

In *Guidelines for Authors of Learning Objects*, Rachel Smith lists a method for finding and evaluating learning objects, and asks readers to ask themselves some questions, for example:

- Is the learning object appealing overall?
- Is the experience of using the learning object a pleasant one?
- Are the technical requirements easily understood and easily met?
- Is it easy to find your way around the learning object?
- Is the content complete and correct?
- Are the activities appropriate to the content?
- Is the scope of the learning object suitable: neither too limited, nor too general for your purposes?
- Does it meet the educational goal you decided upon?

She goes on to state that "if you answer yes to the above questions, you've found a pretty good learning object." (Smith, 2004, p. 26). Indeed, most Pachyderm authors can answer yes to these questions. Pachyderm naturally satisfies many of these questions, or at least offers methods for assistance with the others, such as gathering and organizing the content (downloadable storyboard forms). Teaming up Pachyderm with a learning management system that includes exercises, quizzes, and other methods of assessment is sure to create a completely successful learning object implementation. No doubt, the creation of the Pachyderm presentation will finally make publishing learning objects the fun it should be. Find it at http://www. pachyderm.org.

References

Howes, D., Shapiro, W., Smith, R., & Witchey, H. (2005, April). *Shaping Pachyderm 2.0 with user requirements*. Paper presented at the Museums and the Web 2005 Conference, Vancouver, BC, Canada.

Leonard, A. (2005). *Pachyderm 2.0 user manual.* Austin, TX: New Media Consortium (NMC).

Samis, P., & Johnson, L. (2005, April). *Taking teaching by the tusks: Introducing Pachyderm 2.0*. Paper presented at the Museums and the Web 2005 Conference, Vancouver, BC, Canada.

Smith, R. (2004). *Guidelines for authors of learning objects.* Austin, TX: New Media Consortium (NMC), with a grant from McGraw-Hill Education.

Wiley, D., & Edwards, E. (2002). Online self-organizing social systems: The decentralized future of online learning. *Quarterly Review of Distance Education, 3*(1), 33-46.

Chapter XV

Using Learning Objects in K-12 Education:
Teachers and QuickScience™

Karen L. Rasmussen, University of West Florida, USA

Abstract

Reusable Learning Object technology offers K-12 teachers and students the opportunity to access resources that can be used and reused in classroom teaching and learning environments. A support tool for teachers, QuickScience™, was developed to help teachers and students improve performance in science standards; resources in QuickScience™ are built upon RLO technologies. Six types of RLOs, including five types of instructional resources aligned to Bloom's taxonomy, are used by teachers to help students improve their performance in science. QuickScience™ offers teachers a model for improving performance, including steps of diagnose, plan, teach, and assess.

Introduction

Teachers face a myriad of challenges and responsibilities in today's accountability and reform movement. They are graded and evaluated in ways that were unknown a short 20 years ago. The No Child Left Behind (NCLB) Act mandates teacher qualifications and student assessment designed to enhance student performance in curriculum standards. NCLB provides opportunities for all students and teachers to succeed and requires that all states increase performance. In the area of science, all states must administer an assessment to students beginning in the 3-5 grade cluster, by the 2007-2008 school year. By 2005, all teachers were to be highly qualified, meaning that teachers must be certified to teach through initial certification, alternative certification, or through professional development (NSTA, 2003). Many teachers have been instructing science without credentials or a deep understanding of the instructional content. It is likely in such cases that students are not receiving challenging content that will assist them in developing strong science-based inquiry skills.

School administrators and teachers routinely analyze data to determine gaps between performance on high-stakes tests and desired performance in the next academic year; many schools pinpoint specific areas of weakness to serve as targets for school improvement. In most cases, teachers are then left with the choice of how to achieve the desired performance in the classrooms and begin their quest for activities, resources, and instructional materials that can meet student needs and curricular requirements. This process has only recently begun for science, as many schools have focused on reading and math, already tested curriculum.

With the implementation of reform and accountability resting squarely on the shoulders of teachers, model interventions must be available to guide, nurture, and spark creative ideas for the classroom. Teachers must take the lead to design learning environments and provide instructional resources that increase student performance. Finding appropriate resources and molding them together is key to success, and, hopefully, increased performance. Teachers search for standards-aligned curriculum resources that are accessible and readily available.

These demands force re-examination of how technology can be used to support teachers and students in classroom learning environments. The challenge of standards is here and waiting for a response. New technologies are available that can be used to support teachers in their quest for resources that both involve science and performance. One of these technologies is based on a reusable learning object model.

The Challenge of Standards

NCLB is very specific in that all teachers must be highly qualified by the 2005-2006 school year. Added to that context, the National Science Education Standards (2006) focus on students having the opportunity to learn through an inquiry model as the context for learning science. This inquiry-based approach requires students and teachers to engage in the same activities and thinking processes as scientists and requires that teachers monitor individual student progress. In this model, students reflect and self-assess on their own processes, procedures, and outcomes as they learn and apply science concepts, techniques, and strategies.

In 2001, *Education Week* concluded that teachers were not getting enough help with training, tools, and support to help students achieve high standards. Fewer than 20% of the teachers in that survey said that they had enough training on using state tests to diagnose learning gaps. Less than 30% said that they had access to resources such as units or lessons that aligned to the standards. Without adequate support, teachers across the United States are being held accountable for student progress at unprecedented levels through high-stakes standardized student assessments. Indeed, some school districts and states (e.g., Denver, New York City, Florida) are seeking to align teacher merit pay and contract continuation with student performance on high-stakes test results (Pinzur, 2006; TC Reports, 2000).

In many schools, teachers are being required to learn new strategies and approaches for teaching and learning in reading, math, and science without being provided with time outside of the classroom during the day for professional development. Ultimately, the improvement of performance comes down to how well teachers understand the reform efforts, the standards, and the content for which they are being held accountable (Sparks & Hirsch, 1997). Absent professional development support, high-quality materials and resources can help fill the gap of knowledge. Teachers must have the tools, support, and training to radically change teaching and to infuse change at the school level (Darling-Hammond & McLaughlin, 1995). With the implementation of reform and accountability resting squarely on the shoulders of teachers, there must be model interventions available to guide, nurture, and spark creative ideas for the classroom.

Purpose of Chapter

In this chapter, the ways that reusable learning objects (RLOs) can be used to support teachers who are faced with the challenges of science accountability and reform will be explored. QuickScience™, a tool created at the University of West Florida, is a system that permits teachers to access and display science resources to students. QuickScience™ was designed, developed, and implemented using the RLO architecture established initially by Cisco and modified to accommodate a variety of teaching and learning strategies. Process, product, and outcomes will be discussed.

The Case for RLOs

Technology, used in innovative and appropriate ways, can be used to provide assistance for teachers facing teaching and learning challenges. One such classification scheme, reusable learning objects (RLOs), defined as digital resources that can be reused to support learning (Merrill, 2000), can be used in the design, development, and implementation of instructional resources. RLOs that are designed to be purposeful and supportive in a learning environment can be easily manipulated and organized to meet learning needs. RLOs can be combined together in a structured fashion so that chunks of learning can be represented in a variety of ways for a variety of purposes—depending on the needs of an individual teacher and classroom of students (Barritt & Lewis, 2001; Leeder, Davies, & Hall, 2002). The value of an RLO is not simply in its inherent usability; rather, for optimal use, learning objectives should be flexible enough to be reused in multiple ways. For ultimate flexibility, users should have the option to reuse resources as well as be able to reduce the size of a learning object to its most granular form, which is identified in Cisco's model as reusable information objects (RIOs). RLOs offer users, in this case, teachers, the chance to select and implement resources that align to goals, objectives, and tasks.

RLOs in Action

QuickScience™ was designed to support teachers as they work to increase student performance in science. QuickScience™ provides a wealth of choices for teachers to select from as they meet individual classroom and student needs. Curriculum and assessment solutions are designed around solid instructional and learning theory and implemented through a modified Cisco model for reusable learning objects (Northrup, Rasmussen, & Dawson, 2001). Using a SCORM-conformant database, the reusable learning objects repository in QuickScience™ maximizes teacher choice in implementing individual concepts of instruction, entire lessons, or assessments, all of which are aligned to National Science Standards, SAT 10 Content Clusters, and selected state standards.

Using QuickScience™, teachers develop personalized Web sites for their classrooms and students to supplement and enhance already in-place science activities and experiences. Based on curricular requirements, teachers determine the content areas or standards that target student weaknesses. Using that information, teachers search for resources. The most effective selection strategy entails using a variety of types of resources (the RLOs) to match all levels of learning outcomes. The curricular resources in are aligned to standards and provide multiple types of assessments. QuickScience™ is a flexible online solution for implementing standards-based science resources in the classroom.

RLOs and a Performance Support System

QuickScience™ is a performance support tool that assists teachers in planning, implementation and assessing student science performance. It contains attributes and behaviors of performance-centered systems, with a strong focus on usability. Intrinsic features support the teacher as the tool is used. There is a scaffolding/coaching feature, *Check with Flo*, which serves as a bridge between the tool and the realities of day-to-day life in the classroom. Other guidance includes a series of questions that link to the uses of QuickScience™, such as "How do I use this?" or "Show me an example."

The QuickScience™ research model (see Figure 1) serves as the framework for the tool (Northrup, Rasmussen, & Dawson, 2001). In overview, the model creates a system whereby teachers can focus on classroom need and access to learning objects in five curriculum approaches and traditional and alternative assessments to fill the

Figure 1. QuickScience™ research model

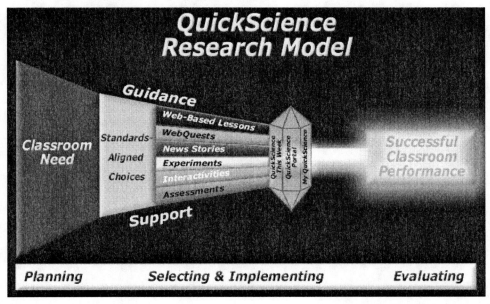

gaps between current and optimal performance. A tracking system helps teachers analyze data that measures performance. Support and guidance are embedded within the tool to facilitate day-one performance.

QuickScience™

As a Web-based tool for retrieving, organizing, and distributing reusable learning objects for use in classroom (see Figure 2), convenience of access is facilitated by delivery via the World Wide Web. When using QuickScience™, teachers make instructional decisions based on the curriculum and associated goals that they have identified for their students, creating personalized learning environments.

Teachers use a process of diagnose, plan, teach, and assess to integrate the RLOs into their classroom curricular resources (see Figure 3). This process facilitates use of RLOs in a structured, purposeful fashion by having teachers select resources that are aligned to curricular requirements and targeted toward student weaknesses. After completing the tasks (the RLOs), student performance is once again assessed. Data

Figure 2. QuickScience™

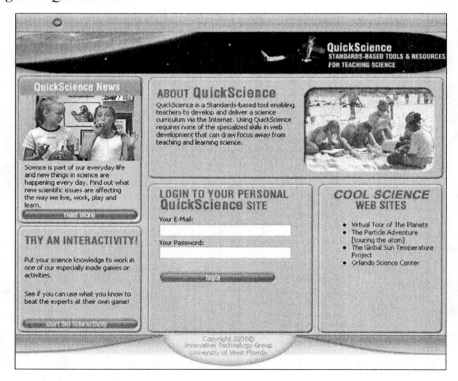

Figure 3. Model for QuickScience™ use

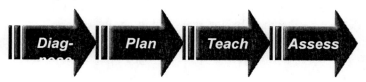

from the assessment are used to re-align curriculum and instruction as needed to support and enhance continued student learning.

Diagnosing Student Weaknesses

Before being able to strategically target resources to improve student performance, student weaknesses must be analyzed. One of the RLOs in QuickScience™ consists of a set of diagnostics reused from previously created items. This reuse functionality of resources permits efficient use of development efforts. Diagnostics are categorized into seven themes of science:

- **The Nature of Matter**
- **Energy**
- **Force and Motion**
- **Earth Processes**
- **Earth and Space**
- **Processes of Life**
- **The Environment**

The items are organized by topic and grade cluster (i.e., 3-5, 6-8). There is also an "overview" diagnostic that teachers can use to review performance from a global perspective. Results of student performance on the diagnostics are captured by Quick-Science™ for teacher analysis. A feature in QuickScience™ also permits teachers to automatically populate resources (the RLOs) to individual students, based on their performance, or teachers can choose to assign resources themselves.

Planning the Learning Environment

Based on performance data from QuickScience™ and traditional classroom assessments (standardized and alternative), along with curricular frameworks, teachers are ready to plan their own classroom Web site and accompanying classroom experience. In this part of the process teachers select RLOs that meet the goals that they have identified. Identified goals, and the learning outcome of that goal, help the teacher determine the appropriate type of object to be used. The different types of QuickScience™ RLOs and their associated outcomes in Bloom's taxonomy are described in Table 1 (Bloom & Krathwohl, 1994). Depending on the results of the teacher's data analysis, RLOs are selected that meet student needs and the goals of the curriculum. At this point, planning the learning environment begins. Selecting resources at all levels of the Taxonomy helps to promote inquiry-based learning.

Teaching Science Concepts and Inquiry

The National Science Standards stress the notion that the scientific method and science excellence should be based on a theory of inquiry. Inquiry as a teaching method incorporates a system of activities that range from low-level concept acquisi-

Table 1. Bloom's taxonomy and QuickScience™'s reusable learning objects

Bloom's Taxonomy Level	RLO Description
Knowledge	News stories are brief narratives of interesting, notable, and current events. Each news story ends with extended practice activities; these practice items include oral- or writing-based assessments directing students to reflect or discuss what was learned in the news story. Many activities are team oriented, helping students to also develop collaborative skills.
Knowledge, Comprehension	Web-based lessons are tutorials comprised of a structure that includes an orientation to a scientific concept and presentation of textual and graphic content. Web lessons are comprised of three reusable information objects: concepts, practice, and quiz. Each lesson has three concepts. Embedded questions prompt students To self-reflect and self-assess to see if they are on the right track as they practice what they have learned. At the end of each lesson is a quiz that can be used to assess how well the student has learned the concepts. Assessment items are formatted as multiple choice.
Knowledge, Comprehension	Interactivities are isolated opportunities for practice. A combination of games and information presentation form this RLO that students can use for additional practice on science topics.
Synthesis, Evaluation, Analysis	Science experiments are printable so that teachers can use them to conduct in the classroom These experiments can be performed with easily located, basic resources. The intent is to present and resolve scientific problems and to be able to discuss results with peers, the class, and the teacher. Tips on discussing results and conclusions are included.
Synthesis, Evaluation, Analysis	WebQuests are inquiry-based experiences where students are provided with real-world situations and real-time data (when possible), along with a structured set of tasks and processes (Dodge, 1997). The intent of a WebQuest is for students to work collaboratively as scientists to resolve real problems such as pollution, weather tracking, etc. WebQuest projects include brochures, presentations, flyers, field reports and other ways to alternatively assess student performance. For reflection and self-assessment, students are provided with rubrics. Teachers can also use rubrics as a grading tool.

tion to high-level, critical thinking for problem solving. The inquiry-based process includes (1) understanding scientific concepts, (2) applying those concepts through inquiry, and (3) participating in self-assessment and reflection. Students must have the opportunity to attain deep understanding of specific scientific concepts through a variety of instructional strategies as they build skills and apply newly learned information to situations where inquiry is the focal point. With a basic understanding of a concept, students can connect the dots by using the knowledge learned to resolve problems.

The RLOs of Web-based lessons, news stories, and interactivities can be used to provide students with foundational science concepts and to supplement already planned classroom activities. Web-based lessons can be further tailored to permit viewing of different elements: content only, practice only, quiz only, or any combination of RIOs. To build upon foundational concepts and to take students to the "next level" of inquiry, WebQuests and science experiments can be used. These resources permit students to explore science questions and problems, working their way through the scientific method. Assessments are designed to permit reflection and decision making as students work together to resolve science questions and problems.

Search and Collect

QuickScience™ models traditional search methodologies, permitting teachers to easily access resources. Boolean searches yield resources that teachers can add to their personal collections. RLOs have extensive metadata tags, including a description, standards, and keywords to facilitate access to resources. The collection is organized into RLO types for easy teacher identification (see Figure 4). From the collection, teachers generate and maintain Web sites for their students. Teachers can view their collection as a shopping cart where all of the items are listed and available to activate for their students. Resources can be assigned to specific students or entire classes.

Figure 4. RLO collections

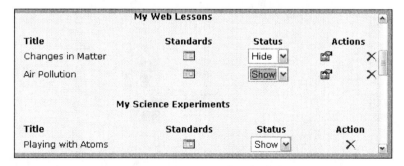

Create and Maintain Instructional Web Sites

Teachers create unique Web sites for each of their classes. They start this process by giving each class and Web site a title (see Figure 5). Next, they write a welcome note where instruction, directions, or other orienting information is entered. Collected resources can be viewed, at this point, for standards alignment and for final selection of to-be-included resources. Teachers can update the orienting information as often as needed or desired.

Once the teacher creates the orienting information and identifies, collects, and shows resources, QuickScience™ resources are ready to be shared with students. Students can access individual resources after the teacher changes its status to show (see Figure 6).

Figure 5. Creating instructional Web sites

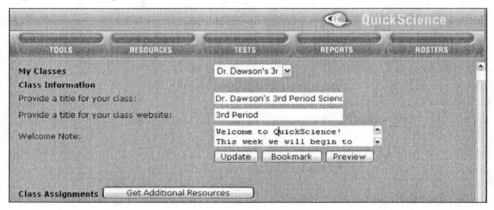

Figure 6. Showing an individual RLO

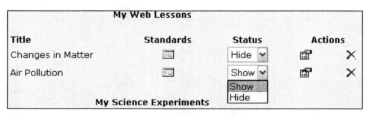

Figure 7. Communicator: Student interface

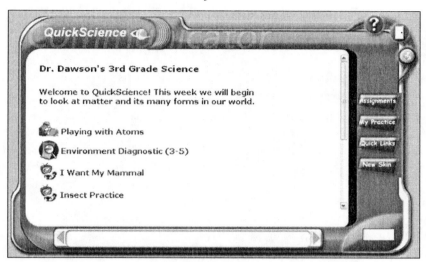

The student views the teacher's instructions and resources through the *Communicator* interface (see Figure 7). On the communicator, students access class resources as well as individual assignments that have been identified by QuickScience™ or assigned by the teacher. Students can view science Web sites, through quick links. Finally, students can change the "skin" of the communicator to personalize their interface. Each RLO is graphically identified by an icon for easy recognition. Students can access the resources that teachers have collected and released individually or in small or large groups, depending on the learning environment structure planned by the teacher.

One feature built into QuickScience™ is the capability of the teacher to further specify and delineate an individual RLO to individual RIOs that comprise the RLO. For example, in Web-based lessons, teachers may activate any or all of the three individual elements of the RLO. Managing RLOs in this fashion, teachers have the flexibility to have students work on content one day, practice the next day, and complete the quiz on a third day. Student performance on the quiz is tracked so that it can later be analyzed.

Classroom Structure and Management

QuickScience™ is completely flexible in how it can be used. From the one-computer classroom to 3-5 computers in centers, to a shared computer laboratory, Quick-

Science™ can be easily integrated into the learning environment. For teachers who have one computer in the classroom and a TV-connection or projection system, QuickScience™ resources can be delivered to the whole class or to small groups. The whole class, group delivery method can be used to present content, ask group questions, and develop strategies for meeting the scientific inquiry or problems under discussion. Small groups can work through lessons or use computer resources to work on group projects.

In a center-based environment, students can rotate between stations that are both online and off-line. Small groups can work together or individually on Web-based lessons, news stories, or interactivities. Most QuickScience™ resources can be printed for ease of use at a center or at an individual student's desk. In this scheme for integrating QuickScience™ into the classroom, groups can be established to work through overall lesson elements (individual resources and in-class activities) for each type and level of RLO. Groups can be given different tasks to complete as they move from one center to another.

A third way to integrate QuickScience™ into the classroom is by using a computer laboratory to facilitate student work on resources. For example, all students could work on the same Web-based lesson at the same time and complete the associated assessments. Once students have acquired the foundational, basic knowledge, groups of students can perform research to resolve WebQuest problems and work together to develop the final project.

Assessing Student Performance

Teachers must use data to analyze performance and then make instructional decisions based on those analyses. Once students have been entered into the roster and either have completed a diagnostic or Web-based lesson, data are available for analysis. This process is supported by several reports that display aggregate class, as well as individual results (see Figure 8). The tracking feature within QuickScience™ enables teachers to diagnose both strengths and weaknesses. Data can be reviewed through examination of individual performance in individual benchmarks. When students miss more items than permitted, individual benchmarks are flagged for easy identification for remediation through QuickScience™ resources or classroom-based activities. Based on results, QuickScience™ can automatically assign practice resources to individual students based on their performance. Curriculum can be realigned and reviewed accordingly. Reports can be printed by topic, by standard, or resources completed.

Figure 8. QuickScience™ reports

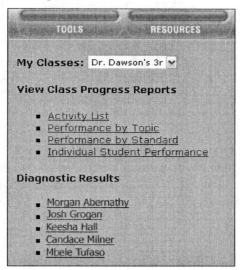

RLOs and Teachers: What Are the Possibilities?

The promise of RLOs and teachers is great. The RLO architecture is an efficient and effective way to design, develop, and implement resources for use and reuse. Focusing these technologies on K-12 environments provides a vehicle for developers and users, whether they are teachers or students, to access materials that can be used in multiple fashions for multiple purposes. The K-12 arena is one setting that is particularly in need of being able to tailor learning environments to specific individual differences and target resources to specific students with specific weaknesses.

Software applications that provide teachers with flexibility, convenience, and support facilitate both teacher performance and the ability of students to access and use high-quality materials that directly align to strengthening weaknesses in performance. Teachers who have access to a wide range of resources that can be used to support learning environments have the opportunity to craft exciting learning experiences for their students. Developers who create resources in such a way that they can be used and reused to support learning and improve performance can be part of a comprehensive solution to the challenges imposed by reform, accountability, and high-stakes testing.

One of the obvious benefits of using RLO technology in the K-12 environment is the ability to quickly retool and rethink the content of the actual resources. In other words, although QuickScience™ has science resources, other content can be quickly, easily, and efficiently integrated into its SCORM-conformant architecture. This design opens the door for all kinds of content to be included. QuickScience™, with content from other sources can become QuickReading, QuickMath, QuickSocialStudies, or QuickAnyContent in a short period of time. This flexibility offers designers, developers, and users a way to meet curricular needs without redesigning an entire system. Rather, the structure is there and content is integrated into the structure. With the amount of materials available, for example, from textbook publishers, museums, other repositories, new resources can be easily created.

Being able to align individual RLOs to student weaknesses is a key benefit to this type of technology. The ability to specifically determine where students are the weakest—and then provide them with specific resources that target those weaknesses—is critical to improving performance. RLOs provide a flexible solution that permits teachers to tailor resources to individual students. This process is facilitated by being able to create small chunks of instruction that are aligned to individual benchmarks. The capability of being able to specifically align instruction to a problem area is powerful as we look to bridging student knowledge gaps.

This type of technology also permits K-12 organizations to structure and create their own resources. Many states, districts, and schools have created their own high-quality materials that are not easily accessible by others. The RLO technology and associated delivery system provides a frame by which those resources can be distributed electronically, through an interface that can be easily learned and used. Districts can acquire the basic technology through licensing and then implement it in their own curricular endeavors.

Use of RLOs in the K-12 environment can lead to an incredibly robust system that facilitates teacher productivity. When designed with the thought for future reuse, the granularity that RLOs provide to a teacher provides maximum flexibility as teachers look for ways to enhance and improve student performance. The power of RLOs permits teachers to do what they do best—help students learn with high-quality instructional resources.

Future Research

There are many opportunities to extend research and development opportunities in the area of RLOs and the K-12 environment. These opportunities range from investigation into the structure of RLOs for maximum flexibility to the composition of the RLO for maximum learning. In the development of QuickScience™ RLOs, the traditional framework of the Cisco model for RLOs was modified and extended to reflect learning outcomes and a template structure based on those RLOs. Further refinement of this system and investigation into its value for teaching and learning would provide additional evidence that RLOs can be used effectively to support teachers as they work with students.

Another area of potential research opportunity is the way that teachers and students interact with the RLOs. Interfaces, support, and access are all issues that influence how users interact with the RLO. Without easy access through interface design, the value of the RLO cannot be realized. On top of the interface, providing teachers with a support system that helps them take advantage of the system features, without requiring extensive professional development, is critical for the system to be integrated into the classroom teaching and learning environment. The idea of systems that are convenient and easily assessable to teachers and students should also be investigated as the convenience of Web delivery expands potential access to systems.

The promise of future research can only lead to systems that are more nimble, robust, and serve users or clients well. Further work into this area can develop systems that can even better serve targeted populations.

Conclusion

The reality of science accountability and testing is here. Teachers need help so that they can prepare their students for high-stakes science tests. The challenge is to provide standards-based instructional resources and innovative instructional environments that increase student performance and provide an environment through which educators may continually seek new knowledge and adapt teaching approaches for inquiry. Teachers are moving in the right direction by planning standards-based science environments that incorporate multiple curricular approaches, as they diagnose and track student progress.

RLO technology offers teachers flexibility not imagined a few years ago. As processes and tools are incorporated into teaching and learning, the potential for efficiency in use and reuse exponentially expands. Systems that take advantage of RLO technology can serve users in ways that can immediately meet their needs and requirements.

References

Barritt, C., & Lewis, D. (2001). *Reusable learning object strategy: Designing information and learning objects through concept, fact, procedure, process and principle templates* (Version 4.0). Retrieved February 8, 2007, from http://www.cisco.com/warp/public/10/wwtraining/elearning/implement/ rlo_strategy.pdf

Bloom, B., & Krathwohl, D. (1994). *Taxonomy of educational objectives: Cognitive domain*. Boston: Addison-Wesley.

Darling-Hammond, L., & McLaughlin, M. (1995). Policies that support professional development in an era of reform. *Phi Delta Kappan, 76*(8), 597-604.

Dodge, B. (1997). *Some thoughts about webquests.* Retrieved February 8, 2007, from http://webquest.sdsu.edu/about_webquests.html

Education Week. (2001). *Quality counts 2001-A better balance: Standards, tests, and the tools to succeed.* Bethesda, MD: Editorial Projects in Education.

Leeder, D., Davies, T., & Hall, A. (2002). *Reusable learning objects for medical education: Evolving a multi-institutional collaboration.* Retrieved February 8, 2007, from http://www.ucel.ac.uk/documents/docs/068.pdf

Merrill, D. (2000). Knowledge objects and mental models. In D. Wiley (Ed.), *The instructional use of learning objects.* Retrieved February 8, 2007, from http://www.id2.usu.edu/Papers/KOMM.PDF

The National Science Education Standards. (2006). National Academy Press: Washington, DC. Retrieved February 8, 2007, from http://newton.nap.edu/html/nses/overview.html

Northrup, P. T., Rasmussen, K. L., & Dawson, D. (2001). *QuickScience™ theoretical framework.* Unpublished manuscript, University of West Florida, Pensacola, FL.

NSTA. (2003). *Key definitions from No Child Left Behind.* Retrieved February 8, 2007, from http://www.nsta.org/nclbdefinitions

Pinzur, M. I. (2006, February 11). State may tie teacher bonuses to tests. *Miami Herald.* Retrieved February 28, 2006, from http://www.miami.com/mld/miamiherald/news/breaking_news/13845297.htm

Sparks, D., & Hirsh, S. (1997). *A new vision for staff development.* Alexandria, VA: Association for Supervision and Curriculum Development.

TC Reports Winter. (2000). *High stakes testing and its effect on education.* Retrieved February 8, 2007, from http://www.tc.columbia.edu/news/article.htm?id=3811

Chapter XVI

Creating a Patchwork Quilt for Teaching and Learning:
The Use of Learning Objects in Teacher Education

Janette R. Hill, University of Georgia, USA

Michael J. Hannafin, University of Georgia, USA

Arthur Recesso, University of Georgia, USA

Abstract

This chapter explores the use of learning objects within the context of teacher education. The authors argue that learning objects can be useful in teacher education if we both create and code learning objects appropriately to the needs of the teacher education community. The chapter begins with framing the teaching and learning issues associated with the use of learning objects in higher education. Next, the chapter introduces a method for generating and marking up learning objects; examples are described where learning objects are created and coded to address the teaching and learning needs of teacher educators and teachers. The authors conclude with a discussion of the issues and prospects for the use of learning objects in teacher education.

Introduction

The challenge with a quilt like this is each of these squares was made by different hands. So I have to bring all these different squares together in a balanced and harmonious design.

~ Anna, Master Quilter
How to Make an American Quilt (1995)

While education and business sectors have been shifting to more digitally-based learning and training environments during the last decade, higher education institutions have been slow to make the transition. Creating and sharing teaching and learning resources has long presented challenges for educators in K-12 and higher education settings (Reigeluth & Nelson, 1997). This is particularly true for preservice educators, who often lack the knowledge and experience to understand where to find resources while beginning to learn the knowledge, skills, and nuances of their practice. Preservice teachers often lack needed resources during the learning (university-based courses) and practice phases (the field-based experience) of their preparation. The needs evolve as teachers refine their practices throughout their careers.

Among available resources, some have been developed to meet the needs of teacher educators and preservice teachers and made accessible via Web sites and digital libraries. (See for example MERLOT http://www.merlot.org and InTIME http://www.intime.uni.edu/.) Unfortunately, despite a growing number of resources, many are underutilized due to limited knowledge of what is available, how they are coded, and their relationship to needs of teacher educators and preservice teachers. With the emergence of learning object mark-up technology, some anticipated increased access and use leading to a transformation of teaching-learning practices (Hill & Hannafin, 2001); to date, however, this has rarely occurred.

Wiley (2001) defines a learning object as any digital resource that can be reused to facilitate learning. Learning objects can be developed once and reused multiple times, enabling a resource-based approach to production and access (Hannafin, Hill, & McCarthy, 2001). Using metatag technology, digital resources can be indexed, retrieved, and repurposed to support the needs of the given audience. The technology has continued to advance, as has overall interest in the use of learning objects.

Thus, to address the needs of teacher educators, as well as preservice and practicing teachers, we need to increase the capacity to both create *and* code learning objects appropriately to the needs of the teacher education community. The purposes of this chapter are to frame the teaching and learning issues associated with the use of learning objects in higher education, to introduce a method for generating and marking up learning objects, and to describe examples where learning objects are created and coded to address the teaching and learning needs of teacher educators and teachers.

The Growth of Learning Objects in Higher Education

Learning objects were described almost a decade ago by the Learning Technology Standards Committee (LTSC) of the Institute of Electrical and Electronics Engineers (IEEE) (1996; see LTSC, 2000). At their core, learning objects can be viewed as components of individual media (text, video, pictures, graphics, etc.) that have the *potential* to support the learning process in a variety of contexts (Hill & Hannafin, 2001). There are four primary attributes associated with learning objects: (1) they are self-standing and Internet accessible, (2) they can be used independently or can be organized to convey a message or provide topic-specific information (Clark, 1992), (3) they are designed to be reusable and shared, and (4) they are searchable via several attributes through the use of metatags (DiStefano, Rudestam, & Silverman, 2004).

The creation and distribution of learning objects was not feasible in a predigital era. Indeed, resources were primarily static and used largely intact due to the technical complexity and effort needed to cut and splice them to meet specific needs. As the ability to break down larger digital media into component objects emerged, the potential to repurpose existing digital media and utilize component learning objects in higher education expanded and transformed how we think about media (Hill & Hannafin, 2001). Existing video resources, such as examples of classroom teaching, need no longer be viewed as fixed length, but rather as a meta-resource comprising a theoretically unlimited number of component objects—segments focusing on specific interactions, exemplars of a given approach or method, or multiple representative snapshots.

While relatively slow to emerge, learning objects are increasingly used in higher education contexts. In Europe, the Joint Information Systems Committee in Great Britain has established the JISC Online Repository for (Learning and Teaching) Materials. The repository is designed as an online bank of materials that is accessible via institution subscription. Individual faculty who create the objects are acknowledged as authors who can deposit, access, and download materials from the repository (Wojtas, 2005). In The Netherlands, a group has developed a learning technology specification, education modeling language (EML), which provides a framework for combining learning objects (Koper & Manderveld, 2004). EML also describes the relationship between the learning objects, how they interact together, and their content. After considerable research, EML was selected internationally for the 2003 IMS Learning Design specification (http://www.imsproject.org/learningdesign/index.

cfm). Team members at the Open University of The Netherlands have continued to expand EML to enhance its capabilities.

In the United States, pockets of learning object use have emerged in higher education contexts. Wisconsin Technical College System was awarded a Fund for the Improvement of Post-Secondary Education/Learning Anywhere Anytime Partnership (FIPSE/LAPP) grant in 1999 to create learning objects related to the general education competencies for students taking classes in the system (Chitwood, May, Bunnow, & Langan, 2002). From initial efforts to create 16 learning objects, the team now has over 2,000 learning objects online, with an additional 100 under development, and new learning objects added weekly (see http://www.wisc-online.com).

Some universities in the United States have adopted learning object technology and standards to enhance their instructional efforts. The OpenCourseWare project at the Massachusetts Institute of Technology (MIT OCW) (see http://ocw.mit.edu for details), for example, provides free access to its online courses. Beginning Fall 2002, MIT OCW published more than 900 courses representing 33 disciplines and five schools at MIT. Underlying the efforts is a commitment to advancing learning object standards and assisting faculty and others in the implementing these standards (see http://ocw.mit.edu/OcwWeb/HowTo/tech-metadata.htm for additional information).

Yet, in most current initiatives, learning objects are quite "large," comprising entire courses or units. In effect, use of large, intact learning objects necessitates more than use or sharing of individual objects; rather, it requires the replacing of local curriculum and pedagogy with those embodied in the course-as-learning object. Consequently, faculty and institutions have been hesitant to simply adopt the values and pedagogy that permeate large, intact learning objects since they fail to address the specific needs, beliefs, and practices embraced locally.

Though disagreement exists related to the centrality of pedagogy to a learning object (see, for example, Merrill, 2001 vs. Hodgins, 2001), greater resource granularity may be needed to realize the as yet largely untapped potential of learning objects across diverse higher education contexts. Downes (2004) defined a resource as an aggregate description comprising and supporting varied functions, distributed across users and locations. In support of teacher preparation, increased granularity of actual teaching practices, for example, enables teacher educators, current teachers, and preservice teachers to identify and codify as learning objects a range of diverse aspects of teaching of specific relevance to particular teaching disciplines and standards, and share and adapt objects to address a wide variety of situation-specific needs.

Codifying Teaching Practices as Learning Objects: The Video Analysis Tool

In the following sections, we describe how the video analysis tool (VAT) (Recesso, Hannafin, Wang, Deaton, Shepherd, & Rich, in press) is being used to capture and codify teaching practice, teach to generate extensible learning objects, and describe current VAT project applications.

Overview

The video analysis tool is a Web-based program designed to capture evidence of teaching and learning. VAT provides users the capability to remotely upload live and prerecorded video into the system. Users can then analyze video evidence as part of a self-assessment, collaborative assessment (e.g., with a mentor or peer), or observation by a rater to define specific needs for improvement. The tool provides for individual or multi-user analysis of the same video using the same or different assessment instruments (see http://vat.uga.edu/ for more complete descriptions and samples of the capture and coding technology). VAT's interface was developed using platform independent code (Java). The current version release is accessible through Internet Explorer 6 and Windows Media Player 10 on a PC (See http://vat. uga.edu). The combination of VAT's open source and industry standard technologies makes the tool accessible wherever broadband (DSL, cable) Internet connections are available.

Teaching and learning evidence is recorded through video cameras either via live, real-time capture, or post-event upload, and stored on a server for subsequent review or analysis. Video analysis enables users to codify key practices. They can view a video of specific events and segment it into smaller sessions of specific interest. Refined sessions, called VAT clips, provide raters granular performance evidence to observe and reflect without the 'noise' or 'interference' of extraneous events. The rater accesses captured practice from a standard computer using the VAT toolkit. Through *create video clips*, initial video segmenting takes place, providing markers as reminders of where target practices might be examined more deeply. Following initial live observation or during post-event review, the user accesses the *refine clips* tool to make further passes at each segment to define specific, finer grained activities.

During refinement, the user defines clips associated with their interests, such as specific activities, benchmarks, or quality rubrics. The user designates, annotates, and certifies specific clips as evidence associated with a target practice. Marked-up performance objects can then be accessed and viewed by either a single individual or across multiple users accessing the *view my clips* tool, providing the capability to examine closely the performance of a single individual across multiple events, or multiple individuals across single events. In the following, we describe each function and summarize the system's affordances and limitations.

Figure 1. Creating learning objects with video analysis tool (VAT)

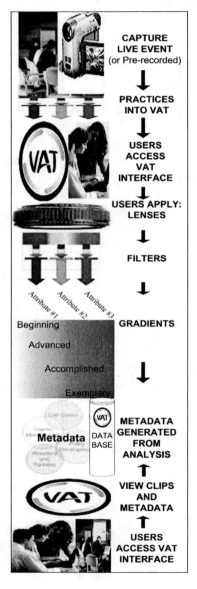

Generating Content: Create Video Clips

- **Live capture:** Through the VAT interface, the user can schedule a remote pre-installed camera to capture events on demand or at specific intervals. Internet protocol (IP) video cameras provide built-in file transfer protocol (FTP) and Web server capabilities, enabling remote configuration and control of the video capture. During live capture, IP video cameras are preinstalled, passing video streams to a server which records the video streams, enabling a rater to observe practices remotely with minimal classroom disruption or interference.

   Figure 2 illustrates live capture settings for classroom observation of an 11th grade Science class (chemical reactions, to be taught January 13 from 10 to 11 AM). The system stores the scheduling data and the remote camera is config-ured to capture classroom activities accordingly. Start and end dates and times can be preset to schedule live captures days, weeks, or months in advance. Users in remote locations can observe the events in real time as they unfold. Using the VAT interface and an IP video camera connected to an Ethernet port, users can simultaneously stream live video to their own local computer and to centralized storage facilities, providing both immediate local and remote access to hypothetically unlimited number of users.

Figure 2. Schedule live capture event

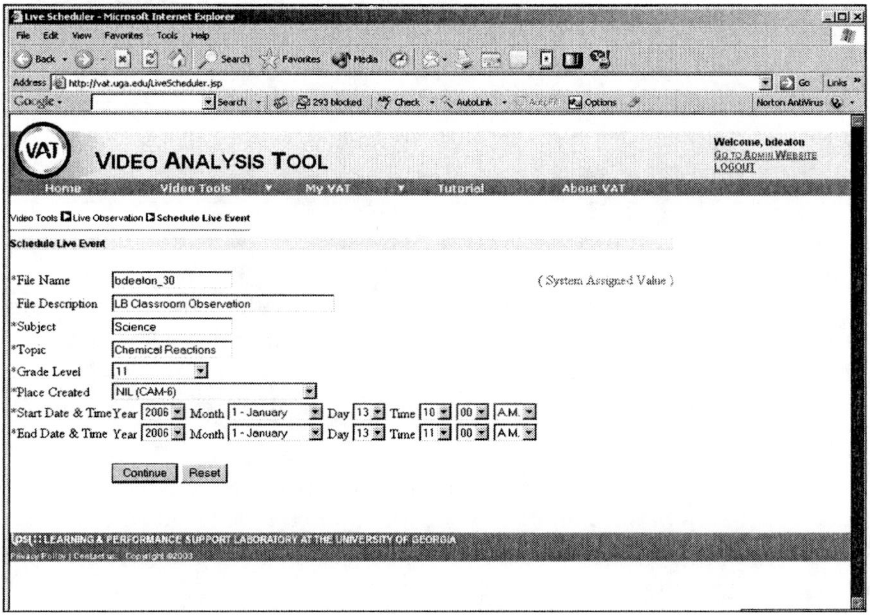

During live capture, the file transfer includes both images of the environment (content) and packets (data) containing metadata such as time, date, and frame capture rate. Data are stored in corresponding database tables after streaming through the VAT interface. Start and stop time buttons, for example, enable a user to segment (chunk) video into clips precisely encapsulating an event. The real-time processing of data through the VAT interface enables a user to initially chunk large volumes of content into manageable segments based on the frames planned for detailed analysis.

- **Prerecorded video:** Post-event upload refers to archiving video files on the VAT server subsequent to recording a practice. VAT users can videotape an event, and subsequently digitize and upload the converted files to the server. Prerecorded video from a variety of media can be accommodated, but must be uploaded manually into VAT, typically increasing the lag between capture and access to content. While increasing the time and effort required to capture video, post-event uploading also provides additional backup safeguards in the event of network or data transfer failures.

Recently, powerful devices (e.g., Webcams, CCD DV video cameras) have emerged that support a wide variety of formats (MPEG2, MPEG4, AVI). Using memory media (tape, microdrive, SD RAM) to which events have been captured, VAT provides a Web interface to browse the media and upload video files. Video files are then translated into a common digital format (MS Win Media 10) using widely accessible codecs (code and decode video for use on multiple computers) to compress the video. This process both reduces storage requirements and ensures broader file access. Immediately following this encoding process, files are transferred to centralized mass storage and referenced by the database for immediate access and use. The entire translation and upload process can be accomplished in less than one hour per hour of video.

System-Generated Metadata

As summarized in Table 1, initial VAT metadata are generated using database descriptors; metadata schemes can also be created or adopted (e.g., international standard such as Dublin Core or SCORM). Use of standard schemes ensures that learning objects (e.g., lesson plan databank, a digital library of area learning activities, resources for teacher professional and practical knowledge) can be shared through a common interface.

VAT system metadata tags are automatically generated for application functions (e.g., date, start/stop times, unique clip identification number), and associated with the source video during encoding or updating. Video content and metadata stored in tables are cross-referenced based on associations created by the user; the video

Table 1. System-generated metadata

Dublin Core Element Name	VAT Name	Example
Date	Date	Date video file was created (taken from upload data of video file into VAT)
Identifier	Clip ID	83 The 83rd clip created by the user for this video
Source	File_name	Video file with which this clip is associated
Coverage	Startime and Stoptime	Start and end time of the clip

files are not digitally altered during the coding process. Maintaining separate content files and metadata tables enable multiple users to mark-up and share results without duplicating original video files.

Modifying Content: Refine Clips

VAT's interface provides control buttons (e.g., start and stop time) that enable its user to further segment video content, that is to create and refine multiple clips (video chunks) by identifying start and end points of specific interest (See Figure 3). Users can then annotate segmented events by associating text-based comments with specific time-stamped segments. Typically, users describe the event, reflect

Figure 3. Refine Clips screenshot

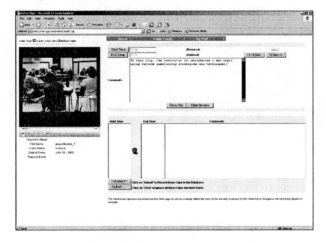

on their practices or student learning, or even assess implementation of strategies. These annotations are stored as metadata and associated with a specific segment of the video content.

Codifying Teaching Practices: Lenses, Filters, and Gradients

Using the metaphor of a camera, VAT progressively guides users in analyzing video segments, simultaneously generating and associating metadata specific to the frame or "lens" through which practices are examined (See Figure 4). A lens essentially defines the frame for analysis. Lenses can be created using existing frames or frameworks (e.g., National Educational Technology Standards), or developed specifically for a given analysis. For example, in Figure 4 the user (an induction teacher) has chosen the Georgia Systemic Teacher Education Program (GSTEP) framework for accomplished teaching as a lens to self-assess his practices. Once a lens has been selected, filters are used to highlight aspects within the frame (in this case, Content & Curriculum Indicator 1.1). The lens amplifies specific attributes of teaching practice (demonstrate knowledge of major concepts, assumptions, debates, processes of inquiry, and ways of knowing that are central to the content areas they teach) and suppresses extraneous noise. Hence, lenses are used to differentiate the

Figure 4. Using a lens to codify screenshot

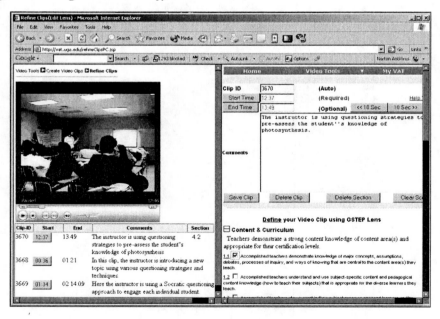

filtered attributes in an effort to identify progressively precise attributes of teaching practices.

Lenses, when applied directly to a specific video clip, enable simultaneous refinements in analysis and the generation of associated explanations (metadata), thus providing contextually anchored indexing standards. Each video clip can have an unlimited number and type of associated metadata from any number of users, thus providing essential tags for subsequent use as flexible learning objects.

Accessing Learning Objects: View Clips

Users can retrieve, view, and modify individual or multiple clips that they (or others) create in VAT.

- **View My Clips:** Users may access existing files and clips—their own or others—as needed and permitted. The View My Clips function activates an embedded video player and a table displaying metadata associated with a selected file. By clicking a start button, the user can identify both system-generated time-stamps for start/end of clips as well as annotations associated with each clip with associated metadata. Thus, the user can examine how they analyzed

Figure 5. View multiple clips screenshot

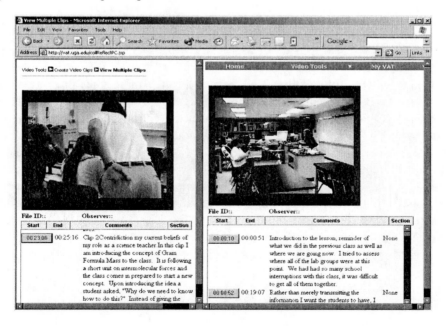

a segment, and an opportunity to see how others analyzed, rated, or associated the event.

- **View Multiple Clips:** View Multiple Clips allows users to select two video files for side-by-side display in the browser window. The associated metadata allows individual teachers to examine their own teaching events over time, compare their practices to others (experts, novices) using the same lenses, filters, and gradients. As shown in Figure 5, a preservice teacher has selected one of her teaching practices (right) to contrast with a more experienced teacher (left) to compare instructional strategies targeting the same concepts. Using metadata comments associated with the experienced teacher, where students are using computers to model their concepts, the preservice teacher compares this with her traditional approach and comments accordingly.

Managing Learning Objects

Given the sensitivities, concerns, and liabilities involved in collecting and sharing video content as learning objects, precautions are needed to ensure security and management of content. Currently, VAT files are controlled by the individuals who generated the source content (typically the teacher whose practices have been captured), who "own" and control access to and use of their video clips and associated metadata. Each content owner can grant or revoke others' rights to access, analyze, or view video content or metadata associated with their individual objects.

Artifacts of Teaching Practice as Learning Objects

We are currently implementing VAT across a range of teacher preparation and inservice efforts in Science Education, Elementary Education Math Education, and Special Education. Preservice teachers in Science Education, for example, are utilizing VAT in methods courses, early field experiences, and during student teaching. Teacher educators have integrated VAT methods to promote self-assessment and systematic observation. VAT has also been incorporated into inservice professional development programs to train mentors and coaches in identifying and supporting teacher development, and to improve the teacher observation and evaluation methods used by school leaders. In the following sections, we describe several VAT applications at the University of Georgia's Learning and Performance Support Laboratory (http://lpsl.coe.uga.edu).

Specifying Embodiments of Practice (E-TEACH)

Participating Evidence-based Technology Enhanced Alternative Curriculum in Higher Education (E-TEACH) faculty and preservice teachers were provided VAT training to collect, organize, and analyze evidence of progress and growth. Preservice teachers and faculty: (1) captured and coded live student teaching episodes from remote locations; (2) systematically examined and analyzed captured video using professional standards and frameworks (e.g., lenses, filters, and gradients); (3) compared and contrasted preservice teachers' analyses with mentors, cooperating teachers, advisors, and other support faculty; and (4) shared best practices with other preservice teachers and across methods courses for further analysis and modeling. Based on VAT-enhanced support, preservice teachers are able to hone their teaching practices by gathering evidence identified in areas of need, systematically analyzing this evidence, and selecting solutions based on their inquiries.

Illustrating, Analyzing, and Sharing Practices (RESA Project)

Enactments of practice—exemplars, typical, or experimental—provide the raw materials from which teaching objects can be defined. This is especially important in making evidence of practice or craft explicit. It is difficult, for example, to visualize subtleties in teaching method based on descriptions or to comprehend the role of context using isolated, disembodied examples alone. The ability to generate, use, and analyze concrete teaching practices, from entire classroom sessions to very specific instances, provides extraordinary flexibility for learning object definition and use.

In an ongoing effort involving regional educational support agencies (RESA), responsible for supporting a statewide movement toward standards-based approaches, VAT is used to capture, then codify, and mark-up key attributes of standards-based mathematics teaching practices. Concrete referents, codified using lenses, filters, and gradients provide shared standards through which elements of captured practices can be identified to illustrate and analyze different levels and degrees of proficiency.

Once embodiments of practices have been defined and marked-up, VAT's labeling and naming nomenclature enables the generation of teaching objects as reusable and sharable resources. Initial teaching objects may be re-used to examine possible strengths or shortcomings, seek specific instances of a target practice within a larger object (e.g., open-ended questions within a library of captured practices). Exemplary practices—those coded for demonstrating high levels of proficiency according to specific standards and criteria—can also be accessed. Marked-up embodiments of expert practices can be generated, enabling access to and sharing of very specific (and validated) examples of critical decisions and activities among the teaching community.

Interestingly, VAT may be ideally suited to determine which teaching objects are worthy of sharing. VAT implementation is being used to validate (as well as to refute) presumptions about expert teaching practices. In the RESA project, we captured and analyzed multiple examples of purportedly "expert" practices. Upon closer examination of the enacted practices, however, many were not assessed as exemplary. Therefore, we continued to seek and capture examples where standards-based practices were reportedly being expertly enacted, and will share those that are validated under close VAT scrutiny.

Training Support Professionals (Knowles Foundation Project)

The procedures used by support professional and school leaders to observe and evaluate teaching practices have come under considerable scrutiny. Often, teacher observations have little focus, thus rarely improve teaching practices. In many cases, school leaders who evaluate teaching practices lack relevant knowledge and experience in the teachers' domains; rather than focusing on the quality of discipline-specific teaching practices, observers tend to focus on general classroom climate, organization, and the like. Codified objects of novice-through-expert teaching practices can help support professionals to identify such practices during their observations, as well as to guide teachers to improve or replicate desired teaching practices.

In the Knowles Foundation project, designed to improve field-based support for student teachers, a faculty supervisor works closely with mentor teachers—that is, cooperating teachers who supervise student teachers in the local school and act as mentor and confidant. During student teaching, the novice is immersed in an everyday classroom environment and relies on the daily feedback from a mentor. Using VAT for collaborative analysis, the faculty supervisor captured the interactions between mentor and protégé. By applying the Lesson Assessment System (LAS) lens (the Knowles Project mentoring lens) to the captured interactions, the faculty supervisor and mentor jointly identified specific instances where the mentor did not demonstrate the targeted support, and where strategies could be improved. By examining mentor-protégé interactions over a semester the faculty supervisor was able to develop new lenses to influence mentoring enactments.

Assessing Practices (Georgia Teacher Success Model)

The Georgia teacher success model (GTSM) initiative focuses in part on practical and professional knowledge and skills considered important for all teachers. As illustrated in Table 2, the GTSM model features lenses (e.g., Content & Curriculum) that amplify specific aspects of teaching practice to be examined, each of which has

Table 2. Sample VAT mark-up scheme adapted from Georgia teacher success model (GTSM) Content & Curriculum Domain lens

Filter	Gradient			
	Basic	Advanced	Proficient	Exemplary
Teachers demonstrate content knowledge appropriate for their certification levels	Relate content to everyday lives of students.	Relate content to student lives and to one or more other areas of the curriculum	Relate content area(s) to other subject areas and see connections to everyday life.	Create interdisciplinary learning experiences that allow students to integrate knowledge and skills and regularly apply them to everyday life situations.
Teacher Attributes/ Descriptions	Invites students to bring their everyday knowledge into the classroom.	Involves students in planning activities that relate content knowledge to their interests.	Involves students in planning activities related to everyday lives of people in their communities and beyond.	Leads interdisciplinary teams to collaboratively plan and share learning opportunities that integrate subject areas and relate to the everyday lives of students
Student Attributes/ Descriptions	Makes connections between content and their lives.	Engages in projects, essays, and research that relate the content area to other subject areas and to his/her everyday life.	Selects and designs projects, essays topics, research, etc. that connect the content to other subject areas and to everyday life.	Articulates how one content area relates to others thematically, historically, and/or conceptually.

multiple associated filters (e.g., Demonstrate content knowledge, etc.) that further specify the focus of analysis. Each filtered indicator will be examined according to specific rubrics (gradients) that characterize differences in teaching practice per the GTSM continuum. Thus in GTSM, teaching objects are defined in accordance with established parameters and rubrics that have been validated as typifying basic, advanced, accomplished, or exemplary teaching practice.

VAT-generated objects support a range of assessment goals ranging from formative assessments of individual improvement to summative evaluations of teaching performance, from identifying and remediating specific deficiencies to replicating effective methods, and from open assessments of possible areas for improvement to documenting skills required to certify competence or proficiency. It is critical, therefore, to establish both a focus for, and methodology of, teacher assessment.

Learning Objects in Teacher Education:
Problems, Issues, and Prospects

The growth in the use of learning objects has been steady over the last decade, but have not yet reached what Gladwell (2002) refers to as the *tipping point*—where a concept or innovation crosses a threshold and spreads rapidly. Several challenges and issues in the use of learning objects in teacher education remain (see Parrish, 2004, for a discussion of the "trouble" with learning objects).

- **Standards for learning objects are not applied consistently:** Considerable progress has been made to create standards for learning objects (McGee & Diaz, 2005). The Advanced Distributed Learning (ADL) Co-Lab was created to improve interoperability and sharing of objects across the Department of Defense. From this work emerged the Academic ADL CoLab helping academic institutions to harness the power of learning objects by utilizing the shareable content object reference model (SCORM). Yet, simply establishing standards is not sufficient. We must also be committed to applying them consistently and systematically. And, those standards need to enable the creation and use of domain-relevant applications, such as in teacher education. Clearly, faculty are developing vast numbers of resources for online environments, capturing classroom events, and requiring preservice teachers develop Web-based portfolios. Applying uniform metadata standards for such resources could dramatically increase usability, providing large repositories of resources that could be mined and adapted to address local teaching needs.

- **The role of context is not fully understood:** The role of context in educational settings is important (Shambaugh & Magliaro, 1996), but rarely understood. For the most part, discussions have centered on *use* rather than the *genesis* of teaching-learning objects. Technologies such as VAT raise important questions about how we *create* learning objects. Context of creation, for example, may ultimately have little influence on context of use (Downes, 2004) if the granular resource is valued over the embedded pedagogy. Different contexts of use may fundamentally redefine the object's meaning (Hill & Hannafin, 2001). As objects are captured and used for diverse purposes (e.g., portfolios, assessment, professional development), we need to further our understanding of how (and under what circumstances) learning objects can be recontextualized.

- **Faculty may be reluctant to share learning objects:** Faculty, both higher education and K-12, have become wary of how, when, where, and for what purposes learning objects comprising their captured teaching practices are used. We have gone to great lengths to define our purpose for capturing teaching events, providing assurances of confidentiality, and distribution control to the "owners" of the source video. Our collaborations to generate learning objects for preservice teaching involve faculty, student teachers, mentor teachers, inservice teachers, and school leaders. In every case we must fully explain the project, obtain permission, and often meet several times to clarify our intent before the work can begin. Further, we need to ensure privacy protection, for the faculty and students involved in the creation of the objects. However, a real potential exists for re-appropriating captured practices and violating agreements (e.g., termination cause, teacher liability, etc). To the extent safeguards are not provided and enforced, the open sharing of practices could be seriously compromised.

- **Technical and resource constraints contribute to the lack of creation and pervasive use:** The resources (e.g., time, technology and funding) needed to capture, analyze, and code objects can prove to be significant barriers (Nugent, 2005). Capturing requires not only access to, but knowing how to use equipment, to identify and extract evidence of specific teaching or learning practices, and the ability to identify and codify qualitative differences in performance. Internet bandwidth can also hamper efforts to implement streaming video support at the school level. Many schools do not have local technical expertise needed to negotiate firewall and digital camera nuances, lack reliable high-speed Internet connection, or have already allocated bandwidth to multiple other priorities. While technical and resource concerns will continue to lessen in the future, they can be formidable barriers to near-term adoption and use.

- **Teachers have not been prepared to integrate learning objects:** Though significant resources exist, both digital and nondigital, evidence suggest that faculty rarely share or utilize existing materials; more specifically, faculty do not know how to use learning objects (Kurz, Llana, & Savenye, 2005). To some extent, this may be attributed to long-standing concerns among teacher education faculty: limited access, little technology preparation, and lack of available software. In this regard, the limited use of learning objects may simply be an extension of generalized reluctance to integrate technology into teacher education programs.

However, teacher educators have also expressed concern over the lack of relevance to actual teaching practice and the immutability of many resources. Systems such as VAT are designed to address such concerns by both generating objects that embody teaching practices and their attributes and supporting customization of such objects. We need to validate both the power and flexibility of systems such as VAT to enable teacher educators to access existing, or create new, high quality reusable learning objects aligned to the needs of their preservice teachers.

Conclusion

Digital technologies, and the vast number of resources they enable access to, continue to expand in terms of their use and viability in educational settings. While considerable work lies ahead, significant strides have been made in refining how learning objects are created and implemented in teacher education. Learning objects have the potential to make contributions to teacher education. To paraphrase Downes (2004), we now need to do the hardest task associated with learning objects: recognize their value and make use of them.

References

Chitwood, K., May, C., Bunnow, D., & Langan, T. (2002). Battle stories from the field: Wisconsin online resource center learning objects project. In D. A. Wiley (Ed.), *The instructional use of learning objects*. Bloomington, IN: Agency for Instructional Technology and Association for Educational Communications and Technology. Retrieved February 5, 2007, from http:/ /reusability.org/read/

Clark, R. C. (1992). EPSS: Look before you leap: Some cautions about applications of electronic performance support systems. *Performance & Instruction, 31(5)*, 22-25.

DiStefano, A., Rudestam, K. E., & Silverman, R. (2004). *Encyclopedia of distributed learning*. Thousand Oaks, CA: Sage.

Downes, S. (2004). Resource profiles. *Journal of Interactive Media in Education, 5*, 1-32.

Gladwell, M. (2002). *The tipping point: How little things can make a big difference*. New York: Back Bay Books.

Hannafin, M. J., Hill, J. R., & McCarthy, J. (2001). Designing resource-based learning and performance support systems. In D. Wiley (Ed.), *Learning objects* (pp. 99-130). Bloomington, IN: AECT.

Hill, J. R., & Hannafin, M. J. (2001). Teaching and learning in digital environments: The resurgence of resource-based learning. *Educational Technology Research and Development, 49*(3), 37-52.

Hodgins, H. W. (2001). The future of learning objects. In D. Wiley (Ed.), *Learning objects* (pp. 281-298). Bloomington, IN: AECT.

Koper, R., & Manderveld, J. (2004). Educational modeling language: modeling reusable, interoperable, rich and personalized units of learning. *British Journal of Educational Technology, 35*(5), 537-551.

Kurz, T., Llama, G., & Savenye, W. (2005). Issues and challenges of creating video cases to be used with preservice teachers. *TechTrends, 49*(4), 67-73.

LTSC. (2000). *Learning technology standards committee Website.* Retrieved February 5, 2007, from http://ltsc.ieee.org/

McGee, P., & Diaz, V. (2005). Planning for the digital classroom and distributed learning: Policies and planning for online instructional resources. *Planning for Higher Education, 33*(4), 12-24.

Merrill, M. D. (2001). Knowledge objects and mental models. In D. Wiley (Ed.), *Learning objects* (pp. 261-280). Bloomington, IN: AECT.

Nugent, G. (2005). User and delivery of learning objects in K-12: The public television experience. *TechTrends, 49*(4), 61-66.

Parrish, P. E. (2004). The trouble with learning objects. *Educational Technology Research and Development, 52*(1), 49-67.

Recesso, A., Hannafin, M. J., Wang, F., Deaton, B., Shepherd, C., & Rich, P. (in press). Direct evidence and the continuous evolution of teacher practice. In P. Adamy & N Milman (Eds), *Evaluating electronic portfolios in teacher education*. Greenwich, CT: Information Age Publishing, Inc.

Reigeluth, C. M., & Nelson, L. M. (1997). A new paradigm of ISD? In R. C. Branch & B. B. Minor (Eds.), *Educational media and technology yearbook* (Vol. 22, pp. 24-35). Englewood, CO: Libraries Unlimited.

Shambaugh, R. N., & Magliaro, S. G. (1996). *Mastering the possibilities: A process approach to instructional design*. Boston: Allyn & Bacon.

Wiley, D. (2001). *Learning objects*. Bloomington, IN: Association for Educational Communications and Technology.

Wojtas, O. (2005, April 29). Jump for jorum. *The Times Higher Education Supplement,* pp. 6-7.

Section IV

Appendices

Appendix A

Theory Under the Hood

David B. Dawson, University of West Florida, USA

Abstract

This appendix provides an overview of psychological frameworks that should be considered in the design and development of learning objects. From acquisition of information to knowledge representation and accounting for types of knowledge, there are multiple ways that psychological concepts are expressed in an instructional product. This appendix is designed to provide an overview of constructs that are closely aligned with learning object-based instructional development.

Introduction

In any learning experience, the underlying psychological constructs frame the design, development, and implementation strategies of the environment. In this Appendix, an overview of psychological frameworks that should be considered in the design and development of learning objects are presented. From acquisition of information to knowledge representation and types of knowledge, there are multiple ways that psychological concepts can be incorporated into an instructional product. These materials are designed to provide an overview of constructs involved; readers are encouraged to extend their knowledge by reviewing psychological-based resources that are listed at the end of the Appendix.

Application and use of the constructs and theories in this presentation of psychological foundations of learning are critical to the success of the learning object and the resulting learning environment. It is not practical that a designer actually apply all of the psychological constructs contained in this Appendix. In reality, designers must devise their own heuristic that includes multiple elements of psychological foundations in the implementation of instructional strategies and embedded learning strategies.

Acquiring Information

Atkinson and Shiffrin (1968) divide the memory system into two categories of components: (a) permanent structural features and (b) control processes. Permanent features include the physical structures representing the basic short and long term memory stores and built-in processes, particularly for sensory stimuli. Control processes are individually constructed cognitive features that are activated in response to specific situations. Atkinson and Shiffrin identify three variables that affect the activation of control processes: (a) the context within which the information is received, (b) the meaningfulness of the information, and (c) the individual's experience and history.

The robustness of information transfer from short-term store memory to long-term store memory is greatest when overt responses from the individual are required during the process. This proposition lends weight to the strategy of interactivity as a powerful instructional tool. Long-term store memory provides the foundation for cognitive structure. It is the place where information is fixed into a knowledge matrix, the permanence of which varies with factors such as decay, interference, or loss of strength (Atkinson & Shiffrin, 1968). Ausubel (1968), Jonassen and Henning (1999), and others propose that these factors are expressions of the relative position of the information in the cognitive structure, its frequency of access, and the robustness of its connections to surrounding propositions.

Atkinson and Shiffrin (1968) identify two common strategies for encoding information into long-term store memory. The first strategy involves the incorporation of the new information into natural language structures. The second strategy facilitates the association of new information into long-term store memory through the use of visual imagery. Both of these strategies can be designed into learning environments when using learning object technology by using natural language structures and rich media that helps learners make links from "old" knowledge to "new." Strategies that focus on these ideas can be implemented beginning with how knowledge can be represented to learners.

Knowledge Representation

Knowledge representation is critical in beginning to display messages to and share information with learners. Knowledge representation can be characterized through concepts of exemplars, generic tasks, and schema.

- **Exemplars:** The exemplar view of concept representation suggested by Bareiss (1989) proposes that concepts are learned by individuals through the collection and storage of examples of category members. The number of examples stored depends on the individual's requirement for precision in the application of the concept; more examples may provide a more extensive set of features whose values appear to be defined with greater resolution (Bareiss, 1989). Rich examples included in the learning object permits the learner to attach meaning to the information and make linkages with currently-held knowledge.

- **Generic tasks:** Chandrasekaran (1989) applies a model similar to the exemplar model for knowledge representation, proposed by Bareiss (1989) to collections of knowledge-based reasoning tasks. He suggests that knowledge-based reasoning is an expression of combinations of generic reasoning building blocks. Each reasoning task, or strategy, possesses three elements: (a) the kinds of information required as an input and the resulting output information, (b) a way to present and organize knowledge required to perform the task, and (c) the process (e.g., algorithm, control, problem solving) that the task employs. Various combinations from among five generic tasks account for most knowledge-based reasoning operations according to Chandrasekaran (1989). The five operations are (a) hierarchical classification, (b) plan selection and refinement, (c) knowledge-directed information passing, (d) hypothesis matching, and (e) hypothesis assembly.

- **Schema:** West, Farmer, and Wolff (1991) build on Bareiss' (1989) exemplar model for knowledge representation and Chandrasekaran's (1989) generic tasks by embracing the notion of schema. They identify schema as information patterns, structures, and scaffolds of two basic types. They describe the first schema type as packets or bundles of either data or information about the state of data. They draw on the work of Rumelhart and Ortony (1977) to describe a second class of schema that represents procedures for handling or organizing data.

The notion of schema activation is especially important in learning experiences. West et al. (1991) suggest that at any given moment, an individual has a certain mind set, literally, a limited set of schema, in consciousness. These active schemas govern what stimuli the individual perceives, and the initial interaction between new stimuli and the active schema determine what new schema are invoked, if necessary, to process and integrate the new information. Since patterns of internal representation drive cognition, the more complex the event or experience, the greater the influence of the schema in its integration. West et al. assert that the effects of poor matches between schema and events may be so profound as actually to preclude the activation of schema that may be the best fit for the new information. Furthermore, other constructs, such as affect and belief, may introduce resistance to schema activation. Knowledge representation is a fundamental building black of how information can be structured for learning. Another building block of this framework involves types of knowledge.

Types of Knowledge

West et al. (1991) propose that knowledge with different properties is processed and organized differently in cognitive structure. They support three broad categories or types of knowledge: (a) declarative, (b) procedural, and (c) conditional. Declarative knowledge is described by West et al. as being factual. This type is stored in the form of propositions and networks of propositions which are subdivided into semantic and episodic. The semantic network represents lists of elements whose access and recall is aided by their relative position in the network. Episodic networks are story related and support Anderson's (1985) notions on episodic networks as representing connected chains of proposition whose relationships with each other are usually in the form of historical narrative.

A second type of knowledge, procedural, concerns processes. Specifically, procedural knowledge consists of order-specific, time-dependent, and sequential instructions that characterize knowing how to accomplish some task (West et al., 1991).

The final type of knowledge, conditional, permits individuals to make decisions. Prawat (1989) suggests that conditional knowledge represents a higher-order cognitive process in that it is concerned with the description of specific criterion combinations and contexts that may be matched to a range of responses to them. West et al. (1991) draw on this concept to conclude that conditional knowledge defines the knowing when and why to use a procedure. These types of knowledge can help designers organize and categorize information that they will use to help individuals learn.

Mental Models

Jonassen and Henning (1999) propose that learners model new knowledge through the adoption of allegory or metaphor to aid in structure mapping. Two assumptions made by Jonassen and Henning stand out when considering the design of a learning object. The first assumption is that the structural position of a concept with reference to others is a critical dimension of its meaning that plays an integral role in the encoding and recall processes. In other words, the organization of a series of knowledge or information concepts is very important to a successful transfer of knowledge from short- to long-term memory.

The second of Jonassen and Henning's (1999) assumptions of interest is that social or collective meaning springs from the intersection of individual models. While variations in experience, prior knowledge, beliefs, and abilities account for individual differences in cognitive structure, the common elements of these features among a number of individuals assume a significance that is important to successful social discourse. Consideration of these elements in the design and subsequent development of learning objects helps to provide context in the learning environment.

The dynamic properties of mental models provide important clues about learning (Jonassen & Henning, 1999). Different contexts or states of activation at the moment new information is introduced may affect what portion of the learner's cognitive structure processes it. The same element of information may play an important role in a number of interconnected submodels in the learner's cognitive structure (Jonassen & Henning, 1999). The more roles the same information plays, Jonassen and Henning suggest, the more likely it is to become a stable point in the learner's cognitive structure. They conclude that linearly structured mental models, lower dimensionality, and less robust metaphors negatively affect the individual's problem-solving ability in a given knowledge domain. These elements provide clues as to how to help learners develop mental models for supporting the learning environment.

Knowledge Organization

Merrill (2000) suggests that for an individual to solve a problem or learn, both a schema for the mental representation and organization of knowledge in the learner's mind and heuristics for manipulating components of that knowledge must be available to the learner. He identifies two sets of problems associated with establishing appropriate mental models and heuristics in the design of instruction using learning objects: categorization, and interpretation.

- **Categorization:** Merrill (2000) divides categorization into two types, classification or generalization. When presented with a series of different examples of subclasses of a particular concept, the learner must recognize the properties and values distinguishing each category. The learner must also be able to assign a new example to the correct category. Conversely, generalizations require the learner to synthesize common properties and values from different examples into a new, previously unrecognized superordinate conceptual class.

- **Interpretation:** The other large set of problems identified by Merrill (2000) relates to interpretation, which is subdivided into three smaller classes of problems: explanation, prediction, and troubleshooting. Explanation requires the learner to use features including property, value, portrayal, condition, and consequence to characterize a mental model of a concept. Predictions involve the identification of the conditions that are relevant to the consequence of the prediction and an *if <condition(s)>then<consequence>* statement, that anticipate changes in property values. Troubleshooting is essentially a sequencing problem for applying predictive conditional statements. Implications of categorization and interpretation to designers who must forecast how their future learners participate in the learning experience.

Knowledge Relationships in Cognitive Structure

Piaget (1952) proposes that "Learning involves the reciprocal assimilation of existing schemata as new objects are subsumed by them" (p. 236). Ausubel (1968) defines subsumption as the "process of linking new information to pre-existing segments of cognitive structure" (p. 58). Ausubel proposes that such modification of cognitive structure assumes a critical role in learning efficiency because associated knowledge at the point of modification of cognitive structure can have direct and specific relevance for subsequent learning tasks. From this perspective, existing structures provide stability for anchoring newly learned details and meanings. Extending this concept to embrace new information, new facts are organized around a common theme that integrates them both with themselves and with existing knowledge.

Ausubel (1968) classifies new knowledge into derivative and correlative propositions. The distinction between the two types is based upon the effect they have on existing cognitive structure in the learner. Propositions are defined as derivative knowledge when new meaning to existing knowledge is implied through a distinct example. Such a proposition increases the density of information clustered around a specific point in the cognitive structure.

Correlative knowledge extends, elaborates, modifies, or qualifies existing knowledge structure because it is neither present nor implied in existing propositions (Ausubel, 1968). Cognitive structure expands in some direction as the result of the incorporation of such knowledge.

Knowledge Relationships in Cognitive Structure

Ausubel (1968) describes the relationships in cognitive structure among propositions implied by his definitions of derivative and correlative knowledge through the use of the terms, superordinate and combinatorial. A new proposition may assume a superordinate position under which several existing propositions may be subsumed or attached in conceptually subordinate positions. Likewise, new propositions may be subsumed under a pre-existing superordinate concept. Propositions are combinatorial when they assume a nonspecific relationship to existing ideas that share a general relevance but have no sharply defined superordinate proposition. Decisions on how to build these propositions are critical to the presentation of information.

Ausubel (1968) summarizes the practical differences between propositions superordinally and combinatorially related as the former representing problem-solving knowledge and the latter being problem-setting knowledge. Superordinally configured knowledge is useful as problem-solving knowledge in that clearly defined structures provide the foundation for an efficient search path strategy. Combinatorially configured knowledge, meanwhile, permits problem setting based on the idea that the introduction of this type of new knowledge forces a re-examination of the loose collection to find a precipitant superordinator (Ausubel, 1968). Ausubel draws support for the role combinatorial relationships among propositions plays from the chunk sequencing research of Miller and Selfridge (1950) who establish that elements of meaningless discourse broken into a sequence of chunks can be recalled better than a continuous stream because the sequence of chunks itself provides relevant cues. Ausubel further explains that related material may be presented in a sequence such that each successive proposition is not dependent on the learner's mastery of the previous one. The learner benefits from the organization of the material itself because the organizational structure orients the learner in subsequent attempts to access the propositions from memory. Overt organization of information, knowledge, data, and so forth facilitates learner performance.

A Cognitive Structure Taxonomy

Ausubel (1968) defines assimilation as the interaction between new information and cognitive structure. He describes taxonomy of cognitive structure variables that define the parameters and character of the assimilation process in a systematic way. It is the properties of these variables that Ausubel asserts influence new learning and resulting information retention. Ausubel derives the framework for the assimilation model from the notions of lateral and vertical transfer proposed by Gagné (1965). He notes Gagné's assertion that lateral transfer of meaning is the extension of generalizable properties to information related tangentially and that the vertical transfer of meaning is the requirement that the learner master subordinate knowledge in order to assimilate related higher order information.

One of the variables Ausubel (1968) describes as critical to the fixing of new knowledge into cognitive structure is relevance (also a strong component in motivational themes). He suggests that learned propositions whose connections to existing cognitive structure are weak or tangential are less stable, consequently, far less likely to be recalled in context, and more likely to decay into inaccessibility than those links with strong connections. He notes that relevance is a measure of the strength of the relationship between existing knowledge and new information, not a property of the new information itself. Furthermore, Ausubel asserts that new information, which may in fact be highly relevant to the learner's existing information, has little chance of gaining stability unless the learner recognizes that relevance.

Another factor that influences the relevance of new information is the stability and clarity of the appropriate superordinate proposition, or anchoring idea. Ausubel (1968) describes a type of cognitive bridge that extends from the anchoring point of general and inclusive information to new propositions, thus fixing it into the learner's cognitive structure. This bridge can be seen in the use of advance organizers which help learners see the relationships between prior learning and the upcoming learning experiences.

An equally important variable affecting the relevance of new material is the degree to which it can be differentiated from propositions that are already part of the learner's cognitive structure. Ausubel (1968) states that new knowledge must be "discriminable from the established ideational system" (p. 169). As the instructional strategies are put into place, careful review of the format of the information and the ultimate presentation of that information helps the learners to make those differentiations and integrate new knowledge into old.

Jolley (1973) capitalized on Ausubel's (1968) notions of anchor points and subsumption to establish an early systematic organizational structure for knowledge that reduces each classification step to a binary choice in perception. The model's aim is to bridge between cognitive structure and search, retrieval, manipulation, and analysis algorithms for computer-based expert systems. While Jolley's effort at a binary knowledge classification system provides an encoding methodology suitable for knowledge base expert systems, its extension to a model for addressing cognitive structure and learning becomes problematic. The issues of accumulated exemplar sets proposed by Bareiss (1989), the role individual experience plays in the schema activation model described by West et al. (1991), and the multidimensional character of Ausubel's anchor point clusters suggest that individual differences play too large a role in cognitive structure to remain unaddressed.

Negotiation in Cognitive System Linkages

Rescher (1979) addresses the nature of interconnecting linkages in a cognitive system by dividing linkages into probative and justificatory. Probative, or evidential linkages, explore the ontological reason of why something is so by defining its specifications. Justificatory, or explanatory, linkages define the epistemological reasons, or why something is believed to be true, for relationships among propositions. Rescher takes care to warn, however, that an explanation of why something should be true, taken by itself, does not automatically make that thing true. He suggests that the negotiation of linkage classification reflects a human predisposition to reconciling the discrepancies between what individuals expect according to mental plans in use and what individuals encounter in reality.

Rescher (1979) proposes that the process of inquiry requires a system that uses a mental map of the individual's cognitive terrain, and that systematization is the prime instrument of error avoidance—a kind of cognitive quality control. He suggests that the cognitive map serves both to keep the wrong things out and to let the right things in, since if a proposition can be integrated into the cognitive system, then it must be accepted as true. The system itself, in Rescher's model, becomes the arbiter of knowledge.

Preferences in Patterns and Styles of Knowledge

Goldman (1986) raises important questions about the implications for cognitive processing that structural organization and systematization theories present. Goldman asks whether there may be preferred patterns and styles of knowledge construction and whether these may impose constraints on mental representation. He proposes that a nearly universal feature of all theories of mental representation, consistent with the notion of patterns and styles of knowledge construction, is the breakdown of experience into discreet parts and the construction of new parts. Goldman (1986) supports the proposition that individuals have preferences for patterns in the creation and segmentation of knowledge by drawing on the philosophical foundations of Gestalt theory in defining five features that characterize preferred or natural patterns of knowledge creation. These features are:

1. **Proximity:** Things that are perceived by an individual to be closer together tend to be associated with each other more often than things that are farther away from each other.

2. **Similarity:** Things that are perceived by an individual to possess characteristics that are like those of others are more closely associated with each other than with those that are different.

3. **Continuity:** Things that follow one another more closely in time or in logical sequence are more likely to be associated with each other by an individual than those which are separated by more time or sequence order.

4. **Closure:** Things that can be grouped together with a sense of completeness are more likely to be associated with each other by an individual than with groups of things that cannot.

5. **Form:** Groups of things that make regular shapes, express symmetry, or balance are more likely to be associated with each other by an individual than groups of things that do not.

Human Preferences for Hierarchical Knowledge Representation

Goldman (1986) extends the idea of organizational preferences and draws parallels between the features of natural language and those of hierarchical knowledge representation by suggesting that sentence structure is an expression of a hierarchy of concepts dependent on semantic memory. He also associates the notion of class inclusion arrays, or taxonomies, with visual and temporal knowledge. Goldman asserts that the natural parts of a collection of propositions in an individual's memory provide strong retrieval cues for the original whole to the extent that good cues are up to five times more effective in retrieving information than bad ones.

Goldman (1986) illustrates the pervasiveness of human preference for hierarchical representation through citation of Restle and Brown's (1970) examination of the way musicians learn music. Restle and Brown found that music is an expression of hierarchical representation, and that musicians learn new music in a top down hierarchy of patterns, not as a sequential string of tones. Goldman addresses the complexity of working from a knowledge hierarchy model by expanding the notion of hierarchy to include features supported by the proposition that the brain possesses an innate computational mechanism for constructing shapes, especially shapes in motion and in three dimensions. He uses as an example of such a feature the common preference for symmetry. The inference Goldman draws from the evidence for human preference for symmetry is that individuals actually employ a rather narrow set of representation-forming operations and have preferences for the sequence in which those representation-forming operations are performed. This inference is consistent with the notion of generic task sets in knowledge-based reasoning as proposed by Chandrasekaran (1989).

Representation-Forming Operations

Goldman (1986) identifies three types of representation that serve as the foundation for the narrow set of representation-forming operations: (a) temporal strings, (b) spatial images, and (c) abstract propositions. Temporal strings involve the fixing of information in sequence along a time line. Spatial images place items of information in relation to each other with varying degrees of proximity. Abstract propositions involve an iterative process of placing new knowledge into relational slots and then attempting to fill in missing slots with existing information or queries for new information.

Linguistic patterns are useful to Goldman (1986) in demonstrating evidence of the pervasiveness of analogy as a form of abstract proposition. He suggests that analogy in the form of linguistic patterns is critical to problem solving and that the abstract proposition feature of relational slot substitution is the key preferred operation in the process.

A significant issue with hierarchies and natural preferences in concept representation is the potential for the rejection of certain propositions when their properties fall outside the range of the individual's preferences (Goldman, 1986). Goldman also suggests that the complete failure to perceive certain propositions as meaningful is another possible consequence of individual preferences in representation formation.

The role that the notion of originality plays in the development of concept representations in the individual is one that Goldman (1986) explores by suggesting that an individual usually finds some new ideas more attractive than others. Goldman suggests that the metric at work in the establishment of a notion's attractiveness as it is processed by the individual has four important features:

1.   The preference ranking of processing operations is not universal for all individuals.

2.   Individuals are persistent in applying existing, familiar operations.

3.   Individuals apply operations in combinations to process information and tend to use familiar combinations.

4.   Individuals tend to apply the same set of operations to different sets of initial ideas.

Recognition that learners have preferences in the manner in which they organize and process knowledge is important to instructional system designers. That those preferences can be persistent, yet open to modification given certain conditions, also informs designers of instructional systems of the criteria for effective system design. These concepts help designers build that extremely heuristic as they approach designing instructional products, especially when applying the learning object construct, using building blocks to structure learning experiences.

Problem Solution Planning

Davidson, Deuser, and Sternberg (1996) suggest that there are three important characteristics of problem solution planning. One such characteristic is that problem solution planning is most likely to occur in cases where the problem has new elements or is complex. In other words, solution planning often follows when preferred cognitive processing approaches, as described by Goldman (1986), prove inadequate. Another characteristic is that planning is an abstract activity, not concrete, and is fluid in that its character is dependent on situational context. This notion is consistent with Chandrasekaran's (1989) ideas about generic task structure. Finally, problem solution planning follows a cost and benefit model. If the problem solver selects a lower order planning strategy for a complex problem, the intended time and effort savings driving such a poor choice are doubly lost if the solution fails and the problem solver has to begin again with a more involved strategy (Davidson et al., 1996). Such a model is facilitated by the multidimensional anchor point cognitive structure proposed by Ausubel (1968). The implication for designers of learning systems is that the problem-solving strategies embedded in the instruction must not only prove challenging enough to trigger solution planning, but must also reflect the varied approaches and cue the learner to invest the appropriate level of effort in deriving the solution plan.

Knowledge and Social Context

One direction of thought in cognitive theory reflects the conviction that since few people ever develop in complete isolation from others, the information processing functions of the individual cannot be meaningfully examined without taking into account the effect of the person's experience. The evolution of this line of thought begins with early concepts of symbolic representation and interaction with the environment.

Vygotsky (1962) addresses concept formation by suggesting that it is a cyclic and dynamic movement of thought between the particular and the general and back again. He stresses that it is not the simple interplay of associations within the cognitive structure that forms a concept, but a specific and unique combination of a diverse range of cognitive functions, taken all together. Scheffler (1965) addresses fundamental issues regarding context by examining the epistemological function of knowledge. He divides that function into two classes, the state of knowing *that* and the state of knowing *how*.

A feature of competence, a measure of knowing how, that Scheffler (1965) identifies as important is concerned with the interpretation of knowledge within context. Furthermore, Scheffler distinguishes between facility and skill in discussing competence. He proposes that facility occupies one end of a spectrum in which activity is routine, or procedural, while the other end of the spectrum is occupied by critical skills that involve an engagement of judgment in performance. Simple facility relies heavily on the assumption of rigidity in the context of performance, while critical skills require a thorough re-examination of situational context, building upon past experience and connections to existing knowledge to estimate the best approach to a new task (Scheffler, 1965).

Ramsey (1992) traces an evolutionary path through empiricist, rationalist, quasilinguistic, and monadic models to arrive at structural holism as a meaningful philosophical account of propositional representation. The essence of Ramsey's discussion lies in the development of one line of philosophical thought about mental representation that has moved from a focus on universal, discrete, granular elements of information arranged in various combinations, through common clustered elements similar to linguistic phrases and idioms, to complete sets of representation structures unique to the individual. Ramsey suggests that it is not possible to pinpoint a single element in cognitive structure that accounts for a specific belief or behavior. The implication is that there are no discrete propositional states; rather, each person possesses a single holistic belief state, individual propositions of which are simply localized, characteristics of that state. In effect, propositions are not components of belief states, simply features of them.

While the structural properties of representation in his holistic model play an important role in cognitive processes, Ramsey (1992) proposes that a more critical element is the degree to which a proposition is activated or "causally implicated in the structure's internal processing" (p. 257). The invocation of different propositions may result in different states of activation of representational elements and thus produce belief states with very different structural properties. Ramsey uses the tenets of structural holism to build the concept of connectionist representation. Connectionism characterizes representational networks in terms of the interaction among units. Ramsey defines these units as the prototypical properties of things, lexical concepts, and propositions arrayed in a network for learning.

Ramsey (1992) classifies them into three different types: input units, intermediary layers of hidden units, and output units. The intermediary units are hidden because the individual is unaware of the associative processes and activation patterns at work in response to the input units and only becomes conscious of the change in state between input and output units. Ramsey proposes, nonetheless, that representations are determined by the activity patterns of the hidden units. An important feature of Ramsey's model that is consistent with West et al.'s (1991) schema activation model and Chandrasekaran's (1989) generic task structure ideas is the notion that a relatively small number of units may produce a very large number of activation patterns, thus producing a very large number of different representations.

Ramsey (1992) proposes that a connectionist view of learning involves the process of modifying the cognitive system so that hidden unit activation patterns formed from unusable initial inputs are replaced with functionally useful states as the individual's network of representational experiences organizes them into portioned classes or groups. The line of thinking that illustrates the interconnectedness of knowledge and the importance of those connections to learning has significance for developers of an instructional design tool based on collections of knowledge objects. Schank and Abelson (1995) carry this line of thinking to a logical terminus by assigning critical importance to the framing of knowledge into coherent stories.

Distributed Intelligence

Petraglia (1998) discusses the dynamic, socially interactive nature of cognition through the concept of distributed intelligence. The individual serves as a node in this model within the ecology of a larger cognitive network. Petraglia suggests that tools and other beings extend the range of our cognition and, in some cases, allow us to bypass normal cognitive processes as in the examples of unconscious awareness of spatial relationships and object significance. The outcome of Petraglia's (1998) discourse on the sociocultural underpinnings of cognition and his general dissatisfaction with other transmission models is his advocation of a constructivist metatheory based on authenticism. He summarizes his position in this way: "Knowledge is constructed from prior knowledge and experience derived from participation in activities distributed across social, cultural, and material dimensions" (p. 55).

Petraglia (1998) proposes that tasks and solutions are always equivocal in the real world and that there are always multiple pathways through the problem space. Cognitive flexibility is a requirement because no single perspective is adequate for representing ill-structured problems. Furthermore, problems are often revisited over time from within rearranged contexts.

Cobb and Bowers (1999) examine the underlying assumptions of situated and cognitive perspectives in terms of the individual in the world, much as material objects are situated in relation to each other in physical space. They propose, however, contrary to the cognitivist assumption, that not all skills require a social context to be learned and that individual actions are elements of a social system and are part of that system even when the individual is physically removed from others in the system. Cobb and Bowers suggest that "learning is synonymous with changes in ways that an individual participates in social practices" (p. 6). They extend this line of thought to suggest that knowledge is embodied in activities such as perceiving, reasoning, and talking. They conclude that the portability of reasoning skills and knowledge is necessarily dependent on the degree of fidelity of the new context to the one in which learning originally takes place. They use this intimate relationship between activity and learning to propose that researchers focus less attention on the relationship between theory and instructional design prescriptions and more attention on the relationship between theory and practice (Cobb & Bowers, 1999).

Jonassen and Henning (1999) also address the proposition that situated social practice shapes cognition and thinking. Their position is that "Knowledge is embedded in the activities and processes that people engage in and the discourse used to make meaning of the activities" (p. 40). They go further to suggest that objects in the world assume a role in cognitive structure. "Knowledge is embedded in physical artifacts that are the objects of activity" (p. 40). These three elements—activities, processes, and objects—play a fundamental role in the development of mental models because they possess the capacity to fix meaning into cognitive structure.

In instances where social construction supports learner performance use of strategies that promote interaction, collaboration, and cooperation in the learning environment can be based on social context and knowledge constructs. As designers consider psychological aspects of social context, they can use appropriate strategies to help learners meet stated goals and objectives.

References

Anderson, J. R. (1985). *Cognitive psychology and its implications*. New York: Freeman.

Atkinson, R., & Shiffrin, R. (1968). Human memory: A proposed system and its control processes. In K. Spence & J. Spence (Eds.), *The psychology of learning and motivation* (pp. 90-191). New York: Academic Press.

Ausubel, D. P. (1968). *Educational psychology: A cognitive view*. New York: Holt, Rinehart, & Winston.

Bareiss, R. (1989). Exemplar-based knowledge representation: A unified approach to concept representation, classification and learning. In B. Chandrasekaran (Ed.), *Perspectives in artificial intelligence* (pp. 1-169). San Diego: Academic Press.

Chandrasekaran, B. (1989). Building blocks for knowledge-based systems based on generic tasks: The classification and routine design examples. In J. Liebowitz & D. DeSalvo (Eds.), *Structuring expert systems: Domain, design, and development* (pp. 215-272). Englewood Cliffs, NJ: Prentice Hall.

Cobb, P., & Bowers, J. (1999). Cognitive and situated learning perspectives in theory and practice. *Educational Researcher, 28*, 4-15.

Davidson, J., Deuser, R., & Sternberg, R. (1996). The role of metacognition in problem solving. In J. Metcalfe & A. Shimamura (Eds.), *Metacognition: Knowing about knowing* (pp. 213-223). Cambridge, MA: MIT Press.

Gagne, R. M. (1965). *The conditions of learning*. New York: Rinehart & Winston.

Goldman, A. (1986). *Epistemology and cognition*. Cambridge, MA: Harvard University Press.

Jolley, J. (1973). *The fabric of knowledge: A study of the relations between ideas*. New York: Barnes and Noble.

Jonassen, D., & Henning, P. (1999). Mental models: Knowledge in the head and knowledge in the world. *Educational Technology, 39*(3), 37-41.

Merrill, D. (2000). Knowledge objects and mental models. In D. A. Wiley (Ed.), *The instructional use of learning objects* (Section 5.2). Retrieved May 2, 2002, from http://reusability.org/read/chapters/merrill.doc

Miller, G. A., & Selfridge, J. A. (1950). Verbal context and the recall of meaningful material. *American Journal of Psychology, 63*, 176-185.

Petraglia, J. (1998). *Reality by design: The rhetoric and technology of authenticity in education*. Mahwah, NJ: Lawrence Erlbaum.

Piaget, J. (1952). *The origins of intelligence in children*. New York: International University Press.

Prawat, R. S. (1989). Promoting access to knowledge, strategy and disposition in students: A research synthesis. *Review of Educational Research, 59*, 1-41.

Ramsey, W. (1992). Connectionism and the philosophy of mental representation. In S. Davis (Ed.), *Connectionism: Theory and practice* (pp. 247-259). New York: Oxford University Press.

Rescher, N. (1979). *Cognitive systematization: A systems-theoretic approach to a coherentist theory of knowledge.* Totowa, NJ: Rowman & Littlefield.

Restle, F., & Brown, E. R. (1970). Serial pattern learning. *Journal of Experimental Psychology, 83*, 120-125.

Rumelhart, D. E., & Ortony, A. (1977). The representation of knowledge in memory. In R. C. Anderson, R. J. Spiro, & W. E. Montague (Eds.), *Schooling and the acquisition of knowledge* (pp. 99-135). Hillsdale, NJ: LEA.

Schank, R., & Abelson, R. (1995). Knowledge and memory: The real story. In R. Wyer Jr. (Ed.), *Advances in social cognition* (Vol. 8, pp. 1-85). Hillsdale, NJ: Lawrence Erlbaum.

Scheffler, I. (1965). *Conditions of knowledge: An introduction to epistemology and education.* Chicago: University of Chicago Press.

Vygotsky, L. S. (1934/1962). *Thought and language* (E. Hoffman & G. Vakar, Trans.). Cambridge, MA: MIT Press.

West, C., Farmer, J., & Wolff, P. (1991). *Instructional design: Implications from cognitive science.* Boston: Allyn & Bacon.

Appendix B

Digital Asset Repositories

Elspeth McCulloch, Brevard Community College, USA

Digital Asset Repositories (Source: http://tux.cdws.ucf.edu/dlss/index.php/Digital_Asset_Repositories)

From DLSS

Repository/Archive	Sponsor	Description	Subjects	Level
Agripedia (http://www.ca.uky.edu/agripedia/)	University of Kentucky	Agripedia is an Internet accessible interactive multimedia instructional resource, developed by the University of Kentucky's College of Agriculture created with a USDA Higher Education Program Grant.	Agriculture	College, Graduate
Annenberg (http://www.learner.org/)	Annenburg Channel	Annenberg Media uses media and telecommunications to advance excellent teaching in American schools. Video streaming and live feeds are available.	Comprehensive	Primary, Middle, High School, College
Apple Learning Interchange - Learning Resources (http://newali.apple.com/ali_sites/ali/)	Apple Computer, Inc.	Sponsored by Apple Computer.	Comprehensive	Primary, Middle, High School
ArtEdweb (http://ase.tufts.edu/arted/ArtEdWeb.htm)	Tufts University	ArtEdWeb is an art education Web site maintained by Tufts University in association with the School of the Museum of Fine Arts in Boston. The Resources link includes Curriculum Resources organized alphabetically.	Arts	Elementary, Middle High
Associated Press Multimedia Archive (http://ap.accuweather.com)	ACCU Weather Educational Division	The AccuNet/AP Multimedia Archive features two photo databases: an International photo archive and a Euro/Asian photo archive. The former features state, regional and national photos from North America, as well as the best of the international photo reporting.	Comprehensive	K-20
Bio-DiTRL (http://bio-ditrl.sunsite.ualberta.ca/)	University of Alberta	Bio-DiTRL operates as an online database with digital media that can be used to assist in teaching biology. In it you will find images, animations, video clips and text excerpts that may be downloaded for use by subscribers. Anyone may search or browse by subject.	Health and Life Sciences	College
BIOME (http://biome.ac.uk)	Joint Information Systems Committee (JISC)	BIOME provides free access to hand-selected and evaluated, quality Internet resources for students, lecturers, researchers and practitioners in the health and life sciences.	Health and Life Sciences	College, Graduate

continued on following page

Name	Organization	Description		
Blue Web'n (http://www.kn.sbc.com/wired/bluewebn)	SBC Knowledge Network Explorer	Part of the SBC Knowledge Network Explorer, Blue Web'n provides users with access to over 1800 educational sites covering all ages and subject matters.	Comprehensive	Comprehensive
Canada's SchoolNet (http://www.schoolnet.ca/home/e/)	Canada	Mandated by the Canadian government to work in partnership with the provincial and territorial government to connect Canadian schools and libraries, SchoolNet provides users with access to over 5,000 teacher approved learning resources for teachers, students and the community.	Comprehensive	Primary, Middle, High School
CAREO (Campus Alberta Repository of Educational Materials): Learning Commons Educational Object Repository (http://careo.ucalgary.ca)	Alberta Learning, University of Calgary, eduSource	CAREO is a repository of over 3,500 educational materials on various subjects and interactivity levels as part of a larger project to create "a searchable, Web-based collection of multidisciplinary teaching materials for educators" for Alberta and elsewhere.	Comprehensive	Comprehensive
Cobris Images for Education (http://education.corbis.com/artandhistory.aspx)	Thomson Gale	In partnership with Thomson Gale, Corbis has made available more than 400,000 digital images from its popular art, historical, nature, science, and space collections for use in a variety of learning-related applications, including class projects and assignments.	Comprehensive	Comprehensive
Computer Science Teaching Center (CSTC) (http://www.cstc.org)	National Science Foundation, Association for Computing Machinery Education Board	The CSTC is a digital library of reviewed resources for teaching computer science. We invite you to submit a resource and browse our collection.	Computer Science	College, Graduate, Continuing
Computing and Information Technology Interactive Digital Education Library (CITIDEL) (http://www.citidel.org)	NSDL	CITIDEL serves to "establish, operate, and maintain a part of the NSDL that will serve the computing education community in all its diversity and at all levels."	Computer Science	College, Graduate, Continuing
Connexions (http://cnx.rice.edu)	The William and Flora Hewlett Foundation, Rice University, and the Hewlett-Packard Corporation	The Connexions project at Rice University has created an open repository of educational materials and tools to promote sharing and exploration of knowledge as a dynamic continuum of interrelated concepts. Available free of charge to anyone under open-content license.	Current collection focuses on sciences and electrical engineering, but the projected collection will be comprehensive	Current collection contains materials for college and graduate level students, through the projected collection will be comprehensive.
Co-operative Learning Object Exchange (CLOE) (http://lt3.uwaterloo.ca/CLOE/)	Edu-Source Canada	A collaborative project of fifteen Ontario universities created to "develop an innovative infrastructure for joint development of multimedia-rich learning resources." CLOE is developing a "virtual market economy" of learning objects.	Comprehensive	College, Graduate, Continuing

continued on following page

continued on following page

Digital Library for Earth System Education (DLESE) (*http://www.dlese. org*)	National Science Foundation	DLESE, funded by the NSF, provides educators and learners with access to thousands of resources that support Earth system science education. The collection includes resources such as lesson plans, maps, images, data sets, visualizations, assessment activities.	Earth sciences	College, Graduate
EducaNext (UNIVERSAL) (*http://www. educanext.org/ubp*)	UNIVERSAL is a brokerage service linking educators and trainers for the exchange and distribution of Learning Resources	EducaNext provides access to thousands of materials on various subjects of relevance to teaching and learning at the college level and higher. Member institutions list their materials on the site as well as fees for those materials.	Comprehensive	College, Graduate, Continuing
Educational Object Economy Foundation (EOE) (*http://www.eoe.org*)	Sponsors of the EOE Foundation	Develop and disseminate the learning-community model; build tools to build communities; promote Java in education; test-bed support for metadata standards; tools for community-based distributed learning; open-source and intellectual-property innovation.	Comprehensive	K-12
Educational Software Components of Tomorrow (ESCOT) (*http://www.escot. org/*)	It is sponsored by Educational social components of tomorrow which means (ESCOT).	This is a test bed for the integration of innovative technology in middle school mathematics. The project investigates replicable practices that produce predictably high quality digital learning resources.	comprehensive	K-12
Eisenhower National Clearinghouse for Mathematics and Science Education (*http://www.enc.org/ resources/collect*)	The Ohio State University, Dept. of Education	Initially developed in 1992 as a collection of K-12 teaching materials within mathematics and the sciences, and information concerning federal funding for education, ENC has come to deliver a wide range of digital content to educators.	Comprehensive	Primary, Middle, High School
Enhanced and Evaluated Virtual Library (EEVL) (*http://www.eevl.ac.uk/index. htm*)	Joint Information Systems Committee (JISC)	Based at Hariot Watt University in Edinburgh and funded by the UK's Joint Information Systems Committee (JISC) as part of the Resource Discovery Network (RDN), EEVL provides users with access to over 10,000 resources useful to teachers and learners.	Engineering, Mathematics, Computer Science	College, Graduate, Continuing
e-Scholarship Repository (*http:// repositories.cdlib.org/escholarship/*)	The University of California	The eScholarship Repository offers faculty a central location for depositing any research or scholarly output deemed appropriate by their participating University of California research unit, center, or department.	Comprehensive	College, Graduate, Continuing

European Knowledge Pool System (ARIADNE) (http://rubens.cs.kuleuven.ac.be:8989.silo/)	European Commission's telematics for education and training program	Developed to deliver educational content throughout Europe, the KPS facilitates the sharing and reuse of educational resources. This encouragement of the discovery and reuse of these materials encourages an increasing recognition that learning object products.	Comprehensive	College, Graduate
Exploratories (http://www.cs.brown.edu/exploratories/home.html)	NSDL, Sun Microsystems	This project, dedicated to producing electronic materials for use within courses has developed 71 Java Applets demonstrating concepts in science and mathematics. The materials are for college and graduate teaching. Materials have no searchable metadata.	Mathematics, Science	College, Graduate, Continuing
Fathom Knowledge Network Inc. (http://www.fathom.com)	Columbia University. Corporate partners are Sun Microsystems and Microsoft	Fathom provides users access to around 300 free "courses," each requiring about 2 hours to complete. The "courses" cover a variety of topics and are meant for learners in higher and continuing education. Users must sign up for an account with Fathom.	Comprehensive	College, Graduate, Continuing
Filamentality (http://www.kn.pacbell.com/wired/fil/)	Knowledge Explorer Network	Filamentality is a fill-in-the-blank tool that guides you through picking a topic, searching the Web, gathering good Internet links, and turning them into learning activities. It combines the "filament" of the Web with a learner's "mentality."	Comprehensive	High School, College, Graduate, Continuing
FLORE (http://www.digital/french.ca/flore)	French Learning Object Repository for Education	FLORE is a free repository of French language educational resources. It is meant to help the user to find appropriate sites and specific learning objects to learn or teach French. FLORE is designed for faculty and students in post-secondary institutions and it offers over 1000 online resources with annotations such as content descriptions and peer reviews.	French Language	High School, College, Graduate, Continuing
Gateway to Educational Materials (GEM) (http://eg2.1school.washington.edu/)	U.S. Department of Education	The Gateway to Educational MaterialsSM is a Consortium effort to provide educators with quick and easy access to thousands of educational resources found on various federal, state, university, non-profit, and commercial Internet sites.	Comprehensive	College
Geotechnical Rock and Water Resources Library (GROW) (http://www.grow.arizona.edu)	University of Arizona	Grow is an award winning collection of civil engineering resources.	Civil Engineering	College

continued on following page

Global Education Online Depository and Exchange (GEODE) (*http://www.uw-igs.org*)		The University of Wisconsin System-Institute for Global Studies (IGS) is dedicated to examining the impact of our ever increasingly integrated world on individuals, communities and nations. By so doing, IGS focuses on comparative and global issues.	Global Studies	College, Graduate
Harvey Project (*http://harveyproject.org*)	US NSF (DUE-9951384), Wayne State University	This site provides users with access to 631 interactive materials within the domain of physiology. The materials are created for college and medical students. Materials can be browsed by subject. Materials are also classified according to domains.	Physiology, Medicine, Life Sciences	High School, College, Graduate, Continuing
Health Education Assets Library (HEAL) (*http://www.healcentral.org/index.jsp*)	UCLA School of Medicine, National Science Foundation, National Library of Medicine	"... such as images, videos, and animations, and textual materials such as cases and quiz questions."	Medicine, Patient Education	College, Graduate
The Hermitage Virtual Academy (*http://www.hermitagemuseum.org/html_En/06/hm6_2.html*)	The Hermitage Museum	A huge e-museum: The site includes a huge number of assets. The Virtual Academy contains several online modules.	Humanities, Art	Elementary, High School, College
Highwire (*http://www.highwire.org/lists/freeart.dtl*)	Stanford University	HighWire Press is the largest archive of free full-text science on Earth!	Comprehensive	College
Humbul Humanities Hub. (*http://www.humbul.ac.uk/*)	University of Oxford. Joint Information Systems Committee. Arts and Humanities Research Board.	Research Board, the Humbul Humanities Hub is a catalog of humanities resources online.	Humanities	Comprehensive
ICONEX (*http://www.iconex.hull.ac.uk/about.htm*)	ICONEX Learning Object Repository	Provides interactive content through technical development, national consultation and exemplar aggregation.	Comprehensive	College, Graduate
iLumina (*http://www.iLumina-dlib.org*)	National Science Foundation	Funded by the NSF, iLumina provides access to nearly 1,500 materials useful for undergraduate teaching of Chemistry, Biology, Physics, Mathematics, and Computer Science.	Chemistry, Biology, Physics, Mathematics, Computer Science	College, Graduate
Interactive Dialogue with Educators Across the State (IDEAS) (*http://ideas.wisconsin.edu/*)	Wisconsin University System	Provides educators with high quality, highly usable, teacher reviewed Web-based resources for curricula, content, lesson plans, professional development and other selected resources. Searchable by subject, grade level and keyword.	Comprehensive	K-20

continued on following page

Resource	Provider	Description	Subject	Level
Interactive University Project (http://interactiveu.berkley.edu:8000 IU)	The University of California at Berkley	A collaboration of several diverse UC-Berkley academic departments, research units and museums. The IU explores how University/K-12 partnerships can best use the internet to support schools and families.	Comprehensive	College, Graduate
Internet Film Archive (http://www.archive.org/index.php)	Internet Film Archive	The Internet Archive is building a digital library of Internet sites and other cultural artifacts in digital form. Like a paper library, we provide free access to researchers, historians, scholars, and the general public.	Comprehensive	K-20
Knowledge Agora (http://www.knowledgeagora.com)	Knowledge Agora	Organizations may list their learning objects on this portal by first registering their institution or organization with Canadian Learning Object Metadata Repository (CanLOM). In December 2003, the portal included 376 LOs for general education, 493 LOs for workforce development.	Comprehensive	K-20
Learning About Learning Objects (http://www.learning-objects.net)	Raven Enterprises	A collection of clean and sophisticated learning objects in a variety of disciplines.	Comprehensive	K-20
Learn-Alberta (http://www.learnalberta.ca)	Alberta Learning	Learn-Alberta contains multimedia learning materials for use by K-12 educators within Alberta.	Comprehensive	Elementary, Middle, and High School
Learning Matrix (http://thelearningmatrix.enc.org)	National Science Foundation	Funded by the National Science Foundation, the Learning Matrix collection provides access to about a 1,000 online resources useful to faculty teaching introductory science and mathematics courses as well as providing instructional and pedagogical training.	Science, Mathematics	High School, College
Learning Object Repository, University of Mauritius (http://vcampus.uom.ac.mu/lor/index.php?memu=1&cat=10)	University of Mauritius	Established to collect learning resources from the University of Mauritius and elsewhere, this English language site, containing materials in both English and French, provides users with access to over 300 learning materials on various topics for students.	Comprehensive	College, Graduate, Continuing
Learning Objects for the Arc of Washington (http://education.wsu.edu/widgets)	Arc of Washington Trust Fund	The materials collected here have been developed as part of the Arc Project, a project dedicated to creating learning objects for learners with learning disabilities or mild retardation.	K-20	Comprehensive
LearningLanguages.net (http://www.learninglanguages.net)	Claire Giannini Hoffman Fund	LearningLanguages.net is a portal that brings together online foreign language resources for English-speaking K-12 students and teachers of French, Spanish and Japanese. The project was created and is maintained and enhanced by staff at the Internet Scout.	Spanish, French, Japanese	Comprehensive

continued on following page

Name (URL)	Institution	Description	Subject	Level
Learning-Objects.net (*http://www.learning-objects.net modules.php?name=Web_Links*)	California Virtual Campus, San Diego Community College District	The collection of learning object on Learning-Objects.net is part of a larger collection of resources and forums that inform educators about the potential uses of learning objects and encourages their use and creation.	Comprehensive	College
Library and Archival Exibitions on the Web (*http://www.sil.si.edu/digitalcollections*)	Smithsonian Libraries	This site features links to online exhibitions that have been created by libraries, archives, and historical societies, as well as to museum online exhibitions with a significant focus on library and archival materials.	Arts	K-20
Library of Congress (*http://www.loc.gov*)	Library of Congress	The Library of Congress is the nation's oldest federal cultural institution and serves as the research arm of Congress. It is also the largest library in the world, with nearly 128 million items on approximately 530 miles of bookshelves.	Comprehensive	K-20
Lon-Capa (*http://www.lon-capa.org*)	Consortium of schools	Open source distributed learning content management and assessment system.	Comprehensive	K-20
Lola Exchange (*http://www.lolaexchange.org*)	Wesleyan, Trinity, and Connecticut College	LoLa is an exchange for facilitating the sharing of high-quality learning objects. It contains materials for use across the curriculum, with a particular focus on modules for information literacy.	Comprehensive	College
Maricopa Learning Exchange (*http://www.mcli.dist.maricopa.edu/mlx*)	Maricopa Community Colleges	Established by the Maricopa Community Colleges in Arizona the Maricopa Learning Exchange provides users with access to over 500 materials on various subjects. Materials, submitted by users within the Maricopa community college network. Excellent resource.	Comprehensive	College
Math Forum (*http://mathforum.org*)	Drexel University	One of the oldest collections of learning materials on the Internet, The Math Forum is a leading center for mathematics and mathematics education on the Internet. The Math Forum is a learning repository for both interactive and text-based materials as well.	Mathematics	College, Graduate
Medieval and Renaissance Manuscripts (*http://sunsite.berkeley.edu Scriptorium*)	The University of California at Berkley	The Digital Scriptorium is an image database of medieval and renaissance manuscripts, intended to unite scattered resources from many institutions into an international tool for teaching and scholarly research.	Literature	College, Graduate

continued on following page

Name	Organization	Description	Type	Level
MIT OpenCourseWare (*http://ocw.mit.edu/index.html*)	MIT has made a long term commitment to the project though initial funds were granted by the Andrew M. Mellon and the William and Flora Hewlett Foundations	MIT's Open CourseWare Initiative is a "large-scale, Web-based electronic publishing initiative" funded by The William and Flora Hewlett Foundation, the Andrew W. Mellon Foundation, and MIT itself.	Comprehensive	College, Graduate
MITE Projects (*http://www.montereyinstitute.org/*)	Monterey Institute for Technology and Education	Monterey Institute for Technology and Education is an educational non-profit organization committed to improving access to education. Although there are few objects, the existing ones are excellent and more are on the way.	Comprehensive	College, Graduate
Multimedia Educational Resource for Learning and On-Line Teaching (MERLOT) (*http://www.merlot.org*)	California State University Center for Distributed Learning	Developed in 1997 by the California State University Center for Distributed Learning, MERLOT provides users with access to online learning materials through a collection of records that now totals over 8,000.	Comprehensive	College, Graduate
National Engineering Education Delivery System (NEEDS) (*http://www.needs.org*)	National Science Foundation	NEEDS is a digital library of resources for educators and learners within engineering. Records are drawn from various smaller collections. Cataloging records contain multiple searchable fields including type of learning resource and publication year.	Engineering	College, Graduate
National Learning Network: Materials (*http://www.nln.ac.uk/Materials/default.asp*)	UK, Department of Education and Skills	The National Learning Network, a government-supported project based in the UK, was inaugurated in 1999 to encourage the adoption of Information and Learning Technology in post-16 education. The NLN collection, which was launched in 2001, exists in order to provide online learning resources.	Comprehensive	High School, College

continued on following page

continued on following page

Name	Organization	Description	Subject	Level
National Science Foundation Digital Library (*http://www.nsdl.nsf.gov'*)	National Science Foundation	NSDL is a digital library of exemplary resource collections and services , organized in support of science education at all levels. Starting with a partnership of NSDL-funded projects, NSDL is emerging as a center of innovation in digital libraries.	Science, Math	K-20
NLN Learning Materials (*http://nln.mimas.ac.uk/login.jsp*)	National Learning Network	A UK initiative to help transform the Further Education (FE) learning environment. £5.5 million has been allocated over two years to develop high quality, Web-based ILT materials designed as small manageable chunks that can be run within a virtual learning environment.	Comprehensive	K-20
Objectopia (*http://www.jiva.org/education sp. digitalresources.asp*)	Objectopia	An innovative initiative that brings digital resources to India.	Comprehensive	K-20
Physlets (*http://webphysics.davidson.edu/Applets/Applets.html*)	Sun Microsystems	Physlets, Ph ysics App lets, are small flexible Java applets designed for science education.	Physics	College
Problem-Based Learning Clearinghouse (*https://www.mis4.udel.edu/Pbl/index.jsp*)	Pew Charitable Trusts, University of Delaware, Unidel Foundation	The Problem-Based Learning Clearinghouse is a "collection of problems and articles to assist educators in using problem-based learning." Materials are accompanied by notes and supplementary materials from teachers regarding their uses in the classroom settings.	Comprehensive	High School, College
Science, Math, Engineering and Technology Education (SMETE) (*http://alpha.smete.org*)	SMETE (National Science Foundation)	A dynamic online library and portal of services by the SMETE Open Federation for teachers and students.	Math, Science	College, Graduate
SciQ (*http://www.sciq.ca'*)	Alberta Consortium	A collaborative partnership that puts multimedia science resources in the hands of teachers and parents.	Science	K-12
School Science (*http://www.schoolscience.co.uk content index.asp*)	Interactive Science Learning Objects	In association with: ABPI, BAMA, British Energy, CDA, Corus, ExxonMobil, GSK, ICI, The Energy Institute, Institute of Physics, MRC, Nirex, PPARC, SGM, Sony, SPE, Unilever.	Science	College, Graduate
SMETE Digital Library (*http://www.smete.org*)	National Science Foundation, National STEM Educational Digital Library Program	The SMETE Digital Library is a portal for the SMETE (Science, Mathematics, Engineering and Technology Education) Open Federation to a collection of materials of use to educators, learners, and policy makers. SMETE is currently developing a number of services.	Engineering	College, Graduate

Resource	Source	Description		Level
SPC RLO Repository (http://it.spcollege.edu:8500/edtech/instructorResources/RLO/search/index.cfm)	St. Petersburg College	One of the goals of Project Eagel at St. Petersburg College. This collection is growing.	Comprehensive	College
Splash (http://www.edusplash.net)	Portal for Online Objects in Learning (POOL)	The POOL Project is a consortium of several educational, private and public, sector organizations to develop an infrastructure for learning object repositories.	Comprehensive	College, Graduate
SunSITE (http://sunsite.berkeley.edu)	Berkley Digital Library	The Berkley Digital Library SunSITE builds digital collections and services while providing information and support to digital library developers worldwide.	Comprehensive	College, Graduate
Teachersource (http://www.pbs.org/teachersource)	PBS	3000 lesson plans and online activities.	Comprehensive	K-12
Telecampus (http://courses.telecampus.edu subjects/index.cfm)	NDBEN Inc.	Organized by NBDEN Inc., Telecampus is a directory of over 60,000 online courses and resources available from pay and free collections. Materials range in length from one hour modules to full semester of year long courses. Materials cover a wide range of disciplines.	Comprehensive	Comprehensive
The Exploratorium (http://www.exploratorium.edu)	The museum of art, science and human expression	Online since 1993, the Exploratorium was one of the first science museums to build a site on the World Wide Web.	Comprehensive	K-16
The Gutenburg Project (http://www.gutenberg.org)	Project Gutenberg	Anything that can be entered into a computer can be reproduced indefinitely.	Comprehensive	College, Graduate
The Inclusive Learning Exchange (TILE) (http://tile.atutor.ca tile)	University of Toronto	The Inclusive Learning Exchange is a revolutionary learning object repository service that responds to the individual needs of the learner. TILE provides the authoring tools, repository architecture, and preference schema needed to support this learner-centered environment.	Comprehensive	College, Graduate
The Landmark Project (http://www.landmark-project.com)	David Warlick	Private site with excellent links to many resources. Includes rubric builder and citation machine.	Comprehensive	K-16
The Learning Federation (http://www.thelearningfederation.edu.au.tlf/newcms/d2.asp)	Federal governments of Australia and New Zealand	The Le@rning Federation is an initiative of State and Federal governments of Australia and New Zealand. Over the period 2001-2006 the Initiative aims to develop online interactive curriculum content specifically for Australian and New Zealand schools.	Comprehensive	K-16
Universitas 21 Learning Resource Catalogue (http://www.edlrc.unsw.edu.au)	The University of Edinburgh and Universitas 21	The Learning Resource Catalogue resource contains both private internal catalogues of member institutions and the shared catalogue for the Universitas 21 Consortium.	Comprehensive	College, Graduate

continued on following page

Name/URL	Institution	Description		Level
University of Wisconsin-- Milwakee (*http://www.uwm.edu/Dept/ CIE/AOP_LO_other.html*)		Various specialized learning objects.	Comprehensive	College, Graduate
VCLIT (*http://vcampus.uom.ac.mu/lor/ index.php?menu=1*)	University of Mauritius.	VCLIT currently develops academic modules for the university and pedagogical prototype projects in line with the national ongoing effort for the promotion of ICT, continuous education and lifelong flexible learning in Mauritius.	Comprehensive	College, Graduate
University of Georgia, Video Resources (*http://www.coe.uga.edu/twt/ resources/instructional-videos.html*)	College of Education, Office of Information technology	A broad range of free online video reources.	Comprehensive	Higher Educaiton
Web-based Learning Resource Development (*http://www.centralschool. ca/web_resources.html*)	Saskatchewan Learning Network	These Web-based resources, or learning objects, were developed by classroom teachers from various school divisions, working with help from Saskatchewan Learning. They can be used as is, but teachers are encouraged to download and make modifications to the	Social Studies	K-12
Wesleyan University Learning Objects (*http://learningobjects.wesleyan. edu*)	Wesleyan University	The Learning Objects Program is in its second year, thanks to a grant from the Davis Educational Foundation.	Comprehensive	College, Graduate
Wisconsin Online (WISC Online) (*http:// www.wisc-online.com*)	Wisconsin Technical College System	The Wisconsin Online Resource Center project is a Web-based teaching, learning, and assessment resource center for instructors to use when designing or revising online courses. The goals of the project are to accelerate the development of quality online.	Comprehensive	College

Appendix C

Learning Object
Authoring Tools

Elspeth McCulloch, Brevard Community College, USA

Product	Web Site	Features	Benefits/Issues
Articulate	www.articulate.com	Articulate Rapid E-Learning Studio provides a comprehensive yet easy-to-use set of tools that seamlessly integrates highly customized Flash-based quizzes, interactions, assessments and surveys into your e-learning courses. Insert selected quiz slides into your course. Set options for how participants navigate your course based on assessment results. And since the Studio Professional suite also includes Articulate Engage, you will easily add stunning interactive content.	Very easy to use, template based tools help you get started quickly. Easy to add audio. Quizzes are somewhat difficult to synch to the LMS test engine. In comparison to some of the other products, it is expensive.
Adobe Breeze	www.adobe.com		
Camtasia	www.techsmith.com	Camtasia Studio is a complete solution for recording, editing and sharing high-quality screen video on the Web, CD-ROM and portable media players, including iPod. Easily record your screen, PowerPoint, multiple audio tracks, and Webcam video to create compelling training videos, screencasts and presentations. Camtasia Studio videos allow you to deliver high-quality content anytime.	Very easy to get started. Easy creation of tutorials. Inexpensive. Does not include a quiz tool, so assessment has to be stand-alone.
Captivate			
Course Genie	http://www.horizonwimba.com/	Quickly and easily convert your Microsoft Word documents into content for your Blackboard and WebCT courses. From one Word document you can generate a set of Web pages that include navigation and interactive features which can quickly be uploaded to your course.	A complete LO authoring tool that installs as a Word plug-in. Easy to get started, but users must understand how to use headings. Relatively inexpensive. Some objects can be awkward in look and feel. Lots of types of exercises and interactive features. Good tool for novice users. Advanced users report frustration with lack of flexibility.
Learning Tools	http://www.learningtools.arts.ubc.ca/mloat.htm	This tool enables content experts to easily combine video, audio, images and texts into one synchronized learning object. All assets are configured to be played back in a preconfigured order. Users do not need to perform any programming tasks, but rather go through a graphical user interface to generate the learning object. A much advanced WYSIWYG "click through" version is being launched in the near future.	Open source and free. Some good specific tools can be helpful. Timeline tool, in particular, is great. Not comprehensive.

continued on following page

Lectora	http://www.lectora.com/	Easy-to-use and rich in features, Lectora provides users with a comprehensive authoring environment for creating and delivering custom interactive multimedia content so you can communicate faster and more effectively.	Loaded with features, versatile and standards based. Lectora is a good choice for intermediate users. Provides a lot of design options. Somewhat expensive.
Macromedia Flash			
Microsoft Thesis	www.microsoft.com	THESIS Professional is a suite of e-learning tools which takes advantage of the SCORM standards and are integrated with Microsoft Office. This combination enables a user to author e-learning resources and objects straight from the familiar Microsoft Office applications such as Word, PowerPoint, Excel, Visio and Producer. The "Learning Object Manager" allows a user to author complete lessons for online teaching and instruction, using multiple learning objects from different sources.	Difficult to assess this tool. Go figure.
Respondus/ Studymate	http://www.respondus. com/	Respondus is a tool for creating and managing exams that can be printed to paper or published directly to Blackboard, WebCT, eCollege, ANGEL and other e-learning systems. StudyMate is an authoring tool that lets you create 10 Flash-based activities and games using three simple templates. The Flash activities are usable with any Web server or can be published directly to Blackboard, WebCT or ANGEL courses.	Affordable and easy to use. Does not allow for content authoring but may be used in conjunction with other tools.
Softchalk	http://www.softchalk.com/	If you can use a word-processing program, you can use LessonBuilder. Designed for teachers and content-experts who do not have time to learn complex software, LessonBuilder is simple, yet powerful, with only the features you need to create exciting, interactive content for your online course.	This is the easiest and best solution for institutions wanting to embrace learning object technology. Lesson Builder offers intuitive lessons resulting in easy to use html files.

About the Authors

Pamela T. Northrup is responsible for all aspects of distance learning at the University of West Florida (USA) including course development, faculty training, student support, marketing the programs externally, and implementation through the online campus. Dr. Northrup holds a PhD in educational research/instructional systems design from Florida State University and has spent her career designing instructional systems. She has led many development efforts for innovative instruction including working with IBM EduQuest to develop children's software; development of a large system-wide multimedia training system for the Florida Department of Corrections; development of a teacher-based tool, STEPS, that was used for K-12 lesson planning; development of a science education tool, QuickScience™ (patent pending) that has been recently commercialized; eLON™ designed for higher education developers; several online professional development courses for classroom teachers in collaboration with local school districts; over 20 online courses and recently implemented a model and the PDA courses for the U.S. Coast Guard. Most recently, Dr. Northrup was awarded a 1 million dollar congressional earmark to further the mobile learning delivery efforts with the U.S. Navy in Iraq and other remote locations around the world.

* * *

Cathleen S. Alfano manages The Orange Grove Project of the Florida Distance Learning Consortium (FDLC) (USA), assisting in the project's wider implementation. Ms. Alfano's background includes thirteen years experience as an instructional designer and project manager with a concentration in the area of distance learning for the past seven years. Before joining FDLC, Ms. Alfano assisted with implementation of Florida State University's (FSU) distance learning degree programs and managed FSU research grant projects for the U.S. Navy. She holds a MS in instructional systems and a BA in English.

Anne-Marie Armstrong was a senior training development specialist for Raytheon in Troy, Michigan, and is currently a program/project coordinator at Wayne State University (USA). She received her PhD in instructional design and development from the University of South Alabama. She spent several years on the Gulf Coast working on various design projects for the U.S. Navy. Later she worked on a multimedia course used by the Federal Aviation Agency. Following this, she became an instructional designer and training manager for Raytheon and Lucent in the Boston area. She then consulted for the Government Printing Office and the Architect of the Capitol in Washington, D.C. and received a certificate in museum studies from George Washington University. She has designed and developed museum Web sites and teacher resources for the Smithsonian Institution.

Charlotte J. Boling is an Assistant Professor at the University of West Florida in the Teacher Education Department. She also serves as a university faculty fellow for the Academic Technology Center at the University of West Florida and a faculty fellow for the Florida Literacy and Reading Excellence program (FLaRE) at the University of Central Florida. Dr. Boling holds degrees from the University of Florida, Johns Hopkins University, and the University of Southern Mississippi. Along with her teaching position, she is a curriculum designer and advisory board member for the Florida Online Reading—Professional Development program (FOR-PD) and content expert and online professional development designer for the Florida Inclusion Network (FIN). Prior to her university experience, Dr. Boling spent thirteen years in the elementary classroom teaching students in Florida, Georgia, Maryland, and DODDS Germany.

Tom Cavanagh has worked on both sides of the academic divide. With a previous career in television entertainment, Dr. Cavanagh is an accomplished instructional designer, program manager, faculty member, and administrator. In the training world, he has developed award-winning e-learning programs for Fortune 500 companies, government agencies, and the military. The projects described in this chapter were produced while he was with the Florida Space Research Institute. Currently, he is the director of online course design and production for Embry-Riddle Aeronautical

University-Worldwide Campus. He is also a published author of several mystery novels. He can be reached at thomas.cavanagh@erau.edu.

Simone C. O. Conceição is an assistant professor for the University of Wisconsin-Milwaukee (USA) School of Education, Department of Administrative Leadership and holds a PhD in adult learning/ distance education from the University of Wisconsin-Madison and a master's degree in administration/ development of adult/continuing education programs from UWM. She co-authored *147 Tips for Teaching Online Groups* (Atwood Publishing), Madison. Her research interests include adult learning, distance education, impact of technology on teaching and learning, instructional design, learning objects, and staff development. Dr. Conceição has keynoted and presented at statewide, national, and international conferences and was co-keynoter with Rosemary Lehman, at the Gallaudet University Videoconferencing Conference (2002).

David B. Dawson develops collaborative instructional design and development tools. He has contributed to the creation of several performance support tools including one for which he is co-inventor in its patent, and one recently adopted University-wide for the development of Web and mobile technology degree programs. Research interests include instructional design support tools and reusable learning object instructional delivery systems. He is also interested in expert knowledge elicitation and documentation through database-driven Web interfaces. Dr. Dawson earned a BA at Florida Atlantic University, an MA from the University of Michigan, and an EdD in Instructional Technology from the University of West Florida (USA).

Vanessa P. Dennen is an assistant professor in the Instructional Systems Program at Florida State University (USA), where she teaches courses in Instructional Design, Learning Theory, Evaluation, and Distance Learning. She earned a PhD in instructional systems technology from Indiana University, and has also been a faculty member at San Diego State University and SUNY Buffalo. Dr. Dennen researches both formal and informal online learning environments, with a focus on online discourse. In particular, she looks at how instructional design and facilitation factors work together to promote success—in terms of both participant satisfaction and participant learning. Additionally, she consults as both an instructional designer and evaluator for Web-based learning projects.

Michael J. Hannafin is the Charles H. Wheatley-Georgia Research Alliance Eminent Scholar in Technology-Enhanced Learning and professor in the Department of Educational Psychology and Instructional Technology at the University of Georgia (USA). He directs the Learning and Performance Support Laboratory (LPSL), an

R&D organization comprising several academic faculty, research scientists, and technical support staff. Currently, LPSL collaborators are actively engaged in federally-funded as well as state-funded research on the uses of technology in teaching and learning. His research focuses on developing and testing frameworks for the design of student-centered learning environments.

Tom Hapgood teaches interactive design in the University of Arkansas (USA) Art Department (2005 to present). Before coming to the University of Arkansas, he worked in a digital arts research and development lab at the University of Arizona and taught there in the School of Art. Dr. Hapgood has presented at Siggraph, New Media Consortium (NMC), Museums and the Web, International Digital Media and Arts Association (IDMAA) and will be presenting soon at College Art Association's (CAA) annual conference. His interests include typography, "Web 2.0," motion graphics, information design, radio frequency identification (RFID), XHTML/CSS, and Pachyderm. Dr. Hapgood has a degree in journalism and a Master of Fine Arts from the University of Arizona.

William T. Harrison Jr. is the Web and systems administrator for the Academic Technology Center at the University of West Florida (USA). His academic focus is in the area of instructional technology and learning objects with an emphasis on usability, accessibility, and re-usability. He is currently conducting research on the design and delivery of college-level courses using a personal digital assistant (PDA) in support of a joint U.S. Coast Guard and University of West Florida project as well as in an additional initiative with the U.S. Navy. He has been developing and conducting online instruction for the past seven years and has expertise in numerous Web development and computer networking technologies. He is a currently on active duty with the U.S. Navy.

Susan L. Henderson is the associate executive director of the Florida Distance Learning Consortium (FDLC) (USA), working with Florida's post-secondary institutions to leverage resources, facilitate cooperation, and develop statewide initiatives. She directs FDLC's Orange Grove Project, a standards based K20 learning object repository for the state of Florida. Ms. Henderson has worked with committees of the Academic ADL Co-Lab, the Online Community Library Center, the Southern Regional Education Board, and MiCTA and collaborated on numerous publications related to learning objects, technical standards, and metadata. A technology and e-learning consultant, Ms. Henderson holds an MS in instructional systems and a BA in psychology and Asian Studies. She is currently directing a Fund for the Improvement of Postsecondary Education (FIPSE) project related to dissemination of repositories.

Janette R. Hill is an associate professor at the University of Georgia (USA), College of Education, Department of Educational Psychology and Instructional Technology. Prior to coming to the University of Georgia, Dr. Hill held academic appointments at the University of Northern Colorado and Georgia State University. Dr. Hill's research interests include community building, resource-based learning and Web-based learning environments. Dr. Hill holds a master's degree in library and information science and a doctoral degree in instructional systems design, both from Florida State University. Her articles have appeared in research and professional publications including *Educational Technology Research and Development* and *The Internet and Higher Education*.

Kira S. King is a freelance instructional systems designer who focuses on developing engaging and interactive learning environments using both computer-supported and face-to-face training. Her training includes a PhD in instructional systems technology from Indiana University (USA) and an MA in computers and education from Teachers College, Columbia University. Dr. King's special interest is in harnessing creativity and storytelling to create impactful instruction that situates learning into real world contexts. Her areas of expertise include: simulation and scenario development, SCORM, and media design. Dr. King has consulted in a wide variety of areas, including the military (modeling and simulation, emergency management, and medical training), corporate learning (guest programs and employee training), and non-profit (museum learning evaluation). She has also taught as an adjunct professor, and also as a K-5 elementary school computer teacher. She can be reached via the Internet at ksking@iag.net.

Rosemary M. Lehman is senior outreach/distance education specialist at Instructional Communications Systems (ICS), University of Wisconsin-Extension (USA) and manager of the ICS instructional design team. She holds a PhD in distance education/adult learning, and a master's in television/media critique. She authored *The Essential Videoconferencing Guide: 7 Keys to Success* (2001, ICS/ UWEX) and edited *Using Distance Education Technology: Effective Practices* (2002, ICS/ UWEX.) Her research interests focus on the relationship of perception/cognition/ emotion to distance education instructional design, educational applications for media/technology, and the development/integration of learning objects. Rosemary has keynoted and presented at statewide, national, and international conferences. She was co-keynoter with Simone Conceição, at the Gallaudet University Videoconferencing Conference (2002).

Nikos Manouselis is a researcher at the Informatics Laboratory of the Agricultural University of Athens (Greece). He has a diploma in electronics & computer engineering, a master's in operational research as well as a master's in electronics &

computer engineering, from the Technical University of Crete (Greece). Mr. Manouselis has been previously affiliated with the Informatics & Telematics Institute of the Centre for Research & Technology (Greece), as well as the Decision Support Systems Laboratory and the Multimedia Systems & Applications Laboratory of the Technical University of Crete (Greece). His research interests involve the design, development and evaluation of electronic services, and their applications.

Elspeth McCulloch is the director of e-learning for Brevard Community College. She has worked in e-learning for over five years and in higher education for over 10 years. She has experience in student advising, LMS administration, faculty development and training, strategic planning and e-learning logistics. She has written several articles, has made numerous conference presentations; and most recently has developed a comprehensive, facilitated online orientation for new online students. Current areas of interest include Web 2.0 technologies, learning objects, student retention and open source learning management systems. McCulloch has a BA from the University of Waterloo and is pursuing graduate studies at Athabasca University.

Ed Morris is a senior lecturer in the School of Computer Science and Information Technology at RMIT University, Melbourne (Australia). As the inaugural online programs leader (2001-2003), he contributed to the development and delivery of first generation online courses. Specifics include a learning management model with demonstrable cost-effectiveness and educational effectiveness. Successful outcomes include an online course portfolio for Open Learning Australia (now Open University Australia) and a tendered learning management architecture for the African Virtual University. Morris has also contributed research in computer ethics, specifically a methodology for analysing ethical issues in cyberspace. He is the lead author of *Information Technology Issues: Ethical and Legal.*

Christine H. Olgren is director of the distance education certificate program, School of Education, University of Wisconsin-Madison (USA). She is responsible for program management, instructional design and development, teaching, evaluation, and marketing. She has taught online (1995 to present) and has developed courses for both collaborative and self-paced learning. Her research interests include learning strategies and the cognitive, metacognitive, and motivational aspects of learning with technology. Dr. Olgren recently completed a three-year FIPSE grant as co-project manager to develop and evaluate learning objects for online instruction.

Kevin Oliver is an assistant professor of instructional technology at North Carolina State University in Raleigh (USA). He holds a PhD in instructional technology from the University of Georgia and a MEd in educational media and instructional design from UNC-Chapel Hill. His research interests include the study of Web-based design objects and cognitive tools in support of student-centered teaching and learning, and applying qualitative methods to the evaluation of programs with intensive classroom technology integrations (e.g., 1:1 computing).

Patricia Ploetz is interim director of the Center for Academic Excellence and Student Engagement at the University of Wisconsin-Stevens Point (USA). She is responsible for developing and maintaining a faculty-driven resource center, the Center for Academic Excellence and Student Engagement, that promotes discussion on issues and trends concerning teaching and learning, provides opportunities for interdisciplinary collaborations, and sponsors professional development workshops, seminars, and brown bags, etc., on teaching, learning, assessment and online technologies for UWSP faculty. Patricia's research interests include teaching and learning with technology and changing faculty roles in a knowledge economy. Patricia was co-project manager for a FIPSE grant that investigated the instructional use of learning objects using standards in online instruction (2002-2005).

Karen L. Rasmussen is the chair of engineering and computer technology, which houses graduate instructional and performance technology programs at the University of West Florida (USA). She has worked extensively in creating Web-based learning environments for online learners through development of academic programs, support systems, and learning object content repositories. She has co-authored a textbook on e-learning and is a co-inventor of two software systems.

Arthur Recesso is an associate research scientist in the Learning and Performance Support Laboratory (LPSL). His research centers on evidence-based methods and tools for decision making. His most recent efforts involve developing a four-stage systematic methodology to support assessment and improvement in performance, practice, and organization structures. The methodology has been instantiated in the video analysis tool (VAT), a Web-based system that enables user to collect evidence from remote locations, interpret it and take a course of action. The evidence-based methods and tools are currently being used in teacher preparation, leadership supervision, and assessment of teacher practices to support growth and development.

Robert R. Saum holds degrees in psychology, biblical studies, and ministry. As a youth, he created gadgets from dismantled household electronic appliances. In 1980, with screwdriver in hand and television in sight, he was promptly promised a computer, preempting his plans. He developed an immediate connection with computers. Since then he has built and fixed computers, and conducted nearly 300 workshops on learning management, content development, and learning object authoring. He served on the Southern Regional Education Board's digital learning content initiative. He is currently the director of the virtual college at Daytona Beach Community College (USA).

Argiris Tzikopoulos is a research associate of the Informatics Laboratory of the Agricultural University of Athens (Greece) (2004 to present). His first degree is in technology education and digital systems (2003) and he also holds a master's degree in e-learning (2006), both from the University of Piraeus (Greece). Currently, Mr. Tzikopoulos is a PhD candidate in the Informatics Laboratory of the Agricultural University of Athens, in the field of knowledge management systems. His main research interests are related to intelligent educational multimedia, learning objects and metadata, and online technologies that may support learning communities.

Riina Vuorikari is currently pursuing her PhD in the K.U. Leuven (Belgium). Additionally, she works in European Schoolnet (Belgium) where she has been dealing with the issues related to digital learning resources, quality, repositories and various aspects of semantic and technical interoperability within a network of European educational authorities (2000 to present). She has a master's degree in education from University of Joensuu (Finland), and a postgraduate degree in hypermedia from Paris 8 (France). Her main research is actually focused on social information retrieval and how it can enhance the discovery and reuse of learning resources.

Index

C

D

E